WITH BRITAIN
IN MORTAL DANGER

Field Marshal Lord Ironside, GCB, CMG, DSO, Chief of the Imperial General Staff and Commander-in-Chief of Home Defence.

WITH BRITAIN
IN MORTAL DANGER

BRITAIN'S MOST SECRET ARMY IN WWII

EDITED AND COMPILED
BY JOHN WARWICKER, MBE

FOREWORD BY
LORD IRONSIDE

CERBERUS

This edition published in 2002

PUBLISHED BY:
Cerberus Publishing Limited
Penn House, Bannerleigh Road,
Leigh Woods, Bristol BS8 3PF, U.K.
Telephone: ++44 117 974 7175
Facsimile: ++44 117 973 0890
e-mail: cerberusbooks@aol.com

011930270

British Library Cataloguing in Publication Data.
A catalogue record for this book is available from the British Library.

ISBN 1 84145 112 6

PRINTED AND BOUND IN UK

Contents

		Page
Dedication		*vii*
Acknowledgements		*viii*
Glossary and Abbreviations		*x*
Foreword by Lord Ironside		*xiii*
Preface		*xv*
Introduction Part I - The problem		*xviii*
Introduction Part II - The scene is set		*xx*
Introduction Part III - The secret weapon		*xxii*
CHAPTER I	The Start of Operations	1
CHAPTER II	'Gubbski' and Friends	9
CHAPTER III	Auxunits Patrols (Parts I and II)	23
CHAPTER IV	Auxunits Patrols(Part III and Poem)	43
CHAPTER V	Coleshill	53
CHAPTER VI	Scout Sections	65
CHAPTER VII	Thuggery!	77
CHAPTER VIII	Myths and Misconceptions	87
CHAPTER IX	Auxunits Operational Patrols – a discussion of their role and that of others 'Going to Ground'	95
CHAPTER X	'Oxo – a sort of Commercial Traveller	113
CHAPTER XI	Auxunits on Active Service and 'Operation *Bulbasket*'	123

CHAPTER XII   Auxunits and Special Forces   137
                  ('Lest We Forget'- by Cyril Hall)

CHAPTER XIII   Auxunits – Special Duties Section   149

CHAPTER XIV   Major John Collings and his SDS team 171

CHAPTER XV   Auxunits (Signals)   179

CHAPTER XVI   Signals – In the Field   195

CHAPTER XVII   Operational Bases - SD Section   205

CHAPTER XVIII   Auxunits ATS – 'The Secret Sweeties' 217

CHAPTER XIX   Stand down   231

CHAPTER XX   Would it have Worked? –   245
                  some remaining questions

CHAPTER XXI   'Werewolves and Gladios'   255

Epilogue   Parts I – V   260

Appendix One   The Museum of the British   275
                  Resistance Organisation

Appendix Two   The Medals Fiasco   276

Appendix Three Hitler's Commando Directive   279
                  (*Kommandobefehl*)

Bibliography   281

Index   283

The following is a discussion and history of the
'MOST SECRET' WWII GHQ Auxiliary Units
and their Active Service Role

Edited and compiled by John Warwicker, MBE
on behalf of –

THE MUSEUM OF THE BRITISH
RESISTANCE ORGANISATION
Parham, Suffolk

With contributions from –

Members of the Auxiliary Units
Their families and friends
and Museum Archives.

The objective is to record, verbatim when possible,
some of the history of Auxiliary Units from existing
archive material and interviews, and by constructive
analysis and deduction using up-to-date research.

Dedicated to the Kindred family of Parham, Suffolk,
and all members of the GHQ Auxiliary Units
who 'Did Their Stuff Unseen' and who,
when their country was in Mortal Danger,
were 'Prepared to Defend it by
Force of Arms and with
Their Lives if Need Be'.

Acknowledgements

Richard Aixill

Yolande Alston

Priscilla Aston

William E ('Bill') Bartholomew

Donald Beaven

The Late Brigadier Geoffrey ('Bill') Beyts, DSO, MBE, MC

David Blair

Geoff Bowery

Geoffrey Bradford, for wise advice and special contributions

Donald Brown and Countryside Books of Newbury

Ann Buckney, for the loan of the Beatrice Temple Diaries

Jean Burnell

Terry Carney

Edward Carpenter

Jim Caws

Gordon Cawthorne, MBE

Reginald ('Rex') Chaston

Philip D Chinnery, author of 'March or Die', and Airlife Publishers of Shrewsbury

Ronald Chisnall

Ralph Clarke

Isobel Collings

Tom Colquitt

Colin Colson

Emma and John Cross

The Late J W Stuart

Edmundson, TD, and his family

Lt Col. Norman Field, OBE

Major Peter Forbes

Roger Ford

The Late Arthur Gabbitas and his family

Eric Gray

C Jack Grice

Cyril Hall

Major R F ('Henry') Hall, MC

Donald Handscombe

Alwyn Harvey

Lord Henniker

The Late David Ingrams and his family

Lord Ironside

The Late Stanley Judson and his family

John Mann

Walter McGowan

Jill Monk

The Late Christine Montagu

Andrew and Paul Mothersole

Ivan Mower

Sally Neilson

Deryck Neville

Joy Oxenden

John C G Phillips

The Director and staff, Public Record Office, Kew

The Late Robert Pitt

Geoffrey Ratcliffe

Peter Robins

David Steed

Doris Steward

Duncan Stuart, CMG, SOE Adviser, FCO

Stephen Sutton

Dennis Walker

Nigel Walker

Dr William Ward

The Late Bill Webber

Peter Wilcox

John Williams

Mick Wilks and Bernard Lowry

Miss E ('Willie') Wilmott

The following kindly contributed information in connection with the Special Air Service and Operation *Bulbasket*

Philip Ashley (brother of Alan Ashley – Dorset Scout section and 1SAS)

Donald Beaven (203 Hampshire Auxiliary Unit, Portsmouth Dockyard.)

George Biffin. (Dorset Scout section and 1SAS)

Jack Blandford (Dorset Scout section and 1SAS)

John Fielding (202 Norfolk Auxiliary Unit and 1SAS)

Joe Schofield (1SAS)

Colin Durrant, and Andrew Taylor, the Chairman and Museum Director respectively, who kept momentum going when energy flagged.

Captain Barbara Culleton, TD is specially thanked for various invaluable contributions and her analysis of Beatrice Temple's diaries.

Tony Evans undertook massive searches in Public Record Office and special acknowledgement is given for his discovery of records relating to Major Nigel Oxenden.

Ann Mary Warwicker – always there when output was threatened by electronic spookery.

...and many, many others.

Glossary & Abbreviations

AFV	Armoured Fighting Vehicle.
All-in-Fighting	Unarmed combat and training in personal Weapons as distinct from firearms.
ATS	(Women's) Auxiliary Territorial Service.
ATTERY	Slang for ATS living quarters.
Auxiliary Units	(or AU's) Generic term including members of the patrols, Scout Sections, Signals, Special Duties and the Organisation generally.
Auxunits	Military abbreviation for Auxiliary Units.
Auxilier	Member of the Auxiliary Units.
Auxunit Patrols	Civilian volunteers enlisted in the sabotage/operational section.
Auxunits (SDS)	Auxiliary Units Special Duties Section.
Auxunits (Signals)	Regular Army troops including Conscripts recruited into the Royal Corps of Signals to design, install and maintain radio communications.
BEF	British Expeditionary Force.
CIA	see OSS.
C-in-C	Commander in Chief.
CO	Commanding Officer.
Coleshill	Coleshill House, in the village of Coleshill, Wiltshire. The national Headquarters of Auxiliary Units.
DLD	Dead Letter Drop.
DZ	Dropping Zone.
FANY	First Aid Nursing Yeomanry.
Fieldcraft	General term for training in cautious movement mainly by night - map-reading, reconnaissance and observation.
GC	Group Commander.
GC & CS	Government Code and Cipher School (sometimes called the Golf, Cheese and Chess Society).
GHQ	General Headquarters.
GHQ Recon. Unit	(See 'Phantom'.)

GHQ Reserve Battalions	201, 202, 203 Battalions. Eventual designation of Auxiliary Units Patrols.
GOC	General Officer Commanding.
GSO	General Staff Officer.
Group Cdr	Commissioned volunteer, nominally in command of several Auxunits' patrols.
'HAM'	A radio amateur who 'speaks' directly to other HAMs by R/T or W/T.
HE	High Explosive.
Highworth	The nearest town to Coleshill; volunteers reported to the sub-Post Office for transport to Headquarters.
HQ	Headquarters.
Intelligence Officer (IO)	Initially recruited to form the Auxiliary Units; subsequently in command of one or more County organisations.
ISPB	Inter-Services Projects' Board.
ISRB	Inter-Services Research Bureau.
ISSB	Inter-Services Security Board.
Jedburghs (Jeds)	Parties, usually of three (British, US and a local national), dropped in Europe near 'D' Day to co-ordinate resistance groups.
LCS	London Controlling Section. Commanded by Sir Stewart Menzies, head of MI6.
MGC	Machine Gun Corps of WWI
MI5	The Security Service. Responsible to the Prime Minister through the Home Secretary - for State Security in Great Britain and the Colonies.
MI6	The Secret Intelligence Service. Responsible to the Prime Minister through Foreign Office for British Intelligence gathering world wide.
MI(R)	Military Intelligence (Research). A pre-war bureau, created by the Director of Military Intelligence, in preparation for WWII. Originally commanded by Colonel John Holland.
MoD	Ministry of Defence.
'Mufti'	Plain clothes.
NCO	British Non-commissioned officer.
OC	Officer Commanding
OCTU	Officer Cadet Training Unit.
OKW	German High Command

Operational Bases (OBs)	Specially constructed underground hideouts used by the Auxiliary Units.
ORs	British Army other ranks.
OSS	The US Office of Strategic Services – later the Central Intelligence Agency
Phantom	'Most Secret' Units on Reconnaissance and Communications missions in occupied territory, or in advance of Allied front line positions.
PL	Patrol Leader.
PoW	Prisoner of War.
PTI	Pocket Time Incendiary (or Physical Training Instructor).
RA	Royal Artillery.
RCS	Royal Corps of Signals.
RE	Royal Engineers.
REME	Royal Electrical and Mechanical Engineers.
RSGB	Radio Society of Great Britain.
R/T	Radio Telephony.
SAS	The Special Air Service Regiment.
Scout Officer	Officer commanding an Auxunits' Scout Section.
Scout Sections	Regular Army troops, recruited from various units, responsible for managing and training Auxunits' patrols in their area.
SDS	Auxiliary Units' Special Duties Section.
SDSIO	SDS Intelligence Officer.
SHAEF	Supreme Headquarters Allied Expeditionary Force.
SIS	(See MI6).
SOE	Special Operations Executive.
SS (*Schutzstaffel*)	Hitler's 'elite' guard, noted for their brutality and ruthlessness.
STC	Special Training Centre (for Special Forces) at Inverailort, Scotland.
TAA	Territorial Army Association.
USAAF	United States Army Air Force.
VAD	Voluntary Ambulance Driver.
'VE' Day	Victory in Europe day – 8th May 1945.
VP	Vulnerable Point.
WO	War Office.
W/T	Wireless Telegraphy.

Foreword
by Edmund, Lord Ironside

'I am trying to piece together an Army in the most terrible crisis that has ever faced the British Empire.'

This is what my father said in his diary on 15th June 1940, just after he had been appointed Commander-in-Chief, Home Forces and had addressed all the leaders of the Local Defence Volunteers – that mixed and hurriedly assembled Force of over 300,000 last-ditch defenders armed with courage and very little else – on their responsibilities for static defence and information gathering in the event of a German invasion. The story of how his initiatives were taken forward and how the formation of a secret army of Auxiliary Units came about is, for the first time, fully described by John Warwicker, so that today's reader and all historians can appreciate the seriousness of the threat that invasion imposed on the Government lead by Sir Winston Churchill and how the underground Forces were mobilised to resist a German occupation.

After describing how all the continental countries had, one after the other, succumbed to the blitzkreig strategy and tactics of the Nazi war machine, he quite rightly notes how the guerrilla warfare knowledge and experience of the many do-and-dare Army officers, such as the celebrated Orde Wingate, Mike Calvert and Colin Gubbins, grew into becoming the backbone of the British undercover operations during the war. Today, as a poignant reminder to visitors, the Museum of the British Resistance Organisation at Parham Airfield in Suffolk, stands in the centre of the vulnerable area of the English countryside which was most exposed to being swamped by the enemy invasion Forces.

Not being able to wave a regimental banner to publicise their presence, the Auxiliers, as they came to be known, silently assumed an identity, which was really only known to the insiders of the British Defence realm. Fortunately for every British citizen the speed of the Nazi advance to the coastlines of Northern Europe and the the Axis boundaries in the South, had stretched the German Army supply lines to such an extent, that Hitler's "*Der Tag*" for the invasion of England was put on hold and buried for good.

So, as the author recounts so vividly, the Auxiliers stayed on the alert until peace was resumed and we can all now read and understand from John Warwicker's detailed study of their role, how they worked, as well as come to appreciate the hidden strength of the asset we held in reserve.

IRONSIDE
(The Lord Ironside)
16th May 2002

Preface

Our arguments can only as good as the source material. If essential evidence is wrong to start with, everything that follows perpetuates and multiplies the error. Here was the origin of the myths which continue to dominate Auxunits' history.

Hugh Verity explained the problem when he wrote about the RAF Special Squadrons in 'We Landed by Moonlight':

'The simple fact that secret agents in the field cannot keep files of archive material and that human memory is fallible, have led to many variations on the details of evidence about particular incidents. I have done my best to match what information I have discovered...'

We too have made every effort to search for truth and distinguish between fact and guesswork. Where there is doubt, it should be clear to the reader but veterans' memories - upon which we have drawn heavily – are not always clear after more than half a century, and accounts given by eye witnesses in good faith sometimes differ. Moreover, Intelligence Officers, the key experts between Headquarters staff and Auxiliers in-the-field, were themselves working to untried guidelines and consequently trained 'warriors' to their own specifications. Different objectives were outlined in different areas and then attained in different ways. A certain confusion was the result; it has proved difficult to penetrate and then co-ordinate into one incontestable account.

Conclusions – always carefully considered – should not however be undermined. In any case, we hope that the goodwill with which this book has been compiled is perfectly clear. Our dedication to the best interests of the men and women, civilians, officers and other ranks, of the WWII GHQ Auxiliary Units – remains unqualified.

★   ★   ★

Unarguably, the most powerful institution in Britain is Cabinet Office in Whitehall.

Focal point for Ambassadors, the Secret Services, Government communications, Private Secretaries to the Royal

Family and Cabinet Ministers, and mandarins of Whitehall Departments and Ministries - Cabinet Office is the clearing house for all the confidential information circulating among them. It is the powerhouse for the Governance of the Commonwealth.

And very much more.

This all-powerful office is overseen by the Cabinet Secretary. As the only non-elected person in Cabinet, the nondescript title seriously understates his role. As well as recording official Minutes and giving Constitutional advice to the Government, he is head of a vast empire of his own, the Home Civil Service. Although conceding up-front influence to Parliament and Downing Street, no serious Westminster watcher doubts that it is the Cabinet Secretary – rather than elected parvenus - who holds all the long-term aces on behalf of his Whitehall Establishment.

Should there be doubt about the epicentre of real power, compare those newly elected Prime Ministerial faces photographed smiling their way into Downing Street, with the elderly, tearful derelicts making a final departure. Some slip away to private hospitals or the Lords, others to 'rest' in the Caribbean, justifying to a skeptical public 'a wish to see more of my family'. In the early hours, their pianos and private furniture are discreetly moved through the back gate of No 10 to pantechnicons ticking over on Horse Guards' Parade.

Ex-Prime Ministers are never happy-chappies as they leave Downing Street.

On the other hand, never having sought bright lights and the excitement of media interest, the Cabinet Secretary will, in his own time, exit quietly to well-deserved retirement, with a properly constituted pension, numerous City directorships and elevation to the House of Lords, free at last to indulge in those intellectual and academic pursuits delayed by commitments to Queen and The Empire since Coming Down from Oxbridge with Honours in Classics, and the forecast of a brilliant career.

So, when our research into the 'MOST SECRET' WWII GHQ Auxiliary Units started in 1992, it was Cabinet Office which gave security clearance at the necessary high level. It was agreed that, after 47 years, there should be 'no residual sensitivity'.

It still took time to work out why GHQ Auxiliary Units' security classification remained so high for so long. The men and women of the Patrols and Special Duties Section, having patriotically volunteered for an unpaid suicide mission when Britain was in mortal danger, had been officially ignored for half a century, shabbily treated under this smokescreen of secrecy and, it seemed, ruthlessly exploited by their good faith in the 'powers-that-be'.

The reasons became clearer when William Mackenzie's '*The Secret History of SOE*', written in 1948 and immediately and officially banned, was finally published by St Ermin's Press (in association with Little Brown), fifty years later. Mackenzie described the Auxiliary Units not just as 'SECRET' or even 'MOST SECRET', but 'one of Britain's nine WWII Secret Services' - the others being MI5; MI6; MI9 (clandestine escape lines abroad); MI13 (double-cross and deception); Special Operations Executive ('setting Europe ablaze'); the Political Warfare Executive (propaganda); the Radio Security Service (interception); and the London Controlling Section (protection of Ultra Secrets).

This placed number nine, the GHQ Auxiliary Units, firmly in the Premier Division for the first time and this book will examine why.

It does not, however, pretend to be the end of the story, or a complete Directory of events.

John Warwicker
Parham
October 2002

Introduction

The Problem

During post WWII de-Nazification, many Germans claimed they had never really liked Hitler anyway. Like him or not, most had certainly *approved* of him. Look at those mid-1930s pictures - the Berlin Olympics, Nuremberg rallies, and the crowds at his speeches and triumphant processions. Every right hand – young and old, male or female – reaches for the sky, straining for recognition, cravenly over-performing with the Nazi salute.

Hitler recreated a sovereign State of German speaking people from the disarray of WWI. By 1918 they had lost more than a million men on the field of battle and – less well known – a further million civilians dead from starvation. Even before military defeat, the British naval blockade brought the German call for peace.

Further humiliation followed the Treaty of Versailles in 1919. African colonies were handed over to the Allies, armed forces emasculated, and severe reparations imposed. Moreover, mainland Germany was separated from German speakers in Alsace, the Rhineland, Czechoslovakian Sudentenland and western Poland. Severe economic depression followed. The value of the Reichsmark collapsed amid wild inflation. Savings became worthless. Unemployment reached crisis level. Stripped of national pride, there was nothing but humiliation for this once great nation.

The late 1920s were a low base point in Germany. The country was primed for political exploitation and fertile ground for ambitious Nazis - young, energetic, nationalistic and ruthless. With the Party prepared to play the race-ace, Jews - ever unpopular and easily condemned as disproportionately influential - were immediately vulnerable, an easy target for brownshirt bullies, the Nazi street pathfinders, glorying in vulgar populism and eagerly exploiting youthful frustration especially among the lower classes. Germany became over-excited by quasi-military spectacle and triumphalism.

While still encouraging his street fighters, Hitler targeted the middle classes, whose votes would not normally have been cast for his Party, They may not have liked him but did gradually see advantages in a leader creating rapid economic progress, financial stability, full employment, modern infrastructure and a steady exchange rate. Many – in the short term at least – discovered that he represented their best interests too.

Hitler cleverly concentrated on other likely political opponents, notably the armed forces. Germany was still formally under draconian embargoes imposed by the Treaty of Versailles, but he financed a programme of secret rearmament. Pocket battleships were removed from drawing boards and translated into the real thing. So was a submarine fleet, the dreaded 'U-boats', which so nearly terminated Britain's war effort in 1942 and 1943. In size, the Luftwaffe overtook the Royal Air Force in 1935; Messerschmitt, Dornier, Heinkel and Focke-Wulf are names still respected by WWII aviation buffs. On the ground, the army - led by Generals not initially welcoming the dominance of an Austrian corporal – were massively funded and given the 'go-ahead' to create the world's largest and best-equipped ground force. Hitler outmanoeuvred his opponents at home and abroad. The nation rediscovered itself.

Germans who disapproved - liberals, artists, academics and intellectuals, for example, were often overwhelmed by the speed of events. Many emigrated.

When he was ready to reunite the German speaking people and create living space (*Lebensraum*) for them, Hitler occupied Austria, the Sudetenland and disputed border territories, without a shot being fired. Not until September 1939, when Germany invaded Poland in the sure knowledge that Treaty obligations committed Great Britain and France to outright conflict, was his aggression resisted by force of arms. Widespread Allied public and political resistance to the horrors of war, and Britain's approved policy of appeasement, well suited his purpose. He had gained time to perfect his war machine and modern blitzkrieg tactics. Hitler never hesitated to deploy them ruthlessly.

In September 1939, the valiant Poles were overwhelmed; Denmark, with a policy of neutrality but strategically important, soon followed; early in 1940, the Germans daringly attacked Norway – as usual without prior notice – and soon outfought Norwegian defences and a supporting British expeditionary force. Shots were now being fired in abundance, and Germany winning on all fronts. The Low Countries came next. Unco-ordinated and sometimes ineffectual Allied armies were further exposed when the King of the Belgians capitulated, against the wishes of his Government. This outflanked a French army in their 'impregnable' Maginot Line defending the border with Germany, as well as British allies. Soon after the miraculous – and, even today, not wholly explained – British Expeditionary Force delivery from the beaches of Dunkirk, Hitler held the European coastline from Norway to Spain.

His Forces had proved irresistible and, by midsummer 1940, were poised to invade Great Britain. The majority of Germans certainly *approved* of that!

Britain was alone. Appeasement under the Premiership of Neville Chamberlain, a Conservative Government and a largely uncritical Parliamentary Opposition, had left us cruelly under-prepared. But behind the scenes the British planned to combat German might with a 'Most Secret' weapon.

He worked for Military Intelligence. His name was Colonel John ('Jo') F C Holland, DFC, RE.

★   ★   ★

The Scene is Set

The 'reluctant' war in France, as it was formally known here – the 'phoney' war or '*Sitzkrieg*' as the Americans called it - lasted from September 1939 until early summer 1940. British Expeditionary Force photographers printed pictures of well-drained trench-works on the Western Front – where there was apparently no way British Army commanders would let their soldiers fight a second war of attrition bogged down in muddy discomfort. German Generals never considered such a possibility. Their soldiers, unconcerned about trench warfare, serviced half-tracks, lorries and Panzer tanks. When the time came they were on the road, riding to victory with 'lightning war' tactics.

At home, even after Dunkirk, Britain was still showing massive disinterest in the war. Encouraged by good weather, holiday resorts were full; work went on unhurriedly in fields and factories; industry was still not tooled up for an urgently needed increase in output. Some signs of war were imposed upon reluctant civilians. Enthusiasm for Air Raid Precautions was widespread. Husbands seeking official, if temporary, separation from carping wives were eager volunteers. Bomb shelters appeared at schools and children were marshalled with new disciplines into cool, damp, dark underground bunkers smelling of fresh cement. Air Raid Wardens in tin hats and siren suits became self-importantly assiduous about blackout infringement. Pillar-box tops designed to change colour with poison gas attack, were painted a dull yellow-green, and everyone, carried a gas mask, by law. The Royal family were pictured with theirs and official spokesmen reported from the Palace that baths had been marked with a five-and-a-half inch Plimsoll-line to economise on fresh water. Not even Royals would undermine the war effort by using more.

Or so it was said.

Barrage balloons made spongy appearances near important target areas; small boys gasped with wonder at the winding winches. Cables parted at a predetermined weak point during the first gale. When the strain of the wind became too great, grey, flappy monsters broke away toward an unfriendly cumulo-nimbus cloudbase – while a hundred meters or so of cable wrought havoc on roofs below. The operators were Balloon Command, and these boys, dressed in Royal Air Force blue, were soon in demand at church socials, replacing husbands conscripted and sent square bashing in Yorkshire.

Evacuees were herded from vulnerable cities to a frequently unwelcoming countryside. Some children took to it and stayed for ever. The majority, seizing an opportunity as a quiescent Luftwaffe kept largely to their own airfields, soon headed back to city homes with enthusiasm – leaving behind country schools never previously supplied with resources such as pencils and rulers. Some rural pupils even became interested in unheard of mysteries such as Algebra and French.

Petrol was in short supply after a while and a new invention called the 'black market' became part of everyday life. Rationing was usually scrupulously fair but citizens with either money or access to the new market did not experience shortages at once. Soldiers in khaki uniform battle dress and boots clomped around importantly and ack-ack teams sandbagged-down around prime targets.

Suddenly, in midsummer 1940, it all became seriously urgent – a new world of pillboxes and instant tank-traps appeared. Fixed defences pointed in the direction from which the enemy was expected to arrive. Constructed with great strength, many remain indestructible more than half a century later. If those clever Germans appeared from the wrong quarter however, with gun ports then pointing at friendly forces, all that digging and cement mixing might have been for nothing. Sandbags were stacked to protect essential buildings such as police stations and Council offices. Dragons' teeth were hurriedly constructed along vulnerable coastlines to prevent tank landings. Local Defence Volunteers became Home Guards and road accidents reached all-time records thanks to the blackout. It proved suicidal to drive at night with limited, officially regulated 'masks' over headlamps. For months it was less dangerous to show a decent light and run the small risk of aerial attack. Unfortunately, real danger did exist as tense Home Guards, mistaking headlamps for enemy invaders, took aim.

Some even fired!

Aerial reconnaissance photographs exposed Hitler's aggressive intentions. Prime Minister Winston Churchill, strongly opposed to Teutonic control of the British way of life, wound-up the nation to a state of awareness and readiness with eloquent speeches. Immediacy was fashionable. The 'Secret Weapon' was waiting as the War Cabinet met on 1st July 1940 to implement counter measures.

In peacetime an army officer gains seniority but not much promotion and this was the opportunity for those professionals who had never taken peace as a certainty. Churchill looked at their plans and gratefully authorised immediate action. One of Colonel 'Jo' Holland's ideas became known as GHQ Auxiliary Units.

This is how it happened.

★   ★   ★

The Secret Weapon

Between World wars, Lieutenant Colonel (Major General in 1943) John ('Jo') Charles Francis Holland, a career Royal Engineer and WWI veteran, was one of a number of underemployed and under-promoted British army officers. His opportunity came as WWII approached.

In spite of distinguished WWI service (among other things as an aviator), his War Office pecking order in 1938 was respectable but not high. But, well ahead of the 1939 crisis, he was preparing for an enemy occupation of Europe when no one else was seriously doing so – including soldiers in the very countries Hitler clearly had his eyes on. He drew up plans, for example, which eventually materialised into Special Operations Executive (SOE), the hugely successful multi-national force of guerrillas which operated in Nazi occupied territory. Informed historians rarely fail to acknowledge the value of Jo Holland's contribution to winning WWII.

In 1938 he was initially declared unfit for active service. But as an officer 'with personal experience of the defensive against irregular warfare in India and Ireland', he was singled out by the Director of Military Intelligence when the War Office finally lost patience with the preference for 'appeasement' voiced in Parliament and by much of the media and the British public. It seemed obvious to the under-funded and under-armed forces that Hitler had Great Britain in his sights as well as much of continental Europe and 'Jo' Holland was authorised to create a small unit, known at first as General Service (Research), or GS(R) to 'carry out research into problems of tactics and organisation under the Deputy Chief of the Imperial General Staff'.

Having limited faith in the cosy theory that German territorial aspirations could be contained by a naval blockade and an economic stranglehold based on a WWI strategy instead of outright military confrontation, and in the absence of official support for recruitment, retraining and rearmament, Jo Holland was allocated a small room in the War Office. With a desk and filing cabinet, a secretary with a 'Royal' typewriter and wind-up telephone, and a rectangle of carpet commensurate with his rank, he was initially tasked as a one-man think tank to work against the massing might of the German Reich. The Treasury thought that - compared with full-scale rearmament - he was good value. Within months his budget would exceed £500,000 however – a truly massive imprest for the times. His staff soon expanded to twenty-five officers.

His unit – formed in December 1938 and with a first programme of work dated 13th April 1939 - was soon renamed Military Intelligence (Research) – MI(R) – and expanded rapidly as the imminence of war became more obvious. A close military associate, Major Colin McVean Gubbins, MC (later Major General Sir Colin Gubbins, DSO, MC), Royal Artillery, was the most significant early appointment to MI(R), for he was to command Auxiliary Units from inception in June 1940 until his transfer to SOE on 18th November 1940.

Through a military and Intelligence fraternity, Holland and Gubbins secretly recruited potential specialists in guerrilla warfare from personal knowledge or indirect recommendation. MI(R) drew up a short list of around 1,000 'potential recruits for unlikely projects' – civilians and service personnel thought suitable for subversive and irregular warfare – and briefing courses, each of about thirty men, were run in London in May and June 1939 and again in the autumn. Gubbins and others – notably his second-in-command, Major Peter Wilkinson (later Sir Peter) – visited Cambridge from November 1939 and, with the collaboration of the University authorities, established a 'Politico-Military' course starting (for about forty officers) on 15th January 1940. The VCIGS was there on disbandment on 9th March, when the course was formally transferred to the Directorate of Military Training.

Holland and MI(R) are credited not only with the development of SOE, but also Independent Companies – later called Commandos; secret Continental escape routes for shot-down aircrew (MI.9); certain aspects of 'strategic deception (MI.10); the use of helicopters as modern army 'cavalry'; and a blueprint for the obscurely named 'GHQ Auxiliary Units'.

They also absorbed a technical section – MI(R)c (later MD1, that is Ministry of Defence 1) – responsible for the development and production of special weapons for irregular warfare. One of Holland's first moves (in June 1939) was to 'pull back from India' his old friend Major Millis Jefferis, RE (later Major General Sir Millis Jefferis, KBE) as Director. Ironically, early in 1940 when the unit title was changed to MD1, there was a Minister of Defence, the new Prime Minister himself, but no Ministry of Defence. MI(R)c therefore became known as MD1 officially and 'Winston Churchill's Toyshop' in the corridors of Whitehall and the War Office. Although technically reporting directly to the War Cabinet, the Jefferis' team expanded so rapidly and with such success as a testing ground for 'dirty tricks' and armaments' innovation, that it operated for the rest of the war virtually autonomously, in spite of attempts within Whitehall to take control of this jewel glowing brightly in the war effort crown.

In the field of irregular warfare alone they invented the 'Sticky Bomb', the PIAT(Projectiles/Infantry/Anti-tank), the 'Blacker Bombard', Push, Pull and Release switches to activate explosives, improved the Time Pencil delay fuse, and replaced it with the 'L' Delay timer.

'Auxiliary Units' was an imprecise title was deliberately chosen to fool the listening enemy, whose agents – according to Lord Haw-Haw on Radio Bremen – were round every corner, but who, it was thoughtfully imagined at the highest War

Office level, might not be able to distinguish Auxiliary Units from Auxiliary Policemen, the Auxiliary Fire Brigade, and the Women's Auxiliary Territorial Service.

These 'GHQ Auxiliary Units' would eventually comprise several thousand civilian personnel and some - contrary to the rules of conventional war – were by midsummer 1940 already being selected, trained and armed to 'stay-behind' in underground Operational Bases (OBs). Their own favourite job description was 'to commit mayhem' behind the lines of invading German troops.

Gubbins, in a War Establishment 'Secret' report dated 26th July 1940, disclosed that there was yet more to the Auxiliary Units:

'...The other role is Intelligence.'

★   ★   ★

Confusion is an inescapable element of war. Brilliant planning at General Staff level may be left in disarray if it comes on to rain, or the enemy reacts unexpectedly, or communications fail. From the Somme to 'friendly fire' casualties in the Gulf, the evidence is incontrovertible.

This was the case in the summer of 1940 when the British, reluctantly, recognised real conflict at last. At the top there were significant uncertainties – was Hitler proposing a secret deal allowing Great Britain to keep the Empire or not? Did we really believe in a crusade against evil fascism or was survival our only imperative?   Were there secret commercial and political interests? If the answers to such mighty matters were unclear to the powers-that-be it was not surprising that confusion also proliferated at ground level. Information available now is often contradictory, especially in the case of Auxiliary Units, whose operations were cocooned in post-war secrecy mainly, it now seems, because of 'the Intelligence role' written about by Colin Gubbins.

To make it worse, in 1940, guidelines were directed at Auxiliers in the field from superiors making up the rules as they went along. It can certainly be a puzzle today.

Sources for Auxunits' research are David Lampe's *'The Last Ditch'*, documents recovered from PRO and local Records Offices, and a number of invaluable eye-witnesses.   Many pieces of the puzzle still remain ill-fitting and a few others entirely missing.   Essential wartime secrecy persists mysteriously into peacetime years and sometimes leads to heated differences of opinion. The noted war historian,

Professor M R D Foot, writes appositely:

> *'Mainly it was due to bureaucratic inertia which thrives on Whitehall's cult of secrecy.'*

In *'Secret Service'*, Christopher Andrew noted:

> *'Malcolm Muggeridge derived from his years in British Intelligence the lesson that nothing should ever be done simply if there are devious ways of doing it...Secrecy is as essential to intelligence as vestments to a Mass, or darkness to a spiritualist séance, and must at all costs be maintained, quite irrespective of whether or not it serves any purpose.'*

The volume of confusion after set-up time in June and July 1940 is often underestimated. For example, instructions to Intelligence Officers (as the first selected leaders were known), had limitations. In spite of a stream of directives from HQ, they often authorised action on untested subject matter, with guesswork substituting for experience. Having no radio communications, operational patrols were always isolated from their HQ, and separate and independent from the 'Special Duties Section' although within the same administration. When factors such as these are absorbed, it is easy enough to recognise the mistake of trying to slot every atom of evidence into some predetermined and well-organised pigeonhole. Once that is under control, the Auxunits story may start to make sense.

The genesis of Auxiliary Units has sometimes been attributed to Winston Churchill himself. Supporting evidence is limited. However, the late Brigadier Geoffery Beyts, DSO, MBE, MC, second-in-command of Auxiliary Units between July 1940 and July 1942, dealt with this point during an interview at the Museum of the British Resistance Organisation in 1999:

> *Q. 'In your book (The King's Salt), you wrote that Gubbins said "...under Churchill's personal direction..." he was setting-up Auxiliary Units. Did it remain your firm impression that Churchill was the overlord?'*
>
> *A. 'Yes, indeed. We gained an enormous amount of pride, wishing to do our level best for England, via Churchill.'*

Whether or not the Prime Minister was actively involved, there is no doubt he was aware, and an early supporter, of irregular warfare in general and 'applied constant pressure for counter-offensive measures against the Germans'. Behind the scenes, and starting more-or-less simultaneously if not always harmoniously with MI(R), the Foreign Office already had 'stay-behind operations in hand under the management of Lieutenant Colonel Laurence Grand (later Major General), a Royal Engineer officer seconded to Section 'D' of the Secret Intelligence Service (MI6). His initial budget was £20,000. The remit of Section 'D' was to operate clandestinely against the enemy in a non-attributable way, and in any theatre of war where the overall war effort would benefit, whereas the Auxiliary Units, fighting ostensibly in some sort of uniform (usually khaki denims), were comparatively recognisable and 'overt', although working from underground as independent guerrillas.

This may not be how critics see it or eyewitnesses on the ground remember things, but records contain overwhelming evidence that these were the respective roles laid down at the highest levels.

On 1st May 1940, the Chiefs of Staff acted to sort out the confusion between various irregular warfare agencies (and, as we shall read, there was a third at work within the United Kingdom at about the same time) by creating an overall authority, not responsible for executive action – the Inter-Services Projects Board (ISPB). Its function was to 'co-ordinate projects for attacking the enemy by sabotage and irregular operations'.

The Board soon rationalised the overlap between MI(R), Section 'D', and XII Army Corps in south-east England (who had organised their own 'stay-behinds'), and other agencies within the remit of the Director of Military Intelligence.

Significantly, the chairman was Colonel John Holland.

On 22nd May 1940, Section D; produced a paper called, appropriately enough, 'Pessimism'. It considered British policy in the case of a 'certain eventuality' – the impending fall of France – and it concluded that the only hope would be in armed rescue by the still un-mobilised USA; in the meantime the best course of action was 'subversion from within to rot enemy held countries'. The paper was discussed by the Chiefs of Staff on 25th May and, on 27th May, the War Cabinet concurred to their recommendations on irregular warfare which led to the creation of SOE. Auxunits were probably a part of the discussion too.

High level policy decisions at last favoured soldiers already working on the potential of irregular activities, such as Jo Holland and Colin Gubbins, It was agreed, for example, that regular defence forces required supplementing with guerrilla-

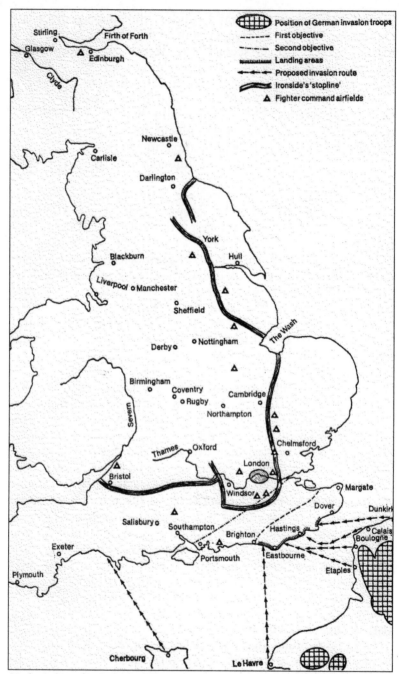

In the event of a German invasion General Ironside drew up plans to show where the 'Stop Line' would be placed.

type troops who would allow themselves to be overrun and be responsible for hitting the enemy in comparatively soft spots behind the zones of concentrated attack. A decision to this effect on 17th June 1940 was the date that Auxiliary Units started to move from the drawing board to operational reality. The ISPB met eight times between 3rd and 20th May 1940 and again on 27th May, 10th June and 5th July 1940. According to SOE records, there is little to be found in its Minutes except the 'organisation of the Auxiliary Units in England'.

Throughout these months, John Holland lobbied his ideas vigorously through the Director of Military Intelligence - from 1939 Brigadier (later Major General) Frederick J ('Paddy') Beaumont-Nesbitt – to the Vice-Chief of the Imperial General Staff; then through War Office to the Right Honourable Anthony Eden, Secretary of State; and, finally, directly to Prime Minister Winston Churchill. In doing so he established his ascendancy, and that of MI(R), in the military/political hierarchy of those crisis days and was influential in a major redirection of aspects of defence policy.

In mid-June, Section 'D' of the SIS was absorbed into MI(R). On 14th July 1940 the Home Defence Organisation of Section 'D' was formally incorporated within the Auxiliary Units administration – to be known as the Special Duties Section – and, at about the same time, so were the two XII Corps 'Observation Units', already training 'stay-behinds' in Kent and Sussex.

It seems probable that General Ironside, Chief of Home Forces early in June 1940, was closely involved throughout, and gave his backing to the growth of MI(R) and the birth of Auxunits. Indeed, in his diary on 20th June 1940, he writes of 'people staying-put in case of an invasion' and 'sabotage behind the lines' – clearly referring to the then unnamed Auxiliary Units. As his former Staff Officer, Colin Gubbins enjoyed direct access to General Ironside and could anticipate his support before these various ideas for the implementation of irregular warfare were pushed uphill for political approval.

It is on record that Churchill and General Andrew Thorne, Commanding Officer of XII Corps, met for lunch at Chequers at the end of June 1940 to discuss defences in the south-east, the possibility of counter-attacking the enemy on the beaches with mustard gas, and the disposition of the only fully-trained Division under Thorne's command. With issues of such dimensions on the agenda, it is improbable that Churchill discussed civilian 'stay-behinds' as an idea of his own.

However, he would have been aware that planning by the ISPB was already well advanced.

Auxiliers in Sussex always stoutly contend, and verify, enrolment *during* early June 1940, before the assumed start-up date. It can hardly be in doubt that they were part of General Thorne's creation, trained by XII Corps Observation Unit, all subsequently being absorbed into GHQ Auxiliary Units proper. To assist him, Captain Peter Fleming, recently returned from the Norwegian campaign as MI(R)s representative, was detached to 'train LDVs to fight behind the lines' as early as 25th May 1940.

The Secret Intelligence Service (MI6) and the Ministry of Economic Warfare were competing for control of SOE as early as 1st July 1940, when the Minister, Hugh Dalton, 'pleaded eloquently at a meeting in the Foreign Office that subversive warfare was a matter better handled by civilians than by regular soldiers'. He was not referring to Auxunits directly but it is another possible *formal* start-date for them. If so, it fits absolutely with the report written by Major Nigel Oxenden, MC, the first Intelligence Officer in Norfolk, cousin of Colin Gubbins, and author of 'Auxiliary Units – History and Achievement 1940-1944', that;

> *'the birthday of the unit can be put at 2nd July 1940'.*

For that reason, the Museum of the British Resistance Organisation chose 2nd July 2000, the 60th anniversary, to hold the final Auxiliary Units' national Reunion at Parham in Suffolk. As far as MI(R) is concerned, however, their official War Diary records Auxunits start date as 17th June 1940.

It is hardly surprising that doubts still persist about these dates; the Ministry of Defence maintains that 'secrecy militated against the survival of papers'. Few have been released. However, Colin Gubbins, part of a thoroughly professional team, would not have created Auxiliary Units without proper authority *in writing* – for the Patrols were in essence an illegal organisation according to international law. As he was responsible directly to GHQ, that authority could only have come from the C-in-C Home Forces, General Ironside. And he would not have given it without political approval from the War Cabinet.

If the official papers dealing with policy are somewhere in Public Record Office at Kew, they might as well have been destroyed. Tens of thousands of files are hidden there without detailed indices, and normally available only at a paltry three in one sitting! The MoD could claim they were holding nothing back in the fairly certain knowledge that – without a lifetime to spare and abundant good fortune – records placed in PRO were untraceable. It is fortunate that Andrew Taylor, Museum Director, can suggest how *some* Auxunits' records did disappear in his text on 'Oxo – a Sort of Commercial Traveller' – in Chapter X.

Documented information of Prime Minister Churchill's Auxunits involvement *after the event* does appear in a famous 'Secret' memorandum – filed in PRO – by Captain Duncan Sandys, his son-in-law, dated 8th August 1940, and Minuted and initialled by 'WSC' himself on 17th August. It describes:

> '...the progress which is being made in the organisation of the "Auxiliary Units" of the Home Guard.'

So, where are other relevant papers? The theory that they *could* have been destroyed in the 1952 fire at Coleshill House, wartime HQ of the Auxiliary Units, borders on fantasy. Were they quietly shredded or lost in official archives? Nigel Oxenden certainly had possession of many, but not all. The existence of further documentation is denied by the Ministry of Defence – but there is not a researcher who would be surprised if that turned out to be an economy of the truth. SOE and Auxiliary Units were intimately related through both John Holland and Colin Gubbins and it *is* known that all surviving SOE files were taken and retained by the Secret Intelligence Service (MI6) after the war.

Did Auxunit records head in the same direction? If so, even in recent correspondence, the SIS is not admitting it.

★   ★   ★

Strictly speaking, Jo Holland was not the only 'Secret Weapon' preparing irregular British counter-measures. Captain John Collings of the Royal Inniskilling Dragoon Guards was another. Also a career soldier with Secret Service contacts, he led British Army Polo players on chukkas to pre-war Germany, ostensibly to play-the-game, but with personal instructions to spy on Wehrmacht dispositions at the same time. Detail is given later.

But, first, we can examine why, early in July 1940, Lieutenant J W Stuart Edmundson, a Royal Engineer Territorial Army Officer on routine defence work in south-west England, was suddenly dispatched to Whitehall Place, London, on a 'Most Secret' Mission...?

NOT TO BE PUBLISHED

The Information given in this document is not to be communicated either directly, or indirectly, to the Press or to any person not holding an official position in His Majesty's Service.

11th June 1940   GENERAL HEADQUARTERS
                                          HOME FORCES

'The war has come closer to us owing to the German occupation of North-east France. This fact should be turned to advantage because the British people are at their best when faced with danger. We are now faced with danger. The attitude that there is little we can do against the invincible German war machine must be stamped out with the utmost brutality...
Any leader who fails to act at once is failing in his duty. Let each leader and each man go out with Cromwell's words in his mind 'It's no longer disputing, but out instantly all you can.'

Edmund Ironside
General
Commander in-Chief, Home Forces

This was part of General Ironside's Decree to his soldiers soon after Dunkirk. The message was clear. The war was not lost. Everyone must do his duty. It could have come from Nelson's flagship.

CHAPTER ONE

The Start of Operations

June 1940 saw the removal of civilian 'stay-behinds' from the drawing board of MI(R) into the real world of political recognition and military authorisation, and the appointment of Colonel Colin McVean Gubbins, Royal Artillery, as Officer Commanding, a leader with special credentials. As he selected his Staff – initially Captains Geoffrey ('Bill') Beyts, MC, an Indian Army officer of the Rajputana Rifles, and Peter Wilkinson, Royal Fusiliers – his watchwords were urgency and secrecy. Urgency because air reconnaissance and Military Intelligence had identified advanced Wehrmacht preparations for invasion; and secrecy for the safety of the men and women he was about to recruit for an experimental, unprecedented and, according to the rules of warfare – such as they were – *illegal* attempt to stiffen Britain's defences. In formal military terms, these were almost non-existent.

As a first step in the creation of Auxiliary Units operational patrols, Gubbins decided early in July 1940 to recruit a dozen Captains as field commanders with the title 'Intelligence Officers' – although not attached to the Intelligence Corps in any sense other than administratively. Indeed, it was not academics that Gubbins was looking for but practical leaders with initiative, ideas and imagination. There were not that many in the army at the time and senior officers were anyway reluctant to lose their best men. One 'stay-behind' 'Observation Unit' comprising regular soldiers of platoon strength under Captain Peter Fleming, was already operating in Kent and Sussex with direct orders from Commander, XII Corps, General Andrew ('Bulgy') Thorne. This was soon absorbed into Gubbins' GHQ Auxiliary Units, but Fleming, his Observation Unit, and any recruited 'stay-behinds' can justifiably claim to be the first of an elite few.

In a progress report on 'HOME GUARD – AUXILIARY UNITS' – to the Prime Minister, dated 8th August 1940, Captain Duncan Sandys, Churchill's son-in-law, wrote under 'Command and Control';

> *9. Contact is maintained with these small scattered bodies (ie. Auxiliary Units) through "Intelligence Officers" appointed for this purpose...There are 12 such officers on the establishment of HQ Auxiliary Units, and each is responsible for one of the areas shown on the attached map.* (Editor's note: This map in not attached in Public Record Office although there can be little mystery about it. Areas generally corresponded to selected County boundaries.)

> *10. The duties of these officers are:*
> *(a) To form Auxiliary Units, selecting localities and personnel.*
> *(b) To distribute and conceal the special stores.*
> *To train personnel in their duties and in the use of the special stores.*
> *(c) To act as liaison officers between the military Commanders and the Units.'*

'Special Stores' is a euphemism, nothing less, for munitions – including firearms, ammunition and explosives. This is the first official evasion, a 'cover up' at the highest level – perhaps an early recognition that civilian enrolment in GHQ Auxiliary Units was in possible contravention of the accepted rules of war.

In 1944, the Intelligence Officer in Norfolk – Major Nigel V Oxenden, MC, cousin of Colin Gubbins and, later, War Office author of the official History and Achievement of Auxiliary Units – the original of which disappeared under mysterious circumstances – wrote from contemporaneous notes:

> *'...About a dozen more were needed, and were appointed during July. They were allocated to coastal areas, from Caithness to Wales, and sent out with vague instructions to form 'cells' as best they could. They were attached, partly for the sake of the pay, to the Intelligence Corps, ...and were known as IOs.'*

In early July 1940, Lieutenant Joshua W S ('Stuart') Edmundson, an Anglo-Irish Royal Engineer Territorial Army officer, was at work on a military defence stop-line between Axminster and Bridgwater in Somerset. Having come down from Cambridge with an engineering degree in 1935, he married Iris Norrington, his boss's daughter, and they were happily established at Plymouth when he was first called to the Colours during the Munich crisis. Released to civil life again as Neville Chamberlain promised 'Peace in Our Time', Stuart was next called upon just before the birth of his first son, Will, on 2nd September 1939, as Britain Declared of War against Germany.

He later claimed he was 'unaware' of being on a pre-war MI(R) short list of personnel suitable for irregular warfare training. Indeed, 'it had never occurred to me' was his disingenuous answer when the proposition was put that Colonel Norrington, his father-in-law and WWI army veteran, may have been the link in a War Office old-boy network stretching from Whitehall to Devon. It had been to his great and unexpected surprise, therefore, when Lieutenant Edmundson was ordered to report to 7, Whitehall Place, London, at 1100 hours on 13th July 1940:

> 'The train had started at Penzance and called at Plymouth, so when it arrived in Exeter it was grossly overfilled. I fought my way on and got into a dimly lit corridor. All the windows were painted out with blue paint. There was a very small light in each compartment and one shaded light in each corridor. The passengers, troops of all ranks and sexes, were crammed in, as many as could fight their way on.
>
> 'Having cleaned up and had breakfast, I reported to a room on the second floor of 7, Whitehall Place. There was – unusually for the War Office – no name of the occupant on the door. Inside I found three or four officers sitting around wondering what it was all about. By 1100 hours we were six in number from mixed regiments, when Major Peter Wilkinson appeared through a side door. He explained that we had been selected for special duties and everything we heard was to be regarded as top secret.'

Stuart Edmundson was probably the only officer of the six without previous Military Intelligence experience. Two were already on Auxunits work in the field – Peter Fleming in the south-east, and Andrew Croft, a famed Arctic explorer and survivor of the Expeditionary force to Norway, in Essex and Suffolk. Both had useful experience of special duties and had attended Auxiliary Units introductory courses with Gubbins during the preceding month. Among other experienced officers was Donald Hamilton-Hill, a pre-war TA Officer, posted initially to War Office department MIL(b) after a course in Military Intelligence at Camberley. He wrote in his autobiography, 'SOE Assignment':

> 'My office was entered one morning by a tall, thin but fit looking major of the Royal Fusiliers – Peter Wilkinson – urbane and self-assured.'

They were already well-known to one another and, as a result:

> 'A call soon followed to report to an insignificant office in Whitehall. This office had nothing on the door – not even a number I sat down in company with six or seven other officers...We listened in silence as Peter Wilkinson entered dramatically and briefed us in

the strict secrecy of what we were about to hear. Then Colin Gubbins came in from a second door...'

The others, as Stuart Edmundson remembered them, were Captain John Gwynn, Grenadier Guards and a Conservative Party Parliamentary candidate, delegated to command Sussex and Hampshire, leaving another Grenadier, Peter Fleming – elder brother of James Bond author Ian Fleming, and himself a gifted writer – in Kent. Dorset and Somerset were allocated to Lord Ashley, Grenadier Guards, Lincolnshire to Donald Hamilton-Hill, Queens Own Cameron Highlanders, and Forth, Berwick and Northumberland to Hamish Torrance, Highland Light Infantry. Serving on the Staff at Whitehall Place until it was bombed, was Major Edward Beddington-Behrens, Royal Artillery, in charge of recruiting, and Captain the Hon. Mike T Henderson, brother of Lord Faringdon, 16/5th Lancers, as Quartermaster.

Gubbins summarised Britain's disastrous military position and announced a fight to the bitter end. It was imperative to form a secret 'stay-behind' force which would not be destroyed by any initial bombing or shore based action. The six were told they had been chosen because of their unorthodox, independent approach to military life.

Donald Hamilton-Hill wrote:

> *'Literally we were to recruit the most reliable local inhabitants in our allotted territories into small patrols...who would go to ground in the event of invasion and only attack, at a crucial given moment and on receipt of a given signal, enemy forces which had managed to establish themselves on any part of Britain's coast.'*

Before heading for the Plymouth train, Stuart Edmundson diverted to see work already in hand at Peter Fleming's HQ – 'The Garth', Bilting, near Charing in Kent:

> *'On arrival in Plymouth I went home for breakfast, ...my wife was surprised to see me believing me still to be in Tiverton. Shortly after breakfast Driver John Alford, RASC, appeared with an army staff car for my use...After breakfast I left for Cornwall and started work. During the day I made several contacts between Plymouth and Helston. I had a wonderful response. All types of men were prepared to come forward and help. They were all prepared to sacrifice themselves, knowing full well that should the Germans arrive their expectation of life would be very short indeed. I thought I had better return home to see if there were any messages, that being the only contact point I had. I found an interesting situation.*

'The night before when I was away, my wife had looked out and seen a 5-ton army truck standing in the drive. An escorting officer came in and asked for me. He said he could only hand his load over to me and must stay. As time wore on she fed him and his driver, who, at her suggestion, took the lorry round the back into the grounds of a Blind Asylum. He thought this was an excellent idea from the security point of view and slept the night on top of his load.'

The contents of the lorry were various munitions contained in cardboard boxes which, according to Major Oxenden, 'disintegrated if buried or left out in the rain', and known (then) as 'packs', 'dumps', or Aux. Units Mark 1. Having the same name as the organisation itself, this created a certain post-war predicament for confused historians.

Having signed for the load, Stuart Edmundson checked the contents and found fifty boxes, each containing:

5lbs gelignite
3 Mills bombs
2 magnesium incendiary bombs
3 oil incendiary bombs
Box detonators
Instantaneous HE fuse
Fast burning fuse
Slow burning fuse
Selection of 'Time Pencils', delay switches ranging
    from 10 minutes to 2 weeks, colour coded.
Pressure switches
Trip switches
Coils of trip wire
A crimping tool
Sticky tape

Collectively, they contained enough explosive to eliminate Fort Austin on Plymouth Sound (in one very big bang), a secure site in which Stuart Edmundson hid them. These 'special stores' had been prepared and supplied by Section 'D' (for Destruction) of the Secret Intelligence Service as it was in the process of dissolution as a separate entity and absorption into the Auxiliary Units. 'D' had already created a widespread network of secret explosive 'dumps', each under the control of one of their selected 'Key men', to await the arrival of the enemy. As things settled after occupation, it was intended that the Key man would recruit local saboteurs to destroy German supplies and transport. Although ingenious in concept, and carried out in a hurry with commendable initiative, the scheme was a secret service operation which found little favour with the War Office or army GHQ, with whose conventional forces it had never been strategically co-ordinated.

In the first instance, no records of any significance were kept on the grounds of secrecy but, by the end of 1941, Devon and Cornwall AUs separated – Cornwall being taken over by Capt. John Dingley, Duke of Cornwall's Light Infantry, and a pre-war banker in Launceston. Stuart Edmundson in Devon, created the first serious records which show he established 32 Patrols in the County under 10 Group or Assistant Group Commanders. Each Patrol had on average half a dozen 'Warriors'. Additionally, a Scout Section of 16 men and a Subaltern was established at his HQ, Lydford Manor on the western edge of Dartmoor.

This set-up was typical of Auxiliary Units development in selected areas.

Stuart – having been instantly promoted although perhaps unsure how it had all happened – remained unintimidated by his new responsibilities and fulfilled Gubbins's hopes for his unorthodoxy. During early operations in Devon, for example, he is on record telling an inquisitive full General to 'mind his own business.' Enigmatic as ever , Stuart explained:

> 'as I was being led away to the Tower of London, I had the good fortune of Colonel Gubbins intervention, followed by prompt release.'

Patrols and Scout Sections were to 'stay-behind' in underground Operational Bases (OBs) in the event of invasion but there was no initial plan for the IO to do so. 'My job would have ended with invasion and I would have returned to duties at GHQ', said Stuart Edmundson. This policy was reviewed under later commands but, although individual IOs disagree, the idea of 'stay-behind' IOs was eventually abandoned, leaving Patrol Leaders as key operational figures.

The claim that Auxiliary Units Patrols were good value for money, employing no regular soldiers, little weaponry and involving minimal expense, is certainly justified by papers in Public Record Office dated 26th November 1942, which show a claim by Captain J W S Edmundson for the sum of £1,416, the total required for the recruitment of 236 men at £6 per head, to be paid to Lloyds Bank Ltd, Tavistock, Devon. As a single Spitfire cost £5,000 this was good value indeed.

Gubbins' proposition that Auxunits were costing the country 'nothing' certainly proved true.

The Intelligence gathering Special Duties Section (the 'other side' of Auxiliary Units) was effectively secret and separate from Patrols, at least up to the rank of Group Commander. Stuart Edmundson always claimed 'I know nothing whatever of the SDS or Signals'. Brigadier Bill Beyts said exactly the same. However, Major Oxenden wrote:

> 'These conferences were held on Wednesdays at Headquarters, 12 (sic) Whitehall Place, and IOs attended, even from the north of Scotland, to report their progress, record this with pins on their maps, and receive their further instructions. On one occasion in July (1940) they found themselves with an equal number of strangers, officers and civilians, and even a woman. "You may as well get to know each other, gentlemen; you are all in the same game." This was the first contact between Ops and Special Duties, and was the last they were to see of one another for some time.'

Until his death in 2000, Stuart Edmundson was Patron of the Museum of the British Resistance Organisation and dealt frankly with our research enquiries. He held a letter of authority from the Ministry of Defence, dated 1st February 1967 allowing him to speak to David Lampe (the author of 'The Last Ditch'):

> 'There is no objection to you describing your personal experiences with the Auxiliary Units. Should you have any official documents of the period concerning these units, they should not be quoted.'

The letter was signed by the Director of Public Relations (Army). There is also a record that Stuart Edmundson visited an Auxiliary Units SDS radio out-station in Devon in 1943 but once again he told us – 'I have no knowledge of Signals or SDS.' The clear inference is of a different and *longer lasting* quality of secrecy around the Special Duties Section and provides some explanation of difficulties experienced in subsequent research.

This tells us a lot, not least that Stuart Edmundson was a man to keep his word about a serious commitment to the Nation's secrecy – *even half a century later*. It is also a useful guide to the significance of the WWII GHQ Auxiliary Units as one of Britain's nine Secret Services.

In autumn 1940, when Colin Gubbins was promoted and became operations Chief of Special Operations Executive (SOE), he wrote Stuart Edmundson a personal letter:

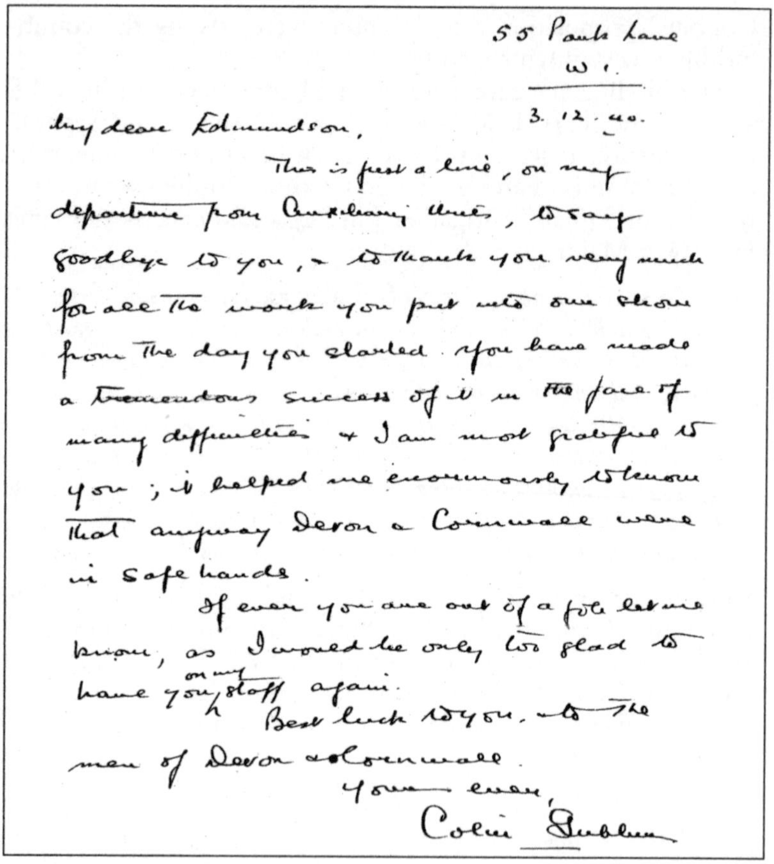

55 Park Lane
W 1.

3. 12. 40.

My dear Edmundson,
This is just a line, on my
departure from Auxiliary Units, to say
goodbye to you, & to thank you very much
for all the work you put into our show
from the day you started. You have made
a tremendous success of it in the face of
many difficulties & I am most grateful to
you; it helped me enormously to know
that anyway Devon & Cornwall were
in safe hands.
If ever you are out of a job let me
know, as I would be only too glad to
have you on my staff again.
Best luck to you, & to the
men of Devon & Cornwall.
Yours ever,
Colin Gubbins

My dear Edmundson,

This is just a line, on my departure from Auxiliary Units, to say goodbye to you, and to thank you very much for all the work you put into our show from the day you started. You have made a tremendous success of it in the face of many difficulties and I am most grateful to you; it helped me enormously to know that anyway Devon and Cornwall were in safe hands.

If ever you are out of a job let me know, as I would be only too glad to have you on my staff again. Best luck to you and to the men of Devon and Cornwall.

Yours ever,
Colin Gubbins.

Gubbins next invited Stuart Edmundson to take part in a special operation with the ill-fated Dieppe landing in the late summer of 1942. Although Stuart was not to able to take part – and the officer who did so instead was killed during the raid – these two patriots had not seen the last of one another. In 1943, Major Stuart Edmundson was transferred to work for Gubbins and SOE in the Far East theatre of war against the Japanese.

CHAPTER TWO

'Gubbski' & friends

'History had helped to make him a man ahead of his time'
(David Stafford – *'Camp 'X'*)

'I never saw him smile', said Stuart Edmundson. He served under Colin Gubbins in Auxiliary Units and Special Operations Executive and they knew one another well – as soldiers if not friends.

According to Lady Gubbins, however, her husband 'really enjoyed parties' and it was sometimes difficult to get him to leave at all! Photographs of Colin McVean Gubbins in uniform certainly show a stern figure, with rarely a glimpse of good humour, although in mufti it looks hard to restrain. Here was a professional who selected his mood-mode for the moment. It was a valuable asset for his country.

Depending on the source, he was either 100% Scottish, Irish-Scottish, a Highlander or an Orkney Islander. Obviously a Celt, Colin Gubbins was born in Japan in 1896, where his father was on British consular duties. Educated at Cheltenham, he joined the army, received officer training at Woolwich, had a distinguished WWI career in the Royal Artillery –both as a gunner in-the-field and on the Staff – and was awarded the Military Cross. John Holland and Lawrence Grand were a year or so junior. They all remained in the army during inter-war years, coming under the Directorate of Military Intelligence in the 1930s.

Some of the success of Colin Gubbins's army career was determined after his selection for General Ironside's Military Mission to north Russia in 1919. From then, he was often called 'Gubbski' – although not to his face when tuned-in to 'Mode – Military'. Recognising his efficiency as Staff Officer to that Mission, Ironside gave Gubbins invaluable support right up to 1940, when he retired.

Colin Gubbins served in Ireland during 'The Troubles' from 1919 and, according to the military historian Professor David Stafford and others, was influenced by the comparative success of small bands of guerrillas there – Irish Volunteers led by

Michael Collins against conventionally commanded British troops. Gubbins was never to forget how effective irregular warfare could sometimes be when deployed against regular formations.

These events persuaded him to specialise in the theory and practice of guerrilla warfare. He convinced himself of the principle that small, resolute bands of men, properly equipped, trained and led, could preoccupy disproportionate numbers of conventional troops under the right circumstances. Today it would also be seen as cost-effective warfare.

★   ★   ★

Meanwhile, John Holland was also at work. He noted the success of irregular tactics in the Boer War at the turn of the century and of T E Lawrence's (of Arabia) campaign, fighting behind the lines against the Ottoman Empire in WWI. He studied Fifth Column activities in the Spanish Civil War and every paper he could find on guerrilla warfare. If he was the 'think-tank' for the Directorate of Military Intelligence, Colin Gubbins was the 'flying squad'.

Gubbins's travels in the 1930s, were for MI(R) rather than the Royal Artillery. He fostered contacts in friendly Intelligence Services – particularly the French, Czechs, and Poles. Together with Captain (later Sir) Millis Jefferis, an MI(R) and Royal Engineer explosives expert, he was also at work in the office and in Spring 1939 they completed three classic booklets – '*The Art of Guerrilla Warfare*', '*Partisan Leaders Handbook*', and '*How to use High Explosives*'. Apparently still classified 'secret' in Great Britain, they were later produced abundantly in several languages to form core training for Allied agents throughout WWII. This completed one of MI(R)s first tasks for the ISPB – 'to produce Field Service Regulations for Guerrilla Warfare' – when they moved into the War Office in September 1939.

English editions, printed on rice paper for unhindered digestion through any alimentary canal, were issued to Intelligence Officers during the briefing at Whitehall Place on 13th July 1940. As far as can be ascertained, only one copy exists in the public domain, No. 7, and that has been kindly donated to the Museum of the British Resistance Organisation by the family of the late Stuart Edmundson.

Gubbins's biographers have recorded some of his travels immediately before the outbreak of WWII – secret missions to the Danube, for instance, where ingenious (but unfulfilled) plans were in hand to block this essential artery of enemy transport; Lithuania, Latvia and Estonia; and several to Poland. In May 1939 – according to SOE records – Gubbins went there to make arrangements for the 'reception of an MI(R) section in the event of war'. Poland was attacked on 1st September 1939 and a visit of special significance, hours before the collapse of Polish defences, has received only limited attention – generally describing him only as 'part of' (or 'Chief of Staff to') General Carton de Wiart, VC's Military Mission (No.4) to the Poles. He was officially GSO(1).

Authors gloss over this slice of Gubbins's career and take for granted his officially subordinate position – when it may well have been one of the most extraordinary episodes in an extraordinary man's life. Indeed, *positive understatement* was still evident in his *Times* Obituary of 12th February 1976, in which Carton de Wiart's military mission, immediately pre-WWII, was described as 'abortive'. Nothing could have been less true.

If leverage was applied to British-based publishers for reasons of National Security, it is simple enough – after reference to Anthony Cave Brown in his book *'Bodyguard of Lies'* – to imagine why. There could still be something to hide but *not,* surprisingly, to cover up a plan that went wrong. On the contrary, British secret services sometimes go to extreme lengths - by hiding yesterday's successful operations – to prevent tomorrow's enemy knowing how clever they can sometimes be. This was a fine example.

Helpfully, authors with access to American records sometimes uncover 'unsanitised sources' and are able to present a freshly laundered viewpoint on 'restricted' subject matter, unencumbered by the Official Secrets' Act.

★   ★   ★

Throughout WWII, Allied operations were heavily dependent upon successful transcripts of enemy coded communications. Hitler, the German armed forces, their Diplomatic Service and Axis allies, employed the 'Enigma' machine in the firm conviction that the system produced unbreakable code. They had explicit trust in the security of their vital communications. It is no secret now that this confidence was unfounded and British experts operating from Bletchley Park, utilising the brilliantly conceived 'Turing Machine' ('The Bomb') and formidable quantities of sheer genius, have rightly been credited with this major contribution to Allied victory.

A measure of 'Enigma' code-cracking existed even before the

war started and on 22nd May 1940 – with the project still codenamed 'BONIFACE' – the GCCS broke the first machine cipher intercept. With this special access to the enemy's thoughts, Churchill enjoyed strategic advantages, not only over the enemy but also Allied governments and political opponents alike, for they – with few exceptions – could never be part of the great secret.

This massive source of Intelligence would have been valueless once the Germans realised their codes were being read. Simply by changing work-input key codes, an invaluable advantage to the Allies would be lost. To prevent this, total responsibility for the security of 'Ultra', the code-breaking programme, was assigned to the head of the Secret Intelligence Service, MI(6), Sir Stewart Menzies, designated within the Service as 'C'. This, and other elaborate deceptions, were brilliantly carried out by a committee, known as the 'London Controlling Section' (LCS), under Menzies' overall command. Gubbins, in his later position as head of SOE and designated 'M', was a member of that committee. The only woman, the secretary and personal assistant to the LCS chairman, was Lady Jane Pleydell-Bouverie, the family name of the Earl of Radnor, owner of Coleshill House, HQ of Auxiliary Units. This was surely more than coincidental – an effective mutual back scratch is evident.

★   ★   ★

The success of the Government Code and Cipher School (GCCS), the 'Golf, Cheese and Chess Society' at Bletchley Park, had not been unaided.

In the early 1930s, Polish Intelligence crypto-analysis experts employed Jerzy Rozycki, Henrik R Zygalski, and Marian Rejewski, outstanding young mathematicians from Poznan University, who made useful progress penetrating 'Enigma' transmissions employing numerical rather than mechanical decode-systems. The product was necessarily slow and limited, as they were working a commercially available 'Enigma' which, it was rightly assumed, had been secretly modified by German experts for official transmissions. From 1937, the French Secret Service Chief of Cyphers – Captain Gustave Bertrand, with different techniques, was also reading a limited amount of encoded enemy radio traffic helped by a paid German informer – Hans-Thilo Schmidt, code-named 'Asche' – who was supplying key-codes. Although an aid to decryption, the product of these traditional methods was usually too slow to be of much operational value.

As war with Germany became inevitable, representatives of the three 'friendly' secret services met near Paris; with both Polish and French defences in danger of being overwhelmed, it was agreed that the British should receive, and be the beneficiaries of, all relevant secrets held in connection with 'Enigma' transmissions.

It was the start of the 'BONIFACE' project, later called 'ULTRA'.

One of these 'secrets' was already in safe hands. Code-named 'Richard Lewinski', he was a Polish Jew, an engineer who had worked in Berlin on an 'Enigma' production line incorporating secret German Government modifications As soon as he was identified as Jewish, 'Lewinski' was sacked and expelled to Poland. Amazingly enough in a country as anti-Semitic and obsessed with State Security as Germany, there was no follow-up. Sensing a unique opportunity, 'Lewinski' – a 'dark man in his early 40s, thin and bent' – persuaded Polish Secret Service agents that he could build a reproduction 'Enigma' machine, single handed.

When the news reached Britain, specialists hurried to interrogate him in August 1938 and, once convinced, were authorised to accept his conditions – £10,000 Sterling, a new identity for him and his wife, and a Residence Permit for France. By arrangement with our Allies, MI(6) moved him to Paris where he came under the control of British 'Agent 2400' – before being transferred to the United Kingdom as French defences collapsed.

He then disappeared, it seems. For ever, and ever, Amen.

★   ★   ★

In 1939, Gubbins was credited with bringing samples of 'time pencils' from Poland, fuse timers for explosives and booby-traps which, after development by Section 'D' and MD1, became the standard workhorse for Auxiliary Units Patrols, the SAS and SOE, and other special forces. Being activated by the effect of acid on copper wire, they had a unique advantage over other timing devices – silent operation.

General Adrian Carton de Wiart's Military Mission arrived in Poland only a week before war broke out. Included were both Gubbins and Peter Wilkinson, continuing a professional relationship which lasted for the duration of war. Gubbins was officially listed as GSO to de Wiart; it was, however, cover for his true role as head of a Mission from MI(R).

In Poland they witnessed at first hand the violent effectiveness of Blitzkrieg tactics and were 'lucky to get away through Romania without capture and internment'. After the Polish capitulation, Gubbins and Wilkinson were reported to be in Paris, 'working with exiled Poles and Czechoslovaks'.

David Lampe in his classic *'The Last Ditch'*, describes Gubbins's specific task in Poland:

> '...to get the Poles and Czechs ready to form some sort of guerrilla warfare...but he barely had time to get started... several nights later the members of the British Military Mission were told to escort their Embassy's staff out of Warsaw. They eventually reached Romania...*where Gubbins was singled out* (Editor's italics) and given a false passport which enabled him to get home.'

This version from Gubbins himself, has some recognisable hallmarks of deception.

David Lampe had a considerable advantage over other researchers in the 1960s – that letter of authority from the Director of Public Relations (Army). The final paragraph raised no objection:

> '...to you describing your personal experiences with the Auxiliary Units...'

Lampe went on to acknowledge;

> 'Major General Sir Colin Gubbins not only started me on the trail of the most important facts in this book but also answered a number of my questions and suggested people who proved to be very helpful.'

The letter and the Auxiliary Units were not in way connected with the 'Ultra' project, of course. And so Colin Gubbins, who was, did not feel obliged to tell the *whole* truth and nothing but the truth.

He had good reasons for not doing so.

★   ★   ★

Colin Gubbins was equivocating – calculatedly and for the best reasons – on essential detail about his final trip to Poland. That he was *singled out and given a false passport* may well have been true, but it was only part of the story. Some secrets are more secret than others. Some secrets are *for ever*, no matter what inducements are made. This special quality appears in many parts of the Auxiliary Units story as well.

Specific information about Gubbins' Polish adventure comes

from American sources in Anthony Cave Brown's book, *'Bodyguard of Lies'*. The author writes of the British Military Mission of *Colonel Colin Gubbins* – and not *General de Wiart*. After a full, at times dramatic, summary of events surrounding the 'Ultra' programme, Anthony Cave Brown continues:

'At a later conference (on 25th July 1939) at a Polish intelligence station in the Pyry forest near Warsaw, the Poles handed over to the British (*headed by Commander Alistair Denniston, Chief of GCCS:* Editor) everything in their possession concerning Enigma, retaining only the material that was needed for operational purposes. It was taken under heavy escort to London on July 24th 1939. It proved a wise precaution. Only a month later the Germans attacked Poland, and the Second World War began. With the capture of Warsaw and the collapse of the Polish government, the key cryptographers involved in Enigma were evacuated from Poland together with the Polish General Staff and the British military mission of Colonel Colin Gubbins. They crossed the Polish frontier into Rumania and the cryptographers were detached by MI(6) and sent...as agreed...to work with the French. But for these precautions the Germans would almost certainly have discovered that the Poles had penetrated Enigma.'

Another Briton – code-named 'SANDWICH' – was reported to be present but not an active participant. It has been speculated that it was either Sir Stewart Menzies of SIS or Gubbins himself, although the likelihood is stronger that it was in fact Commander Humphrey Sandwith, codebreaker for the Directorate of Naval Intelligence.

Colin Gubbins' 'most secret' role in the summer of 1939 is amplified in *'A Man Called Intrepid'* by William Stevenson, again using American sources. On page 42:

'A British intelligence mission was sent to Warsaw early in 1939. Mystery still surrounds it. The operation, like many others, was conducted in defiance of official British appeasement policy. The Warsaw mission was led by an unusual man-at-arms, the Scot named Gubbins, otherwise known as Colonel Colin Gubbins, of the Royal Artillery, who had been working for some time in a shabby office near Stephenson's St. James's Street headquarters (probably Caxton House). Gubbins dressed immaculately, wore a red carnation in his buttonhole and carried kidskin gloves. One acquaintance remembered him as *an amiable, rather vague sort of chap with no particular talents and some sort of desk job in the War Office.*' (Editor's italics.)

Gubbins had again played an impeccable deception.   No one directly involved *ever* thought of him – even privately – as 'rather vague'.

Further description follows on Page 44:

'Gubbins and his men flew back to London from Warsaw on August 22 with a companion *and a prize that would remain secret for another thirty-five years* (Editor's italics). The very next day...Gubbins was already on his way to Warsaw again. One of his colleagues, Eric Bailey, a legendary secret agent himself, commented to Stephenson later: "It seemed madness". Only Stephenson and one or two others knew that, crazy or not, Gubbins had to do it.   The coming world war might be won or lost in consequence.'

In August 1939 when the staff of Government Code and Communication Section moved from London to Bletchley, they found an Enigma machine waiting. It had been 'acquired' by the Polish Secret Service – according to Stevenson – after the 'failure of the Polish engineer's mock-up'.

Perhaps that was why Lewinski disappeared? Anthony Cave Brown thinks not, however:

'The accuracy of Lewinski's creation would later be confirmed when *the Poles were able to obtain an actual Enigma...*' (Editor's italics).

William Stevenson continues:

'It was a week before Germany attacked Poland...(the) *prize was the greatest gift one nation could give another* (Editor's italics)...It more than compensated Britain for signing the Anglo-Polish Treaty three days later, on August 25, committing Britain to make war on Germany if she invaded Poland...So strong was Gubbins's sense of obligation and comradeship that he was already leading a thirty-man team straight back into Poland...Then, *in October 1939*, (up to a month after German occupation: Editor), Colin Gubbins made good his escape from conquered Poland.   He had slipped into Romania and from there traveled (*sic*) through the Balkans to the Mideast.   He brought with him the nucleus of a Polish secret Army.'

The 'prize' was one of the Wehrmacht 'Enigma' machines built by the Poles – another had apparently been temporarily 'requisitioned' by the Polish Customs service. The Poles revealed their array of de-cyphering techniques to several Britons – together with Key Codes - and delivered one machine

to the British and another to the French. They were removed
via Romania – and the Poles smashed the rest.

During the last week of August 1939, Gubbins was on the
spot to orchestrate removal of the acquired 'Enigma' from
Poland to Bletchley. *He then went back again for his Polish
friends, to whom the Allies owed so much – and nearly got
caught.* Stevenson asserts that Gubbins was behind enemy lines
for *up to a full month.* It was certainly the right time to be
singled out for that false passport.

In the face of all this drama, and the secrecy surrounding
'Enigma' and 'Ultra', it is not surprising that some sequences
overlap, or show minor differences of timing. They do not,
however, seem significantly to undermine the main thrust of
Gubbins's involvement.

He was never on routine attachment to a military mission (it
was once described as 'agricultural') coincidentally in Poland
before the outbreak of war. Instead, he headed a number of
non-attributable adventures specifically tasked to acquire
Intelligence about the construction, operation and decoding of
enemy Enigma transmissions. The unique cocoon of secrecy
surrounding these episodes is founded on the fact that
Gubbins's missions – on direct War Office orders through the
Director of Military Intelligence – *were in direct 'defiance' of
official Government policy.*

The quoted versions corroborate one another in general and,
fortunately, recent confirmation comes from the official SOE
diary records.

25th August 1939	Gubbins left by air for Poland.
3rd September	Gubbins arrived (nine days later and two days after the German attack – Editor)
18th September	The Mission was evacuated (but if William Stevenson was right, without Colin Gubbins – Editor)

The bonus was the recovery of a working 'Enigma' machine –
narrowly ahead of the Germans – from Poland to Bletchley
Park in August 1939, the exclusive result of Gubbins's long-
term, personal cooperation with Polish Intelligence. This
achievement certainly influenced the outcome of the war in
favour of the Allies.

But, if Gubbins had later been taken by the Germans, he
would have been formally disowned. MI(6) policy since WWI
was clear:

'Any act was permissible, even assassination. The only crime
was to get caught; if an agent was caught, he was disowned.'

('*Bodyguard of Lies*', page 29)

Perhaps it is less than extraordinary that, after all these years,
official disclosure is still restricted and then usually sourced
from overseas. Even less so that Gubbins chose not to explain
it all to David Lampe.

In fact, he never did openly refer to his work in Poland or
write an autobiography. His official biographers, Sir Peter
Wilkinson and John Holland's secretary, Joan Bright-Astley, in
'*Gubbins and the SOE*', also avoided specifics, although both
were professional intelligence officers and involved with him
either directly or indirectly. Only a massive and everlasting
quality of secrecy could have persuaded them – and other
British authors – against disclosure. The temptation was
resisted even *after Gubbins died.*

A significant slice of Gubbins's war service and a proper
place in history, were therefore sacrificed to protect the 'Ultra'
project. The well-tested Secret Intelligence Service maxim that:

'To be effective, a secret service must be secret'

– worked faultlessly. Some of these events still seem to remain
'Most Secret' and the evidence presented here is mainly from
work published abroad.

The 'Ultra' operation was necessarily secret at the time – it
gave obvious strategic and tactical advantages to the British and
Americans, members of the 'Special Relationship' on
Intelligence matters – and had to be kept from other Allied
combatants such as General de Gaulle and the Soviets, as well
as the enemy. Someone with influence must still see advantage
in keeping a lid on these secrets – in a quiet way. In a
democracy, elected representatives are the top pinnacle of
Government; the military their subordinates; and secret
services somewhere in between. But, in August 1939, frustrated
by prevarication and appeasement from the Palace of
Westminster and Whitehall – Foreign Office in particular – an
initiative was taken which deviated from the rules and was
contrary to official Government policy.

It very much appears that it is still against certain interests to
rock the boat and draw attention to it all now.

Nevertheless, let's hear Three Cheers for Colin Gubbins.

He was soon back in front-line action. Early summer of 1940
saw the beginning and end of a disastrous British military

expedition to Norway. The army had a bad time before the Royal Navy ferried them out. The only success, a moderate one, was another of John Holland's ideas, the 'Independent Companies'. Under Gubbins they lived to fight another day as Commandos. He was awarded the Distinguished Service Order (DSO):

> 'Lieutenant–Colonel Gubbins...displayed sterling qualities of leadership in the handling of his troops operating in a strange and difficult type of country. On several occasions he personally led troops which were fighting a rearguard action in contact with the enemy, His courageous example of devotion to duty, though greatly overworked, was an inspiration to his men and their safe withdrawal was due to his inspiring leadership.

Another incident, not formally applauded, demonstrated his special talent for opportunism. During the height of the campaign, Gubbins found time to mount a dawn raid on GHQ Officers' Mess. Last seen in a staff car at speed, heading back to his men, he had sequestered the final whisky supply. Typical of his man-management skills – although the Staff were not ecstatic – it did miracles for his soldiers fighting in bitterly severe weather.

Leo Marks was chief cryptographer for SOE as the Second Front approached, working directly for Colin Gubbins, then near the peak of his power. Here is a digest of Marks' comments on 'the Mighty Atom' taken from his book '*Between Silk and Cyanide*':

> '...Gubbins's eyes made de Gaulle's seem placid...the intelligence in that room was like vibro-massage...described as a real Highland toughie, ...he was short enough to make me feel average, with a moustache which was as clipped as his delivery, and eyes which didn't mirror his soul or any other such trivia...his eyes reflected the crossed swords on his shoulders, warning all-comers not to cross them with him...there was a warning gleam in those forbidding eyes...the General closed the report and without pausing for breath, proved he was a field-marshaller of facts...was the bloody man telepathic?...he shot his next question as quietly as a machine gun...he then made a statement which caused a drop of perspiration to parachute from the end of my nose and land on the edge of his desk...the spiky little bastard with an MC on his tunic and an Intelligence department in his head...in many ways mortal, Gubbins was unable to conceal his intense fatigue, but a single glance from him was still the equivalent of a brain-scan.'

★   ★   ★

This was the first commander of GHQ Auxiliary Units – no backroom theorist but a decisive, practical, experienced soldier of the highest calibre and a measure of the men and women recruited as Auxiliers in the summer of 1940. They were no Dad's Army.

He selected two outstanding soldiers as joint second-in-command. Major Geoffrey ('Bill') Beyts, an Indian Army officer of the famous Rajputana Rifles, had won a Military Cross in 1932 in Burma, leading patrols against rebel insurgents in a long jungle campaign. He also served in Norway. An expert in camouflage, silent killing, stealth and stalking, he was ideal as Officer Commanding Auxiliary Units' Operations and Training. He served for two years before returning to the Far East, where he earned a DSO with special forces in combat behind-the-lines against the Japanese.

In charge of Organisation, Planning and Liaison with various secret departments, was (Sir) Peter Wilkinson. He left Auxunits in October 1940 to move with Gubbins to SOE, having his own adventures behind enemy lines, mainly in the Balkans. After the war, he entered the Foreign Service, reaching Ambassador's rank; his final Whitehall appointment was as Intelligence co-ordinator at Cabinet Office. He was awarded a knighthood (KCMG) and a DSO, he also held many foreign decorations.

Peter Wilkinson and 'Bill' Beyts died in Millennium year. Brigadier 'Bill' was Guest of Honour at the final Auxiliary Units Reunion at the Parham Museum in July of that year, and Peter Wilkinson sent a message which was read on his behalf, for he was then blind.

Major General Sir Colin Gubbins, KCMG, DSO, MC, predeceased them. He died in 1976 and left an Estate of £27,114. Either he had a talented Inheritance-Tax advisor or was seriously under-rewarded for dedicated service to his country.

The end of WWII had brought the immediate dissolution of SOE and the destruction of his power base. On the other hand, The Secret Intelligence Service, under 'C' – Sir Stewart Menzies, grew from strength to strength as the Cold War developed. In WWII, the two men fought the same enemy, the Axis powers, but in doing so had fallen out. In 'The Secret Servant', Anthony Cave Brown makes a comparison:

'Both were spirited men, although Gubbins was the more evidently to be believed, as he wrote, that...the best thing to do with an informant was to kill him quickly. 'C', on the other hand disliked noise and violence in his work, preferring silence and stealth. When Menzies captured a spy, execution did not necessarily follow immediately: he preferred to keep the man alive on the grounds that a live spy had utility, a corpse had none. This was a difference of tradecraft, and it was a difference that caused much of the trouble between the two men and their Services.'

SOE records were taken over in 1945 and became the gift of MI(6) to release or not. Normally secretive, 'C' ensured that Gubbins never got another job in the army – and made no effort to disguise it. Here was one battle even Gubbins could not win and he moved first to the business world and, then, retirement. Generously recognised with foreign honours, the emergence of the Gubbins' story at home was at best, drip-fed to the public.

If his enormous contribution to 'ULTRA' was embargoed by Sir Stewart Menzies, could it be justified on grounds of State Security alone? Was there also an element of personal vindictiveness? Were quasi-official inducements subsequently employed to constrain detail of Gubbins's Polish adventures?

Such interesting speculation involves distinguished and successful SOE authors as well as Gubbins himself. Christopher Andrew in his book 'Secret Service' gives full credit to Polish Intelligence for its part in breaking the 'Enigna' codes – but none to Gubbins.

But, if it ought to be over-and-done-with more than half a century later and you would prefer to read all about it yourself, go to your bookshop and buy the latest edition of Cave Brown's 'Bodyguard of Lies'.

It will not be there. You could, however, order it from America at $17.95 and it might just have slipped through the net and into your public library.

★   ★   ★

Sequence of significant events

1939

24th July	the Poles handed over everything in their possession concerning 'Enigma' – retaining only material needed for operational use. (ACB)
August	'Enigma' machine *in situ* at Bletchley) Park (WS)
22nd Aug	Gubbins flew from Warsaw to London – with a 'prize' that would remain secret for another 35 years (probably the Engima machine acquired by the Czechs and Poles) (WS)
24th Aug (?)	(probably 22nd) – 'a week before Germany attacked Poland – the prize was the greatest gift one nation could give another.' (WS)
25th Aug	(or the 'very next day') – 'Gubbins and a thirty man team (WS), left by air for Poland (SOE). '...it seemed madness...Gubbins had to do it. The coming world war might be won or lost in consequence.' (WS)

Anglo-Polish Treaty committing Britain to make war on Germany if Poland was invaded.

1st Sept	Germany attacked Poland.
3rd Sept	Gubbins finally arrived (nine days after departure and two days after the Germans attacked). (SOE)

Britain declared war on Germany.

17th Sept	capitulation of Warsaw.
18th Sept	'The Mission was evacuated' (SOE) but (if WS was right) without Gubbins.

'...with the collapse of the Polish Government, the key cryptographers involved in 'Enigma' were evacuated...together with the Polish General Staff and the British Military Mission of Colonel Gubbins.' (ACB)

Oct(?)	Colin Gubbins made good his escape from Poland. He brought with him the nucleus of a Polish secret army. (WS)

AUTHORITY:
(WS) William Stevenson, (ACB) Anthony Cave Brown
(SOE) Special Operations Executive records

CHAPTER THREE

Auxiliary Units' Patrols

by Andrew Taylor, Museum Director

*'We shall defend our shores – whatever the cost may be.
We shall never surrender...'*

(Winston Churchill, 1940)

Suffolk farmer Herman Kindred's first contact with Auxiliary Units left him in no doubt of the fate about to befall Great Britain in 1940. He was sure the Germans were on their way across the Channel:

'They told us – "The Germans are coming, they'll soon be here. They are a ruthless lot"...'

As he repeated that simple sentence more than half a century later, it still portrayed his frightening certainty that Britain would be the next to endure Hitler's onslaught.

For the same reason, Fred Simpson, a Dorset farm worker, joined the Local Defence Volunteers almost as soon as recruitment started in May 1940:

'...one rifle appeared for about twelve of us, with five practice rounds every few weeks. One night there was a rumour that the Germans had landed. I was the only one with a gun, my father's 410 shot gun, and other chaps had sticks and farm tools or nothing at all. It was a good job the scare came to nothing.'

In the midst of the Dunkirk crisis, Prime Minister Winston Churchill and the War Cabinet, had approved an Inter-Services Project Board assessment – dated 27th May – that:

'The regular defences require supplementing with guerrilla type troops, who will allow themselves to be overrun and who thereafter will be responsible for hitting the enemy in the comparatively soft spots behind zones of concentrated attack...'

This led directly to the formation of Auxiliary Units operational patrols and Colin Gubbins was selected to establish a network of *civilian* 'stay-behind' saboteurs (rather than 'troops') to attack invading German forces from behind their lines. He had the pick of those army officers previously identified by MI(R) as suitable candidates – which he called Intelligence Officers (IOs) – to raise and train 'cells' to operate behind German lines mainly in assigned, vulnerable, coastal areas. These Patrols, as they became known, were provided with an operational hideout and the best available equipment – explosives, firearms, ammunition, fighting knives. They were to leave their homes and go to ground when the order was given by their IO.

These specially selected and trained saboteurs, formally known as Auxiliers, would then emerge from cover and, acting alone in their individual patrol areas, carry out guerrilla operations in the heart of enemy held territory. In no other European country had such a defence force been created *before* the Nazi assault.

The unit that Gubbins commanded in 1940 would not entirely resemble the one stood down more than four years later. Auxiliary Units Operational Patrols were to undergo procedural and administrative modifications throughout the war. For the purposes of this study, their historical existence can be broadly divided into two distinct periods – from summer 1940 to the end of 1942 – by which date it was widely considered that the threat of invasion was over – and from 1943 until Stand Down in November 1944.

Within these two periods the operational development of Auxunits Patrols was directly influenced by the appointment of successive Commanding Officers, the main effect of which saw both the discontinuation and reinstatement of Gubbins' original cellular method of operation. As we shall see, at one stage the maintenance of essential secrecy surrounding the Patrols experiment had been irretrievable compromised.

The early days – 1940

Major Nigel Oxenden, one of Colonel Gubbins' original twelve Intelligence Officers, served in Norfolk until the middle of 1941 and his document – 'Auxiliary Units, History and Achievement' written in October 1944 - is an authentic source of information. In this extract he briefly explains the orders issued to IOs and some of the problems faced in setting up this unique force in the early days:

'Their mission was to find reliable men, about thirty each, to leave with them a "dump" of assorted explosives and incendiaries, to help these "dump-owners" to form their cells of five desperate men, to train them in the use of weapons that were as new to them as to their trainees, and to provide the cells with some form of "hideout"...

'...Faced with a form of warfare that they had probably never contemplated before, IOs automatically looked for the gamekeeper or poacher type of recruit, as being already trained in everything but explosives. If these men were also last war veterans, so much the better; they were probably steady, and well aware of their own limitations...'

At least one instance is recorded of both gamekeeper *and* the local poacher belonging to the same patrol – their combined expertise in stealthy pursuit and evasion no doubt being invaluable to their comrades. Other recruits included farmers and labourers, ghillies, miners and factory workers – even a vicar was out training in the art of sabotage when not administering to his congregation. Specially tasked 'Pals' units were also formed, for example, in Marconi's factory in Chelmsford and within the Admiralty administration at Bath.

Like Fred Simpson – and a million others not yet called to the armed forces – a young Herman Kindred joined the LDV in May 1940. For three months he was rostered to patrol and protect the village communities of Parham and Little Glemhan in Suffolk. Patrols were a three hour stint on a pedal cycle armed with a shot gun and three-inch cartridges that would 'make a nasty hole in a sheet of iron at one hundred yards' – but which would have been little defence against a squad of German Storm Troopers.

At the end of August, Herman was approached by the local commander of the (now renamed) Home Guard, and asked if he would be interested in a specialist role that would relieve him of his normal duties? If he was keen, he was to report to the village hall at Little Glemham the following Sunday.

Admittedly bored by endless nights cycling around the area or staring for hours into darkness on lonely guard duty, Herman was intrigued and duly reported to the village hall on time. There, met by two regular army officers he had not seen before, he and a handful of other men from the area were given a demonstration – slicing a lump of solid steel in half with a carefully placed explosive charge. After being assured they did 'not need to stand so far back', the huge bang and resulting clean cut through the metal, convinced Herman that this role, whatever it was, would be a lot more exciting than 'ordinary' Home Guard duty. When told that anyone still interested should report back to the hall on the following Tuesday, Herman Kindred had no doubts:

'When we got there we were absolutely amazed. There was an armed guard on the door, and another patrolling the building to see that nobody came anywhere near...

'We met the Officer in charge again, and then he disclosed to us what we were expected to do. He said – "we've cleared up most of the south of England and are moving fast up this area to build hideouts for you people. You will be trained to operate behind the lines when the Germans come, to observe what's going on, know where to report it back to and, after they have gone through, to be able to sabotage and be a perfect nuisance to them.

'He was a chap by the name of Croft. He wasn't really concerned with our military abilities. He wanted chaps who knew the countryside and could get about by day and by night.

'He told us to go back to our places and pick up a few others we could trust. "Give us their names and we can vet them and their families and see if their pedigree is OK. Make sure they are suitable and try to get men who haven't already joined the Home Guard". He told us that secrecy was paramount, secrecy was everything.'

Captain Andrew Croft held a reserve Commission in the Essex Regiment and, after University, had been awarded the coveted Polar Medal for his part in the 1933 British Trans-Greenland Expedition. He had also attended Gubbins's pre-war MI(R) courses and served with him in the Norwegian campaign.

The Operational Bases (or 'hideouts') he was intending to provide were no longer called 'hideaways', that name having been officially dropped as incompatible with the role of the Patrols. They would be *operating*, not *hiding*, behind the lines. The understandable urgency with which Auxiliary Units' Patrols were being raised in the first few months after July 1940, meant that it was impossible to establish a standard design for the network of underground bases. Although this was attempted and partly achieved much later, during the first frantic days patrols everywhere were expected to use their own ingenuity and cunning to conceal their actions and stores of weapons and explosives from an ever vigilant nation as well as the enemy. In this, the IOs helped as much as possible and, after October, the establishment of Auxunits' Scout Sections of regular soldiers in each area provided much needed full-time manpower.

The form that OBs took in these early days varied

considerably around the country. Virtually in no area were they even similarly constructed. Andrew Croft appears to have encouraged a standard design concept throughout south Suffolk and north Essex, the area he established before leaving Auxiliary Units in November 1940. Virtually all Croft's Patrols dug for themselves a simple, rectangular OB, lined out with corrugated steel sheets on rough timber supports, the roof consisting of railway sleepers and more steel sheets covered with earth. A simple trapdoor allowed access into the cramped, badly ventilated, and often damp interior. Some enterprising Auxiliers constructed tunnels leading a safe distance from the main chamber, through which they intended to escape if enemy soldiers forced an entry. A grenade thrown back up the tunnel might have prevented them from giving chase.

Two hundred miles to the south-west, Fred Simpson who, like Herman Kindred and hundreds of other brave men, had answered the Auxiliary Units' call, was also scaling the learning curve of OB construction:

> 'We were to hide when the Germans invaded and come up behind their lines to play merry hell with them. This involved blowing up petrol dumps, laying mines and booby traps across roads and paths, cutting railway lines, blowing down trees across roads or anything that we could think of to hinder the German advance. To do this, we were first of all to dig an underground hideout – our first one in very dense forest very quickly collapsed, but we dug another and I made some hurdles from hazel, backed with bracken as it was sandy soil. Five of us spent two and a half days and nights in this one to test the air – and we found it foul. We cooked meals on a primus stove, just boiled potatoes and eggs mainly, and nothing fried because the smell could be detected on the surface some distance away. It was very primitive and damp, but we stayed below anyway, urinating in a corner which soaked away in the sand.'

In Devon and Cornwall, Stuart Edmundson's 'warriors' made use of the network of underground tin mines and tunnels that crisscross the area and through which they assured him the Cornish Peninsula could be traversed without once emerging from below ground. Old colliery workings were another predominant choice of OB for Auxiliers in suitable parts of the country. In Scotland, natural caves were favoured, with at least one having its entrance masked by a waterfall. In another part of Britain, Auxiliers broke through into the disused basement of a house and from there carried out operational training throughout the war, the occupants above remaining blissfully unaware of their clandestine guests. It is also known that at least one church crypt was utilised.

The men chosen to form the patrols, whatever their backgrounds or from whatever part of the country, possessed similar qualities. Almost every single one was tough, resilient, resourceful and patriotic. But perhaps their most understated quality was the sheer bravery required to volunteer for this virtually suicidal role. After the call to action, they would have left their families and loved ones without being allowed to disclose the true reason, but intending to face their last days alive harassing and being hunted by a ruthless enemy.

Auxiliers' training in 1940, centred mainly on two essential aspects. The first was to stay alive as long as possible. The second, the reason for their existence, was the skilled use of explosives and weaponry. The harsh reality was that any significant lack of competency in either could only mean catastrophe for a patrol. In this respect, a number of men initially considered to be of the required calibre, proved during training not to be so. Discharging the men, and those who developed second thoughts about the task, apparently gave more cause for concern among Auxiliers than their commanders.

Nigel Oxenden wrote:

'Security was the keynote of the IOs activities, and covered a multitude of sins. Fortunately, the general excitement that followed the fall of France, and the anti-invasion preparations, blinded the public to many unavoidable lapses. Dump-owners, after forming their cell, or patrol, and doing a fortnight's training, were recovered after a struggle by their (Home Guard) battalion, and left Auxiliary Unit with full knowledge; hopeful recruits, after witnessing most of the tricks in the IOs bag, preferred the comparative safety of road block and rifle.'

If these 'unavoidable lapses' were believed by IOs to be adequately covered by the situation of the times, then the same cannot be said of the Auxiliers, who depended for their very lives upon the security surrounding their role. Although steeped in controversy and mythology, there is nevertheless significant evidence to suggest that some Auxiliers, realising the potential threat to their lives, made plans to 'deal' with certain unreliable individuals who had knowledge of their existence as saboteurs. It has been confirmed by a number of Auxiliers recruited during 1940 and 1941, that they considered the elimination of potential informants against them as essential to their chances of survival after an invasion. In action, it was more than likely that the instinct to survive would have played an important part in their decisions.

For excellent reasons of safety, the concept established during 1940 under Colin Gubbins, centered on individual patrols operating in designated areas, independently and with little – or preferably no – awareness of others nearby. However, if Herman Kindred's experience of collective recruitment and search for suitable local personnel was typical, and being repeated elsewhere, some official allowance appears to have been made for a degree of overlap. This may either have been an elementary security lapse or an understanding that men, thinking they were entirely on their own, could hardly have been instilled with serious determination to carry out their task.

Even in the very earliest days and weeks of their existence, the men of Auxiliary Units Patrols were issued with the best equipment possible at a time of severe shortages within the armed services. Initially, each patrol received a cardboard container packed with enough explosives and associated equipment to last a patrol for about one month of operations. Known variously as 'Dumps', 'Packs' and finally (and very confusingly) 'Aux. Units', the use of the equipment contained was explained in a small booklet compiled under the supervision of Major Peter Wilkinson in 1940, simply entitled *'Calendar 1937'* – so named to provide a degree of security against inadvertent scrutiny. It is doubtful, however, whether this simple ruse could have provided more than short-term protection against an inquisitive and efficient German search party.

The contents of this intriguing booklet provide a clear idea of the equipment available to patrols during 1940 and 1941. It contained explanations on the use of the Paraffin Incendiary – a small device containing a petrol/paraffin mix, struck like a match to ignite, and which then melted, releasing its burning contents; Magnesium Incendiaries; Liquid Phosphorous Bottles; Detonators; Safety Fuse; Detonating Fuse; Instantaneous fuse; Time Pencil Fuses; Plastic Explosive; Blasting Gelatine; Grenades, and Sticky Bombs. The booklet also contained details of how and where all these devices could be placed to maximum effect.

Fred Simpson remembers the first consignment of stores issued to his Dorset patrol:

'The stores to be kept were ammunition, explosives, a certain amount of food and a gallon of rum in a stone jar. At the end of the war all these were collected by the Ordnance Corps, but one of the patrols had drilled a hole in the bottom of its jar and drunk the rum. Then they filled the hole up with cement but, like fools, we allowed ours to go back.

'We had a good assortment of armaments. The first delivery was of a case of phosphorous grenades, these being a make-do affair of lemonade bottles, two thirds full of phosphorous and topped up with mutton fat. As phosphorous burst into flames when exposed to air, our officer said the safest way to store them was under water, so we buried them in a bog and forgot to mark the spot. I have prodded the bog with a stick several times since, but they were never found. My first personal weapon issued to me was a Stanley kitchen knife, which I still have.'

This is now in the Museum of the BRO.

Some 'Packs' contained a bronze casting looking like a lump of coal, holding about two ounces of High Explosive – a 'museum piece' according to Nigel Oxenden. Contrary to popular belief, this period did not see the widespread issue of 'Tommy' Guns, Sten Guns and sniping rifles. Oxenden provided an insight into the kind of weapons issued in the early days:

'Col. Gubbins recommended the issue of revolvers. Mr. Churchill added a note, "these men are to have revolvers".

'Accordingly four hundred .32 Colt automatics were distributed at once, and the next month a 100% issue of .38 revolvers was made, followed much later by ammunition that fitted them. These, and hunting knives, were a great source of pride... They enhanced a reputation for toughness that the unit was building up, as opposed to the 'church parade' activities of the ill-equipped Home Guard proper. American rifles, on a scale of two per patrol, were an early issue, nobody quite knew why, and this item was never afterwards changed.'

Once instructed in the correct use of the items contained in their Packs, Auxiliers had then to be taught how to select and attack targets without detection by an enemy. This most important aspect of their training was to become the trademark of Auxiliary Units Patrols when tested against regular military units and secure installations. In movement by stealth, an IO's original selection proved a major contributing factor. Herman Kindred:

'We were taught to avoid confrontation with the enemy if at all possible. The most important thing was to be able to move up to a

target, set your charges or booby traps in place, and withdraw back
to the safety of the OB. If confronted by an enemy sentry, we were
trained in a certain amount of unarmed combat and in the use of
the knife, so we would have dealt with him that way. But we were
taught not to get into a firefight unless it was unavoidable. Our
most important weapon was the cover of darkness.

'We had plain denim suits and special rubber ankle boots with
smooth soles that didn't leave a footprint, and we would black up
our hands and faces with burnt cork. I also wore a balaclava which
was knitted by my mother. I had her make a pattern of holes near
the ears so I could hear better; she thought it was for my Home
Guard work. We were taught that you cannot be seen at night if
you stand perfectly still, and this was correct. Many a time we had
Home Guard or Army people walk past within inches of us
without even knowing we were there.

'We were taught to move slowly, one step at a time. It was
amazing what we could do at night if we kept perfectly quiet and
took our time. For instance, when we needed to replenish our
water supply, we would send a couple of chaps down with two
Jerry cans each to a certain farmyard. They had to pass the yard
dog, enter the cow shed, fill the cans up and pass the dog on the
way out without waking it.

'And they could do it!'

Most training was carried out in and around Patrols' local
communities, either by the IO or, after October, by members of
the regular Scout Sections assigned to each area. In addition,
many Auxiliers were sent in rotation to the national HQ at
Coleshill House, near Swindon, where their training was
consolidated.

Basic procedure laid down by HQ in 1940, called for one
Auxilier to act as observer throughout the day, while the others
slept in the OB. Each man, in his turn, would observe from a
concealed position and survey the surrounding countryside. At
nightfall, he would report back to his Patrol Leader, who
prepared details of the attacks to be carried out that night. Both
the returning observer, and the man detailed to take his place
the next day, would be excused the forthcoming raid.
However, this original system contained many drawbacks,
some of which were outlined in Nigel Oxenden's 1944 report:

'Everyone realised from the outset that the activities of the
patrol were dependent upon the finding of suitable targets during
the day, but it was optimistically expected that one man, watching
from a well concealed observation post, would be able every day

to locate something worth attacking. All exercises began with the assumption that a remote and concealed target had been satisfactorily picked up, and it was two years before any doubts were thrown upon the probability of a single static observer proving adequate to this most important task.'

The problems outlined by Oxenden were to form the rationale behind almost all the changes to Auxiliary Units Patrols' operational procedures throughout the remainder of their existence. The man who instigated perhaps the most fundamental changes was Lt Colonel C R ('Bill') Major, who replaced Colonel Gubbins as OC in November 1940.

Those changes were inadvertently to ensure that the survival of an Auxunits Patrol from then – although issued with vastly improved equipment – would never again be in direct proportion to its own skill and expertise alone.

From then they were working with a built-in handicap and, if called to action, it could have been disastrous.

★   ★   ★

On the crest of a wave – 1941 - 1943

'Guerrilla warfare...should in favourable circumstances cause such a diversion of enemy strength as eventually to present decisive opportunities to the main forces.'

(An MI(R) assessment)

'The first year had been a blaze of wild priority; then in 1941 and 1942 had followed a period of organised power, guarded by a security that nobody could get past...'

(Major Nigel Oxenden)

The beginning of 1941 saw the introduction of a more standardised type of operational base. Although by no means provided to all Patrols, the 'elephant' shelter was to become the main form of OB construction until stand down. These portly constructions were first used as overt Home Guard check point shelters, the name being derived from the grey, self-supporting corrugated sheeting, about fourteen feet in length, in the shape of a Nissen Hut. Originally designed for use in the construction of culverts, the heavy-gauge material was to prove an ideal shell for underground operational bases.

The construction expertise and manpower required to dig these structures into the ground meant that Auxiliers were generally no longer required to build their own OBs. The use of Pioneer Corps and Royal Engineer labour had long since

(top left) Major General Sir Colin McVean Gubbins, DSO, MC, founder of the GHQ Auxiliary Units. *(Museum Collection)*

(top right) Major General Lawrence Grand, RE, head of Section 'D' of the Secret Intelligence Service, who created the 'Home Defence' civilian stay-behinds, later to be incorporated into the Auxiliary Units as the 'Special Duties Section'. *(Museum Collection)*

(lower left) Major General John F C ('Jo') Holland, DFC, RE, the 'think-tank' of Military Intelligence (Research). *(Museum Collection)*

Lieutenant Colonel Sir Peter Wilkinson, a pre-war Royal Fusilier. As Auxiliary Units' Second in Command he was responsible to Gubbins for Administration and Liaison. After the war he became a distinguished diplomat and security co-ordinator for the Cabinet Office in Whitehall. *(Museum Collection)*

The Late Brigadier Geoffrey H R ('Billy') Beyts, DSO, MC, MBE, a career Indian Army soldier with the 6th Rajputana Rifles, was joint second in command to Colin Gubbins, responsible for training and operations until he returned to active service in 1942. He is seen here at the final Auxunits' national reunion at Parham on 2nd July 2000. *(C Jack Grice)*

(top left) Lieutenant Colonel
Joshua W S ('Stuart')
Edmundson, TD, RE. Here seen
officially opening the Museum of
the British Resistance
Organisation at Parham Airfield
in Suffolk on 30th August 1997.
(Will and Marcus Edmundson)

(top right)
Major General Sir Millis Jefferis,
KBE, MC, Director of MD1.
(Colonel R. Stuart Macrae)

(bottom left)
Colonel R. Stuart Macrae,
F.I.Mech.E, Second-in-
Command at MD1.
*('Winston Churchill's
Toyshop/Stuart Macrae)*

Captain Norman Field was the Intelligence Officer in Kent (later a Lieutenant Colonel on Field Marshal Montgomery's staff). Seen here with the highly prized Staff car which went with the job! *(Norman Field)*

An archetypical Auxiliary Units' Operational Base. This picture by Arthur Ward was presented in his book – *'Resisting the Nazi Invader'*.

(top left) The well-hidden entrance to a Cornish OB, custom built by quarrymen personnel of a patrol near Wadebridge.

(top right) John Warwicker, representing the Museum of the British Resistance Organisation, researcher Alwyn Harvey and Perranporth Auxilier, Trevor Miners, seen among the post-war underground detritus. *(Ann Warwicker)*

(bottom left) Operational patrols used the Home Guard as cover. This battledress with four service chevrons, and ostensibly belonging to a WWI veteran, provided cover as a Caernarvon HG officer. *(Terry Carney collection)*

Auxunits; Intelligence Officers and Group Commanders for Devon and Cornwall under the overall command of Stuart Edmundson, *(fourth from right, front row).* On his right is the Cornish IO, Captain John Dingley, DCLI, who operated from Polhilsa House, Callington after his safe return from the Dunkirk evacuation. Between them in the second row is Captain Roy Bradford, Scout Section officer for Devon, later IO for Sussex, who was killed in action with the SAS in 1944. *(Geoffrey Bradford)*

Covers intended to fool the enemy, or snoopers, for secret operational manuals issued to Auxiliary Units operational patrols. *(Museum collection)*

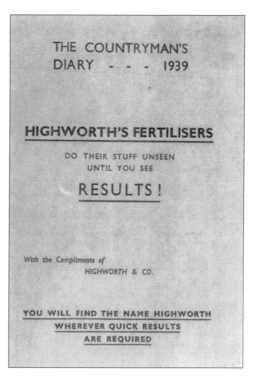

THE COUNTRYMAN'S
DIARY - - - 1939

HIGHWORTH'S FERTILISERS

DO THEIR STUFF UNSEEN
UNTIL YOU SEE

RESULTS !

With the Compliments of
HIGHWORTH & CO.

YOU WILL FIND THE NAME HIGHWORTH
WHEREVER QUICK RESULTS
ARE REQUIRED

Coleshill House, near Highworth, Wiltshire. This 17th Century mansion, the home of the Pleydell-Bouverie family, was Auxiliary Units HQ after the move from Whitehall, in the late summer of 1940, until January 1945. *(Eric Gray)*

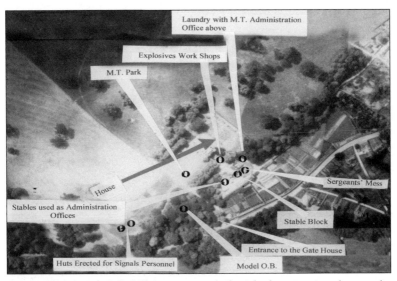

Laundry with M.T. Administration Office above

Explosives Work Shops

M.T. Park

Sergeants' Mess

House

Stables used as Administration Offices

Stable Block

Entrance to the Gate House

Huts Erected for Signals Personnel

Model O.B.

An aerial view of Coleshill House *(marked with the arrow)* and grounds, believed to have been taken by the RAF Photo Reconnaissance Unit in 1942 to establish that soil from the demonstration OB had been successfully camouflaged. The locations have ben identified by Eric Gray. *(Joy Oxenden/ BRO Museum collection)*

Hannington Hall, half a dozen miles from Coleshill. The first Headquarters of Auxiliary Units' Special Duties Section under Major Maurice Petherick and, later, the 'ATTERY' for ATS Auxiliary Units. *(Barbara Culleton collection)*

Melville House, Ladybank, Fife, Auxiliary Units' HQ in Scotland. *(David Blair)*

been adopted in some areas as the best way of providing the necessary numbers of OBs required; many Auxiliers neither wished, nor had the time, to dig OBs in addition to their full-time professions and training commitments. The widespread use of soldiers, including regulars in the Auxiliary Units' Scout Sections, became standard in most areas, and the expertise that these gangs of men developed was illustrated in the increased speed and sophistication of the constructions.

When Herman Kindred was promised a 'hideout' by Captain Andrew Croft in August 1940, what he and his Patrol colleagues initially got was a wheeled shepherd's hut, 'hidden' in a nearby wood, from which to plan their assault on Hitler's occupying forces. Only after some weeks was the Patrol supplied with an OB that would have afforded them anything like realistic protection:

> 'Our dugout was put down, I think, in the October. The Engineers camouflaged it extremely well, with a vertical shaft and trap door at the front and a tunnel that went out about 18 yards, well camouflaged with bushes and so on. The Engineers dumped timber down there, so we could build our own bunks, that folded down to make seats. It was extremely dry because when they first picked out a site, I objected to it because we would be in water in the winter time. I told them we must get on to the sand further up, about three quarters of a mile to the east. As it turned out, when the airfield was built (for the USAAF at Parham), the bomb stores were put right over the spot where they were first going to put our dugout.'

Excavations by BRO Museum staff in 1997 revealed that Herman Kindred's patrol OB was constructed with corrugated steel-end walls – the entrance shaft from the main trapdoor being of the same material. Of the many OBs discovered around Britain during the 1990s, only a few are of similar construction, the majority having brick end-walls and entrance shafts, highlighting the rapid development in building techniques that continued well into 1942 – by which time OBs had reached a level of sophistication undreamt of by the men recruited into Auxiliary Units Patrols two years earlier.

The corrugated steel tunnel went out at an acute angle from Herman's main underground chamber, to absorb some of the blast from an enemy grenade. Of the six storage bays built into the sides of the tunnel one was left with an earth floor, an obvious 'facility' for men kept underground, perhaps for days, while enemy solders searched for them in the woodland above.

The two aspects of OB development to which Auxiliers themselves paid most attention were the escape tunnel and the trap doors. To the Auxiliers who were expected to exist literally underground inside these constructions, their means of escape and the concealment of their points of entry were vital elements in safeguarding against the unthinkable. Another possible breach of their security was created when landowners' permission and co-operation was sought for OB construction. The fewer people that knew about it the better and in isolated cases the whole construction was carried out, if the territory was suitable, without consulting them at all.

The main change that Colonel Bill Major's appointment as OC brought to the operational procedures of Auxiliary Units Patrols, was one that would irretrievably compromise the high secrecy surrounding their role.

Lacking the same level of subversive warfare expertise as Gubbins, Bill Major reorganised the Patrols along more conventional military lines. Patrols now worked in groups of approximately six or seven, led by Group Commanders (GCs). These were usually former Patrol Leaders – Sergeants – promoted to the 'Home Guard' rank of Lieutenant and initially given direct operational control over the whole group. The Corporal would then usually gain promotion to Sergeant and Patrol Leader, while a new recruit would bring the patrol back up to strength which, since the introduction of 'elephant' shelters, was now about seven men.

Bill Major's 'Group Attack' theory called for the abandonment of the system of individual patrols selecting and attacking targets within their local areas. The new technique involved the selection of targets by the GC from reports provided by all his patrol observers and other sources. Once targets were selected, patrols within the Group were to rendezvous at a given map reference before proceeding to the target area. The irony of Nigel Oxenden's quote at the beginning of this chapter is highlighted by another extract from his 1944 report:

> '...GCs were expected to maintain contact with all their patrols and to use this extended command to bring off ambitious attacks with their whole strength, plus, sometimes a scout section. This meant that their remoter ones would have to travel considerable distances, possibly devoting a night to the journey, neglect any targets of their own that might crop up, fight on ground that was utterly strange to them and spend a third night getting back.'

Although satisfied with 'a security that nobody could get past', and not highlighting the direct damage to Auxiliers' security by 'Bill' Major's scheme, Oxenden is clearly skeptical about this new system.

The cellular system established under Gubbins, minimised the number of people with knowledge of any particular patrol. Only the IO possessed any comprehensive detail of his network and there is conclusive evidence that IOs and Divisional Army Commanders were to decide whether the IO should remain with his 'warriors' after invasion – and be vulnerable himself – or try to liaise with them from Divisional HQ. Therefore, under Gubbins, a captured Auxilier in-the-field *could only divulge details concerning his own patrol* – allowing others to remain at large.

Peter Wilkinson articulated his disapproval of the group system under Major and, although also deriding the 'fleabite' value of cellular attack as carrying less punch, was in no doubt it had the overwhelming merit of vastly improved security, and associated longevity for each patrol.

The introduction of the Group Attack system had the immediate effect of stripping away the vitally important concealment of individual patrols, The all embracing cloak of secrecy was made redundant, and it can now be seen that any realistic chance of the Auxunit Patrol experiment working in practice was lost.

Despite the abandonment of Gubbins' cellular system, the standard of equipment and training throughout 1941 and 1942 was to improve dramatically. The most significant was in the evolution of operational bases, as parties of Engineers and Pioneers gained in experience and refined the construction techniques.

Many of the OBs hurriedly built by the Auxiliers themselves were now replaced by constructions that were strong, waterproof and better ventilated. Although ventilation was never satisfactorily or widely perfected, the generalised use of a system of clay water pipes during this period was a vast improvement on the attempts of 1940 to prevent asphyxiation – which ranged form the extraordinarily rudimentary to the virtually non-existent. A number of early OBs could only be adequately ventilated by leaving the trap door open, detracting absolutely from the concept of underground concealment.

Auxiliers were now provided with underground bases boasting brick entrance shafts and end-walls. In East Anglia, tunnels tended to continue to be constructed from timber and corrugated steel sheeting, but in a number of areas concrete pipes were eventually favoured as an easier and ultimately safer method of construction. Some fine examples built in this way remain largely intact in areas including Sussex and Lincolnshire. In Cornwall, quarrymen built their own OBs – under Royal Engineer's supervision – of such strength they remain intact today.

An important element of OB camouflage remained the trap doors through which Auxiliers were to enter and leave without detection. Many of the more ingenious designs, although often attributed to 1940, were dreamt up by Auxiliers and Scout Sections during 1941 and beyond. The main problem had always been to maintain their camouflage after being closed *from inside*. A widely used solution was to base the construction of the door itself around a shallow wooden or metal box which, when filled with earth and turf, or even shrubbery in some cases, would blend with natural surroundings.

Hinged at one end, the box would fit snugly into a frame at the top of the entrance shaft and, when closed, be concealed from all but the closest inspection.

In Suffolk, the Scout Section at Cransford established a production shed for the manufacture of their own unique version of this concept, in which a concrete counterweight was attached to the underside of the trap door box. A hidden trigger mechanism was activated via a wire which terminated at a convenient nearby feature, usually a fence-post or bush. When the end loop was pulled, the perfectly balanced door, rotating on a gas-pipe swivel, would slowly and smoothly open. Once the men were inside, the door could be closed with the pressure of one finger. To prevent an obvious clue to the OB's whereabouts, 'grass box' trap doors sometimes had to be watered to prevent discoloration. A feature of many excavations of Suffolk OBs is the routine discovery of the home-produced, extremely heavy, trap door counterweight.

Other ingenious designs included a log on a particular pile of firewood which, when lifted, activated a wire mechanism to open a concealed door. On another, a system of cantilevers and wires allowed the complete trap door to rise on four corner posts. In Norfolk, a last ditch escape hatch was created in the OB roof at Kings Lynn. A mushroom shaped roof fixture rested permanently on four posts. Escape was effected by four of the patrol heaving upward simultaneously, one to each post. This forced the 'mushroom' and its camouflage up – exposing a hole big enough for a man to climb through. James Bond himself would have been proud of some of the ideas.

In Dorset, Fred Simpson's patrol no longer had to endure the foul air and damp conditions of their first 'successful' OB. 1941 would bring many changes to Fred's clandestine life:

'Troops from the Pioneer Corps were sent to build us a proper bunker. They came down from the north and were not in a position to tell anything about our location. The new bunker consisted of two rooms built of concrete blocks and curved steel sheets. The first room was for living and storage, and the second – connected by a small passage set at an angle so that any grenade or other explosion would not affect both rooms – was for sleeping.

'Here we had naval hammocks erected star fashion – the times we fell out on the concrete floor bring back painful memories – and at one end of this sleeping area we had a bolthole to the surface, the main entrance being the trap door, on which was planted grass, ferns, and a small tree for camouflage. To enter from outside, one had to look for a cotton reel hidden in a clump of bushes and, on pulling this, a steel wire raised the trapdoor just a little so that it could then be swiveled round on its support, exposing a shaft with a ladder.'

Hitler's attack on Russia in June 1941 appeared initially to spell the end of the road for Auxiliary Units, as it was widely thought within HQ that the events in Eastern Europe would almost certainly be seen in Whitehall as ending the threat to British shores. In the event, the War Office took the opposite view and, on the assumption that enemy raids at least were still a likelihood, sanctioned expansion into the Borders, Durham and Northumberland. In all, one hundred new patrols were formed within these and the original areas, some of which were now divided to ease the burden on individual IOs staff – including Suffolk and Essex, and North and East Riding. There were now twenty-two areas, each containing approximately fifteen to thirty-five patrols.

In September 1941, the practice of posting one static observer to locate potential targets was upgraded by the introduction of the one-man OB – sometimes referred to as an Observation Post (OP). Although varying in design, these have been described as a corrugated steel telephone box, large enough for just one man, and sunk vertically into the ground. The purpose was to allow one member of a patrol to observe the immediate area by daylight and report back to the main OB by field telephone. In typically Auxunits fashion, many aids to concealed observation soon developed, including mock rabbit burrows with glass inserts through which strategic points such as main roads, could be kept in view. Many patrols were also issued with simple wooden periscopes to check the surrounding area before emerging. An excellent summary of this revised method of operation is given in a series of training lecture notes co-written by Major 'Billy' Beyts in October 1941:

> 'Function of the Observer's OB.
>
> 'Firstly, this is to provide a "hide" to enable the observer to go to ground, if the enemy are nearby, and to save the necessity of opening up the Patrol's OB, which would inevitably disturb its camouflage, and which might jeopardize the lives of the whole Patrol by bringing a closely pursuing enemy on to its OB.
>
> 'Secondly, his one man OB affords the observer an opportunity to keep in touch with his Patrol by means of the telephone. Without the telephone he would be cut off from (the Patrol Leader) throughout the hours of daylight.
>
> 'Thirdly, the one man OB forms a rendezvous for the neighbouring Patrol's message carriers to meet. The whereabouts of Patrol OBs need not therefore be disclosed to personnel of other Patrols...'

This last point vividly highlights, perhaps more than any other, the potentially calamitous nature of the Group System of operation. The idea of patrols having access to neighbouring one-man OBs would be to build into the system a most dangerous source of insecurity. Any Auxilier captured and interrogated under pressure, would now know the whereabouts of others, and divulging the location of 'secure' one-man OBs would in practice mean the almost certain capture of an entire Group – as an enemy search party would need only to trace the telephone land lines to discover the location of each patrol's main chamber.

With the same astuteness about personal security which had seen Auxiliers identifying the threat from potential informants, many patrols now searched for ways to conceal this 'guideline' between OBs. A technique often adopted was to run the telephone wire through a series of underground pipes, forcing an enemy at least to expend more effort in following the trail, and allowing more time for escape.

Herman Kindred's patrol, whose OB was situated in a wood

near the village of Little Glemham in Suffolk, found an ingenious and possibly unique answer to the problem. By 'crimping' cables from both phones to the metal wire of a surrounding fence, they made the astonishing discovery that the link worked perfectly, thereby removing the need for a buried line, and all the attendant work. This method was possibly the nearest that any patrol came to countering the new threat imposed from HQ, as an enemy patrol would have had to carry out a minute examination of nearly a mile of fencing to locate the virtually invisible telephone lines.

The irony surrounding the implementation of the Group Attack system is that throughout 1941 and 1942, Auxiliers in all areas were better trained and supplied with an increasingly diverse and sophisticated array of weapons and sabotage equipment, all of which – had the advantages of the cellular system not been lost – would have afforded Auxiliary Units Patrols the genuine possibility of success if called to arms.

★   ★   ★

'When Colonel The Lord Glanusk, DSO, took over command of Auxiliary Units from Colonel Major in February 1942, it was on the crest of the wave. Priority was not what it had been, but this was not reflected in the areas. IOs could get all the RE stores they asked for... and they were in a position to demand any recruit they wanted for making up their numbers.

'The greatest service that Lord Glanusk did for the unit was to throw doubt upon the wisdom of the elaboration, both in essentials and details, that had grown up... and that liaison between patrols was little more than wishful thinking, and of questionable use at that. At one stroke our policy had been cleared of much hampering undergrowth. From now on the patrol was self-contained and would fight alone; from now on the rank and file would not be asked to think.'

Nigel Oxenden's comments regarding the return to a cellular system, appear to suggest that the potential risk to operational security of the previous system had finally been noted at HQ level under Lord Glanusk. Possibly, GHQ was alert to the danger and he was the go-between. It can be seen now that however much equipment was issued to Auxiliers, however much training in unarmed combat they received or however deep the security surrounding their network, their chances of survival in combat had one year earlier, been seriously compromised from within.

Whether this fact was widely obvious to Auxiliers in a matter of conjecture, but what is certain is that they did continue to grasp the technique and use of new equipment with ever increasing proficiency.

By 1942 Auxiliers had become adept at stealth by day and night to a level of competency unknown outside regular special forces. They had become highly proficient in the art of preparing and deploying a vast array of booby traps, ambushes and attacks on static targets. They had been taught how to approach an enemy stronghold without detection and how to deal with challenges from enemy soldiers. Many a British or American sentry completed a tour of guard duty totally unaware that Auxiliers with the potential to kill him silently within seconds had only been inches away. Auxiliers were taught the psychologically challenging practice of holding their ground if shot at, resisting the temptation to dive for cover or to return fire. The theory was that an enemy sentry, after firing and hearing no response, would either retire or feel brave enough to investigate – whereupon they would be silently dispatched.

Increased sophistication of equipment and training meant that by mid 1942 the Auxiliers' original training manual *Calendar 1937* was outdated and replaced by the *Calendar 1938*. An obvious difference between the two was the amount of information given to Auxiliers in the application of their stores. Many ideas developed by experience over the two previous years were detailed, including novel booby traps such as a No. 36 grenade placed with its pin removed and contained inside an empty food tin. The tin was tied to a tree or convenient post and a wire attached to the grenade stretched across a path or road. When 'tripped', the wire simply pulled the grenade out of the tin – and exploded. In another, a 'double' trap allowed an enemy to find one wire only to walk into another.

The equipment issued to patrols to enable them to set these traps included such ingenious wartime inventions by MI(R) under Millis Jefferis as the Pull Switch, the Release Switch and the Pressure Switch. All fired a detonator by means of a spring loaded pin; the former when pulled by a trip wire and the latter when trodden on. The Release Switch was designed to be placed under a moveable object strategically located. When picked up, the switch released a spring and fired the attached explosive charge.

Perhaps the most fearsome of all was the AP (Anti-Personnel) Switch, also known in macabre military parlance, as the 'Castrator'. This malevolent weapon consisted of a bullet placed inside a shaped steel tube and pushed into the ground point up. When trodden on, a barb-trip fired the bullet through the unfortunate man's foot, if he was lucky! In most areas the AP Switch was considered too dangerous to deploy on training exercises, in case they were misplaced and later trodden on by members of the public.

The most significant aspect of the *Calendar 1938* was the inclusion of the new 'Unit Charge', which consisted of 1-lb of High Explosive – either two 8-oz or four 4-oz sticks of Gelignite, Nobels 808 or Gelatine. Nigel Oxenden provides a summary of its development:

> 'Attempts had been made at intervals to produce a charge that was universally applicable, that could be made up beforehand and fastened to any sort of target...1lb was fixed as a weight of explosive that was light enough to carry in reasonable numbers, and powerful enough for all practical purposes. A simple make-up was adopted as official, universally taught, and illustrated in our revised textbook, the Calendar 1938. Briefly, the charge had one ounce of primer and a twelve-inch tail of detonating fuse to which were taped two time pencils with detonators.
>
> 'The auxilier would not now be asked to play with bits and pieces in the target area, or to devise 'booby traps' under the noses of enemy sentries...his work would simply be to get in and place a unit charge, a form of field craft that had reached a very high standard.'

The last important change introduced to the operational procedures of Auxiliary Units' Patrols came towards the end of 1942. Patrols were once again employing the cellular system of operation. Group Commanders, although still in existence, were now no longer in operational control of Patrols; their role had been reduced to administration of personnel and stores. Attention was once again turned to the limitations of posting single observers to locate targets. The selection of targets for individual patrols had become secondary during the Group Attack period but, since the abandonment of that system, it was clear that in order to have any reasonable chance of locating prime targets, patrols would have to undertake reconnaissance missions beyond the immediate area of their OBs.

It was now decided therefore, that patrol leaders would

dispatch teams of observers during the day; the number of men sent out was governed by operational expediency. These missions became known as scout patrols – a throw back to the name given to many Auxunts' Patrols in July 1940, and one that, not unreasonably, is still confused with the regular Scout Sections – who were themselves intended to sub-divide into operational 'Patrols' as they went to ground after invasion. The new system reversed the original concept in which the observer locating the target did not participate in the forthcoming attack. He would now be needed to guide his colleagues onto 'his' target by night.

A major consideration of the new procedures was to conceal Auxiliers on scout training or reconnaissance from the suspicions of an ever-vigilant population. The need to move within their communities was an important pre-operational factor and it had been realised, as early as 1940, that to allow Auxiliers to train with inadequate uniform, or no uniform at all, was the simplest route to exposure, capture, and death *after* invasion. While it might have been equally easy for an occupying force to identify either Home Guards or non-Home Guards *who had disappeared* as invasion started, the danger of leakage from the general public was thought to be reduced for Auxiliers who had previously been seen in uniform in their locality.

Perhaps such a 'masquerade' would forestall one of the Nazi's main potential, if inadvertent, sources of information – the general public. To enable Auxiliers to carry out their main operational function after invasion, concealment within the framework of the Home Guard was a prerequisite.

But it would come as their continued existence was once again being questioned.

CHAPTER FOUR

Auxunits Patrols - Ultimate Concealment

by Andrew Taylor, Museum Director

'As I see it, the degree to which we are justified in retaining the Auxiliary Units organisation must be measured by:-

a) The likelihood of invasion

b) The "vital area" if invasion came.

'As regards (a), we are working on the assumption that invasion is not possible in 1943. It is highly unlikely at any future date.

'As regards (b), Home forces' recent appreciation showed that nothing serious could be attempted outside the area, roughly, Norfolk – Hampshire.

'The deductions from these two facts are that:-

(a) Auxiliary Units are unlikely ever to be required; and

(b) If they are required, they would only be necessary in,

and possibly slightly overlapping the flanks of, the "vital area".'

(War Office, January 1943)

1943

In the event, Auxiliary Units was never reduced into a 'vital area'. Moreover, following this War Office analysis dated January 1943, the secrecy surrounding the Patrols function was actually being reinforced by the further concealment of civilian Auxiliers under a Home Guard' blanket. The irony of this situation would continue to be played out over the next eighteen months, during which Auxiliary Units would be forced to justify their continued existence, in the face of growing scepticism within Home Forces Army Commands and certain officers in the War Office.

In this period, Auxiliary Units HQ, through GHQ, would cling determinedly to the very existence of the organisation, as well as maintaining the high secrecy surrounding its role.

The introduction of scout patrols – reconnaissance missions as opposed to Scout Sections – was the last major change to the operational procedures employed by Auxiliary Units Patrols. In September 1942, by which time Auxiliers were expected to 'scout' for targets in daylight, there had been considerable discussion within Home Forces Command regarding the need to further enhance the concealment of Auxiliers within their own communities.

Nigel Oxenden, in his *'History and Achievement'* , provides an outline:

> 'A long disputed point was the flash to be worn by auxiliers. The alternatives hitherto had been to wear that of the local (Home Guard) battalion, when permanent absence from parade caused comment; to wear, with the consent of the commander concerned, the number of the battalion to which the men belonged on paper, when many would be seen at the wrong end of the county: or to wear none at all, which aroused the deepest suspicion.
>
> 'However arrangements were made for three TAAs (Territorial Army Associations), located at Invernesss, York and Reading, to administer all the HG personnel of Auxiliary Units. Three Battalions were formed. The 201st included Scotland and Northumberland, the 202nd carried on southwards to the Thames – Severn line, and the 203rd covered S.E and Southern (Army) commands... the name Auxiliary Units need never in future appear in Pt II orders, which simply showed auxiliers as belonging to this or that G.H.Q. Res.Bn.'

The 'Reserve' Battalion title was to stick fast, and many documents in PRO are still indexed as such.

By the beginning of 1943, Auxiliers in all areas were being issued with shoulder flashes indicating attachment to one of the three new 'Home Guard' Battalions. For the first time, all Auxiliers were wearing a standard form of identity that would allow them to undertake training in their revised operational procedures, with minimum risk of suspicion from the public, or ordinary units of the HG. That the flashes they now wore represented non-standard, perhaps even bogus, Home Guard units is made apparent by the huge geographical area covered by each 'battalion'.

In understanding the relationship between Auxunits and the HG it should be borne in mind that whether Auxiliers themselves were fully, or nominally enrolled as HGs is, in many respects, irrelevant; but that the unit to which they were attached, and for which they worked – Auxiliary Units – was never part of or under any HG control or command.

In March 1943, Colonel F W R Douglas, Royal Artillery, was appointed the fourth (and final) Auxunits Commanding Officer. As 1st General Staff Officer to the previous

Commander, Colonel The Lord Glanusk, who had stood down through illness, Douglas had a good working understanding of the organisation, and was the ideal candidate to steer it through what would be two difficult final years to Stand Down in November 1944.

Throughout 1943 and into 1944, Auxiliary Units continued to request and, in most cases obtain, large quantities of arms and equipment. In explosives and booby traps alone, the organisation used more in one month of training than a regular infantry battalion in six months. However, as requests for equipment continued, skepticism - now building within War Office regarding the continued justification of Auxiliary Units – began to threaten the highly classified status enjoyed since 1940. During the first two and a half years, Auxunits had been considered within Home Forces Commands as a secretive curiosity, of which it was unwise of anyone not in-the-know to ask questions. It had been allowed almost any equipment it requested, limited only by availability.

By the third year, patrols had amassed a formidable array of weaponry. They were now designated, either for administrative or obscure operational reasons, as Type A (equipped with the American .45 Thompson Sub-Machine Gun) and Type B (with the British 9mm Sten Machine Carbine). The latter weapon gradually replaced the former, which had been in issue at least since 1941. Much has been written regarding the relative merits of these two famous weapons and nothing conclusive can be added to the debate from Auxiliers' experience. Many have testified to the superiority of one over the frequent unreliability of the other, although, interestingly, a number of Auxiliers found the Sten preferable when firing from the prone position – its side magazine, unlike that of the Thompson, allowing the operator to take aim without exposing his head above ground.

In Suffolk, the Leiston Patrol developed an ingenious modification to their Stens to fire single rounds. The idea worked perfectly, with the additional benefit of curtailing the weapon's alarming habit of firing off a whole magazine on its own volition. Through their IO, the Patrol shared details with HQ. Although they received no acknowledgement, a surviving document notes HQ's objection to Auxiliers carrying out 'unauthorised' modifications to their weaponry.

In addition to coshes, truncheons and fighting knives, American .300 rifles, Colt .32 and Smith and Wesson .38 revolvers were issued from 1940 – many of which dated from

1930s prohibition days in America. Auxiliers were later supplied with a weapon destined to become the focus of many researchers' perception of operational patrols. The Winchester .22 'sniping' rifle, issued with a silencer and telescopic sights which, according to Nigel Oxenden, added little to accuracy, even when carefully zeroed, was to take out enemy sentries, and to 'fill the larder'. The latter use was confirmed by many former Auxiliers, some quietly admitting to the weapon's continued larder filling service for many years after the war. So it cannot have been all that bad?

Whether War Office appraisal of their continued usefulness was ever officially communicated to Auxiliers is not on record – but most of them worked it out for themselves. With the establishment of the special Reserve Battalions, came the introduction of parade drill. Until the end of 1942, the potentially highly dangerous voluntary role of Auxunits had spared them the seemingly inane military square-bashing endured by Home Guards. Now, although ostensibly intended to further enhance their cover, it was also an indication of their reduced importance. The privileged position enjoyed since 1940, above any civilians with Home Forces, was in decline.

For the remainder of its existence, Auxiliary Units' HQ remained locked in a struggle with War Office and Area Command Quartermasters, over the level of equipment required to continue operational training. That the organisation was able to sustain and even develop its level of training throughout 1943 and into 1944, was largely due to the tenacity of its new CO in his dealing with those in authority who constantly barraged his Command with demands to justify its procurement levels. Often requested to state the intended use of equipment on order, he staunchly refused to compromise the high security which continued to surround Auxiliary Units, and often drew upon the backing of his allies within the War Office and GHQ Home Forces. The Director of Quartering at the War Office wrote to GHQ Home Forces in September 1943.

The following is an extract from a letter received from Southern Command:

'Under instructions from GHQ Home Forces, demands for stores from IO Auxiliary Units have to be met. In view of the special nature of the Units the purpose for which the stores are required is not revealed when the demand is made.

'It is requested that you will confirm that the work in which these Auxiliary Units are employed is essential for Home Defence...Would you also please say from what War Office branch information concerning...these units can, if necessary , be obained.'

Extracts from two surviving documents written shortly afterwards, suggest that the Director of Quartering probably failed in his demand for information:

'It was agreed in Jan 43 that reserves of stores should be held by GHQ Aux Units. Owing to the super secret role of Aux Units it is not possible to show what their strength is or how many patrols or sections are concerned.

'We presume that we can safely say that the work of Aux Units is essential for Home Defence, but we do not know to which branch of the War Office Q.1.c should refer for information.'

After the War Office appraisal of early 1943 regarding the likelihood of invasion, there is no evidence that any official sanction was given to Auxiliary Units HQ to continue operational development of the network. However, it is doubtful if the 'super secrecy' protecting their function, and the ongoing high level of training and procurement of stores, could have continued without support from the highest level. In this respect, perhaps Nigel Oxenden's view of a continuing development towards a definitive *'final teaching'* explains an otherwise paradoxical situation.

Is it too outrageous to propose that Auxunits' founder, Brigadier Colin Gubbins, now in desperate need of explosives and weaponry to 'set Europe ablaze' with SOE around 'D' Day, was buttressing his supply state in a roundabout way through his own very special network of personal contacts?

Of all issues to Auxiliers, the '1939 *Countryman's Diary* has the most durable mystique and, due largely to David Lampe's own interpretation of its relevance, often remains misunderstood and historically misplaced. This fascinating booklet was a direct development of *the Calendar 1937* (produced in 1940) and *Calendar 1938* (1942) – as a brief comparison of the respective contents will confirm. On the balance of probabilities, the most likely period for its issue – certainly before 1944 – was toward the end of 1943.

A fashionable attraction for the booklet has developed around the rather 'tongue-in-cheek' wording of its front cover: *'HIGHWORTH'S FERTILISERS do their stuff unseen until you see RESULTS! You will find the name Highworth wherever quick results are required.'* It appears that the paradoxical situation of Auxiliary Units in 1943 was not lost on whoever produced those words, as the cover design is clearly a humourous departure from the original concept of a simply titled booklet that no-one, especially an enemy, would bother to pick up and read - in favour of one advertising a known ingredient in the manufacture of home-made explosives.

The contents of *The Countruman's Diary* remained much the same as that of *Calendar* 1938, including the 'L' (Lead) Delay, an advanced version of the Time Pencil which, instead of acid, relied upon a spring-loaded lead wire. When broken, it fired the attached detonator. The main changes were in the exclusion of the 'Sticky Bomb' and the highly dangerous AP Switch; and the inclusion of the 'Fire Pot' – a magnesium incendiary which, once lit, was almost impossible to extinguish – and the Pocket Time Incendiary (PTI). Both were issued exclusively to Auxunits. The reduction in weight of the Unit Charge – the standard explosive weapon used by operational patrols since the middle of 1942 – provides further indication that this booklet was the last in the evolutionary line of 'Calendar' training manuals, as the new half pound charge also features in Major Nigel Oxenden's 'Final Teaching' – detailed later in this book.

The inclusion in the booklet of the No. 77 'Smoke Grenade' is one whose issue provides a clue to the period of production. This unpleasant weapon – which showered burning phosphorus on anyone within ten yards – had hitherto not been widely issued to Auxiliary Units and, like the half-pound Unit Charge, was ultimately included in Oxenden's 'final' appraisal as a preferred weapon for the saboteur. In November 1943, a request from Auxiliary Units HQ for *fifty thousand* No. 77 Grenades almost caused uproar within the War Office as it exceeded their issue recommendation by some 2,500%. After much deliberation and the well-practised ritual of justification, only on the 10th January 1944 was the issue agreed - and then subject to supply phased over three months.

Although there is no corroboration, the evidence – including the timing of requests for the issue of Fire Pots and PTIs, suggest that possible publication dates range from mid-1942 to the latter half of 1943.

★   ★   ★

The Pace Slackens – 1944

This is an extract from the 'official history';

'IOs were finding it increasingly hard in the Spring of 1944 to fill the (training) course vacancies allotted to them (by HQ)...everywhere labour was increasingly scarce and men therefore busier in their civilian lives.

'The approaching opening of the second front gave the Home Guard a chance to prove their value by taking over from the army certain coastal defences and VPs (Vulnerable Points). Wherever possible Auxiliary Units co-operated......and discontinued all other forms of training.

'Some of the remoter areas...were sent in relays to the Isle of Wight, where they formed guards and patrols for about a month.'

One of the last entries contained in Major Nigel Oxenden's 'official history' indicates the rapid decrease in activity within Operational Patrols in early 1944. While the impending Allied landings in Europe created a genuine strategic role for the Special Duties Section – dealt with later – albeit followed by a dramatically rapid stand-down soon after the actual invasion, Ops Patrols were to drift quietly towards a yet undetermined finish, not quite Home Guards and yet now obviously never to be required in the role for which they had trained so competently for almost four years. Whether the pre-invasion deployment to certain 'vital areas' was one of genuine military necessity, or intended as a metaphorical 'pat-on-the-back',' is open for debate, but what is certain is the pride many Auxiliers felt at being able to contribute in some small, but positive way, to Eisenhower's 'Great Crusade'.

Dorset farm worker Fred Simpson was among them:

'One thing which we were very proud of was being chosen on D-Day to guard one of the radar and wireless stations working at that time, which was in the Purbeck Hills, and buried underground. A telephone call came the day before the night of D-Day – a night full of aircraft towing gliders. We were allowed to make our own choice of weapons, and I selected my Smith and Wesson revolver and a Tommy Gun. Our instructions were to meet at Wareham, where we had a store concealed behind the local auctioneers office, at 2.00pm. We had high hopes of a quick parachute course and of being dropped in France. But no. We were picked up in army lorries and taken to the hills above Swanage.

'Out task was to mount guard duty during the night and, as we had done a bit of drilling by that time, we were fairly orderly. We set trip wires with alarm charges and booby traps on all approaches to the installations, except for the main approach, but left the safety pins in. Then as the RAF guard with their Alsatians came off duty at dusk, we took over and pulled the pins out. We selected our stations – lying down, not standing – and manned a triangular area which was best for fire power. We had three OPs and fully loaded arms, the reasoning being that Jerry would probably land saboteurs in the bay and try and blow up the sites. We weren't a bit nervous, but between, say, 2.00am and 4.00am every bush seemed to move and one chap shot at one with his Sten Gun, which caused a bit of a scare. It was cold too and we had two weeks of this. This was the only time we were put to actual use.'

In mid-July 1944, Auxiliary Units HQ commenced preparations for disposing of all weapons and equipment held by operational patrols. The organisation held at this time no less than seven thousand Aux Unit Mk II 'Packs' - containing a total of *seventy tons of high explosive, nearly a quarter of a million detonators and more than one and a half million feet of detonating fuse*. Initial plans for each patrol to deposit their stores at a convenient central collecting point very soon met with hostility from Area Command Ammunition Depots (ADs). The discovery that some explosives held by Patrols had been stored incorrectly and were in dangerous condition resulted in one final challenge to the high secrecy surrounding their role when ADs insisted that Ordnance Officers be allowed to inspect the stores held within individual OBs, before being handled by regular AD personnel. Even now, the highly classified Operational Patrols, as with the whole Auxunits' organisation, remained impenetrable to anyone who did not 'need to know'.

In the event, it was suggested that Auxiliers, who did not appear to share the reluctance of the regular army in handling suspect explosives, would themselves dispose locally of anything they 'deemed' unfit to hand in and, over the next few years, many a tree stump would be levelled on a farmer's land with the aid of a Unit Charge.

In August, virtually all the IOs in the twenty operational areas around the coast of Britain were withdrawn and Auxiliary Units was divided into four regions – Caithness to Northumberland, Durham to Suffolk, Essex to Hampshire, and Devon to Carmarthenshire. A Training Cadre remained 'on circuit' in each area and Patrols were allowed to retain one Aux Unit Mk II for training purposes. Although by now severely depleted of stores and regular personnel, Colonel Douglas ensured that, as far as possible, his men would retain their identity as Auxiliers up to and beyond stand down in

November 1944. More significantly, the secrecy surrounding their true role, the real triumph of Auxiliary Units, would remain for another two and a half decades.

Fred Simpson:

'Nobody, not even our parents, knew what we were doing, and we kept our silence. We had no disbandment parade, as did the Home Guard. We just gave up our supplies, though we kept our great coats and two pairs of boots (leather and rubber) and just went home. Later came a letter of thanks from the War Office and after one reunion dinner we ceased to be. The REs blew up our bunker and it was back to the plough.

'I don't know what would have happened if the Germans had invaded. After the initial repulse on the coast, the Home Forces and Home Guard were to be withdrawn inland (and) we would have gone to ground waiting to be overrun. The worst of it was knowing that our families would have been in enemy hands and liable to have been shot if we started anything.

'Anyway, we had our gallon of rum, didn't we?'

Dedicated to the men and women of the
WWII British Resistance Organisation
known as

The GHQ Auxiliary Units 1940 – 1944

By W.A. Joyce, 203 Devon Auxunits
(with apologies to Henry Wadworth Longfellow and Prologue of
'*The Song of Hiawatha*')

Should you ask me whence these stories?
Whence these Legends and Traditions?
With their nasty sounds of banging and
Their smells of smoke and almonds,
I should answer, I should tell you:

Tales they are of Home Defences –
Of a very secret movement.
Frowned upon at first by Big-Wigs,
Looked upon as underhanded!
"T'wasn't done," they said, disgusted
Turned their Army noses upwards
As a sign it was beneath them

But our persevering leaders
Stood their ground and asked no favours,
Trained their men with scanty weapons,
Gave them strange ideas of fighting!

Till at last the pompous Big-Wigs
"Thought there might be something in it"
Condescended to consider,
Questions that concerned equipment.
Saw results in other quarters and
At last began to praise us!
So our work became quite pleasant
Once we felt we were approved of!

CHAPTER FIVE

Coleshill - The Focal Point

'...The aim of the guerrilla must be to develop their inherent advantages so as to nullify those of the enemy. The principles of this type of warfare are therefore:–

(a) Surprise first and foremost, by finding out the enemy's plans and concealing your own intentions and movements.

(b) Never undertake an operation unless certain of success owing to careful planning and good information. Break off the action when it becomes too risky to continue.

(c) Ensure that a secure line of retreat is always available.

(d) Choose areas and localities for action where your mobility will be superior to that of the enemy, owing to better knowledge of the country, lighter equipment, etc.

(e) Confine all movements as much as possible to the hours of darkness.

(f) Never engage in a pitched battle unless in overwhelming strength and thus sure of success.

(g) Avoid being pinned down in a battle by the enemy's superior forces or armament; break off the action before such a situation can develop.

(h) Retain the initiative at all costs by redoubling activities when the enemy commences counter-measures.

(i) When the time for action comes, act with the greatest boldness and audacity. The partisan's motto is –

Valiant but Vigilant

★　　★　　★

These *nine points of the guerrilla's creed* were laid down by Colin Gubbins in his MI(R) publication *'The Art of Guerrilla Warfare'* – one of the three booklets for which he was responsible to the Directorate of Military Intelligence. Although regarded as 'Most Secret', they are not visibly marked with any security classification.

The fountainhead for his guerrillas was Auxiliary Units' Headquarters, originally at 7, Whitehall Place in London. Although centrally situated for the War Office, it was not equipped for operational training either in size or location, and he soon organised a conspiracy of Lords to find something more suitable.

With his usual impeccable touch, Gubbins despatched a selected officer from his Staff – Captain (later Major) The Honourable Michael T Henderson, 16/5th Lancers, the younger brother of Lord Farringdon – to trawl for somewhere suitable in the centre of England. It was not an immensely difficult business because the noble Lord's neighbour in Wiltshire was the Seventh Earl of Radnor, who owned one of England's great country buildings – Coleshill House, a 17th Century Palladian mansion and extensive estate, created by the amateur architect Sir Roger Pratt – apparently with a hint or two from Inigo Jones – as well as nearby Longford Castle. These certainly kept him off any housing waiting-lists and, as he preferred life in the Castle, the only occupants at Coleshill were the sisters, Mary and Katherine Pleydell-Bouverie and their dogs.

A financial accommodation was reached with the War Office and, at the arrival of Auxunits in the summer of 1940, the Pleydell-Bouverie's contribution to the war effort was an unpremeditated change in lifestyle.

The conspiracy of Lords was consolidated when Lord Glanusk became Commanding Officer in 1942, with Lord Delamere his appointed second-in-Command and Transport Officer. In support, were a number of officers with double-barrelled names.

Initially intended as a training HQ, administration was moved down to the country too after 'blitz' damage in Whitehall. Coleshill House, near the town of Highworth and less than ten miles from the railway station at Swindon, was in most respects an ideal location, remote from the point of likely enemy invasion and with plenty of space for operational training. The postal address – GHQ Auxiliary Units, c/o GPO Highworth – is immediately recognisable to any 'warrior' – of whatever station – as well as any interested historian or researcher.

The plan was to develop the estate as a training area for Auxiliers. Dummy tanks and aircraft, damaged beyond repair, and enemy transport – some real, others simulated – were dispersed in the grounds and a massive collection of firearms assembled, a number of which were German, as well as booby traps and explosives. Demonstration OBs were dug – one is still there. Classes were prepared in close combat, map reading, stealth, night cross-country movement, the use of firearms and grenades, and camouflage. In due course, competitions were prepared. At first, officers responsible for training had to commute from London for the weekend – the only time their students, the Auxiliers, could conveniently absent themselves from work. It is generally accepted that Coleshill was a quiet place during the week and seriously noisy at weekends. By the end of 1940 the whole Auxunit HQ War Establishment had settled at 'GPO Highworth'.

All this required officers to supervise the administration and organise a training programme, and other ranks – men for transport and engineering and women as secretaries, cooks, clerks and orderlies – to provide routine spadework-and-support services. Officers were in the big house and other ranks at first lived and worked in, and over, stables and outbuildings. Later they moved into newly erected Nissen Huts, a disappointment for the rats which had plagued the stables. The soldiers, however – previously without heating – saw it as a definite improvement in lifestyle.

Life in the big house was no less hearty at times. Eric Gray, who served at Coleshill for two years as an RASC technical and mechanical clerk, remembers just one telephone – Highworth 85 – until Auxunits (Signals) built an adequate network. He is pretty sure too that there was no electricity at first until a supply was installed through temporary cables suspended in passages and the main rooms. Heating was negligible and not in any sense coordinated. The water supply was pumped from a main reservoir, more than thirty feet below ground, under a series of cellars and tunnels. This, and the ancient appliance – man-handled and pumped by half a dozen men either side of a master lever – was the only protection against fire hazards. Eric was not surprised that shortage of water was still a major factor when this otherwise magnificent building – then in the ownership of millionaire Mr Ernest Cook, one of the partners of the well known travel agents, was finally burned to the ground in September 1952.

The training rationale was described by Nigel Oxenden:

'COURSES. With the idea of standardising the teaching, and at the same time building up everywhere a personal contact with headquarters, it was decided to hold four weekend courses. Coleshill House was considered suitable; the servants' hall and kitchen were taken over as a mess, and lofts over the stables as billets for (visiting) officers and men. The HQ staff came down on

Fridays from Whitehall Place, laid on the programme and catering, and returned to London on Sunday evening. The first course was held on August 22nd 1940; the series of four stretched to one hundred, with surprisingly little deviation from the original programme.

'...The first effect of instructing the auxiliers, was to clarify the ideas of the instructors...'

Auxiliers, with emphasis on Patrol Leaders first, were selected to attend a Coleshill course as soon as administratively possible. Some made several visits and a few never got there at all. A number were able to travel by car, if the IO could wangle a few petrol coupons for them, and first reported to Highworth Post Office, a security cut-out to identify visitors – whose intention was reported to 'Highworth 85' by telephone – before they were guided on to the main house.

But the vast majority came by train to Swindon. From there they were brought directly to Coleshill in RASC transport – usually a three-ton truck – marked with the GHQ Home Forces insignia, an Heraldic Lion Rampant, and the unit identification number 490. If there was a yellow blob on the bonnet it was, like the tops of pillar boxes, intended to change colour when poison gas was detected.

Highworth Post Office still receives frenetic cover in daily newspapers as the clearing house for *all* visitors to Coleshill, and postmistress Mrs Mabel Stranks role, useful though it undoubtedly was, overstated. (The 'Mabel Fable' is outlined in Chapter Eight). She and her staff were well known to the regular other ranks at Coleshill.

The late Kenneth E Burnell volunteered for unspecified 'secret duties' directly after training at Aldershot, and before a regimental posting – with no idea what he was volunteering for. He served at Coleshill for two years from November 1940, first arriving by train at Swindon:

'The RTO (Rail Transport Office) there had us transported to GPO Highworth. The Postmistress, Mrs M A Stranks, got on the phone and a car soon arrived and we got to Coleshill. Until then we just had no idea as to our destination!

'(Later) I had to stay the night at the PO at Highworth in case an urgent phone call came through from the War Office. Mrs Stranks said she would be awake on duty all night and let me go to sleep in the bed upstairs after a very nice supper. Even brought me tea in bed in the morning!'

Eric Gray recalls:

'Her post office was merely an accommodation address for Coleshill House and her only involvement was to contact Auxunits by telephone whenever anyone arrived asking for them. In any event, this was usually delegated to one of her two charming lady assistants. I often spoke to them over the telephone but unfortunately I have forgotten their names. They used to allow Corporal Johnny Banks and myself to leave our cycles at the Post Office for safety whenever we went to the dance at the local school. Mrs Stranks I remember as a shadowy figure in the background...'

★ ★ ★

The main remit for Auxunits' HQ was to teach the nine points of the guerrillas' creed to the men in the sharp end, those civilians in the operational patrols, and the Scout Sections of regulars; and to provide refresher courses for Intelligence Officers. Instruction started from a zero base point – it had never been attempted before. Moreover, it had to happen in a hurry – 'the Germans were coming'.

This required permanent staff. By 1943, Auxiliary Units' HQ War Establishment totalled ninety-seven personnel. Ten officers included two Royal Engineers responsible for OB design and construction – for both Patrols and Special Duties Section – and to 'teach bangs'. The eighty-seven NCOs and other ranks listed a musketry instructor, carpenters and bricklayers, four officers' mess staff, drivers and motor cyclists, ATS switchboard operators, quartermasters and clerks.

Hidden away under 'Notes' at the end of the Establishments were seven officers and sixty-nine NCOs and other ranks, including 41 signalmen – *additional personnel allowed for the special duties branch 'to be filled as and when required'*. Some lived at Coleshill - others were privately billeted in areas. These specialists were responsible, through their own Auxunits (Signals) OC, to nearby Hannington Hall (HQ of Auxunits' Special Duties Section), and the purpose will be explained in following chapters. For the moment, it is enough to describe their work as very specially secret with some of them, from 1942, assembling secret radios in huts at Coleshill, after moving from Bachelor's Hall at Hundon in Suffolk.

Finally, the 'Notes' referred to fifty-six 'subalterns and second subalterns', and their support staff – equally secret

Control Station operators for ATS (Auxiliary Units) radio communications network.

Hannington Hall was under the supervision of Major Maurice Petherick and Senior Commander Beatrice Temple – in their respective roles as head of Auxunits' Special Duties Section and overlady of the ATS – both of whom were regularly in conference at Coleshill, although representing absolutely distinct and separate parts of the complete Auxiliary Units organisation (these are also detailed in later chapters). From 1942, after this very close affiliation with Britain's Secret Services, Hannington Hall became an 'ATTERY' for ATS personnel, with daily motor transport provided for those working at Coleshill.

The support staff of all ranks at Coleshill were back-ups for the instructors, the men who had to put the guerrilla's creed into practice. The musketry instructor, with varieties of arcane weaponry, operated from a firing range in a quarry half a mile away from the main house. Lectures were given in the old servants' hall, and demonstrations in the estate grounds included those important 'bangs' which guaranteed Auxiliers' interest – grenade throwing and firing explosives. Practical exercises were set up on subjects such as camouflage, stealth, night movement and Close Combat. This training is still fresh in the memories of many Auxiliers. As usual, there is some conflict of evidence.

There are, for example, indications that Major 'Dan' Fairbairn himself (See Chapter VI) was in charge. Others, downgrading the importance of Close Combat, remember training under regular army Physical Training Instructors. Knife fighting was reported to be under the command of Captain (later Major) W W ('Bill') Harston – whose first official post was 'transport officer'. Other indisputable evidence points to instruction from a five feet, two-inch Scots sergeant-major, specially released for the purpose from Barlinnie Jail in Glasgow, and yet more eyewitnesses attest to CQC instruction from a Russian – a gifted knife fighter!

From 1942, Welsh Guards officers predominated on the Staff and it is hardly conceivable – lampooned as they were by the cartoonist Ian Fenwick – that they would have been acceptable to Commanders other than Lord Glanusk, who arrived in his Rolls Royce with a young wife and his wine cellar. Any previous association between instruction in irregular warfare and the Brigade of Guards seems entirely improbable.

David Lampe ridiculed this set up:

'Glanusk invited the young officers on his staff to share his wine and pay no more for each bottle than he had paid when he laid it down. From then...more and more of the staff officers at Coleshill were to be the wealthy, the well-to-do and the titled. The place became like a guards' mess in peacetime, public school accents predominated, and there was more talk of shooting animals and less of shooting Germans...the officers were unwilling to talk about anything except horse-racing...'

In his personal copy of *'The Last Ditch'* Stewart Edmundson noted – 'This is unfair. Toby Glanusk had a fine war record'. However, a surviving Intelligence Officer from those days agrees more with Lampe. On a visit of inspection in-the-field, Glanusk's first question to the IO was 'Do you have any Gentlemen I could meet?' As opposed to Players, presumably.

Glanusk certainly created a 'Guardee' (meaning 'Brigade of Guards') atmosphere at Coleshill with the introduction of Lord Delamare as his Transport Officer, and Marcus Wickham-Boynton, who owned the largest racing stables in the country, in charge of administration. *His* order requiring patrols to lay out their kit in Guards fashion was deeply unpopular. Instructions were also sent out that all auxiliers should learn arms drill (Guards style), for a competition that later took place at Coleshill. They took great exception to this utter waste of their time.

Outsiders in the Mess found a very hostile and uncooperative atmosphere and it is difficult to envisage how pragmatists such as Major Oxenden, in charge of Training, fitted in with it all. As he was living-out with his family, it is a fair bet that he avoided it all at every opportunity.

Major Peter Forbes was to become GSO(2) to the later CO, Colonel Frank Douglas. But as the IO for The Borders he remembered:

'...drilling at my HQ.....just for two or three patrols who had come out on top in the other events (in Coleshill competitions)... To decide the overall winner. That patrol...was done out of it by the drill judges, Wickham-Boynton and Tom Delamere. This still rankles!!'

Fortunately for Auxiliers, basic training groundwork had been very securely laid by Major Geoffrey Beyts and continued in the safe hands of the pragmatic Nigel Oxenden. 'Brigadier

Bill's' previous combat experience with the Rajputana Rifles in Burmese jungles was to be the sure foundation for all the significant instruction at Coleshill, as well as the demonstrations, exercises, and competitions which he devised. His lecture notes are masterpieces of detail, based on his own personal experience of real combat.

'Bill' Beyts had other invaluable assets. Conscientious and energetic in a unit where these qualities were often lacking, his was a real seven-day week during the two years he was responsible for training at Coleshill. And, unusually, *all* ranks spoke well of him. Most officers must have had respect for his first hand experience of close quarters' fighting and – in spite of all the pressures of travel, lectures, advice, administration – he remained unfailingly courteous to all ranks. Auxiliary Units of all stations have everything to thank him for.

★   ★   ★

Commanding Officers carried the rank of Colonel. Colin Gubbins was followed in November 1940, by C R ('Bill') Major, of the Dorset Regiment, who had spent much of his career with the Directorate of Military Intelligence. He moved on to form the RAF Regiment in February 1942 and was replaced by Lord Glanusk of the Welsh Guards. When he had a heart attack in August 1943, his deputy, Frank Douglas, another former member of the MI Directorate was promoted, and remained in charge at Coleshill – through stand-down – until close-down on 15th January 1945.

While these officers were dealing with strategy of stratospheric significance, others at Coleshill soldiered on at a more conventional level.

For example (as can be seen in Chapter IX), Intelligence Officers in the field may not have been too sure whether to stay behind when the Germans arrived, or not. And their staff may, or not, have been trained to fight from OBs. But there was no confusion on the point for personnel at Coleshill.

The support staff there were *not* trained to stay behind after invasion and did not expect to be ordered to do so. Moreover, if there was any unit where cellular secrecy was totally effective it was Auxunits' HQ. None of the other ranks cared what was going on nearby or had the slightest idea what 'staying behind' was all about, duties and interests being confined exclusively to their own special trade. With a comparatively 'cushy' number there was no point in rocking the boat.

One warrant officer, Class I, having recently moved his wife into the area, was unwise enough, to upset the newly appointed transport officer, Captain The Lord Delamere. No doubt with some concern for the legendary power of senior NCOs – usually 'old soldiers' with a wealth of practical know-how – and actual eye-to-eye confrontation, Delamere used his personal influence at War Office in a roundabout way to get the Warrant Officer Establishment *downgraded* to Class II, leaving the powerless victim either to accept a reduction in rank and pay, or a posting elsewhere. At the time, 'elsewhere' was likely to be a well-defended Normandy beach.

Delamere's arrival in August 1942 also brought discomfort to long serving Coleshill personnel, when he decided they would all benefit from the unique instruction opportunities which Coleshill could provide. This led dispirited non-combatants to a day of spirited activity in the quarry and on the assault course.   One night, someone, strongly suspected of being female, was sick in the back of a staff-car. Captain John Collings was reported to the War Office when *his* staff-car was seen by a civilian watchdog, parked outside a cinema. Although he couldn't apparently confirm or deny that he was on duty it was deemed, at the right level, a case for 'no further action'.

1st Class Staff Sergeant Major Twelves was considered a 'nasty bit of work' by some of his soldiers, and a Quartermaster sergeant, 'an old sweat and heavy drinker', obtained a full list of the staff, took it to the cobbler in Highworth and tried to claim for boot repairs for the whole HQ. He received a prison sentence and 'reduction to the ranks'.

Orderly room private Delaney caused quite a stir when he complained to the Priest at Shrivenham that no provision was being made at Coleshill for soldiers of Catholic faith. The priest approached the Camp Commandant, Captain A R C ('Andy') Anderson, who:

> '...blew his top. He blew Delaney up for giving away the secret location of the Unit. He then arranged that all the Catholics should attend Mass at 6am each morning and transport to Shrivenham was laid on for them at 5.30am.'

Four RASC drivers, enjoying a 'joyride' in Captain Anderson's private car, were in a head-on collision with Captain Tracey in his sports car on the Highworth/Coleshill road, after swerving violently to miss the infant Joy – daughter of Major Nigel Oxenden – while she was being wheeled along in her perambulator. The five principal protagonists were all conveyed to an emergency ward at Stratton St Margaret's Hospital and the transport pool was short of drivers for a week.

Rumour abounded that some officers were trying to fiddle their car expenses but, over and above this domestic nonsense, real advances in training were taking place. A suggestion by an IO that the champion patrol of Great Britain should be found by competition, bore fruit in the winter of 1941/2. Areas were given several months in which to find their county champions, who met in the semi-finals, five or six at a time, at Coleshill, on four successive weekends. The four winning teams returned a month later for the finals. These tests were largely the inspiration of Major Beyts. Nigel Oxenden wrote:

> 'The principal event was a night patrol, in which there was inevitably a strong element of luck, but the others, night-firing, grenade throwing, an efficiency race and explosive problems, were a good test of knowledge and skill.'

Initiatives were still encouraged. During one weekend event, when 'Home Guards' were set to attack the HQ building, two men in white overalls arrived through the main gate pushing a wheelbarrow loaded with ladders and tins of paint. The disinterested sentry took no notice. They entered the building, moved up the stairs to the library on the first floor, pointed at the CO and said, with respect:

> 'Sir, you are dead!'

Credit was given to the Auxiliers involved although not, it is reported, by the sentry as he doubled away to the 'cooler'.

A second competition was held in the autumn of 1942 and a third in the autumn of 1943 – in which a drill element was introduced. Problems arose when old men were discredited by the young, after which there was a tendency among IOs to recruit 'boys' to fill their gaps. Repercussion came when they, in turn, were conscripted into the regular army at a time when replacement was getting harder.

These competitions helped maintain interest in the patrols when events were making it daily less likely that the Germans would invade. Fortunately, the possibilty of enemy raids was adequate justification for Auxunits' continued existence.

The first series of courses for Group Commanders was held from March 1941. They continued until early 1943 – with no less than 142 GCs attending Coleshill between November 1942 and January 1943, by which time their function was becoming increasingly administrative. It was clearly impossible for every Auxilier to attend. But it was possible for the majority of Patrol Leaders and they passed on what they had learned. New courses started for them in February 1943.

From that time, GHQ attention was increasingly focused on the Second Front. Some Coleshill personnel were redirected to active service and the pace slackened. When it was no longer practicable to operate from Auxunits' HQ, a skeleton network of 'circus visits' travelled to the areas. Six were made in June and July 1944 by a small training staff with their own demonstration gear and stores.

Since August 1940, Coleshill had seen 100 Auxunits' weekend courses, including twenty-five for Patrol Leaders, nineteen for Group Commanders, fifteen for complete Scout Sections, eleven for new intakes, 5 for Scout Section officers, 4 for Royal Engineer corporals and 3 for Intelligence Officers' HQ staff.

Further instruction and demonstrations had taken place in Scotland, centred on Melville House, the seat of the Earls of Leven, situated between Ladybank and Cowper, Fife, having extensive surrounding areas suitable for training and ideally within reach of a railway. It had courses on hand-to-hand combat, its own pistol range, and researcher David Blair has recently discovered a stretch of railway line in the grounds – part of a demolition practice area.

After stand-down in November 1944, the only Coleshill personnel in residence were Colonel Douglas, and Major Nigel Oxenden – by then working from a cottage in the grounds under directions to compile the final Auxunit history for War Office – and a very small support staff. 15th January 1945 was final close down day.

It was also farewell to the nine points of the Guerrilla's creed. There is no sign of their re-emergence until the end of the century – although it is inconceivable that both the creed and Oxenden's final report were not the focus of later analysis by today's Special Forces.

To avoid catastrophe for 'behind the lines' irregulars, they are still invaluable guidelines.

★   ★   ★

Memorial trees have been planted at Coleshill – now in the stewardship of the National Trust – since 1996. Individual dedications are kept in a Dedication Book in the Coleshill Estate Office and can be viewed by visitors. The trees – oak and beech – are located in small groups out in the Park.

Dedications – all to Auxiliary Units - include two to former

Auxiliers killed in action with the SAS in enemy occupied France; the 'Lads' of the South East Essex and East Anglian Groups who were trained at Coleshill House; the men and women of the British Resistance movement; the survivors of the Somerset Group; Auxunits (Signals); members of the Sussex Auxiliary Units; the 'Legion of Frontiersmen' and 'Churchill's Secret Army'.

CHAPTER SIX

The Scout Sections

'I have never known such secrecy...we trained ourselves and
became fitter and fitter...It was nothing to be on the go all day and
most of the night...The men moaned.'

(Geoff Bowery, NCO, Suffolk Scout Section)

'Scout Sections' of regular soldiers, although significant
contributors to Auxiliary Units history and training, often
remain overlooked by writers and researchers.

David Lampe, for example, left them out entirely in 'The
Last Ditch' and it has to be assumed that no one briefed him.
The omission is otherwise difficult to understand because they
were – together with certain personnel from Auxunits' Signals
– the only 'regular' soldiers scheduled to 'stay-behind' after
invasion. Moreover, several members of the Sections were
involved in Special Operations at the time of the Normandy
invasion, including SAS behind-the-lines action in France.

Both Ops Intelligence Officers and Auxiliary Units ATS radio
operators *might* have stayed behind after invasion as well.
However, although the women subalterns were provided with
highly secret 'Zero' Stations, no provision was usually made to hide
the IOs. In any case, neither was *scheduled* to stay behind; whether
or not they did so in the event depended on last minute orders.

The lack of interest in Scout Sections is partly the product of
routine administrative army procedure. After withdrawal from
Auxiliary Units in 1942/3, these soldiers were fragmented as
units, mostly re-absorbed into the mainstream army, and finally
demobilised from different centres, dispersing homeward in
every direction. This happened with other regular soldiers on
Auxiliary Units War Establishment too, including those Signals'
personnel who created and maintained a secret GHQ
communications network. At stand-down, there was no need
to remind these regulars of the continuing need for secrecy; a
well oiled technique calculated (or not) to divide and rule,
worked wonderfully as they disappeared from regimental duty,
never to he heard from again. Well, almost.

Another factor was preoccupation with the 'stay-behinds'

organised by XII Army Corps Observation Unit and Section 'D', a department of the Secret Intelligence Service (MI6) under the command of Lawrence Grand. When Auxiliary Units started functioning – to all intents and purposes in July 1940 – it was not the precise beginning of guerrillas or 'stay-behinds'. In splendid anticipation, caches of arms and explosives had already been secreted by Section 'D' in vulnerable areas of mainland Great Britain. This was not an unqualified success and their irregular activities overlapped and upset other agencies. It seems reasonable to assume the regular army was among them. Counter-productively, they overlooked the need to recruit and train personnel to fire the guns and detonate the explosives; the operation therefore petered out in disarray. Section 'D' was soon disbanded as an independent unit and absorbed, together with many skills and talents, at first into Military Intelligence (Research) and, later, Special Operations Executive.

Another 'stay-behind' force was created by XII Corps, defending front-line counties in south east England, under Commanding Officer, General Andrew ('Bulgy') Thorne, Grenadier Guards. Only too aware of the inadequacy of his fixed defences, troops and armour after the Dunkirk evacuation, Thorne – with unusual interest in irregular warfare for a regular soldier – authorised the creation of a 'stay-behind' force, on the assumption that the 'crust' of coastal defences envisaged by General Ironside, then C-in-C Home Forces, would soon be overwhelmed by the enemy. Retreat to an organised defence line running east-west along the north Kent Downs would follow. To help with the creation of civilian 'stay-behinds' in the theoretically occupied Weald below, the War Office despatched two officers from MI(R), Captains Peter Fleming, Grenadier Guards, and Mike Calvert, Royal Engineers.

Operating from headquarters at 'The Garth', Bilting, on the edge of the Kentish Weald, these two officers, extraordinary personalities who would each achieve fame in Special Operations later in the war, vigorously set about creating a guerrilla force even before a formal start to Auxunits operational patrols. Their activities were confined to Kent and Sussex. With no slavish precedents to follow and unlimited scope for innovation, they booby-trapped piers and bridges and selected prospective civilian 'stay-behinds'. Regular soldiers responsible for training them in those early days were squads known as XII Corps 'Observation Unit'. Not dissimilar to Scout Sections formed shortly afterwards under the Auxiliary Units, they were soon absorbed by Colin Gubbins.

It is no real surprise to find historians focussing on Section 'D', General Thorne and XII Corps Observation Unit, and the imaginative, charismatic activities of Peter Fleming and Mike Calvert. The first 'stay-behinds' were organised by Fleming, a noted traveller and writer, whose wife was Celia Johnson, darling of London's wartime west-end and heroine of the film-weepy *'Brief Encounter'*, and whose brother Ian wrote the James Bond series. Mike Calvert, acknowledged hero of the second Chindit long-range jungle penetration behind Japanese lines in Burma, was later CO of the re-formed SAS. Together, they were a hard attraction to ignore.

Yet another distraction was the presence in Kent – arranged by Robin, another Fleming brother (later killed on active service) – of a number of Lovat Scouts to assist the Observation Unit. It has been incorrectly reported that they were headed by Lord Lovat himself. This unique Regiment, founded in 1900 from Highland stalkers, gillies and shepherds, specialised in field-craft, stalking and reconnaissance. They provided invaluable experience at the Special Training Centre at Inverailort, distinguished themselves in the Italian campaign and, in peacetime, have been amalgamated into 23 SAS (TA).

Without in any way underplaying the significance of XII Corps Observation Unit, which could with all justification claim to be first among Auxiliary Units' operational 'stay-behinds', the proposition here is to give long overdue attention due to the mainstream Scout Sections.

★   ★   ★

In a War Establishment report, Colin Gubbins' recommendations for Scout Sections of regular soldiers were committed to paper as early as 26th July 1940:

> 'Three weeks experience has shown that the IO of an area requires a small nucleus of regular troops under his command for the following purposes:
> (a) Assistance in the training of Auxiliary Units.
> (b) Construction of hide-outs, main dumps etc.
> (c) Supervising distribution and security of concealed dumps.
> (d) Special fighting patrols and aid to Auxiliary Units if invasion comes; sniping of stragglers.'

Only *three weeks* were needed to identify this urgent need. Gubbins went on to describe the background:

> 'As an experiment, in one sub-area of XII Corps, the IO (Fleming) has been given an RE Officer (Calvert) and a section of

Lovat Scouts to work under him. The Corps Commander has now reported that the result has been excellent, and has asked for similar sections to be provided for his other sub-areas.'

He then added a plug for his new Units:

'In his (General Thorne's) opinion, as the organization of these Auxiliary Units is not only urgent but must remain to some extent secret, the necessary preparations can only be completed if a small regular nucleus is provided throughout.

'The number of such sections required is two per IOs area, i.e., 24 in all. Each should consist of one Scout officer and eleven Scouts, plus one car with driver, one M/C and eleven cycles.

'At the same time the IO requires one confidential clerk to assist him, plus one RE officer and one sapper, one truck and driver.'

Gubbins was outlining an ideal and, in the event, the pattern was not always consistent. Nevertheless, indications of the important role he had in mind for his Scout Sections are clear enough.

Further early evidence comes from a letter filed in Public Record Office:

From:- Brigadier N M RITCHIE, CBE, DSO, MC

HEADQUARTERS
SOUTHERN COMMAND
SALISBURY

SECRET

There exists an organisation, in reality a part of the HG's, which works under one Brigadier GUBBINS and whose role is highly secret. GUBBINS you may possibly know already as he was in NORWAY.

The Chief is most anxious to help GUBBINS' show by getting hold of five good young officers, one for each of our areas, to train this personnel in intensive scouting and battle patrol training.

As your Division is not charged with the particular supervision of any HGs, whereas other Divisions are, the Chief asked me to write and find out from you whether you can provide these five officers?

Details of the precise amount of time these officers will have to spend on the job I have'nt (*sic*) yet got, but I don't imagine it will be absolutely full time. But I would like to make it clear that if operations commence the officers would at once rejoin their units.

As soon as you can let me know I will get all details.

(signed) NMR

(To) Major-General J A H GAMMELL, DSO, MC
Commander, 3rd Division

A number of significant points can be identified. There is, for instance, no specific mention of Auxiliary Units themselves – an example, on security grounds, of a limited distribution of the title even at Staff level. The date, just one month after Auxunits came on stream, demonstrates the 'blaze of wild priority' (see Nigel Oxenden's Auxiliary Units, History and Achievement') generated by Gubbins and his HQ staff and the influence he carried with the 'Chief'. The 'Chief' was probably General Ironside, but may have been his newly appointed successor as C-in-C Home Forces, General Alan Brooke, or GOC Southern Command, General Claude J E Auchinlech. There is no evidence to be read here, even between the lines, of political influence from Winston Churchill, the Prime Minister.

The idea that the loaned officers would return to their units when the balloon went up seems to be an example of Gubbins's pragmatic approach to an implacable problem. From the earliest days, his Scout Sections were intended to 'stay-behind' and not be returned to their regiments – and there is no evidence that subalterns were exempted.

Finally we see an Old Boy Network in action – the hallmark of Auxunits at every level - from Colonel Gubbins up to the 'Chief'; down to Brigadier Ritchie and up again to Major General Gammell. This was surely not a normal chain of command.

Scout Sections of Auxiliary Units were an urgent necessity in the summer of 1940, while the threat of imminent invasion was still in the forefront of military minds. Auxiliers had to be trained immediately if they were to be of tactical use and – as operational Patrols were rapidly expanding around coastlines and training facilities at far away Coleshill still at an initial stage – professionals were at once needed on the spot.

Colonel Gubbins first required a nucleus of twenty-four Sections of regular troops, to work under the direct command of IOs. By November 1940 there were fourteen Auxunit Areas – each usually (but not always) corresponding to a County boundary. Devon and Cornwall – initially one area, for example – were separated later. Each Area was scheduled to have two Scout Sections of a dozen regular soldiers under a subaltern – preference being for troops of local County Regiments although, as we shall read, Mike Calvert had doubts about this preference.

In Cornwall, for example, the Duke of Cornwall's Light Infantry was assigned and in central East Anglia (where Areas were not defined precisely by County boundaries), the Suffolk

Regiment. Peter Fleming and Captain Norman Field, his successor in Kent, benefited for a while from the presence of Lovat Scouts to help the Observation Units – now two in number, East and West Kent OUs. Many Sections also had a Royal Engineer in the squad and a RASC driver. Transport was usually a 15-cwt truck, supplemented by an establishment of one motorcycle and eleven bicycles.

Postings were flexible and dependent upon available troops. One Suffolk Scout Section – at least – included a Sergeant cook, known affectionately as 'Bottles' Worby. Unanimously applauded, he was a great boost to morale after a hard day in-the-field.

Subalterns were the officers referred to in Brigadier Ritchie's letter. It will be helpful to define 'regular' troops as those who were *paid*. They were not necessarily career soldiers and included Territorials, Reservists and conscripts, as well as time-servers. They differed from Auxiliers and Group Commanders specifically over pay, for Colin Gubbins's civilians were never to receive any form of remuneration, other than minor expenses often grudgingly handed over. Gubbins was certainly right when he said they 'cost the country nothing'. Jim Caws, an Isle of Wight Auxilier, was incensed at stand-down in 1944, when he was charged sixpence for his Auxunit lapel badge – after 'giving four years of my life for free!'

To avoid the administrative confusion evident sometimes at even the highest official levels, it is useful to propose some definitions – for our purposes at least. It was later intended that Operational Auxunit Patrols should organise Observers, or Scouts, from their own number, specifically tasked to discover enemy targets on a daily basis. They could fairly be referred to as 'Scout Patrols' whereas 'Scout Sections' were regular soldiers responsible for instruction. (There is a further possible complication as some Scout Sections, splitting into two groups to retreat to their own 'funkholes' (OBs), sometimes called themselves 'Scout Patrols'.) For the purposes of this book, professional 'stay-behinds' will therefore be referred to as 'Scout Sections' and civilian 'scouting' Auxiliers as 'Observers'.

However, official correspondence, and some researchers, do often misleadingly confuse 'Scout Sections' and Scout 'Patrols'. Major Beyts, OC Operations at Coleshill and the man most likely to know, was clear enough in 'Secret' Lecture Notes dated 25th October 1941, in which he identified 'Scout Patrols as Observers dispatched daily from OBs to search for targets'. Less likely to get it right was the Director General of the Home Guard (1941 – 1944), Major General The Viscount

Bridgeman, CB, DSO, MC, who announced, in a 'Most Secret' letter dated 20th January 1941 to Territorial Army Association secretaries in all Auxunit Areas (copied to General Officers Commanding-in-Chief regular Forces):

'I am directed to forward the following instructions regarding the control of Auxiliary Units of Home Guard known as "Scout Patrols" or "Observation Units"....'.

A number of instructions follow and it seems clear the Scout Sections had until then been administratively perched unsurely, midway between the regular army and Home Guard. The letter emphasised that they were operationally responsible to GHQ Home Forces while borne on the strength of the Home Guard. Enrolment Forms AF W 3066 'will be endorsed to show membership of Auxiliary Units but no more detailed endorsement will be made.' The letter concludes:

'This letter will be kept in a safe and will not be reproduced or its contents communicated to other than addressees except in so far as it is absolutely necessary. It is important that the existence of these units should be mentioned as seldom as possible.'

As TAAs are involved, it seems most probable from the date that the evolution of the three Reserve GHQ Battalions, 201, 202, 203, later to become fact, was under consideration.

Scout Sections completed Auxunits' operational chain-of-command. HQ handed out orders to Intelligence Officers, and through the subaltern they had overall command of Scout Sections. Officers at a level below IOs were Home Guard Group (and Assistant Group) Commanders. They and the Patrols were unpaid and therefore, for practical and legal purposes, of civilian status, although sometimes wearing uniform.

It was an unfortunate fact that the men of the Scout Sections often came to irregular warfare almost as untrained as Auxiliers themselves. Their elementary knowledge of firearms could be put to use at once but, thereafter, they systematically extended their own knowledge of explosives, map-reading, night fighting and close quarters combat, to a format circulated from Coleshill – sometimes managing to keep only one step ahead of their part-time pupils.

Their real significance was that they were among the few regular soldiers scheduled to 'stay-behind' after invasion. For this purpose they generally built thir own OBs, sometimes with help co-opted from local pioneers and sappers. A later scheme for Intelligence Officers to stay behind was apparently abandoned, although Captain Peter Forbes, IO in the Borders, and Norman Field in Kent, made their own plans to do so with or without the knowledge of HQ.

★　　★　　★

On 9th September 1940, Colin Gubbins wrote from Whitehall Place to Lieutenant-General C J E Auchinleck, CB, etc., GOC-in-C., Southern Command.

> My dear General,
>
> I am very grateful indeed to you for the loan of the officers to help us in the training of the Auxiliary Units of the Home Guard. The 3rd Division produced a first class lot of officers who have been of enormous assistance and have worked their hardest to give us a good start. It has all been a tremendous help to me and to my officers with whom they were co-operating.
>
> I have seen General Gammell and thanked him personally.
>
> Yours ever,
C McV Gubbins

By early September 1940, Scout Sections were certainly up-and-running - with their subalterns getting high level appreciation.

★　　★　　★

Nigel Oxenden, in *'Auxiliary Units – History and Achievement'*, is clear that the Scout Sections:

> '...after three months' training by the IO, should in turn train the patrols by lectures, demonstration and night exercises. A good deal of this (initial three-month) period was spent in constructing their two OBs, since they would be split into two patrols of normal strength for operational purposes.'

With the job description outlined, Nigel Oxenden continued:

> 'By the time they had built these, it was only natural that they should be considered by the IO as his working parties, and be employed in digging for those of the Home Guard who firmly declined to do it for themselves.
>
> 'Both scout officers and other ranks were chosen for their youth and toughness...all the sections went through a course at HQ within their first few weeks and courses were held twice a year thereafter for fresh intakes.
>
> 'Nearly all of them did more than their share of digging, and some did little else during the years of their attachment the Auxiliary Units.'

As Scout Sections were the IOs private army, Major Oxenden was possibly writing from unusually isolated experience. His version – uniquely – is not corroborated by survivors. Other experiences support the proposition that most OBs were dug after local arrangements with Royal Engineers or the Pioneer Corps and that Auxiliers turned-to willingly enough. If they did not, certain sanctions were available. Although it was bad security to train a 'warrior' in secret and then return him to ordinary HG duties, it was within the gift of the IO to do so, and looked upon as a disgrace for both the Auxilier and his Patrol. It did not, moreover, need the formal backing of Military law or the usual paperwork.

Scout Section veterans are not unanimous in their accounts; they were after all what their IOs made them, and memory is naturally fallible after more than half-a-century. Geoff Bowery certainly built two OBs in Suffolk, and helped with others, but it was far from a total commitment, as he made clear in audio-taped evidence to the Museum of the British Resistance Organisation. Geoff got his call-up papers in February 1940, with initial training at the Suffolk Regimental Barracks at Bury St Edmunds. He did not enjoy the experience.

> 'I began to get fed up with barrack life. I am not the sort who likes to march up and down and be shouted at. On the company notice board I saw that positions were offered for Special Military duties and, disregarding the advice "never volunteer for anything in the army", I put my name down. After interview and a stiff medical, I reported with all my kit to (then) 2nd Lieutenant McIntyre and was driven, with other volunteers, to the Mill House at Cransford. Jack Steward, a regular soldier, was the sergeant and he and his corporal, Cyril Hall, were soon sent away on foreign postings (to West Africa, initially) and I was made sergeant.'

Sergeant 5825095 John ('Jack') Steward enlisted in the 2nd Battalion, Suffolk Regiment, in 1930 and was brought home from Regimental Service in India a few days before the outbreak of WWII. He met Doris at Cransford; they married in 1941, before he was attached to the Royal West African Frontier Force and posted to the India/Burma campaign. Jack has since died, but Doris Steward still lives within a few hundred yards of the Mill House.

Cyril Hall has retired to Lincolnshire and his later WWII Service with the 'Chindits' can be read in Chapter Twelve.

The Mill House stands on the edge of the small village of Cransford, deep in Suffolk countryside. A detached building of several *siecles,* it remains unchanged. Ideal for a Scout Section HQ, with adequate accommodation, woods and pits nearby for training, and a garage with hard-standing opposite as a workshop, it was requisitioned in 1940 and remained in army hands until 1942, when a flurry of unexploded bombs forced hurried evacuation. An Royal Engineer NCO specialised in the design and construction of finely balanced trapdoors, which were distributed in his Area as OBs neared completion.

Men and women of Suffolk are much attracted to superstition and the mysterious WWII history of Mill House is still spoken *sotto voce.*

Group Commander Captain G Scott-Moncrieff operated from the Mill House and lived in the nearby village of Hacheston. 'He was 'rather a gin-palace' and, unknown to the Scout Section, was targeted as 'unreliable' by one Patrol. Creating their own authority, an Auxilier was delegated to execute him if the enemy arrived. The garrotte was favoured. Captain Holberton, their IO, not on the 'danger' list was:

> '...a fine example of a young English gentleman. A peculiar sort of fellow. A flippant aristocrat who would have done well when aristocrats were running the country. Very impatient, he had to be waited upon hand-and-foot. He had a batman/driver he tore the inside out of nearly. He had a large staff car, a Humber Snipe. A revered possession.'

The Humber Snipe staff-car was a serious and much sought-after status symbol. Captain Norman Field succeeded to one at Bilting but it was not the last time Peter Fleming, his predecessor, travelled in style. While serving on secret Military Intelligence deception duties in the Burmese jungle, he avoided the Japanese by a nose, exiting the front line at the very last moment thanks to accelerated departure *'in his staff* car', another Humber Snipe.

In Norfolk, the Scout Section was established in a large house near Wroxham Broad, when Tom Colquitt was posted with the Norfolks early in 1942. Captain Oxenden had left for Coleshill by then and the IO was Capt. G Woodward ('he had a Humber Snipe staff-car'). Tom found a motley crew of adventurers including Corporal Leslie Long, a London hairdresser (whose service record with the SAS can be read in Chapter XI); and regular private soldiers, 'Chalky' White and Alfie Barffe, who:

> 'had absconded from the (pre-war) army while serving in Gibraltar. They swam to Spain and joined Franco's forces. At the

outbreak of war they worked their passage back to Britain as stokers on a tramp-ship and gave themselves up. After a short period of detention they joined Auxiliary Units.'

Tom Colquitt found a Section with two OBs, one of which had a radio with callsign 'Bowling Nine' for use in 'emergencies only'. Tom was on the fringes of Auxunit Special Duties Section, for the radio network was theirs, and contact with them should never have been below 'Key Man'/Group Commander level. The Section, under Lieutenant Percy Pike, planning to stay-behind after invasion, were well equipped and trained. They had little contact with the 'Home Guard patrols and regarded them as 'greatly inferior'. Tom mistakenly thought they 'did not even have their own OBs. They came later'.

This was not how Geoff Bowery found things in nearby Suffolk.

'I have never known such secrecy. McIntyre ....only passed to me things which directly affected what we were doing. It was difficult to train men without being able to tell them anything. During the week, Monday to Friday, we trained ourselves and became fitter and fitter. It was nothing to be on the go all day and most of the night. With the Auxunits...we hardened ourselves without usual refreshment or rest. The men moaned.'

After one long day, Geoff was anticipating a good meal and rest in the 'lovely lounge at Mill House', when 'Mac' told him to prepare immediately for a long trip on his motorcycle – a 350cc Triumph. He was on his way to Coleshill House for training. He took his Tommy gun and went in darkness with just a hooded light to see the way ahead. Arriving at 3am, he checked into the guardroom and slept soundly before starting a training course for non-commissioned officers. They were introduced to black plastic High Explosive:

'The instructor just rolled it about and said it was completely safe. He took out his cigarette lighter and, to our consternation, lit the end. It just flared like a firework. But place a detonator in it and it is a different thing. The pistol instructor was a Captain Henderson, one of the best shots in the Army. I asked when we were to get some action and he shouted "NOW!" – and fired a bullet into the ground about an inch in front of my army boot.'

Major Oxenden recorded thirty-one courses for regular personnel at Coleshill – 'fifteen for complete scout sections, eleven for new intakes and five for scout officers.'

Geoff Bowery recalled:

'...at weekends we trained Auxunits all round Suffolk. Local people became attuned to the noise of our explosions and firing. The AUs were first class, good at moving at night. A few were awkward, some good at one part of their training and duffers at others. Some were mechanically useless but bright in other ways. One fellow was doubtful about grenade throwing and his bomb bounced back into the trench. I picked it up and threw it the second time and it went 'WHAM' almost before it got to the target.

'We experimented with the sticky bomb, it was the product of a madman...you had to throw it over-arm like a cricketer. If you flung it underarm it could stick to your trousers...We tried everything possible in the way of weaponry. We had trials of the PIAT (Projectile Infantry Anti-Tank). It projected a bomb towards a tank...a queer thing...It was one of the first rocket-propelled things we ever saw...We experimented with paratroopers' collapsible cycles, wonderful things.

'Then along came two small Triumph motorcycles; we drove along all sorts of back paths between roads, along the side of fields. We got our own little maps and plots of the locality to tell us where they were...Army discipline disappeared altogether. We used our own initiative to prepare for anything that might be coming.'

As the Second Front approached, the soldiers were needed for more active service and GHQ wanted them back. The late William Webber of 'Badger Patrol', remembered a Patrol Leaders' meeting at Allington Farm, Sussex, under Captain Benson, on 16th February 1943, at which he was notified that Lieutenant William Ashby and the Scout Section were leaving Auxiliary Units and returning to their regiments.

Bill said:

'It was the beginning of the end for the Scout Sections and us too.'

★   ★   ★

But for many Auxiliers and Scout Section personnel, it was only the end of the beginning. Len Edwards and John Fielding, conscripted after Auxunit service in Norfolk, remember many 'warriors' in a holding camp at Northampton. The Second Front was still a year away but Special Forces were already looking for soldiers trained in irregular warfare.

Men from Auxiliary Units were ideal.

Chapters XI and XII will record some of their adventures. Unfortunately, the casualty rate was high.

CHAPTER SEVEN

Thuggery!

Compiled with material specially provided by Major R F ('Henry') Hall, MC, and Peter Robins, Karate black belt and senior instructor with the British Combat Association.

'All of us who were trained by Major Fairbairn soon realised he had an honest dislike of anything that smacked of decency in fighting'.

(Richard Dunlop, US Office of Strategic Services)

'If you think our methods are not cricket, remember Hitler does not play the game.'

(Major William Ewart Fairbairn)

Major Geoffrey Beyts preferred the word THUGGERY for the 'dirty tricks' he taught. Other professionals had a different Lexicon – 'Close Quarters Combat', 'The Art of Silent Killing', and 'Unconventional Warfare Training', for example. Peter Robins sums it up as 'Close Combat'. 'Dan' Fairbairn called it 'Gutter Fighting'.

For his Coleshill lectures, 'Bill' Beyts prepared no less than four pages of 'Thuggery prompts'. Followed by Instructors' demonstrations and in-the-flesh participation, it was a real measure of the importance he attached to close quarters skills in guerrilla fighting.

The subject is usually avoided by Auxiliers themselves. Ask about explosives and their elderly faces are rejuvenated. They describe with undisguised glee the effectiveness of time pencils or plastic high explosive, and how to blow up tree stumps or throw a sticky bomb. They are cheerful enough too on firearms – although a touch reticent about the use of the .22 snipers' rifle, preferring to describe targets as 'bunnies' ('...we knew we might have to live off the land.....'), or Alsatian tracker-dogs, rather than German sentries or British collaborators. Interesting detail can emerge about life in Operational Bases as well.

But ask about thuggery and the response is likely to be a disarming smile and change of subject. The dangers of limb dislocation, and death by stabbing or strangulation, have never been forgotten and Auxiliers are still well aware that detailed information on killing the enemy – hand to hand – can literally be lethal even in peacetime, for there are still plenty of bad boys who would like to benefit from their special know-how. For just that reason, in 1999 Independent TV 'pruned' an explicit close combat demonstration, pre-recorded with Major R F Hall, in their programme 'The Spying Game'.

The man who contributed most to the arcane science of thuggery was William Ewart Fairbairn. 'Foul methods help you to kill quickly' – he recommended. This put him in much the same category as Colin Gubbins ('Informers should be killed quickly'), his commanding officer when both were in SOE. Other similarities are evident. While not exactly an Official Secret these days, or subject to 'D' Notice guidance, quasi-official *discouragement* to write about Fairbairn is apparent. In the latest PRO 'Secret Files' publication – 'SOE Syllabus' of four hundred pages he is, for example, summed up in less that twenty lines.

Gubbins, as we have know, had the benefit of similar treatment.

Most British writers go little further than acknowledging him as one of two former Shanghai policemen who, from July 1940, were instructors at the WWII Special Training Centre (STC) at Inverailort in Scotland. This hugely underestimates their remarkable history which, although not specifically *banned* in Great Britain, is usually only sketchy in outline and 'hush-hush' in lack of detail.

Close Quarters Combat specialist William Cassidy, – in 'The Art of Silent Killing – WWII British Commando Style' – may have put his finger on it:

> 'The history of British unconventional warfare training is an epic which, will require several volumes and still the story will not be told in its fullness. So vast were the British programs, so painstakingly detailed and so secret, that historians now find they must of necessity console themselves with mere sketches, as the greater tale has been lost.'

Men-in-the-know describe 'Dan' Fairbairn as 'The Forgotten Master, Father of Close Quarters Combat' or 'The World's Toughest Cop from the World's Toughest City'. Different things to different people, he was monosyllabic on subjects unconnected with combat. Described by one source as a slight and elderly figure with mature charm, he put aside all pretence when it came to fighting. He was lively and entertaining company to enthusiastic students of his special interests, who admired him as 'The Deacon', or 'Delicate Dan', or 'The Shanghai Buster' or 'Fearless Dan'. To some he was 'The Shanghai Connection'.

Fortunately, Americans are both better informed and more outgoing in praise. Fairbairn trained US agents and special forces and, from their publications, we learn real detail of the incredible contribution made by 'Dan' Fairbairn, and his Shanghai Municipal Police colleague, Eric Anthony ('Bill') Sykes, to close combat training. Employing systems still taught by special forces throughout the western world, including police services, their basic techniques have hardly been improved upon to this day. The Auxiliary Units learned much about 'thuggery' from the same expert source – directly or indirectly

★   ★   ★

Lieutenant Ronald F Hall – often known as 'Henry' after the popular 1930s dance band leader ('...and tonight is my guest night'), was a pre-war Territorial in the Artists' Rifles. Called to the Colours for the Munich crisis, in 1940 he was serving with XII Corps in Kent as a Lieutenant in the Dorset Regiment (in accordance, perhaps, with Mike Calvert's theory that County Regiments, being reluctant to destroy their own towns and friends and relatives while fighting in the national interest, *should never be stationed near home*).

In February 1941 he was sent to the Special Training Centre (sometimes known as the Irregular Warfare Training Centre – IWTC) at Inverailort:

'...our course travelled in a steam train from Fort William. Just before arriving at Inverailort the train came under fire from machine guns and mortars. The driver, obviously in the know, slammed on all brakes and we were thrown forward in heaps. The train was surrounded by instructors yelling at us to get out. We were then doubled to the Big House, still under fire and struggling with our kit.

'We gathered at the foot of a large staircase in the house and two old gentlemen in their late fifties, dressed in battledress with the rank of Captain and wearing glasses, appeared at the top of the stairs. They proceeded to throw themselves down the stairs together, landing in a battle-crouch position at the bottom with a handgun in one hand and the Fairbairn-Sykes knife in the other which, I later learned, they carried in their modified trouser pockets.

'From that time we were under fire most of the time, wet through, and rarely stopped running. The ablutions were in the open with only cold water. To attend lectures we had to wade across streams to huts on islands in the river.'

David Niven – Hollywood celebrity and pre-war regular army officer – attended an Inverailort course and says in his autobiography – '*The Moon's a Balloon*':

'...they concentrated on teaching us dozens of ways of killing people without making a noise.'

Henry Hall learned skills from Fairbairn and Sykes which he later put into deadly effect against German troops in Normandy and near Arnhem, earning a Military Cross and only missing a Croix de Guerre by the toss of a coin. Of the Dorsets who had landed in Normandy, only two officers were left. With just one medal on offer from the French, it was his fellow officer who called 'heads' correctly:

'They (Fairbairn and Sykes) taught instinctive 'double-tap' handgun shooting from the navel; the modification of handguns for quick drawing and firing; the use of the knife which they designed ...; silent killing with sticks from four inches to six feet long; coshes, longbows, crossbows, catapults, garrotting, shovels and tin hat strikes, and neck breaking. They taught the vulnerable parts of the body – mouth slitting, ear-trapping to break eardrums, eye-gouging, the grallock (or disembowelling), rib-lifting, "lifting the gates" – temporary dislocation of the jaw, ear-tearing, nose chopping, shin-scraping with the edge of a boot, shoulder jerking – a sharp pull downward to dislocate the shoulder, and releases to get away from any hold. They also taught the 'grape vine' by which a prisoner could be secured without ropes to a slender tree or pole by a forced position of his knees and ankles. Fairbairn said – "The average man in this position would collapse in ten minutes, and it was not at all unlikely he would throw himself backwards. This would kill him"...

'Every directive was followed by the order – 'and then kick him in the testicles!'

Or words to that effect.

Back in Kent with his battle patrol early in 1941, Lieutenant Hall was instructed by Brigade to contact a Captain – unnamed – at a certain grid reference. It turned out to be a house in woodlands off the A28 between Ashford and Canterbury. There can be no doubt it was 'The Garth' at Bilting, Auxunits' Scout Section HQ, formerly that of XII Corps Observation Unit. It was stacked with steel bows and arrows, crossbows, and other 'impedimenta' which Peter Fleming was known to have collected. The Captain said he commanded the 'Kent Observation Unit'. (Even after absorption into Auxiliary Units, the title remained in use locally.) Peter Fleming had been posted back to Military Intelligence by then and this was almost certainly his replacemennt IO, Captain Norman Field. He remembers the day of his arrival at the Garth:

> 'Lunch was held up as a wounded German fighter pilot lay on the only available table until an ambulance turned up from Canterbury. Colonel Major was there for lunch too.'

Dorsets and the Observation Unit combined to put on a demonstration for officers of 130 Brigade. 'Henry' Hall and Norman Field have since spoken. Both remember the demonstration, if not one another.

Lieutenant Hall was then invited unofficially – the 'old boy network again – to help train Auxiliary Units. It was all very 'need to know' and names were never exchanged, but he was put in touch with a number of Auxiliers and helped train them in dirty tricks. He gave advice about siting their 'hidey-holes' but was never shown a full-scale, proper OB:

> 'I can remember some of the locations and a few years ago I looked, but could find no trace. All the men I came across were of the highest calibre – intelligent, dedicated, real men of the soil and most efficient. I am sure that had the Germans invaded, they would have caused havoc.'

Although not specifically a 'dirty trick', Major Hall may well have passed to Auxunits another recommendation – tested later under active service conditions:

> '...always carry a handful of good old regulation issue condoms.
> 'They can be used over the muzzle of any weapon, over the lenses of binoculars or over the open ends of magazines. They keep out all the dust and dirt and keep them dry. They are also useful for carrying such things as detonators...'

Fairbairn-Sykes's training syllabus was the prototype of that drawn up by 'Bill' Beyts at Coleshill - although he placed more emphasis on defence. Nevertheless, Auxiliers were not taught half measures.

WRIST RELEASES. Effect release by sudden pressure against the thumbs. Follow up with a quick knockout blow, or pull his head quickly downward and smash his face with your knee.

ARM BREAK. ...swing your left shoulder round vigorously and strike it against the back of his upper arm. A fracture can easily occur from a well-delivered blow.

(to effect release) WHEN HELD AROUND WAIST (from the front)...If wearing a steel helmet, smash him in the face with vicious head movements...Gouge his eyes or use your knee at his "fork".

Both schedules recommended specially prepared dummies and urged caution during practice – although certainly never when in action. Fairbairn, for example, under 'Special Occasions', deals with 'Killing a Sentry':

(a) if you are armed with a knife
(b) if unarmed
(c) spinal dislocator

NOTE: *This last exercise requires great care when practising.*

You bet!

★   ★   ★

Peter Robins tells us that William Ewart Fairbairn was born in Surrey in 1885. One of fourteen children from a working class family, he was christened after Gladstone, the great nineteenth century Liberal Prime Minister. Under-age, he enlisted in the Royal Marine Light Infantry in 1901, and served in the Far East. Having bought himself out of the Marines in 1907, he joined the Municipal Police in Shanghai, where Britain and France supervised a Settlement of a million or so wealthy, international inhabitants, situated in the centre of the Chinese city of more than three million – many of whom lived in poverty.

Crime and violence were endemic and, after being badly beaten up on duty, Fairbairn dedicated himself to a study of defensive training. With outstanding natural ability, massive application, and the best instruction, in 1926 he became the first European outside Japan to be awarded a Judo Black Belt. He also mastered Jiu-Jitsu and Chinese Boxing, as well as conventional western boxing and wrestling.

Fairbairn commanded a supremely efficient and vitally necessary Shanghai Municipal Police riot squad, revolutionised its equipment and training, and retired before WWII with the rank of Assistant Commissioner.

To extend his knowledge of martial arts, he drew heavily on the experience of his older colleague, 'Bill' Sykes – big game hunter, firearms expert, agent for Colt and Remington, and one-time head of the SMP sniper unit. Together they developed training schedules for close combat, with and without weaponry, while remaining in the sharp end of everyday action on the Shanghai waterfront. Both retired before the Japanese invasion of 1941 and were soon recruited by the 'War Office' (probably MI(R) on their return to the UK. 'Dan' Fairbairn's son was still in Colonial Service and – together with others who 'stayed on' – was imprisoned by the Japanese and severely maltreated by the *Kempei Tei* (Secret Police). It is understood he survived the occupation and served in Borneo after the war in Colonial Police Special Branch, but died in the early 1950s – never having fully recovered from wartime privations.

Fairbairn and Sykes were senior instructors at Inverailort, teaching unarmed combat, pistol and 'Tommy-gun' shooting, and knife fighting. Major 'Bill' Beyts was a frequent visitor from Coleshill, to share training problems connected with sabotage and 'living off the land'. Sykes remained there when it came under the direction of Gubbins and SOE. However, in March 1942 Fairbairn was sent by Gubbins as senior instructor to Camp 'X' near Oshawa, Lake Ontario, just on the Canadian side of the border - covertly established with the Americans to train US agents and special forces even before their entry into the war. It is reported that President Roosevelt personally asked for Fairbairn after witnessing an impressive demonstration of his various skills, but details were kept secret even from Canadian Prime Minister, William L Mackenzie King.

Legends in the western world, it has been claimed that Fairbairn and Sykes trained the whole of the instructor cadre of Anglo-American special forces in WWII. They are, however, generally given more credit abroad than at home. Their most enduring legacy is the Fairbairn-Sykes fighting knife, issued sparingly to WWII special forces, and now a most sought-after blade among martial arts' buffs, Americans see the knife as 'symbolising the fighting spirit of Britain's elite raiding forces'. A few Auxiliers managed to 'commandeer' theirs at stand-down. The exclusive product of F/S design, the commando fighting knife was produced by Wilkinson Sword.

The First Pattern, hand-ground and checkered, can now fetch £1,000. Estimates are that 2,500 were produced. A long time ago, 'Henry' Hall bought his from Wilkinson Sword in

Pall Mall for 13/6d. A Second Pattern – quicker to manufacture – was modified but retained the Wilkinson Sword logo. Both models were of steel, with checkered hilt, 'S' cross-guard, and double-edged, seven inch, spear-point blade honed razor sharp. Later still, they were mass-produced as Commando knives, blackened, and without logo or ricasso.

Major R F Hall recommends:

> 'Never use a knife with a wooden or leather handle. It will slip when your hands are wet or bloody. Only a checkered metal handle will do'.

★   ★   ★

Auxiliary Units Patrols, undoubtedly special forces, were trained accordingly. None have been identified directly at 'The Castle', Inverailort, and 'Henry' Hall's battle patrol admittedly operated only with 'warriors' in Kent – but David Lampe (page 121 of 'The Last Ditch'), deals with a relevant change to British Resistance under the second CO, Colonel 'Bill' Major:

> '...he introduced hand-to-hand combat training at Coleshill, and a team of instructors from the Army Physical Training Corps turned up every Saturday afternoon to hold classes. Most of the members of most of the patrols were taught at least a few of the tricks of killing with bare hands as well as with their Commando knives.'

Perhaps Mohammed came to the mountain? Peter Robins, who has traced nearly every breath Fairbairn took, has reports of at least one visit by him to Coleshill and he is in no doubt that the close combat instructors, working to Major Beyts' directions, were moulded from the STC programme – and not just PT Instructors in well-pressed kit supervising reluctant press-ups.

Jim Caws, an Isle of Wight Auxilier, found himself – fifty-five years after stand-down – still reacting instinctively, parrying an (imagined) threat after a sudden movement from a public house companion. His training had remained that deeply ingrained. Many instances of such reaction are on record, notably unsuccessful attempts to rob WWII Special Forces leaders Sir Fitzroy Maclean and David Stirling – when they were in their late 60s – by muggers who had unwisely failed to search their WWII records in Who's Who?

In addition to close combat instruction, Auxunit Patrols and Scout Sections were generously supplied with material for booby traps and dirty tricks from standard military hardware, and trained to use trip wires, pressure and pull-switches, 'stun' grenades, timers, fuses and high explosive. Encouraged to experiment for themselves, Patrols decided whether to protect their OBs with booby traps or not. An explosion could certainly be useful forewarning of an approaching search party. On the other hand, an enemy patrol might conclude that big bangs hid something significant, and spend time looking for it instead of just passing by.

The Carlton Patrol in Suffolk devised a booby trap suited, it was hoped, to both objectives. Rex Chaston describes it:

> 'Take a large beer bottle, soak the base in very hot and cold water alternately until it can be tapped off. Insert a standard Mills Grenade with the safety pin removed, and the activating lever held in place against the edge. Stand the bottle upright near approaches to the OB and lay bait – such as a page from a 'girlie' magazine. When an inquisitive, or lonely, enemy soldier lifts the bottle the grenade drops out, the firing pin activates and his patrol should be left in disarray.'

At least.

Tom Colquitt's Norfolk Scout Section developed a trap for vehicles. It involved tin cans nailed to trees either side of the road, holding grenades similarly prepared but with instantaneous fuses, and connected with a tripwire. An experiment with their subaltern's car was successful, even with de-activated grenades. The officer, however, with extensive collateral damage to his car and a broken windscreen to account for, was less than ecstatic.

Tom also devised a method of destroying trucks. Two 8-oz sticks of Nobel's 808 were taped under the driver's seat with a 36 detonator. This was connected by instantaneous fuse to another 'det' taped out of sight under the exhaust manifold. Once the engine warmed up, heat would blow the detonators which then exploded the Nobel's. His Section also prepared an explosive package in a bicycle inner tube, with detonator and time pencil, to lay along the wing of an enemy aircraft. Motor car inner tubes, with the valve section cut out, were adapted to carry prepared charges, complete with fuses and detonators – leaving out the time pencils during exercises, for safety. One end of the tube was tied with rope; a noose round the other created a sling

The Carlton Patrol used plastic explosive which, although normally benign enough, could be lethal when rolled and shaped like a piece of coal, and primed with a detonator to explode when shovelled onto a fire. Anti-personnel Bakelite grenades, smaller than a tennis ball, had lengths of tape attached to a safety pin. Thrown with the end of the ribbon secured, or utilising a small lead weight, they created a violent detonation, especially indoors. They could also be used to booby trap a door by cutting the tape to an appropriate length and suspending the grenade, allowing it to drop and activate with a 'horrible bang' when the door was opened.

The Castrator' (or 'de-bollicker) was available too, ready-made. A pencil-like device with lugs, it held a .303 bullet and was pressed into the soil vertically. When trodden upon, the bullet was discharged upward but, admittedly, indiscriminately. Another random defence was the phosphorus bomb – in early days a half-pint bottle with a crown cork, the contents of which ignited and spread venomously when in contact with air. The patrol practised suspending these bombs from trees, hidden by foliage, with trip-wire attached and instant detonator fuse.

Speaking from personal experience, Major Hall emphasises;

> 'The psychological attitude to Close Combat work, or any other type of fighting, is of paramount importance. With the example of 'Dan' Fairbairn and 'Bill' Sykes, and all the other instructors, you became convinced you were better at anything than anyone else! You must have the right psychological attitude and instinctive reaction so that you know that whether you are out for a man, a machine gun post, or even a tank, you will win whatever happens. The enemy is dead as soon as you see him. He who hesitates is lost – or dead!'

In total war, no justification for unorthodox dirty tricks and traps was necessary. This approach would have horrified many officers in WWI – and affected even a few diehards in 1940. Rex Chaston and the Carlton Patrol worked out their own philosophy:

> 'We thought we were right and had God on our side; and the Germans were wrong and didn't!'

Fairbairn and Sykes would have agreed with that!

CHAPTER EIGHT

Myths & Misconceptions

With material specially prepared by Devon Auxilier, Geoffrey Bradford, and Museum Director, Andrew Taylor

'One, the more modern (myth), bears witness to the boundless credulity engendered by the media age. The second, older and wiser, stands as a testament to the...desperate need of a beleaguered population eager to see light at the end of a dark tunnel.'
(James Hayward, 'The Bodies on the Beach')

James Hayward was persuaded by all the evidence that rumours of burned enemy bodies washed up in 1940 on the beach at Shingle Street in Suffolk were nothing more than a myth. Although most details of Auxiliary Units patrols can by unequivocally authenticated by survivors, they have not been exempt from their own fair share of myths and misconceptions

The stop/start, shifty attitude of the authorities has been largely to blame – giving sustenance to 'the credulity of the media age' as well as 'feeding the need of a beleaguered nation...' – who, with few facts to work on, were vulnerable to the easily recycled amateur dramatics favoured by the Press. They simply rewrote old records, added a little unattributable guesswork, and hurried along to the pub' after an easy day. However, leading articles in the 'Times' and quasi-official publications such as 'The Last Ditch', on one hand, and complete information embargoes on the other, proved an irresistible provocation for researchers.

The 'Myth of the Moment' is the 'Mabel Fable'. Mabel Stranks role at Highworth sub-post office has already been outlined. She was a useful cut-out, a half way house for arrivals at Coleshill, giving the staff there some useful moments to check the credentials of visitors before uploading them into whatever transport was available. There is, by the way, nothing on record to indicate that this identity check was a requirement demanded of officers as well as other ranks.

In 2001, the late Mrs Stranks was to be the beneficiary of a good idea by Highworth Town Council. They decided to erect a plaque to her memory on the old post office. It was simple enough, as can been from the photograph in the illustrations.

In the absence of any evidence or corroboration, newspaper editors decided that she '...*ran the secret war against Hitler*', and was chosen by Churchill to recruit the British Resistance, or vetted applicants for Britain's secret service; and that she kept a 'Tommy Gun' behind her post office counter. Former Auxilier, Eric Gray noted that '*her lips were sealed*' – and explained why:

> 'She didn't know anything!'

★   ★   ★

Auxiliary Units Patrols have been described by the media as '*Commandos*', '*trained assassins*', and '*silent killers*'.

Instructed to avoid direct conflict with the enemy - and in the absence of formal enlistment, uniform and a rank structure - they did not qualify as *Commandos* proper, although some of their training and operational techniques did run along parallel lines. Their true role was sabotage and, following Lawrence of Arabia's dictum that men were easier to replace than materiel, sought to destroy or disrupt enemy supplies, transport and communications.

Although they were well capable and usually determined enough, *assassination* was never their primary function. It is true that enemy sentries, and perhaps selected officers, might have become targets as well as collaborators threatening their safety, but their execution was more likely to be in pursuit of patrols' primary objectives than assassination for its own sake. It would, after all, certainly have exposed them to determined pursuit and the local population to vicious reprisals – such as those meted out to the Czechoslovaks at Lidice or the French at Oradour-sur-Glanes. Random assassination would have been essentially counter-productive to their GHQ commitment.

Silent killers? This one is nearer the mark. Although they would have resisted assassination as part of their function, when the time came silence was an integral part of Auxiliers assault technique. They understood the advantages of a fighting knife and, with Fairbairn/Sykes know-how, intended that death should come to the enemy both instantly and quietly. Indeed, silent action was so importantly prized that the final recommendations based on experience gained in training, were that all firearms – except one silenced hand-gun – and conventional grenades should be withdrawn from their inventory.

★   ★   ★

(L) *Pills*. Another myth concerns the issue of lethal pills or cyanide capsules to be swallowed if captured. It is admittedly something of an academic point however. While there is no record of these being issued, fallback plans certainly included an expectation that wounded comrades could not be left to the mercy of the enemy, and would be 'dealt with' if they represented a threat to the Patrol's effectiveness, or the security of their Operational Base.

Sergeants Alan Hollingdale in Monmouthshire, Herman Kindred in Suffolk, and Norman Steed in Kent, all independently stated that their first-aid kit contained sufficient morphine to enable any wounded to be silenced. Its use was regarded as standard operating procedure.

★   ★   ★

The Exploding Water Closet – has recently enjoyed renewed celebrity status.

The current myth describes the booby trapping of a wc situated in a stately home likely to be used by German Commanders as an HQ. Auxunits, it was claimed, had surveyed the house with intent to commit grievous harm to the officer while at rest on the throne. The device would explode as the seat was occupied. Perhaps this was how the 'thunder-box' euphemism started?

It cannot be doubted that Auxunits were adequately trained and equipped to install such booby traps and it was also within a patrol's remit to survey any potential target in their area.

However, the use of booby traps in this manner was both unlikely and impractical. The necessary 'Pressure' switch would be difficult to fix under the seat, and the explosive charge impossible to camouflage. A more likely booby trap – suitably waterproofed with a condom – would have been placed inside the overhead water cistern and actuated by a 'Pull' switch.

★   ★   ★

The *Gamekeeper* legend, probably originating in Sussex, was then recycled through newspapers in other counties.

A Gamekeeper discovers the activities of a Patrol and the whereabouts of their OB. Representing a threat to their safety after invasion, he was placed on their 'hit-list' for assassination. Such decisions would usually have been made by individual patrols after consultation with their IO. If a true representation

of the Auxunits function, the 'hit-list' would have been a
lengthy one in many cases. While some OBs and the activities of
their occupants were never detected by the home population,
others were constantly in jeopardy – usually from schoolboys.

At Stradbroke in Suffolk, for instance, Ernie Blaxall and
David Bowen regularly 'bunked-off' from school and were
untraceable, even when their classmates were 'scrambled' to
find them. The two rascals, safely hidden in the local patrol's
OB in Valley Farm and surrounded by fuses and phosphorus
grenades, were having the time of their life instead of studying
for the eleven-plus. Ernie and patrol members Ralph Clarke
and Ivan Mower, met nearly sixty years later to confirm it.

Gamekeepers, more evident and important then than now,
were often obliquely in the picture and, if not enrolled into a
patrol directly, warned to say nothing of any discovery to
anyone, and sometimes threatened that – in the event of
invasion – there were enough Auxiliers around to deal with
them. The point is that suspects were not placed randomly on
a 'hit-list' and the Press are wrong to infer that it was a
preoccupation with the patrols.

In Yorkshire, according to Jack Caddy, an unsporting liaison
developed between a schoolboy and the local gamekeeper. Jack
actually witnessed, from his hiding place in woods, the
construction of an Auxunits' OB by Sappers – until they caught
the watcher watching. In an unfortunate lapse of security, the
soldiers befriended the 10-year old and he saw much of their
work, including trap door construction and the location of an
associated Observation Post (or one-man OB).

Jack kept occasional watch in the area but never saw the
patrol there. He regularly worked his way through one of the
trap doors – but could not open the second. Inside the OB were
boxes of grenades, fuses, time pencils – all the usual Auxunits'
paraphernalia – and a lot of 'shiny things' – probably
detonators. When the roof caved in later, he persuaded himself
he had some sort of claim to the 'shiny things' and removed a
number, and some highly dangerous items, to a private hide –
and others to school where the older boys created a 'hell of a
bang' in the playground with his detonators.

Unfortunately for him, the local gamekeeper had seen his
mischief in the woods but, handicapped by a wooden leg, could
never match Jack for acceleration or speed along the straight.
Taking advantage of the gamekeeper's special affection for his
grandson, Stephen, the 'apple of his eye' was persuaded to throw
a live hand grenade one day in the woods – an adventure which

Jack and his mates had been too fearful to indulge in themselves.

Either the playground explosion or, more probably the gamekeeper, put the police on Jack's trail. A constable carrying a list of missing stores - provided by the army, detained him and together they went to the scene of the crime:

> 'There was one thing missing from his list as I felt around in the dark hide. It was a sort of tube, half khaki and half black. When I went to hand it to him, all I could see were his boots. He was shouting - "Put it down. Put it down!" That policeman was no hero.'

Jack was presented before three magistrates at the local Juvenile Court. Two of the exhibits were extremely powerful magnets (for attaching charges to enemy tanks). When examined by the Bench, these crashed themselves irresistibly together, to the Justices evident consternation – fearing they had started off some irreversibly explosive process.

Not unwisely, however, they found for the defendant on the grounds that the quality of army security was so lax that any passer-by could have discovered the OB and its special stores. Unhappy with the verdict, there was an ante room scuffle after the case, when a soldier - made to look foolish in Court - came to blows with Jack's grandfather, himself a retired gamekeeper...

★   ★   ★

Although there was some limited pre-war planning, in an 'instant' organisation such as Auxiliary Units – dependant upon trial and error rather than precedent – extraordinary secrecy was always an essential. It has led, not surprisingly, to a number of *misconceptions*.

Breaking both old rules and new ground, GHQ did not want this special force talked about, and initial communications were always highly secret. While he was Intelligence Officer for Devon and Cornwall, Stuart Edmundson understood:

> '...regarding the conventions of war, nobody ever questioned the legality of what we were doing. There was a job to be done. In the event of capture these men would have been given no quarter. They would have been screwed first, then immediately executed'.

If secrecy was paramount for Auxiliers' immediate safety, it was only marginally less so, long-term, for those giving the orders, the officers responsible for breaking the Conventions of War.

But the name – Auxiliary Units – was not in itself always secret. From the available official correspondence of the day, there was confusion about this – even at upper levels, until

clarification appeared in a GHQ instruction dated 7th
November 1943, signed by Lt Col. M Telfer, for Major-
General, General Staff, and sent to Command HQs, Corps
HQs, and the HQs of Divisions, Districts and Sub Districts in
touch with Auxiliary Units:

> 'Knowledge of the existence of Auxiliary Units should be
> confined to persons who need it in the course of duty. As however
> a considerable amount of correspondence of a purely
> administrative and non-committal nature refers to these Units, it is
> not necessary for documents containing a bare reference to them
> to be marked SECRET.
>
> 'The functions of Auxiliary Units are MOST SECRET and any
> document which refers to, or in any way suggests their functions, or
> gives any indication of their strength, will be graded MOST SECRET.'

Anything to do with the function of Auxunits was only to be
dealt with at officer level and a permanent distinction was
acknowledged between the mere *existence* of Auxiliary Units –
and their *function* (or role).

In the field, the secrets were – after their careful selection –
largely in the hands of the most vulnerable men, those in the
operational Patrols. However, there is indisputable evidence
that their existence was – through no fault of their own – not
always as closely contained in their own localities as it should
have been. By 1940, for example, the 6th Battalion, Suffolk
Home Guard held a complete list of personnel 'currently
attached to Auxiliary Units'. Another, pre-dating it, is entitled
'Scout Patrols' – the name by which Auxunits Patrols were
sometimes known in the very earliest days. Confusingly,
although Suffolk HG command knew of Auxunits, it is equally
certain that the local platoon officer did not.

To complete their protection locally, a simple, very effective
deception was allowed to happen – namely that they were no
more than Home Guards in some minor specialist role. It was
so effective that more than sixty years later, historians
sometimes find difficulty in prising Auxiliary Units apart from
the history of the Home Guard itself.

In understanding the relationship between Auxiliary Units
and the Home Guard, comparisons can reasonably be drawn
with the modern Special Air Service and the regular army or –
as we shall read later at an official level – 'the Brigade of Guards
and the Salvation Army'. But it had become strikingly clear that
simply to recruit men straight from civilian life and pitch them
into guerrilla warfare training, right under the noses of the local

communities, had the effect of arousing deep suspicion. The inescapable conclusion, as obvious now as it must have been in 1940, was that to maintain the real secret of their *function*, it was necessary to arrange for Auxiliers the freedom to move and train within their communities and without suspicion.

This was achieved in a stroke by issuing them with Home Guard uniform.

Whether or not they used it in their guerrilla role was not necessarily an important factor in this deception. Intelligence Officers came to varying agreements with local HG commanders on what insignia, if any, could be worn by Auxiliers operating in their area. Some allowed the display of local battalion insignia while others agreed to its use – but only outside their direct location. Major Nigel Oxenden pointed out in 'History and Achievement' that some Auxiliers:

> '....wore none (insignia, that is) at all, which aroused the deepest suspicion.'

With uniform came another bonus, probably not unforseen by the Adjutant General's Department of the War Office. Stuart Edmundson:

> 'The reason for the issue of uniforms was because the Government got cold feet, as they were raising an illegal army and Auxiliary Units had no legal status...There was no uniform in 1940. They were given denims to protect their clothes...I never trained a man in uniform and never intended them to fight in Home Guard uniform.'

In Suffolk, Herman Kindred received identical instructions and confirmed that:

> '...our Home Guard uniform was our "walking out uniform", just to let us get from A to B, or when we were doing a spot of reconnoitering during the day. You see, our job was to know the land and this couldn't be done if the Germans had arrived. So we had to be able to move about beforehand. Our "real uniform", if you like, was just plain army denims, but then they were only really to protect our ordinary clothes...'

All this fits with 202 Battalion Standing Orders that no denims were to be worn by day, and no uniform at night or near the Operational Base.

Wearing uniform legitimised Auxiliers within their communities and reduced the suspicion of members of the public, especially during the crisis days of 1940 and 1941.

Some misconceptions about the patrols resulted from

misinterpretation of known facts. Perhaps this is because of the considerable amount of sometimes overlapping information available and a general failure to appreciate the evolutionary development of Auxiliary Units. This has led in turn to an over complicated view of their history – creating a further myth that there was no 'rhyme-nor-reason' to patrols' operations. The truth is very different with error exacerbated by the assumption that most, if not all, memories and experiences of individual Auxiliers pertain to the height of the invasion scare.

This rather romanticised view is a significant myth-maker.

There has also been a failure to expand on David Lampe's, 'The Last Ditch', as researchers benefited from increasing amounts of available documentation during the 1990s. As far as Signals and the Special Duties Section (dealt with in later chapters) were concerned, Lampe apparently had little to go on. And he omitted the significant Scout Sections altogether. This is understandable as he was apparently working alone on a subject, both complex and still largely secret – and dependent upon information fed to him by circumspect witnesses. However, although justifiably considered a masterpiece of its day, Lampe's work was flawed in its failure to appreciate the evolutionary development of the Patrols.

His significant mistake was to assume that the diverging experiences and memories of his sources were due to a disjointed and entirely individualist command structure. This is also, to an extent, understandable because of the autonomy delegated to Intelligence Officers. In the event, his book has been either considered the bedrock of historical accuracy, from which all additional research could safely stem – despite increasingly available documentary evidence to the contrary – or unfairly vilified in order to promote modern theories of dubious accuracy. It is, of course, somewhere in between.

David Lampe did not set out to create misconceptions. The obvious enthusiasm shown in his book, suggests that, working alone, he became engrossed in the mystique of his subject but, in doing so, failed to assemble diverging memories into a chronological sequence. The myths which emerged were, perhaps, the product of his unquestioning enthusiasm, then perpetuated by a new generation of researchers seemingly reluctant to provide the disinterested, retrospective analysis his work deserves.

Even giving the Media the benefit of some doubt, perhaps it is just too much to expect a hack looking for a quick headline and 250 words of easy text to grasp?

CHAPTER NINE

Operational Patrols of the Auxiliary Units, 'Going to ground'

'They keep their thoughts to themselves, for they learned self-control in a hard school and they realised long ago how difficult it can be to explain the concepts of service and loyalty, as they understood them, to a more liberal, less reverent and perhaps more self-indulgent generation.'

('*To the Last Man*', Lyn Macdonald)

Lyn Macdonald was writing about WWI veterans but her words could be applied with equal relevance to men of the Auxiliary Units operational Patrols.

One such man, a gentle, intelligent Suffolk farmer, the late Herman Kindred, could keep a secret when convinced it was important enough to do so, and followed orders as long as they made sense. He and his brother Percy, and colleagues in the Stratford St Andrew patrol in Suffolk, men of high personal integrity, typically kept silent about their Auxiliary Units service for more than forty-five years, honouring allegiance to binding commitments entered into on enrolment.

In any analysis involving this amorphous organisation, the need for caution against putting everything into nice, neat research pigeonholes has already been advised. When evidence is inconclusive, massaging facts to fit conventional military thinking leads only to yet worse confusion. In early days, however, the men in the Patrols – having no precedents to go on – were not much affected by a certain confusion of directives. Sceptical though many naturally were, they trusted the 'powers-that-be' and took it for granted the officers knew what they were doing.

It should therefore be no surprise that confusion continues about many details – dates of enrolment, for example, and whether signatures were, or were not, given under the Official Secrets Act. Some Auxiliers remember facts well, others not at all. One new recruit recalled an invitation to sign the *back* of an

Official Secrets Act form. At the same moment, he cunningly glimpsed other familiar names – having been at school with some of them. This was both an early breach of basic security and an unusual example of formal, pre-war type War Office administration, usually being set aside in 1940 to get things done in a hurry. One Intelligence Officer in what is now the West Midlands, not only called for signatures but also instant oaths of loyalty to King and Country sworn on his pocket bible. It was, perhaps, a personal idiosyncracy intended to impress the new man with the importance and secrecy of his duty, rather than in slavish pursuance of a Headquarter's directive.

(Yesterday's 'flexible' administration is sometimes counterproductive to today's applications for the Defence Medal, often making it impossible to prove the Ministry of Defence wrong in refusing bona fide cases, even when it is as clear as daylight that they are.)

Post-war discretion progressively became less difficult for Auxiliers as successive generations – each more liberal, less reverent, and certainly more self-indulgent – showed obvious disinterest in any connection between their own comfortable standard of peacetime living and the sacrifice of older kinsmen.

As we have already seen, however, Herman Kindred certainly never forgot the impact of his induction interview at the end of 1940, when invited to volunteer for 'something less boring than the Home Guard'. Half a century later he vividly still recalled the regular soldiers on armed guard at the doors and that:

> 'Secrecy was everything and at first we were only told the basic essentials.
> ' "The Germans are coming", they said. "They are a ruthless lot. If they get here they will castrate and deport all the men and our women will be 'spread' by their elite".
> 'We were really taught to hate the Germans.'

Once aggressively motivated, Herman and his colleagues were at the start of something big. The British, having previously fought wars cleanly and, by and large, under accepted rules, held the moral high ground after atrocities by Germans troops during Continental battles early in WWII, but were about to adapt themselves to the needs of modern irregular warfare. In the vanguard, many Auxiliers discovered special aptitude for 'dirty tricks' now regarded as everyday ingredients of military training but, in 1940 – when bayonet practice was the nearest a soldier ever came to the unorthodox – something really new.

Jim Caws, an Auxilier in one of the two patrols on the Isle of Wight, remembers his training in unarmed combat:

'Chiefly, we were taught how to tear someone to pieces. It sounds strange but that's a fact.'

The Patrols' war-objectives were gradually revealed in piecemeal fashion during verbal briefings. Orders were never confirmed in writing. Indeed, notes made privately by Auxiliers, in secret and against instructions, are now collectors' items. As a result, not a single man can produce written evidence of commands conflicting with War Conventions. Odd scraps of official paper did appear from above with the issue of stores or weaponry and an administrative need for receipts, for not even the imminent arrival of a savage enemy could deter a quartermaster from keeping his books balanced.

Eventually, secret training manuals appeared – such as 'Calendar 1937'. Although covers were disguised, the contents were principally a digest of training techniques for the regular army. The 'powers-that-be' – discriminating between lawful orders, with no after-taste if we lost the war, and what might later be defined as unlawful ones – were careful to cover their tracks from an early stage.

The 'stand-to' call would follow proclamation of the code word 'Cromwell' – can there be doubt it was coined by General Ironside himself? Auxiliers were then to muster in their OBs, well aware that their mainstream role for the few weeks it was supposed they might survive, was to commit mayhem behind enemy lines. They expected to find targets by day – aircraft at dispersal points, laagered tank units, fuel and ammunition dumps, or enemy patrols – and lay plans to destroy them at night. It was clearly understood they were to avoid engaging the enemy in firefights or open combat. Instead they were to use organised stealth, reconnaissance and observation, to plant timed explosives or set booby traps and then, like phantoms of the night, withdraw to their secret operational bases as quietly as they had come. If they had to eliminate a sentry, they were trained and equipped to do so silently. If there was *anything* straightforward about the patrols, it was here.

Nigel Oxenden wrote:

'The organisation of a guerrilla force had the double advantage of building up a body of men to work behind the enemy's lines with much more success than would probably attend the road block efforts of the Home Guard, and of doing it, moreover, without drawing upon the country's scanty supply of small arms. Their mission was to create havoc and destruction among the enemy's supplies and communications.'

Peter Wilkinson, initially second-in-command under Colin Gubbins, conceded in 'Operation Sealion':

'In early days, Auxiliers were regarded as immediately expendable.'

Later, in a waspish interview with Stephen Sutton, Wilkinson referred to the famous memo from Duncan Sandys to his father-in-law, Winston Churchill:

'I think you grossly exaggerate their (the Auxiliary Units) importance at this stage because at the very best they would have been a flea-bite behind the enemy lines. They might have sown a certain amount of confusion and insecurity but they were never on a scale that would have been of any decisive importance and, I think, that in the cold light of reason, it is at least arguable, as many senior officers held, that they were not worth the effort that was put into them.'

This crushing assessment has to be read in context. Sir Peter was involved in rubbishing the short-cut adopted by Captain (later Sir) Edward Beddington-Behrens to get to Winston Churchill directly through Duncan Sandys, who was not in any way authorised to receive such highly classified information. At other times, Peter Wilkinson articulated a more balanced point of view. Indeed, by November 1940, he was already making plans, with Colin Gubbins's approval, for an inner-circle of specially selected members of Auxiliary Units who would be really secret and who might form the nucleus of a future Resistance organisation (with long term prospects, that is) – if they survived the first month. He saw himself as Chief of Staff but was moved to SOE before the plan could be put into effect.

Colin Gubbins declared, post-war, that Auxiliary Units would have gone into action as guerrillas when the balloon went up, and make immediate contact with the Germans. In effect they became stay-behind parties with instructions to do or die. He anticipated that they would have been wiped out after a few weeks at the very best:

'None of the men had any illusions about their role...'

There is no serious dispute, even from the most reticent Auxiliers, that this was a fair 'job-description' – one for which they were individually selected, trained, and equipped. Keith

Seabrook, a Patrol leader in Essex, and later Group Commander, remembered:

> 'It was not a blueprint for a long life. We were completely expendable and never thought of the consequences.'

Only a few Intelligence Officers were explicit about 'going to ground' themselves, and patrol leaders usually understood that final authority was delegated to them when the chips were down. A Suffolk farmer might therefore be called upon to make life and death decisions rarely faced by regular soldiers.

Guidelines in Kent were equally draconian. Auxiliers had targets such as lorries, tanks, fuel dumps and enemy stores. Interference with communications was added later. They all received Home Guard uniforms. Membership of the HG was used as cover to reduce local suspicion about their activities. Killing Germans was secondary – and only if necessary. Given Fairbairn-Sykes fighting knives, they were taught to kill silently. Absolute secrecy was essential 'to protect wives and families'.

Less clear, however, was their authority to execute collaborators or traitors, even wounded comrades or *their* families, who might under pressure be a threat to continued operations, and to do so *entirely at their own discretion*. This was a sensitive subject, and Herman Kindred at first stuck to a story that the Patrols' .22 rifle with telescopic sight was only to replenish food stores by shooting 'bunnies'. 'Tracker dogs' as potential targets were included next. When pressed, he accepted that the rifle could be 'for eliminating enemy sentries when we were unable to get close enough to use a fighting knife'. Finally, he conceded that 'selective execution' was also part of his remit – *even Britons* if they were a danger to his operation.

It was, anyway, an academic point because his patrol preferred the garrotte. Their Group Commander, a Commissioned officer in the Home Guard, headed an unwritten target list after collective agreement that he drank too much, was fiddling their expenses, knew the whereabouts of half-a-dozen other OBs, and could not be trusted to resist betrayal if caught by the enemy and interrogated under pressure. He was 'number one' when the balloon went up.

Not every Patrol included assassination or execution as a prime objective; but many certainly did. As usual, it depended upon the IO. Jim Caws lifted the lid in a recorded interview:

> '...if there was ever any Fifth Columnists or anything like that,

we could either sort of tear them to bits to start with or shoot them first and then tear them to bits. Which was pretty unusual. Gouge their eyes out, or split their nose up, or their mouth. And we went all the way round their body like that. The purpose of that, I presume, was that if somebody was helping the Germans and you could catch up with them we would make a mess of them and leave them on the side of the road to deter other people from doing it...I don't think I would have done it actually. I don't see the point of that. You might just as well shoot the bloke and call that it.'

Captain Peter Forbes, IO for The Borders, later identified another problem – as a result of Auxunits operations, the Germans would have taken hostages in the villages. He was not sure how members of the patrols would have dealt with their wives and children being rounded up and shot. At the time it wasn't seriously thought about.

With a similar line of thought, Donald Handscombe, from the Essex 'Thundersley' Patrol, became involved in a general policy discussion during his Coleshill weekend and said the thing that stuck in his mind:

'...was reprisals on our acts. The Staff admitted they were concerned about it too and said they would get an official ruling...If we thought by our action that reprisals would be particularly severe, should that stop us? They said they would make sure all patrols got an answer and I remember some months afterwards my Group Commander coming to me and saying – "Yes, whatever the reprisals, you are to continue and that has come from Churchill himself".'

In a Press interview after the war, Colin Gubbins confirmed from German sources that resistance *would* have led to reprisals against civilians of the kind which terrorised Europe:

'Yes, there had to be a Cabinet decision there. There was nothing for it. We were facing total war.'

When Don Handscombe was asked about his understanding in respect of collaborators, he remembered:

'We would have killed without compunction. Our patrol might have made that decision about local people, Quislings or collaborators for example, without having orders from above. You will notice in the Stand Down orders, Colonel Douglas said; "We know you would fight with orders or without". Authority was delegated to each patrol in that respect. Absolutely.'

Other serious issues were confronted. When they went to ground without backup or communications, and provided with only a basic First Aid Kit, contingent plans were needed for injured men. Herman Kindred was instructed in the use of morphine:

> 'One-quarter grain to reduce the pain of wounds or injury; one-half to bring about unconsciousness; and a full grain to self-destruct. A terrible thing to have to do to a comrade but they were our instructions. In other words, none of our six was to be captured alive. Otherwise he could be forced to divulge who and where the rest were.'

The Thundersley Patrol had no poison pills but:

> '...we had morphine (and were instructed) on how to deal with members if they were too badly wounded to survive. That was an order.'

Norman Steed, a Kent Patrol leader, was ordered to shoot or kill wounded patrol members some way or another, if they could not otherwise be saved. He found this 'very worrying':

> 'They were all my friends. One was my brother.'

Auxiliers at the cutting edge were prepared to inflict and suffer all extremes of modern warfare. According to another reliable source, even more could have been involved – although Auxiliers knew nothing about it.

★ ★ ★

Norman Field was the IO in Kent from November 1940, taking over from Peter Fleming when he moved to SOE with Colin Gubbins. To understand the context in which the army had to operate in 1940, Colonel Field says it is important to remember what life in the country was then like.

Kent was only indirectly affected. Air Raid precautions were introduced, a 'blackout' imposed at night, gas masks issued, and giggling school children taught to struggle into them. Rationing was talked about and petrol was already in short supply for the few men who owned cars. Conscription for national service had not yet been ordered and farm work was, anyway, a reserved occupation. Generally, life went on placidly. People were oblivious to far away battles.

With few private cars, personal mobility was on foot or bicycle. Buses passed infrequently, but on time. There were no main roads as known now. Quiet country lanes were the normal arteries of communication and public houses the favoured meeting places. Most people drank rough, cheap, locally brewed cider. Summer weather was warm and pleasant.

Agriculture was the main occupation, whole families being involved during the harvest – men carting and stacking; their wives 'stooking' sheaves of corn – cut and disgorged from horse-drawn binders; and daughters gleaning corn heads spilt round the threshing machine, to store as chicken-feed for winter months. Small boys with sticks, and dogs, joined a noisy chase for rabbits as the last strip of corn was cut. Other mechanised help on the farm was almost unknown. Stacks were built by hand and thatched to keep out the weather. Horses and carts were vital and horsemen the accepted elite of the workforce.

Londoners arrived by the trainload for the hop-picking season, dossing in happy family groups in lean-to accommodation provided by their holiday employer. Until war came, aircraft circling the skies were a rarity.

Nearly everyone was poor and lived in a tied cottage. Many were dependent upon the patronage of landowners or church charity, but not everyone resented it. Trade Union activity was almost unknown. Schools were nearby, and bussing to school not an available option. Classes, usually commanded by upright and not necessarily unkind spinsters, were large and disciplined. Children's toilet arrangements were unembarressedly unisex. School milk was free and, if a family failed a means test, so were school dinners.

People, in general, were not seriously unhappy although standards of living incomparable with today's. Medical services had to be paid for and an avuncular doctor – sometimes arriving in horse and trap – carried his own bag filled with mystery medicaments, and often charged what he thought a family could afford. Sometimes that was nothing.

In the late 1980s, Mike Calvert – one of the officers delegated from MI(R) to create civilian 'stay-behinds' in Kent in summer 1940 – recorded his memories. Anticipating early German attack and that Kent would bear the brunt, the high-ups wanted:

> '...to leave a number of people behind who were trained in sabotage to create as much havoc as possible.
>
> 'Our job was to raise and train civilians to carry out demolitions and I was given a very free hand. We prepared at least four "cuts" in every road going from the sea toward the North Downs, where

the stop-line was and where they hoped to hold the enemy. Our job was to raise a guerrilla force between the coast and the North Downs. The idea was that when the Germans had crossed the area they would find the roads behind them effectively destroyed, cutting their main lines of supply.'

Captain Calvert was known as 'Mad Mike' because of his casual but expert handling of explosives at Inverailort when – to demonstrate its perfect safety – he ordered a Lovat Scout to fire at a wad of guncotton he was holding.

Four parties of civilians were recruited to deal with each main road and 'cuts' – milk churns filled with guncotton, left under bridges and culverts – were hidden for them to fire. He was not sure how effective the men would be:

> 'I expected that three out of four would think of some jolly good reason why they didn't take action. These were farmers whose names were given to us by the Controller (probably the Regional Commissioner) or the General, and we trained them. All they had to do really was to put the explosives in place and press the time fuses and then go away.

> 'We found some of these people reluctant to do this destruction. They had known Britain for so long and when we wanted to blow up a bridge they said – "But that bridge was built in 1400," or something. We found this worst in Kent and when Sir Eric Geddes (later Lord Geddes, Regional Commissioner for the South-East) came and asked me if there were any problems, I said that the land-owners of Kent were very reluctant to help us. They weren't co-operating. I remember him saying that the landed property owners of Kent were always willing to sacrifice their only sons for their country but not one square yard of their property.'

Army commanders therefore:

> '...avoided putting Sussex and Kent battalions to defend Sussex and Kent, fearing they would be reluctant to shell their own homes. Most of the troops in Kent and Sussex were from outside.'

(This is corroborated by Major R F Hall, whose Dorset Regiment battle patrol was posted to Kent early in 1941, where they joined Auxiliers in a 'stealth' demonstration to penetrate the army's barbed wire defences on the outskirts of Canterbury.)

Mike Calvert went further;

> '...and then we got the Lovat Scouts down to act as pump primers.'

In November 1940, Norman Field inherited just a couple of Lovat Scouts – Sergeant MacDonald and Corporal MacKenzie – but remembers that a useful number, possibly of platoon strength, had assisted with earlier training. They were led by Peter Fleming's brother Robin and not Lord Lovat himself (as often recorded), and brought to the area through Fleming/Lovat family connections.

Calvert concluded it was 'difficult to get farmers to shoot Generals'. Unable to imagine that Germans would behave politely and pay for everything, he 'wanted to start the ball rolling':

> 'The idea was we got these Lovat Scouts, Scotsmen, and their job was to shoot Germans in the back and that sort of thing. And then the Germans would have had retribution and shoot men of Kent and Sussex in the back and this would arouse the anger of the local population, who would then start shooting Germans.
> 'It struck me as an interesting development of war.'

Mike Calvert is acknowledged as one of Britain's bravest WWII soldiers. Promoted to Brigadier, he later took command of the Second Long-Range Chindit Penetration Raid deep into the Burmese jungle. After the war, he was CO of one of the re-formed Special Air Service Regiments. His opinions command respect.

He was not alone in his assessment. Stephen Sutton headed his Dissertation on the Auxiliary Units in Kent and Sussex – *'Farmers or Fighters'*. In fairness to the men of Kent, Calvert and Sutton and recent researchers all concluded that the Auxiliary Units, when formally brought under the command of Colin Gubbins, did very much want to help their country and formed an important ingredient of the defence force.

(If there is an inference that 'Scotsmen' were looked upon as barbarians acting with unthinking cruelty, it must immediately be dismissed. It is well recorded that the Lovat Scouts, widely respected since formation in the Boer War and as a Territorial unit between the wars, specialised in stalking, camouflage, and sniping. They were later to achieve recognition and honours as special forces, particularly in the Italian campaign. In today's peacetime, they remain part of 23 SAS, a Territorial Army Regiment.)

The 'Calvert' theory was unknown to the men in Auxiliary patrols who would, nevertheless, unknowingly have been the active *provocateurs*. It may all have originated from war game talk with Peter Fleming – imagination was an important ingredient if enemy planning was to be pre-empted. Norman

Field found it 'quite extraordinary' and insists he 'found nothing down there (i.e., in Kent) which fitted'. In fact, he did not hear of the 'Calvert' theory until 2001. Sir Peter Wilkinson stated:

> 'The only people who might have been in danger (from Auxiliers) were local big-wigs who had evinced strong pro-fascist tendencies and refused to help the cause because they really wanted Hitler to win.'

This moderate conclusion is circumstantial corroboration, at least, that execution *was* sometimes on Auxunits' agenda. Although not explicit, for this part of their function, the targets were definitely British rather than German. The fear that civilians were sometimes less than dedicated to total war, was taken on board by the Ministry of Economic Warfare and other official agencies, who produced a poster and radio campaign to move the nation into top gear. Real concern at the highest level became clear when General William Edmund Ironside, as Commander-in-Chief, Home Forces, wrote:

> 'The attitude that there is little we can do against the invincible German war machine must be stamped out with the utmost brutality...'

Until the Dunkirk evacuation, disinterest in war was still commonplace, particularly among some of the upper class and within academic circles. General Ironside noted in his personal diary for 20th June 1940, as the nation was finally becoming war-motivated:

> 'I ran up to Cambridge in the evening and dined at Corpus Christi with Will Spens, a most efficient Regional Commissioner (for East Anglia). He told me there were many intellectuals who were already defeatists. He then tackled me about the people 'staying-put' in case of invasion. He had it on his conscience that we were arranging sabotage behind the lines if the Germans succeeded in landing. He wanted it stopped. A most upright attitude, I thought. But treating the Germans as though they were civilised beings...'

It is likely that Professor Sir Will Spens had heard about 'people staying-put' either from his Section 'D' contacts in the Secret Intelligence Service or his former pupil, Peter Wilkinson – recently in Cambridge seeking influential support for the Auxiliary Units – who, in an interview recorded in his latter years, declined to elaborate. He did agree, however, that while recruiting, he came across people who would not have minded much if the Germans had won the war:

> 'They certainly felt it was not worth the effort or cost to continue the battle and we might as well make terms with the Germans while we could on a fairly reasonable basis. And that once France had fallen, we were without allies and there was no chance of invading the Continent for the foreseeable future and, really, there was not a lot to be said for the Churchillian stance of utter defiance.'

Whether Calvert was fully justified in his understanding of Auxunits' functions or not, a volume of circumstantial corroboration does exist to justify the conclusion – although a diverse range of targets is identified – that operational patrols were intended to include assassination on their agenda and, as such, were unwitting provocateurs.

This places them at a very special level in the hierarchy of Special Forces.

★   ★   ★

At 'Action Stations' the 'stay-behind' role of the regular soldiers of the Scout Sections was intended to be identical to that of Auxunits' operational patrols.

In the ascending chain of command – Auxiliers, Patrol leaders, Group Commanders (and Assistant GCs), Intelligence Officers, HQ at Coleshill, and GHQ Home Forces – there were two other groups of potential 'stay-behinds' – GCs (and AGCs), and IOs.

It is doubtful whether Group Commanders commissioned in the Home Guard were ever seriously considered as potentially 'operational' and, if so, only on a temporary and experimental basis. Many were retired army officers, some on medical pensions, and their principal, long-term function was administrative. They did admittedly attend Ops courses at Coleshill but evidence that they regularly trained below ground is inconsistent, although some made supervisory visits to OBs. Moreover, their generally middle-aged and sedentary occupations in civvy street, would hardly have equipped them for rigorous manoeuvres, let alone the rigour of protracted active service.

This leads to consideration of the IOs role. As long as the threat of imminent invasion loomed, unusually direct access was available between Coleshill and GHQ – with commensurate status for Auxiliary Units in the military pecking order. This special arrangement was confirmed by Stuart

Edmundson, IO for Devon, who was in no doubt that his duty with Auxunits in-the-field terminated with invasion, when he expected to be returned to duties at GHQ. Paradoxically, but undoubtedly, Norman Field in Kent:

> '...would have joined the Patrol of HQ Staff and taken up residence in one of two OBs known as "Big Kate" and "Little Kate". My administrative staff tended to take part in all demonstrations, exercises, and lectures and practised living underground. They were just as knowledgeable as the other Auxunit Patrols.
>
> 'That is what we did in Kent in 1940, and at least the first six months of 1941.'

While IO in The Borders, Peter Forbes was also prepared to stay-behind:

> 'I can't remember any instructions from Coleshill as to whether we should go to ground. I just assumed we would. Luckily, there was an old castle with very little above ground but heaps of rooms below with connecting passages needing very little work. I first put a patrol there and then decided it was also ideal for our own HQ. We had all the stores, my staff was trained and we went to ground for long weekends with others and carried out exercises as a unit against airfields, etc. When the balloon went up, all patrols knew they would be acting entirely on their own, although I might have been able to liaise with those within, say, five miles. With hindsight, I realise we would have been putting all twenty-one OBs in jeopardy as we (the IOs, that is) were the only people who knew where all the OBs were if captured.
>
> 'All other Group Commanders I gradually promoted from patrol sergeants, who would have stayed with their patrols.'

Directives from HQ were therefore inconclusive, with the 'stay-behind' decision delegated to IOs by default. These 'flexible' procedures inevitably lacked uniformity. Irregular warfare might demand unorthodoxy but this sounds like chaos. If the IO did stay behind and was captured, he could be forced to disclose the whereabouts of all his patrols. If he stayed at HQ and tried to make regular forays through the lines, he was equally exposed and they were equally vulnerable. Without the IOs presence in the field at all, the patrols were once again entirely on their own, isolated from the regular army, and deprived of any useful tactical information. Enter 'Bill' Beyts to try to sort it out before he left.

'Most Secret' correspondence (reference AU/13) recovered

from Public Record Office and dated 19th May 1942, indicates that some IOs were by then directed to 'stay-behind' *at the discretion of their Corps Commanders*. The clear inference is that, once the threat of invasion had passed, responsibility for 'stay-behinds' was downgraded from GHQ to Corps. Perhaps this was an opportunity seized upon to leave some IOs – not all of whom had made themselves popular with the regular army and now lacked the special protection provided by the influential Colin Gubbins – out 'in the field'.

Two AU/13 letters, signed by Major Geoffrey Beyts less than two months before he was scheduled to leave Auxiliary Units, were addressed to DCGS (Deputy Chief General Services), GHQ Home Forces – Major General P G S Gregson-Ellis, OBE. As one was a summary of difficulties surrounding IOs 'stay-behind' role, and the other a requisition for stores and money in consequence, it is not impossible to deduce which was left on top in his 'In' tray. Both are awash with useful evidence and inferences.

Letter number one (it is assumed) was headed – 'Function of IOs Headquarters, Auxiliary Units, on 'Action Stations'.

It is a clear statement that the role of the IO was, at that time, left to the discretion of his Corps Commander who, in the majority of cases, had directed he should go to ground and maintain touch and control of the patrols *in the enemy-overrun area*. However, the Intelligence Officer had, in a number of cases been directed *to remain in close contact with his Corps Commander*, to be in touch with events, and available to order 'destruction work' against suitable targets.

It had been different for Norman Field in 1941 and, when he heard of this, he responded positively:

> 'At no time did any local army command issue any order or requests to us. We were entirely independent as to what we might do and where. Hints did occasionally come from Coleshill.'

A number of reasons were tabled by Major Beyts in a proposal that *in all* cases the operational IO should go to ground, together with his HQ staff - *who had been trained to operate in the same manner as the Scout Sections and operational patrols* – and exercise direct control in his area.

The issues are clear. Coleshill had relinquished absolute authority over their IOs and were trying to regularise that loss. They were also assuming, disingenuously perhaps, that the IOs staff, seven in strength, clerks, dispatch riders, drivers, engineers, and signallers, were trained to 'stay-behind'. It would certainly have been a surprise to the staff, who had particular skills but not – in most cases – that of guerrilla warfare as practised by the patrols and Scout Sections.

To understand the politics involved, it is worth quoting the second letter in full:

My dear General,

Lord Glanusk asked me to write to you on his behalf on the subject of our operational IOs going to ground on the same lines as our Home Guard and Army Scout patrols (even Major Beyts had lapses!) have to do. In the majority of cases, this is what they already do, but they are short of the necessary Operational Base, Arms and stores to fulfil their purpose. Above all, there is an urgent want of a No. 17 R/T set, which we have so far had to beg or borrow from benevolent Corps or Army Commanders. This is not very satisfactory as they may be taken away at any time, as indeed is now happening with our IOs in SE Command. Unless they have this R/T contact they will, I think, never be able to be in touch with their military commander, as running to and fro in the midst of the enemy's position is an impossible ideal to attain.

These letters, signed 'Bill Beyts', request a special issue of arms and equipment, stores, and £2,000 in cash, to provide Operational Bases for nineteen Auxunit IOs, each with seven staff. They are a positive indicator that – even if the staff had attended lectures, demonstrations and exercises – they had not generally practised living underground. The OBs were simply not there.

In May 1942, Lord Glanusk had recently arrived at Coleshill – as the third Commanding Officer – and Geoffrey Beyts was preparing to leave to campaign in the Far East. Renewed interest in the IOs role may have come from either of them. Glanusk, a new broom, possibly detected a weakness in the operational control of Auxiliary Units. Major Beyts was probably aware from early days.

The correspondence shows the downgraded role in which GHQ regarded Auxunits by 1942. IOs had not seriously been regarded as 'stay-behinds' and their staff generally not trained to do so either. Although Patrols were consolidating and in some cases still expanding, the purpose of sending IOs to ground in the event of invasion seems not to have interested GHQ, where minds were concentrating on penetrating the Atlantic Wall. In any case, the proposed OBs did not materialise and a number of IOs were shortly detached to

Special Forces or regimental duty.

Between-the-lines interpretation leads to the probability that this correspondence was a roundabout way – by the energetic Bill Beyts – of securing equipment and funds for Auxiliary Units for deployment after his departure and, in particular, creating an opportunity to indent for No. 17 RT transceivers. Unsuitable because of their short range and lack of security, these were *never* intended for operational Patrols. But they *were* urgently needed by the expanding Special Duties Section and it is possible to conclude that – as very specially secret and not in any way militarised - they were not easily able to obtain army supplies in their own name or through normal channels.

Perhaps Bill Beyts acted deviously on their behalf?

As a professional soldier, Major Beyts would have been well aware of the operational weakness created by a lack of any dependable communication between IOs who, it has been firmly established, were categoric that radio communications were not needed – and patrols in-the-field. He may have felt obligated to depart with the subject committed to paper, highlighted and passed upwards for determination. It never was, however, and the weakness remained to the end.

Nigel Oxenden was aware of the absence of collective operational role directives from the top:

> 'THE RAID ROLE. In the early summer of 1942, the Home Guard was warned that local raids might be expected upon our priority coasts, and all units worked out their raid roles.
>
> 'This warning was a gift to IOs for although no universally applicable directive could be issued from HQ, they were able to formulate their own (directives) in conjunction with their local military commander, and the rumour of a renewed threat to our shores was a wonderful tonic for fading enthusiasm...'

Answers are indicated here to some of the questions Major Beyts may have wished to address before he departed. No substantial evidence has come to light that IOs and Group Commanders were ever seriously intended by GHQ collectively to 'go to ground'. This means that civilian Patrols and the Scout Sections would have been alone in their operational bases when the alarm sounded and the balloon went up.

With no knowledge of the whereabouts of the front line, without communications to find out the state of battle, or contact with an Intelligence Officer, not only would they have been alone - they would have been effectively abandoned.

Although, at high level, the regular army knew they were there – *they did not know where.*

This hiatus did not involve Norman Field at the start of 1941, however:

> 'In my time, IOs required no radio, which was insecure anyway, or any other communications. Judgement as to the best actions were left to the individual concerned. Occupation of OBs would not have occurred until 'Cromwell' was sounded. Auxiliers wished to be left alone and did not regard it as being abandoned. Nothing seemed to be gained by the Army knowing where they were. The more who knew, the more vulnerable became security.'

But local, independent operations, accepted – and even encouraged - in 1940/1941, were soon replaced by the more formally structured and highly insecure Group system. It also created a temporary operational role for GCs – although not necessarily below ground, presumably as the link between the IO and his patrols. 1942 was the year which saw the dissolution of both the 'Group' system of operation *and* any indication that IOs were to 'stay-behind'.

Were any of these changes for the better? As it was not put to the ultimate test, we will never know. But the overriding conclusion must be that the unfailing confidence which the men in the OBs – and especially the Patrol Leader – had in their 'powers-that-be', was seriously flawed.

★ ★ ★

Another group of 'stay-behinds' has not been forgotten – those men and women hurriedly recruited in 1940, some possibly earlier, by Section 'D' under Lieutenant Colonel Lawrence Grand on the instructions of the Chief of the Secret Intelligence Service (MI6), simultaneously and in parallel with the creation of the Auxiliary Units patrols through MI(R) and the Director of Military Intelligence.

However, although 'dumps' of explosives and firearms had been independently prepared for them throughout Great Britain, the Section 'D' agents were never to become operational. Instead, as 'D' was absorbed into Special Operations Executive in the autumn of 1940, its recruits formed the nucleus of the Special Duties Section, assimilated as Intelligence agents into the Auxiliary Units administration as a going concern in the winter of 1940/41.

As such they will receive detailed cover later on, mainly in Chapter Thirteen.

'Dirty Tricks'; illustrations of recommended CQC techniques.
(W E Fairbairn/Geoffrey Bradford.)

CHAPTER TEN

'OXO' - A sort of commerical traveller...

by Andrew Taylor, with additional research
by Joy Oxenden and Tony Evans.

'How lucky we are that he came when he did in the Lazy Tide
of History'

(Homer's *Iliad*)

Portelet Bay nestles idyllically into the end of a natural land
spur, formed between the much larger bays of St Brelade's and
St Aubin's on the south coast of Jersey. It provides the setting
for the oldest holiday park on the Island and was, in the early
nineteen fifties, the location of the first known Auxiliary Units
memorial to be erected anywhere in Britain. It reads:

In Memory of
Our Beloved
Major N V Oxenden, MC
Presented by
Norfolk Aux.Units

Supported on three stone pillars, the horizontal millstone –
probably linked to the windmills of East Anglia – was placed by
former Auxiliary Units men of Norfolk upon learning of the
death of the man who had raised and led them during the first
crucial year of their wartime existence.

It is sometimes said that, to be effective, a Military Officer
should not seek to be liked by his men, but to be respected. In
keeping with, and perhaps because of his natural unorthodoxy,
Nigel Oxenden attained both. This was not a sign of weakness.
Indeed, he did not suffer fools gladly, and was someone with
whom it was unwise to cross swords. His propensity to speak
his mind in the highest company was well known and, coupled
with an enviable WWI record, engendered respect from those
on the receiving end.

It is perhaps surprising therefore that this maverick,
outgoing character should, for over half a century, go virtually

unnoticed in the history of Auxiliary Units. This in itself would not be of particular historical significance if it were not for the fact that Oxenden was the man given the task of writing the official history of Auxiliary Units at stand down in November 1944. The full document remains undiscovered in 2001; that he even wrote it remained unknown for almost as long as Oxenden himself. He was the last person to have access to the 'lost' HQ records, believed - almost certainly wrongly – to have been destroyed in the Coleshill House fire of 1952.

So how did this important piece in the Auxiliary Units jigsaw get overlooked? The genesis of the oversight can be traced to a minor misinterpretation of facts more than twenty years after the end of WWII. That misinterpretation would indirectly help create and perpetuate a myth that nothing concerning Auxiliary Units was ever committed to paper, or that all records were either destroyed in the 1952 fire, or shortly after stand down.

The true fate of the Coleshill records, as we will see, is almost certainly much less clandestine or mysterious.

★   ★   ★

Nigel Oxenden, known as 'Oxo' to officers and men alike, received his first recorded Military Cross on 7th January 1917, as a twenty-one year old 2nd Lieutenant, for gallantry in action in the Battle of the Ancre, the final convulsion of the horrifically ineffectual Somme offensive. He was to receive one recorded Bar to the decoration, although colleagues would later contend that Oxenden was actually the holder of *three* MCs and Lt Colonel Stuart Edmundson placed on record his belief that he had won *four*.

He joined the Royal Northumberland Fusiliers as Nigel Vernon Gallwey at the outbreak of the Great War, taking his mother's family name at about the end of 1916, when he was serving with the 5th Company of the Machine Gun Corps (MGC). Records show that on 13th November 1916, the day of the Ancre Battle, 5 MGC Company took part in a semi-successful attack on German trenches at Serre and Puisieux, north east of Corselles-au-Bois. The unit sustained nearly forty casualties. Oxenden (Gallwey) was in command of 'A' Section during this action. His award was Gazetted on 13th February 1917:

> 'Temp 2nd Lieut N V Oxenden – MGC. For conspicuous gallantry in action. He displayed great courage and initiative in the placing of his machine guns during an attack on the enemy's

trenches. He later rescued a wounded man under very heavy fire.'

Oxenden was wounded himself on 18th August 1917 during a machine gun attack on 'selected targets', a euphemism for harassing fire into enemy positions. After recuperation he returned to 5 MGC Company on 14th September.

On 21st March 1918, Oxenden was caught in the massive German counter attack which precipitated the Second Battle of the Somme and during which, in just eight days, the British were temporarily to lose many of the gains made in 1916. A letter written in 1959 to Nigel Oxenden's widow, Pat, provides insight into these events – in which confusion and panic all but overwhelmed the entire British front line. Its author, Eric Bird, also highlights something of Oxenden's character, and sheds light on an apparent promotion to Captain. He and Percy Bell served with 'Oxo' throughout the First War, the three men remaining lifetime friends:

'(Percy) had a great affection for and admiration of Oxo. They were quite dissimilar in their habits, Percy being very correct, public school, and invariable most correctly dressed. But they were two of the toughest and most stout hearted fighting men I met during the whole war. Nothing ever rattled either of them and the worst crises left both of them apparently unmoved. I was happy to tack on behind and draw moral strength from two such self-reliant characters.

'Their strength was most apparent in the great German offensive of March 1918 during a fighting retreat for 8 days against tremendous odds, in which my total amount of sleep was 5 hours and I suppose theirs was much the same...I did not see Oxo for the first 3 days of that battle as he was away fighting on a flank, but then he was ordered out of a position which had become impossible. He just walked up to Percy and me and said "Hullo" in his usual calm way. There had been some doubt whether we should ever see him again, but Percy merely grinned and said "Ha! Oxo!" – and then told him where he wanted him to place his guns and men for the next rearguard action.

'We were at that time in a desperate position. Yet the two of them were entirely calm and collected. Percy was a born natural commander and he ran a company of 240 men as if he had had 20 years' experience. Oxo was much more of an individualist and preferred his little gang of 24 men and 4 machine guns. He was promoted to Captain and second-in-command of another company but after a month of it he gave it up and came back to Percy and me, as a Lieutenant...We were having tea one afternoon in a peaceful spot behind the trenches when Oxo walked in among us and sat down. Five minutes later someone noticed he had only two stars on his shoulder instead of a Captain's three. Oxo said – "Oh, I couldn't stand that lot any more and came back here". Only then did he hand over to Percy the official order of his appointment.

'Percy was delighted and, from then on, the three of us remained together...perhaps you may see why I loved and admired these two men so much and why they got on so well together.

'The world could do with more like them.'

The 'bulge' forced into Allied lines was finally held on 28th March 1918, and Germany's last great gamble in men and equipment – like Hitler's in the Ardennes more than a quarter of a century away – marked the beginning of her humiliating defeat eight months later. During the general Allied advance which followed this first 'Battle of the Bulge', Nigel Oxenden was involved in numerous actions and for his part in one is recorded as receiving a Bar to his MC on 5th October 1918, and Gazetted on 2nd December:

> '...For conspicuous gallantry and ability while commanding a section of machine guns in an attack. He led his men forward with great dash and took up an advanced position from which he was able to cover the line reached by the infantry with enfilade fire. When the enemy attempted to counter attack he materially assisted in breaking up the attack.'

In April 1919, after serving with the Allied Forces of Occupation in Germany, Lt Oxenden, now twenty-three years of age, was demobilised, returning home to the Channel Islands.

Between the wars, Nigel Oxenden found many ways to utilise his natural energy and satisfy his zest for life. Most involved danger – which he believed should be practised to overcome fear – or personal endeavour. In 1920, finding civilian life on Jersey too tranquil after years of war, he went off to travel the world. Among other adventures, he tried tobacco farming in South Africa, where he also competed in cliff diving competitions, becoming a national champion. He would later say that although his South African record of 70 feet sounded good, it was far easier than diving had been on Jersey.

His travels took him to Australia and Hawaii where he developed a lifelong love of surfing - which he is credited as pioneering in Britain. Upon his return to Jersey in the early 1920s he put his engineering qualification, gained before the war, to good use and built his own bungalow, 'Four Winds', where he housed his collection of cars and motor cycles, competing in trials and sand racing events. In 1922 a holiday camp was set up on land owned by Nigel's mother, Flora, at Portelet Bay, which he ran with his wife, Pat, whom he married in 1926. For wedding gifts, they gave each other new motor cycles; Pat shared Nigel's love of racing and competed successfully in her own right.

When re-mobilised in September, 1939, Oxenden was first sent to Alderney to train a token contingent of troops, before being ordered to withdraw to the mainland in June 1940, as Britain prepared to abandon the islands to German occupation. Oxenden provides his own unique perspective on these historic events and his subsequent attachment to Auxiliary Units in a letter to a friend, written in October 1940:

'...Pat left Jersey on June 19th, in an RAF plane, with Joy (their new daughter) in a carry-cot, and three suitcases. Mother left the next day by Jersey Airways with 28lbs of luggage. Pat had 30 hours warning from me and packed very cleverly. But her actual departure was on receipt of a phone call from the airport, where our MO (doc) had wangled a seat for her. Everything was just left. Pat's car and mother's were in everyday use, but my MG was on blocks, and out of running order. The cats were taken to the animal shelter, where there was a queue of people having their pets blotted out. The whole affair was a complete heartbreak, and we all feel as sore as hell at the way the thing was mismanaged by the government.

'...Nobody feels that we should have held the islands, but all troops were withdrawn on June 20th...I never managed to get back home, although I would have given anything to do so.

'...I was still a 2nd loot (Lieutenant). I got seven days leave from Salisbury to look after Pat and Mother, and stayed with some Gubbins cousins in Sussex. I heard that my young cousin Colin, who used to spend his holidays with me in Jersey, was a Brigadier at the War Office. He was thought to be reorganising the Polish army. I asked his sister to tell him that if he wanted any colonels for it, I was waiting. I thought no more about it until, a month later, I was ordered to report for an interview at room 213 (in the War Office). I had forgotten Colin, and had no idea whom I was going to meet, but it was he, and he offered me a sort of hush-hush job which he couldn't tell me about unless I would definitely accept it. The pay was pretty good and I should be a captain at once. I said yes and even managed to bring another subaltern along with me.

'So here I am, working for Colin, and with Norfolk as my area, a car and driver and clerk, with prospects of getting within the next month, three subalterns, two more cars and one 15-cwt truck, and 28 assorted other ranks...I am a sort of commercial traveller, travelling in explosives, with after-sales service, and bangs grow on one to such an extent, that I just hate a silent day.

'I am not fighting a very heroic war, but nor is any soldier at the moment. I have said for years, that in this war I should be a climber (seek promotion) and now Joy makes it necessary. I was terribly happy last time as a cross-snatcher (front line soldier) but then I only had myself to think of. Of course, if Hitler lands round here, I shall find it very hard to stay alive. There is no prospect of me becoming a major but, on the other hand, there is no reason why the twelve of us scattered around the coast, should not eventually get up a step. We are directly under GHQ Home Forces, and there is no fixed Establishment like there was in the 341st MGTC...

'We are a unique show.'

Although it appears that Oxenden had accepted that his age and the welfare of his family forbade heroic deeds, he found it difficult to suppress the old soldier within. He was deservedly of the opinion, outwardly at least, that he had 'done his bit' twenty odd years earlier and that this was a young man's war:

'Now we are up against a most unpleasant bunch, and I feel it should be our duty to kill as many as possible, so as to eliminate Hitler's brutal upbringing of the youth of the last twenty years. There can be no good Huns under 45...'

Oxenden was never at ease with Britain's conduct towards the enemy during the early months of the war. He noted with irony that while the Great War had been fought with massive brutality between combatants who retained a degree of respect for each other, in his opinion the war against Hitler was being conducted too leniently:

'...The spirit of the thing is all wrong. I look back with regret at the days when a plane brought down meant a crew roasting or falling, not just baling out and being rescued by police and given a cup of tea...'

Everything Nigel Oxenden did, and the standards he expected from his Auxiliers, was governed by a comparison with what he considered *real* war. He never quite managed to suppress his naturally tenacious attitude to fighting. He instilled a fearsome attitude into the men of Norfolk in a way that gained him their lasting respect. He insisted that Hitler's Germany should be met by, if not the tactics of WWI, then nothing less than an all-out approach to war. This uncompromising stance and his forthright opinion is clear in a letter to his wife, written in May 1941 while still serving as IO for Norfolk:

> '...I have just been up to Div. While we were waiting for the GOC to come, there was an alarm, so we went outside, nominally to the trenches. A Heinkel came past at 1000 feet and, when he was passing us – not directly overhead – he let go two bombs. A dozen of us, and two dozen troops, were watching. The bombs floated away from us, and I turned to say something and found myself completely alone. It was like a conjuring trick. (They made a couple of huge craters in a wheat field about a quarter of a mile away.) I am rather disgusted. I suppose that I ought to be proud that no one was sick or fainted, but judged by last war standards, it was a revolting exhibition and has given me rather a shock. There were several majors, but no one as old as me.'

His mention of majors is interesting as it could suggest that he had gained promotion by this time. This would have been prior to his move to Auxiliary Units HQ at Coleshill in around the summer of 1941, an appointment offered to him by Colonel Bill Major in March:

> '...There are two faint possibilities of my getting a job as a major somewhere else. One through Colin Gubbins, who got me into this show, and has now moved on and up, and the other through his successor, our new CO, who asked me the other day whether I would like a certain job in MI5 if it became vacant, as he didn't want to drag me away from Norfolk if it was my home. I assured him it wasn't.'

Whether or not the position Oxenden eventually took at Coleshill was with MI5 is not certain, but it is known that within two or three months he was ostensibly at Auxunits HQ as a training officer. If Oxenden *was* seconded to Britain's counter espionage organisation, it adds credence to the suggestion of joint secret services' involvement in Auxiliary Units. The probability is addressed elsewhere in this book.

Little is recorded of Oxenden's work at Coleshill House between the middle of 1941 and the end of 1944. However, he was apparently a member of the operational training staff under Major Geoffrey Beyts until the latter left Auxunits in mid-1942, when 'Oxo' was promoted in his place. His initials appear on a number of training and operations directives, and he lectured on weaponry and explosives as part of the standard weekend courses for civilian patrols and Scout Section regulars. It is also confirmed that he frequently went to nearby Hannington Hall, HQ of Auxunits Special Duties Section, helping to train ATS subaltern Control Station radio operators in map reading and field craft.

There are uncorroborated suggestions that he was involved in training French SOE operatives at Coleshill prior to D-Day in June 1944. The historical link between Colin Gubbins, the eventual chief of SOE, and Auxiliary Units is firmly established, and Oxenden could have proved valuable to his illustrious cousin – having been a fluent French speaker since boyhood days 'endured' at Wellington College.

If details of Oxenden's service at Coleshill House are sketchy, it is conversely certain is that he was given the task of producing for War Office what amounted to an 'Official History' of Auxiliary Units from inception through to stand down. The authority was noted in 'TOP SECRET' correspondence dated 27th November 1944, from C-in-C Home Forces to The Under Secretary of State, The War Office:

> 'Historical Record: The Commander HQ Auxiliary Units has been instructed to prepare, for the information of War Office, a report on all aspects of the raising, organisation, training and closing down of the Auxiliary Units. This report has not yet been completed. In connection with this report, the sorting of the records of HQ Auxiliary Units for destruction or retention is still proceeding.'

The final 20,000 word version of this document was, according to Oxenden himself, to be a blueprint for setting up similar units in the event of another war in Europe. An earlier 8,500 word draft, entitled 'Auxiliary Units, History and Achievement' and discovered on Jersey Island in 1998, set out the evolution and operational development of Auxiliary Units throughout the war and contains clear and concise recommendations for the establishment of a similar network if the need ever arose again.

The draft document, which was published by the Museum of the British Resistance Organisation in September 1998, contains nothing that, in itself, could be considered sensitive to national security; nor does it give any definitive indication that it was a draft of the *final* version. Controversial or not, the continued unavailability of the latter deserves further analysis.

Although full investigation of possible 'quasi-official' intervention to seize the document is beyond the scope of this book, events in early 1998 – leading to the unresolved disappearance of papers entitled *'Auxiliary Units, History and final Teaching'* from a property on Jersey Island - lend credible, if circumstantial weight to the possibility. The mystery is deepened by the fact that, only a few weeks prior to the intended donation of this history to the Museum, Ministry of Defence officials had been notified of Oxenden's own indication, contained in a letter written in 1947, *that he had retained a carbon copy of his final report.* The maintenance of private and possibly legal discretion dictates that full details of these events cannot be divulged here; but it is reasonable to surmise just what Nigel Oxenden's final document could have contained to prevent its disclosure more than half a century after it was written.

The fact is that the myths, uncorroborated reports and theories that permeate Auxunits' history, cannot be resolved while this document is retained in secret. For example, did an explosion at Coleshill House cause the deaths of men supposedly serving in the 'Home Guard'? Did civilian Auxiliers die in an ill-conceived operation in occupied France in 1942? Were civilians given discretionary powers of assassination? The validity of some of these propositions may never be satisfactorily proven, but in all probability *the reason for its existence,* rather than any perceived sensitivity of content, may account for the continued classification of Oxenden's document. In this respect, his own eloquent explanation could suit the Ministry of Defence line for as many years as it sees fit:

> '...The unit has just evaporated, and nothing now remains but a 20,000 word account of our history and final teaching, which I had the honour of writing, filed away in the secret archives of the War Office until the next time that hostile troops are sitting on the other side of the Channel...'

Whether Nigel Oxenden's 'Official History' has been lost, or is indeed still classified 'TOP SECRET', one fact is inescapable. While, during 1967, author David Lampe prepared his classic Auxiliary Unit history – *'The Last Ditch'* – his minor but fundamental error in assuming that Capt. Andrew Croft served during 1940 as Intelligence Officer for the county of Norfolk, as well as Suffolk and Essex, ensured that Lampe would never know that the evolutionary detail of Auxiliary Units, lacking in his book, and the elusive written word on subjects to which he often refers, were resting undiscoverd in a house on Jersey:

> '...I myself left Aux Units in October last, and as you know, by Christmas even the IOs who had been left to collect arms and equipment, had been posted away. Col. Douglas and half a dozen HQ staff left on Jan 16th (1945), and that was the end of everything...'

Nigel Oxenden's letter, written in February 1945, while still billeted in Coleshill Village, gives a clue to the fate of the mysterious HQ records. During investigations into the whereabouts of his final document, Museum researchers discovered that in the 1970s, during clearance of his house, thousands of WWII documents were found in an attic; many contained illustrations and details of unarmed combat techniques. The eventual fate of this extraordinary find has never been established, although there are unconfirmed reports that everything was burned on a garden fire along with miscellaneous items from the house. It would appear that in a sad irony, Oxenden's wartime fears regarding the effect of enemy occupation on his Island homeland, were prophetically borne out by the fact that British wartime documents now generate little historical interest in the Channel Islands.

Whatever happened, it is reasonable to assume, due to Oxenden's almost exclusive service with Auxiliary Units throughout WWII, that these papers were charged to his care as the last man left at Coleshill after stand down. Moreover, this suggests that the widely held, and always unlikely, view that the wartime records of Auxunits HQ perished in the 'mysterious' fire at Coleshill House in 1952, is wide of the mark.

The truth is almost certainly more straightforward. Nigel Oxenden, once again the last man standing, and faced with a mountain of papers to dispose of in 1945, simply took the most interesting home to Jersey.

CHAPTER ELEVEN

Auxiliary Units on Active Service. 'Operation *Bulbasket*' and the disappearance of Trooper George Biffin

With material specially provided by Geoff Bradford, John Fielding and George Biffin. Acknowledgement is made to Paul McCue, the author of 'Operation Bulbasket'.

'I have always felt that the Geneva Convention is a dangerous piece of stupidity as it leads people to believe war can be civilised. It can't!'

(Captain John Tonkin,
Officer Commanding 'A' Troop,
'B' Squadron, 1st Special Air Service
Regiment on 'Operation *Bulbasket*'.)

★　　★　　★

Did the Auxiliary Units ever go to war? Argument based on the limited evidence available still 'rages' among researchers.

One controversial example comes from private post-war correspondence between Major Nigel Oxenden, then back in Jersey, and a Norfolk Auxunits' operational patrol leader – continuing a wartime friendship based, perhaps, on a mutual interest in Freemasonry. Some of the correspondence is straightforward enough; a few parts deliberately use a personal code however.

'Between-the-lines' interpretation, admittedly inconclusive, gives a strong hint that sabotage *was* conducted against the enemy by Norfolk Auxiliers under the leadership of Nigel Oxenden. The target was approached in a sea-going launch. After landing to set explosive charges with time-delays fuses, the team hove-to offshore at dawn, waiting to confirm a successful firing. The saboteurs apparently returned safely.

A further possibility, although still speculative, is that the target was an enemy installation on one of the Channel Isles. If so, as a former resident, an engineer and soldier, Oxenden knew the land better than anyone. Is there something still so

secret about the operation that apparently unrelated papers
about him, and details of his WWI medals for bravery, have
been withdrawn from Public Record Office? More than fifty
years after his death, they are, unusually, *retained within the
Ministry of Defence*? Could it all be connected with the strange
degree of otherwise inexplicable secrecy surrounding
operational Auxiliary Units as a whole? Does someone still
fear the bright lights of public scrutiny?

Although there is no known record of this action, it would
be a brave man who claimed that Auxiliary Units were
definitively *never* on active service. However, David Lampe –
in days when less corroboration was available – boldly
declared:

> 'Auxiliary Units personnel were parachuted into France, but not
> civilian members of the Patrols.'
>
> (the 'Stand Down' chapter of '*The Last Ditch*')

Although David Lampe was *nearly* right, Joseph Ogg, a
Scottish Auxilier, and Fred Rowe from Monmouth, would have
disagreed. It was also a surprise to John Fielding. A student
chartered accountant when war broke out in September 1939,
John transferred from the Home Guard to a Norwich Auxiliary
Units' operational patrol early in 1941. He trained at Coleshill
and, during weekends, with the Norfolk Scout Section at
Wroxham until call-up at the end of 1942, when Auxunit
enrolment no longer deferred him from military service. He
was aged 22.

Together with 'fifteen to twenty other Auxiliers' he was first
garrisoned in a holding unit at Northampton, where suitably
qualified men were invited to volunteer for Special Forces. Len
Edwards, another Norfolk Auxilier, remembers about a
hundred there in his time. John Fielding volunteered to 'go
over the other side' with the Special Air Service Regiment (SAS)
and was sent to Scotland for extra training, and Ringway, near
Manchester, for parachute instruction.

> 'I joined the SAS when the 1st and 2nd Regiments came home
> in the winter of 1943 after the Italian campaign. 'At the end of
> 1943, we occupied an old weaving factory at Darvel, near
> Kilmarnock (now Strathclyde), the area where we did the majority
> of our training. We were extremely fit; later, in action, it would
> stand us in good stead. We got used to travelling long distances on
> foot at night, and without sleep.
>
> 'At Ringway, after ground practice in a hangar, we dropped from

a balloon – this was more difficult than jumping from an aircraft. The only way your parachute opened was by the speed of your fall whereas in an aircraft the slipstream activates it quickly. We trained in Stirling aircraft. They were better to jump from than a Halifax, which you left through a smallish hole – and had to keep absolutely upright or your head smashed into the side. The SAS encouraged Troopers to work in pairs, and I teamed up with veteran Sam Smith, a maverick Liverpudlian.'

John Fielding and his comrades of A Troop, B Squadron, 1 SAS, were being prepared for Operation 'Bulbasket', one of a number of schemes devised by Supreme HQ, Allied Expeditionary Force (SHAEF), to delay the relocation of German reserves – particularly the feared 'Das Reich' German SS Panzer Division – toward the Normandy beach-head after 'D' Day. To ensure secrecy and their safety, he and his SAS comrades were – for several weeks before the drop – secluded within a 'sanitised' depot known as 'The Cage' at Fairford, Gloucestershire. Special training with explosives concentrated on the destruction of bridges, culverts, trains and railway lines.

Captain John Tonkin, in his early twenties but already campaign-hardened with Special Forces and SAS service in North Africa, Sicily and Italy – where, he escaped German army captors after being taken prisoner – was commander of 'Bulbasket'. He parachuted into the Vienne Region of France during the night of 5/6th June 1944 – as 'D' Day forces set sail from the English coast – and was shortly joined by the rest of his advance party to reconnoitre targets and prepare suitable Dropping Zones ('DZs'). During the early hours of 11th June, John Fielding dropped with the main party, carried in two RAF Stirling aircraft. When asked to recall his thoughts he replied:

'What's it like? I'll tell you. It's exciting!

'You're in your early twenties. Your first trip abroad. You jump into blackness. It's impossible to know just what to expect. A few seconds later you hit the ground – in my case hard. I thought I had broken my foot. The first man I spoke to was M Albert Dupont from the French Resistance reception committee. We are still friends – nearly sixty years later.

'Yes. It is exciting. We were thoroughly trained. We trusted the RAF and our comrades. And had confidence in ourselves too.'

The 'stick' jumped from 300' to give enemy soldiers less chance to aim as they floated defencelessly down. They were also less vulnerable to drift, and separation from colleagues.

Sam Smith followed on so immediately, he snagged the top of John Fielding's parachute canopy:

> 'I felt a tug in the moments before he steered clear.
>
> 'Each Trooper had a heavy kit bag full of explosives suspended from a cord. It was designed to hit the ground a moment beforehand. As some weight was momentarily taken from the parachute's load, the canopy billowed briefly, giving a theoretically 'soft' landing.
>
> 'My bag failed to clear properly and we hit the ground more or less simultaneously. Sam Smith was right alongside. With no broken bones after all, I was soon on my feet again.
>
> 'We collected our gear and marched off into the night.
>
> 'Yes. It was exciting!'

Unfortunately, a German army convoy, highly visible, was moving through the area and this led to scattered 'drops' as 'DZs' were missed. Surviving many dangers, John's group eventually joined John Tonkin and his advance party some days later.

One sub-group of 'A' Troop – led by former Dorset Auxunit Scout Section officer, Lieutenant Peter Weaver - was dropped way off target at 0220 on 11th June 1944. Their immediate objective, before scheduled re-join with John Tonkin, was a vital section of railway line code-named 'Lot 4'. Landing to the west of Parthenay and almost 90 kilometres from the main party, they were equipped with pistols and explosives but no food other than ration packs – so they prepared to live-off-the-land for a few days. None of the party spoke French. Locating their target successfully, they blew up a section of track, and de-railed a train before starting the long cross-country walk to join their colleagues at main base.

Moving quietly through a wood one night, they were startled to hear *American* voices and came across an officer and sergeant in US uniform – surrounded by stocks of weapons, equipment, radio gear, food and money. The Americans had failed to rendezvous with the French Maquisards for whom the material was intended. Declining offers to help themselves, the troopers moved on. Later, they encountered a group of French guerrillas – untrained to use the weaponry and sabotage equipment with which they were well supplied – and decided to stay with them for a few days' rest and recuperation. In return for home cooking, they coached their French 'hosts' in weaponry skills. When they moved on a few days later, it was with reluctance on both sides.

Peter Weaver's team eventually joined the main group without loss.

Corporal John Kinnivane, a veteran western-desert SAS campaigner, and ex-Auxiliers Joe Ogg, 'Sam' Pascoe and George Biffin, were also dropped off target. They escaped initial capture and eventually joined the main party – except for Trooper Biffin, who 'disappeared'. His parents were notified that he was 'Missing – believed killed in action'. After being night-dropped *into* the village of Airvault, he had vanished without trace.

On 25th June, as battle raged in the Normandy bocage, about thirty-five SAS 'A' Troopers bivouacked in woodland near the small town of Verrieres, in the Poitiers region – together with eleven Maquisards and a shot-down American airman. Four Jeeps, equipped with long range fuel capacity – and mounted with twin Vickers 'K' machine guns ranging ahead, and a third aft, firing tracer, incendiary and armour-piercing bullets at about twelve hundred rounds a minute – were received from successful RAF Halifax night drops to a DZ prepared and lit by 'A' Troop.

John Fielding identifies no less than eleven former Auxiliers in the *'Bulbasket'* team. To be fair to David Lampe, only one other was a 'civilian' – Trooper Joseph Ogg, who had served with an operational patrol in the Alves, Spynie and Elgin, Morayshire, region of Scotland.

Most, if not all, of the rest were Scout Section regular soldiers – Corporal Les Long and Trooper Victor ('Chalky') White from Norfolk, and several from a remarkable group – all volunteers from the Dorset Auxunit Scout Section – under Lieutenant Peter Weaver. The dramas of 'A' Troop – their adventures, successes and failures are graphically detailed by researcher Paul McCue in his book, *'Operation Bulbasket'*. Major Joe Schofield, for the SAS Regimental Association, wrote in their journal, *'Mars and Minerva'*:

> 'A well researched book recommended to be read by all present and future members of the SAS as a salutary lesson on what, and what not to do, when operating in an enemy occupied country, whether the natives are considered friendly and trustworthy or not.'

Early *'Bulbasket'* reconnaissance and intelligence communications to their HQ in England, together with sabotage directly against the French railway network, are estimated to have kept 'Das Reich' from the Normandy front for up to seventeen days – and liaison with the RAF resulted in a formidable attack on 15th June 1944 on the Panzers' essential fuel supplies stored in railway sidings at Chatellerault, north of Poitiers.

In the field, SAS Troopers gained confidence as each day passed. Morale was high although undermined at times by boredom. Coded, plain language broadcasts over the BBC, preceded by the music of 'Sur le Pont d'Avignon', were greeted with energetic jiving and finger wagging, the dance fashion of the day. The Maquisards liaised with other French Resistance fighters to provide valuable local knowledge.

By early July, however, security had become careless and the encampment compromised. Aware of this, John Tonkin planned a location transfer but faced a number of problems. Alternative drinking water sources were scarce for example, and delay was unavoidable as they anxiously waited at a well-proven DZ nearby for urgently needed supplies.

★   ★   ★

Feeling under-utilised, Sam Smith proposed a sabotage operation against 'Lot 2', the code-name for a vital stretch of railway. John Tonkin authorised the action and Sam, John Fielding and a third trooper, prepared to depart at dusk on 2nd July. John will never forget that day:

> 'When you are successful and have a low casualty rate, you are liable to drop your security precautions. We thought it was too easy and our security was not as it should have been. During the day, I was guarding one of the entrances to the Foret de Verrieres, lying behind a fence. I could see up the road and there was a motorcycle combination coming down with two men, one riding the bike and one walking behind. They had a puncture. They stopped at a footpath leading into the forest and I left them there for a while before showing myself and asked them what they were doing?
>
> 'They claimed they were French Resistance people, so I took them up the footpath, about a quarter of a mile into the forest, and handed them over to our Maquisards who questioned them. They had their story absolutely correct; they gave our men a lot of information about other Resistance groups a long way away, with which our people had no contact at all. They convinced our liaison people that they were genuine and were released.

The classic photograph of the staff and IOs taken on the steps at Coleshill, in January 1942 with Colonel 'Bill' Major (centre, front row) in command. On his left is Major Maurice Petherick and Senior Commander Beatrice Temple and, at the end of the line, the imposing figure of Major John Collings. On Major's right is Major 'Billy' Beyts. *(Eric Gray)*

This second photograph shows Major Mike Henderson on Colonel Major's left and Billy Beyts and Nigel Oxenden on his right. Stuart Edmundson is arrowed and Ian Fenwick prominent in the centre, back row. *(Miss E.M. ('Willy') Wilmott)*

(top left) Ernest Blaxall *(left)* describes to Suffolk Auxunit veteran Ralph Clarke how - to avoid school - he hid in the latter's local Auxunit OB. *(Paul Mothersole)*

(top right) Major William Ewart ('Dan') Fairbairn, a pre-war Shanghai police chief and 'father of Close Quarters' Combat'. He was the lead instructor at Inverailort and later at Camp 'X' in Canada, and the co-designer of the Fairbairn/Sykes fighting knife. *(Peter Robins)*

(bottom left) Four of the NCO permanent staff at Coleshill. (left to right) Corporal Johnny Banks, RE; Sergeant Leonard Smith, RASC; Acting Sergeant Eric Gray, RASC; and Sergeant Singleton, RASC. *(Eric Gray)*

The plaque commemorating the role of Postmistress Mabel Stranks, erected by Highworth Town Council, on the wall of the post office through which many Auxunits patrols passed on their way to Coleshill House. *(Geoffrey Bradford)*

'The Garth', Bilting, Kent, today. Peter Fleming created the first Scout Section here, to train 'stay-behinds' for XII Corps commander, General 'Bulgy' Thorne, even before the formal creation of Auxiliary Units. *(Ann Warwicker, courtesy of the owners)*

The XII Corps Observation Units, as they were known even after absorption into the Auxiliary Units, pictured in 1943. *(Imperial War Museum)*

The Suffolk Scout Section operated from the Mill House, Cransford, Woodbridge. Lieutenant McIntyre *(top centre)*. To his left, Geoff Bowery, and right, Sergeant Jack Steward and (then) Corporal Cyril Hall. *(Geoff Bowery)*

The Suffolk Scout Section toughening up on a cycle cross country during the bitter winter of 1940/41. *(Geoff Bowery)*

In 1941, Suffolk Rgt. Sgt John ('Jack') Steward, married Doris, a local girl, while with the Scout Section at Cransford. Doris still lives in the village. *(Doris Steward)*

'The Big House' at Inverailort, in the West Highlands of Scotland. Originally the Irregular Warfare Centre for Commando training, Inverailort was later the SOE Special Training School under Colin Gubbins. *(Major R F Hall, MC)*

John Warwicker *(right)*, representing the Museum of the British Resistance Organisation, thanks Major R F ('Henry') Hall, MC, for his first-hand description of Close Quarters Combat in action against German troops near Arnhem. *(Ann Warwicker)*

(top left) Major William ('Bill') Sykes, big-game hunter, firearms expert, former Shanghai police officer, and a senior instructor at Inverailort. *(Peter Robins)*

(top right) Brigadier Mike Calvert, DSO, of later 'Chindits' and SAS fame, had his own ideas of the role of the Auxiliary Units. Apparently, his radical opinions were not widely shared. *('Mad Mike'/David Roone - a 1944 sketch)*

(lower left). A snapshot of 'Pat and Oxo' taken in Jersey on 16th September 1925 – their wedding day. *(Joy Oxenden/BRO Museum collection)*

The Dorset's Auxunits' Scout Section was disbanded in 1943 when seven joined 'B' Squadron, 1 SAS and took part in the ill-fated Operation 'Bulbasket'. *(Front row)* Tpr George Cogger; *(second row)* Lt Peter Weaver, Cpl Jim Rideout and L/Cpl George Biffin; *(top row)* Tpr Sidney Ryland Tprs Alan Ashley and 'Sam' Pascoe. Peter Weaver, Jim Rideout, and George Biffin survived the Operation. *(Paul McCue/George Biffin)*

The SS Panzergrenadier Barracks on the banks of the Vienne River was destroyed by 14 Mosquito aircraft on 14th July 1944, without significant damage to adjacent French property. *(Air Commodore E. Sismore/Paul McCue)*

'Of course they were not and I should have shot them both!'
These two Milice – despised French collaborators with the
Boche - alerted the Germans, who probably had corroboration
after capturing and torturing two other *Bulbasket* troopers.
Sam Smith's three-man sabotage team left by Jeep at nightfall
as scheduled. If the SS were already deploying round the wood
to attack, they may have astutely allowed this uninterrupted
departure to avoid alerting the main body of SAS. At any rate,
when the Jeep driver later got lost near the target area, Sam
Smith dismissed him and the team continued on foot. It was
John Fielding's first full scale action. Four days later, with their
target destroyed, they marched back to Verrieres to report to
John Tonkin.

As they approached, they were warned by friendly local
Frenchmen of disaster at the SAS encampment. The sabotage
operation had saved their lives.

★ ★ ★

At 7am on Monday, 3rd July 1944, large numbers – reports say
five hundred - of skilfully deployed SS troops, opened fire on
the main SAS party with mortars and firearms. Unprepared and
uncoordinated, many of the troopers surged about in the
forest, unwisely trying to escape in a group. Captain Tonkin
destroyed radio codes, returned fire with the Vickers, and blew
up the Jeeps while calling to his men to split into smaller
parties.

Four were injured – including two ex-Auxiliers, Joe Ogg and
Henry ('Sam') Pascoe. After capture, they initially received
medical treatment, but were later criminally neglected before
being forcibly removed from Poitiers hospital by the Nazi
Feldkommandantur. Never seen again, there is compelling
evidence that three troopers were murdered by lethal injection.
The injured officer, 'Twm' Stephens, was beaten to death by
Germans troops, in front of French citizens assembled in the
town square.

Thirty-three SAS men were captured, together with the
'downed' American pilot. On the 6th or 7th July, 1944, they
were all taken by truck into the forest of Saint Sauvant, lined
up, shot, and buried in shallow graves. German reports claimed
they were permitted to say goodbye to one another and then
died calmly and with dignity.

Sam Smith and his team, returning after the SS attack,
regrouped with survivors including John Tonkin, Peter Weaver
and Corporal Jim Rideout. In a remarkable display of

airmanship – by Flight Lieutenant A H C (later Sir Alan) Boxer – fourteen men (and five from a 'Phantom' communications team), were evacuated from a rough airstrip by RAF Hudson aircraft on the night of 6/7th August 1944.

After a fortnight's leave, John Fielding returned to duty and served in Italy and Greece – compensating guerrillas who had helped other SAS teams. Then, with allied units advancing into Germany, he was among the first to enter and warn of the horrors of the death camp of Belsen.

At the end of the war in Europe, John was rounding up German stragglers still garrisoned in Norway. During a day of rest in Bergen, on a makeshift pitch before hugely bewildered Norwegian spectators in a sports stadium, he opened the batting for 'B' Squadron SAS v 'A' Squadron. (He later played minor counties cricket for Norfolk.) Peter Weaver, a post-war County cricketer for Hampshire, scored a duck for 'A' Squadron, but was voted demon bowler of the day – taking five wickets for seventeen runs.

★   ★   ★

Of the 33 SAS soldiers captured and executed, John fielding identified the following former Auxiliers;

Trooper Alan Ashley	Dorset Scout Section
Trooper George Cogger	Dorset Scout Section
Corporal Les Long	Norfolk Scout Section
Trooper Sidney Ryland	Dorset Scout Section
Trooper Victor ('Chalky') White	Norfolk Scout Section

These murders and those of the four wounded, including ex-Auxiliers Joe Ogg and 'Sam' Pascoe (also of the Dorset Scout Section), were carried out under the authority of Hitler's notorious *Kommandobefehl* (See Appendix THREE) of 18th October 1942. Paragraph 2 specifically identified 'sabotage troops of the British' and Paragraph 3 stated:

'I therefore order:
From now on, all enemies on so-called Commando missions in Europe or Africa, challenged by German Troops, whether armed or unarmed, in battle or in flight, are to be slaughtered to the last man...'

While this command was carried into effect enthusiastically enough by the SS and their henchmen, Wehrmacht officers raised objections and, after 'D' Day, Hitler was petitioned by senior commanders who were finding it increasingly difficult to distinguish between 'sabotage' troops and soldiers engaged in operations which the Germans themselves accepted as legitimate.

In an Appendix to the *Kommandobefehl* dated (significantly enough) 25th June 1944, Hitler ordered that:

> '...only sabotage troops caught behind the rear Corps boundary of a German Corps in action with the enemy, were to be slaughtered'.

Analysis of Hitler's new thinking, may have led to the delay between capture on 3rd July 1944 and execution of the SAS soldiers on about the 6th. In any event, no matter how exercised German commanders might have been, it demonstrably failed to save the men of 'A' Troop.

★　　★　　★

'Memories are notoriously short and images are inclined to fade.'

(Donald Hamilton-Hill)

Revenge and retribution

Radio messages to HQ by Captain Tonkin and a 'Jedburgh' team (code-named 'Hugh'), called for retaliation by the RAF on an SS Panzergrenadier barracks identified alongside the Chateau de Marieville, Bonneuil-Matours, on the east bank of the River Vienne, 15 miles north-east of Poitiers. Special Forces HQ passed the messages to HQ/SAS Brigade who, in turn, contacted 2 Group, RAF.

140 Wing allocated fourteen Mosquito fighter-bombers for the attack – six equipped with new American M76 phosphorus incendiaries, effectively the first napalm bombs. The remainder carried instantaneous or fused high explosives. SS troops were at supper on July 14th as the precision raid took place; casualty reports varied from 80 – 200 killed, with the target left blazing and awesome destruction. The camp was abandoned two days later – when the SS left for good.

Tracked down by a post-war SAS team known as 'The Secret Hunters', a number of German perpetrators of the *'Bulbasket'* massacre were convicted by a War-crimes Tribunal. Two were sentenced to death by hanging and long terms of imprisonment imposed on others. On review, however, all the sentences were reduced – the longest served was five years. No hangings were carried out.

Memorials and burial sites at Verrieres, Saint-Sauvant and

Rom are still honoured. In July 1994, fifty years on, commemorative ceremonies, attended by representatives of local Resistance fighters, the United States Air Force, and the British and French armies, were held at Verrieres and Rom.

Auxiliers were conditioned to expect no mercy if captured after a successful German invasion of Great Britain – indeed they were instructed to prevent their wounded from falling into enemy hands. If proof were needed of the foresight of that training, it was abundant enough with 'Operation Bulbasket' – an innovative adventure and so nearly a success, but destined nevertheless to enter the records as one of the most tragic WWII actions involving the SAS, and its nucleus of Auxiliers

★   ★   ★

Timetable of Events:

(compiled from published sources and individuals' personal accounts. Where dates or numbers are uncertain, the most probable are given)

1944

5th June	Captain Tonkin's advance party.
11th June	Main party arrives. Special targets ('Lot 4') assigned to Peter Weaver and Corporal Kinnivane.
15th June	RAF Mosquito strike on Chatellerault sidings.
17th June	Jeeps dropped successfully by parachute.
25th June	Main camp established in Verrieres Forest.
2nd July	Milice succeed in identifying the camp. Sam Smith and his two colleagues leave on a sabotage mission
3rd July	SS troops attack Verrieres. Twm Stephens and seven Maquisards killed. Three more SAS Troopers wounded and thirty-three captured.
6th or 7th July	SAS troopers executed.
13th July(?)	Three wounded troopers killed by lethal injection.
14th July	Reprisal RAF Mosquito attack on SS barracks.
6th/7th August	Evacuation of survivors by air.
December	Mass grave discovered.

Two Memorial trees have been planted at Coleshill.

No. 1, an oak tree – is dedicated to the memory of Alan George Ashley, aged 24. A member of Auxiliary Units (Dorsetshire Regiment), trained at Coleshill, and 1st SAS Regiment ('A' Troop, 'B' Squadron) who was executed on 7th July 1944 in the Forest of Saint Sauvant, France, whilst in action behind enemy lines on Operation *Bulbasket*.

No. 6, a beech tree – is dedicated to the memory of Henry James ('Sam') Pascoe, aged 28. A member of Auxiliary Units (Dorsetshire Regiment) and 1st SAS Regiment ('A' Troop – 'B' Squadron) who was wounded and captured whilst in action behind enemy lines on Operation *Bulbasket* on 3rd July 1944 in Verrieres Forest, France. He was hospitalised at Poitiers and executed by lethal injection on 8th July 1944. Resting place unknown.

Remembered with Love and Pride by his family.

★　　★　　★

These dedications are recorded in the Memorial Book at Coleshill Estate Office. Each is written in calligraphic script and illuminated in colour with the regimental badges of the Dorsetshire Regiment and the Winged Sword emblem of the SAS

★　　★　　★

Trooper George ('Biff') Biffin

'...George Biffin disappeared when he parachuted into the town square at Airvault with Corporal Kinnivane's party.'

('Operation *Bulbasket*', p 185)

Here is Trooper George Biffin's own recollection.

Soon after the outbreak of war, aged 21, he joined his County Regiment, the 5th Dorsets (No: 5727819) and after initial training volunteered for the Auxiliary Units, serving under Peter Weaver in the Scout Section. Early in 1944, with invasion no longer a probability, he volunteered for the SAS and was posted to 'A' Troop, 'B' Squadron, 1st SAS for 'Operation *Bulbasket*'.

During the night of 10/11 June 1944, together with Joe Ogg and Henry Pascoe, George was dropped from an RAF Stirling aircraft with a 'stick' commanded by desert veteran Corporal Kinnivane – an independent unit tasked to destroy a vital section of railway line before joining Captain Tonkin and the main party. However, the drop was delayed when their aircraft was caught by searchlights and anti-aircraft fire. After missing the assigned DZ, they parachuted – unintentionally – *into* the village of Airvault, which was heavily garrisoned by German soldiers. George managed to steer clear of a river, landing in a private garden and losing touch with his comrades – who miraculously escaped unharmed from unscheduled landings in the town square.

Hearing shouts, he quickly released his parachute harness and grabbed the kit-bag containing his essential supplies. He hid his parachute, avoided a patrol and moved cautiously away. George was soon forced to chance crossing a bridge, but a sentry saw him and fired. After a struggle, he was captured by a section of German soldiers.

Although handled roughly, he was not otherwise initially maltreated, and answered questioning about his unit, and the purpose of the explosives in his kit bag, with only his name, rank and number. Frustrated, an officer moved behind him during interrogation, inserted a stick – or bar – through his camouflage neckerchief and twisted it until George passed out, asphyxiated. Dragged to his feet as he came to, George still refused to answer operational questions and the treatment was repeated.   He lost count of the number of times he was throttled but, when he finally recovered consciousness, he was alone in a locked room.

The same officer eventually returned and said :–

'Biffin. You have got yourself into a difficult situation but we have no quarrel with you. If you want to get away, now is your chance!'

He unlocked the window and left the room, closing the door behind him. George moved to escape but saw an armed sentry hiding behind a bush outside. Fearing a trap, he waited to see if the sentry moved away, but the officer returned first, re-locked the window and told George he might live to regret not making the most of the opportunity. However, had he done so, he would probably have been shot 'attempting to escape' – with the German officer then excused responsibility for deciding whether to execute him or not. George still refused to answer questions and, although his captors seemed uncertain whether to shoot him or not, he was not tortured again.

Prison conditions were foul, but his morale was raised when a friendly prison officer gave him cigarettes – and they talked together of happy pre-war days in England. French prisoners also lifted his spirits, singing the 'Marseillaise' during exercise breaks. In due course, as he was a parachutist, the Wehrmacht decided to hand him over to the Luftwaffe. An officer came into his cell and said:

> 'So you are the man the SS are looking for. If they find you, you know what will happen! You will stand a better chance without these.'

He cut off George's shoulder tags and SAS wings and told him, if questioned, to claim he had been captured during the battle for Normandy. Things were slowly moving his way until, on a journey with German guards and other PoWs, their truck was strafed by machine gun and cannon fire from 'friendly' aircraft. Badly injured in the left shoulder and leg, George survived, although the lorry was wrecked and most of the others killed. After a gradual recovery from his wounds, he was sent to PoW Stalag 9C to work in a salt mine.

The front line moved nearer in the early summer of 1945 and, as gunfire was heard, the prisoners were marched away towards the Harz mountains. Conditions were severe and the food inadequate in quantity and quality. At one stage they refused to go on – until guards fired shots in the air. When they reached the Bavarian Alps, their captors disappeared and the PoWs were soon liberated by the advancing American Rainbow Division.

George Biffin's parents had been notified their son was dead – 'Killed in Action'. This was later amended to 'Missing – believed Killed in Action'. They remained unaware of his survival until he sent them a telegram, (delivered by a telegram boy with pillbox hat, and riding a bicycle) and, at first, they were too apprehensive to open it. George was soon flown to England for extended home leave. His wounds prevented any return SAS duty and he was eventually *demobilised from an infantry regiment at Bedford.*

That appeared to be the end of George Biffin's war.

Having been parachuted at night, on active service into a foreign country occupied by a ruthless enemy, he was captured within a few hours and brutally interrogated. Avoiding a stratagem to shoot him while 'attempting to escape', he was then seriously injured by 'friendly fire', before enduring further hardship as a Prisoner of War. Partly by a change of regimental identity, he avoided inquisitors from the SS. This was of later significance.

Although routinely demobilised in due course, it was as a

regimental soldier and not an SAS Trooper. Although the SAS was aware he had survived, due to administrative confusion George slipped through research nets when Operation Bulbasket was released to Public Record Office in the mid-1990s. Indignation was evident when it appeared he might still be 'Missing in Action' and unaccounted for.

He was not in fact 'missing' in any sense other than administratively. Indeed he was living quietly on the Hampshire/Dorset border and now, aged 81, he is proud to record his time in both the Special Air Service and Auxiliary Units.

The final drama of his many adventures is that he never came to notice until half a century after he was reported to have disappeared!

It is gratifying to have this opportunity to contribute to his true story.

CHAPTER TWELVE

Auxiliary Units & Special Forces

With special material provided by Cyril Hall and Geoff Bradford

'The legion of the faceless ones who died in the Allied cause may never, alas, be counted – except – one hopes – in a better world. The Valhalla of the unsung heroes. There were many of them.'
(Donald Hamilton-Hill, '*SOE Assignment*')

In a description of service in the Special Operations Executive (SOE), Donald Hamilton-Hill wrote:

'SOE was the cover name given in 1940 to an amalgamation of organisations which directly, or indirectly, and subject to British Cabinet control, operated eventually in virtually any enemy occupied and many unoccupied territories throughout the world. Its function included every conceivable form of military, para-military and economic activity which would assist Britain and their Allies in defeating Germany and their Axis Satellites.

'Assassination, sabotage, prisoner-of-war escape routes, female seduction, sophisticated blackmail, resistance armies build-up, gun-running by parachute drops, by land, by sea, forgery, currency deals and the making – and sometimes breaking – of foreign leaders and even governments. Such were some of the headings on files marked Most Secret in the various Country Sections within SOE Headquarters spread round the world.'

A serving officer in the Queens Own Cameron Highlanders, Captain Donald Hamilton-Hill was called to Whitehall Place on 13th July 1940 to be briefed as an Auxunit Intelligence Officer by Colin Gubbins and Peter Wilkinson. Stuart Edmundson went to Devon and Cornwall from the same meeting. Donald Hamilton-Hill was allocated Lincolnshire – from the Humber to the Wash.

At the end of 1941 – before becoming operational himself – he was absorbed into SOE by Colin Gubbins, then Chief of Operations, as second-in-command, SOE training schools. He served in Tunisia, Sicily, Italy and on the island of Vis, off the

Dalmation coast, a joint Allied-Partisan fortress and the launch pad for a number of raids against neighbouring German-held islands. They successfully diverted Wehrmacht forces trying to eliminate Marshall Tito, the effective Yugoslav partisan leader, and his British mission. Hamilton-Hill then went to Greece as second-in-command of the Force which liberated Athens and Salonika.

He survived the War and settled in Kenya.

★ ★ ★

In research for his book – '*Fire from the Forest*' – on the SAS at war in France at the time of 'D' Day, writer Roger Ford concluded that the approach for Auxunits' recruits into the SAS was not a haphazard affair:

> '...though no record of such a system being in place has ever been discovered. There is certainly a mysterious element here, and after more than a half-century, during which it seems that all the documents in question have been destroyed, and memories have dimmed, it is impossible to be entirely sure of the facts of the matter.'

This certainly fits with much of the rest of Auxunits' history.

Nevertheless, Roger Ford must have been very close indeed to those facts when he found (from Otway's '*Airborne Forces*') that some three or four hundred former Auxiliers had joined the SAS in 1943 and 1944. This disproportionately large number is recognition of the special skills which both civilian Auxiliers and regulars of all ranks had acquired.

Moreover, they were called to volunteer for the SAS at a time when, under Colonel 'Paddy' Mayne (a heroic figurehead who, like Mike Calvert and many other WWII mavericks, is said to have been unfairly deprived of adequate recognition) was seeking to get the Brigade up to strength before the cross-channel assault on fortress Europe.

Apparently, there were four paths for recruitment. One was informal – when Auxunit officers learned of the SAS search and stepped forward after returning to their regiment. One belief is that Colonel Mayne visited Coleshill as well looking for officer material. The next to be targeted were former Intelligence Officers and personnel from the Scout Sections who, since 1943 had been returned to their regiments. Officers were addressed in the Curzon Cinema in London's Mayfair in March 1944 and other ranks at the (long requistioned) Grosvenor House Hotel in Park Lane. Having described the role and needs of the SAS, volunteers were called for and – as 'Tiny' Kidner of the West Dorset Scout Section was to say many years later – 'it would have taken real guts to remain seated!'

The final call was upon Auxiliers rather than regular soldiers. It is not clear whether, during 1943 and 1944, suitable men were called to volunteer while still with Auxunits – and then had their exemption from military service lifted, or were deliberately singled out as 'volunteers' *afterwards*. In any case several hundred former Auxiliers (including John Fielding and Len Edwards) were assembled over a period in a camp at Northampton for assessment and, after selection processes, many were invited to volunteer for special forces, including the Special Air Service.

★　　★　　★

In early Auxunits' days, regular soldiers of the Dorset and Wiltshire Scout Section trained local operational patrols in the western half of Dorset and part of Wiltshire. Early in 1944, after 'Paddy' Mayne's Grosvenor House Hotel session, eight volunteers from the Section were accepted for the SAS Regiment and posted to 'B' Troop, 'B' Squadron, 1 SAS. They were:

Private C. ('Dusty') Beckford
Private Leonard Blackwell
Private Jack Blandford
Corporal Bob Burgin
Private Roy Handford
Private Charles Stark
Private Lionel Stoneham
Private Jack Straker

Monmouthshire Auxilier, Private Fred Rowe, was in the same Troop.

The Dorset and Wiltshire Scout Section Officer, Captain Geoffrey Brain, also a volunteer, joined a secret GHQ Reconnaissance Regiment, code named 'Phantom'.

'B' Troop and the remainder of 'B' Squadron, six officers and forty-six other ranks in all, were employed in 'Operation *Haggard*' which – like *'Bulbasket'* – was intended to delay the movement of German armed forces toward Normandy. The start date, initially put back because SOE feared reprisals against the local population, was the 10th August 1944, when an advance party dropped by parachute between Gien and Nevers, near the River Loire. They were met by a reception

committee from the local Resistance, who reported a large
number of German troops passing through, but only a few
garrisoned in the area. This provided excellent opportunities
for operations.

The main party parachuted in on 14th August and a base was
established in the Forest of Ivoy, north of Bourges; later the
remainder of 'B' Squadron was dropped near Villequiers, south
of the main base, to sabotage roads leading to the east, toward
which American troops were already advancing. From the 21st
August, for more than thirty days, the SAS carried out
successful ambushes, with active co-operation from the
Maquis, killing some 120 German troops and destroying 25
vehicles – at the expense of one British casualty killed and four
wounded.

After Operation '*Haggard*', 'B' Squadron was re-equipped
with armoured Jeeps carrying 6-pounder guns, and remained
on active service in Holland, Belgium, Germany and Norway.
The former Auxiliers among them had been able to employ
their sabotage and demolition skills against the enemy with
considerable success.

★   ★   ★

Roy Bradford, born in 1916 in Barnstaple, Devon, trained pre-
war as an architect and in April 1939 – at the time of the
Munich Agreement – enlisted in the Devonshire Regiment,
Territorial Army. He was formally called up at the outbreak of
WWII. Commissioned in March 1940, Lieutenant Bradford
joined Auxunits as Scout Officer in Devon, under Stuart
Edmundson, on the 9th June 1942, before transferring to
Sussex in February 1943. Promoted to Captain, he took over
as Intelligence Officer there on 16th August 1943 before joining
'A' Squadron, 1 SAS Regiment, on 8th February 1944.

On the 21st June 1944, as part of '*Operation Houndsworth*',
Roy Bradford and his troop parachuted into the Morvan area
of France, a wilderness in the Nievre Departement, 150 miles
south-east of Paris. They were ordered to attack German
forces and assist the local Maquis.

On   19th July 1944, together with three of his troop,
including REME Craftsman Devine as rear-gunner and a young
Maquisard, he set off by jeep to contact a *reseau* – a group of
French partisans – north of Clamecy. On the way he diverted
to debrief Captain Chevalier, head of the local Maquis, who
was anxious to pass on important operational information. The

RAF was strafing anything seen to move, so his party avoided main roads and usually travelled by night. At about 8am on 20th July they passed through the village of Lucy-sur-Yonne, crossed a single railway line and turned right along an unmade secondary road. After a few hundred yards they came face to face with a German officer and NCO on foot. Not realising they were British, the officer signalled them to halt – and dived for cover as the SAS opened fire. A few yards further on they ran into a stationary German convoy of considerable size, with troops breakfasting on either side of the road.

Too late to turn back, they shot their way through, soon coming under heavy return fire from troops in the trucks and on foot. As they were passing the last truck of the convoy, a burst of Spandau light machine gun fire hit the jeep, killing Roy Bradford and Craftsman Devine and wounding Sergeant White and the Maquisard. Round a left-hand bend, behind a wood and only just out of sight of the Germans, the damaged jeep finally broke down and came to a standstill. Hearing Germans running toward them, Sergeant C ('Maggie') McGinn, the sole unwounded survivor – after checking the dead – helped his comrades into the wood. Two adventurous days later, they made good an escape and were cared for by friends in the Maquis.

Sergeant McGinn was awarded the Military Medal. Captain Roy Bradford and Craftsman Devine are buried in carefully tended graves in the village cemetery at Crain. In 1994, on the 50th anniversary of this action, a memorial stone was erected by the local community at the place where they were killed.

The road was re-named – 'Rue du 20 Juillet 1944'.

★   ★   ★

In his book '*Somerset v Hitler*', researcher Donald Brown writes:

> 'Captain Ian Fenwick of the Kings Royal Rifle Corps, was the Intelligence Officer directly in charge of Somerset's Auxiliary Units. Winchester College knew him best as a demon bowler. From Cambridge University he went to pre-war Berlin as an honorary Attache at the British Embassy where, alongside undefined diplomatic activities he studied art.'

This description has classical hallmarks and associates Ian Fenwick, vicariously at least, with a British Secret Service network. After war was declared, he hurried home to join the elite 60th Rifles, Kings Royal Rifle Corps. On 30th June 1940:

> '2nd Lt Fenwick's entry in the Army List, noted his transfer to a specialist appointment.'

His pre-war Intelligence associations, having secured his place on the priority list, he was absorbed by Gubbins into Auxiliary Units – a fortnight before even Stuart Edmundson – and posted as Intelligence Officer, Auxiliary Units, in Somerset. Professional neighbours, Ian and Stuart also became friends and Fenwick and his wife joined the Edmundson family, on holiday in a hired cottage on the north Devon coast in the summer of 1942. During this break, Will Edmundson, (Stuart and Iris's first son – born the day before War broke out), aged three, featured with his mother in a pen and ink drawing by Ian Fenwick, already a respected cartoonist for magazines such as '*The Tatler*', '*Men Only*', '*Strand*', and '*London Opinion*'.

Both men left Auxunits for Special Forces – Stuart Edmundson to SOE and, in February 1944, Ian Fenwick to the SAS. He commanded 'D' Squadron, 1 SAS and parachuted into the Forêt de Fontainbleau, south of Pithiviers, as part of 'Operation *Gain*' on 16th June 1944. His unit was ordered to attack and disrupt German communications and railway lines in the area near Orleans. On one occasion – having successfully attacked a troop and ammunition train at night, chasing alongside in Jeeps and firing until it was burnt out – he ended his radio report to SAS HQ:

> 'We are happy in our work!'

However, on 7th August, after numerous successful operations and shortly before planned evacuation, Ian Fenwick – while visiting an SAS base to the east of Orleans – heard that German soldiers had attacked the main camp in his absence. He promptly left by Jeep on a rescue mission with his driver, a sergeant and two Maquisards, unaware that his small group of troopers, although surrounded by six hundred of the enemy for no less than seven hours, had all fought clear in a bitter battle and broken clear from what looked a certain death-trap.

Confusingly, as he approached the base, he received garbled reports that most of the troopers had been captured. A Frenchwoman also waved a warning that Germans were waiting in ambush in the next village, Chambon-la-Forêt. Fenwick, his temper roused and still hoping to rescue his men, drove on at high speed, guns ready, unaware the movements of his Jeep had been reported by a German spotter plane. He met

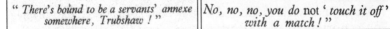

" There's bound to be a servants' annexe | No, no, no, you do not ' touch it off '
somewhere, Trubshaw ! " | *with a match ! "*

the ambush with all guns firing and was almost through the
first body of Germans when a 20mm cannon shell struck his
head. Death was instantaneous. The two Frenchmen were also
killed. His driver was concussed but escaped later.   The
sergeant – led away and presumably executed – was never
heard of again.

(In *'The Last Ditch'*, David Lampe has Ian Fenwick killed on
5th July, a dozen of his men captured, and their eventual
execution. From the sketchy information then available, he
may have confused Operations *'Gain'* and *'Bulbasket'*.)

On 1st October 1945, Stuart Edmundson on leave, was
browsing in Bhawani and Son, Stationers and Booksellers,
Connaught Place, New Delhi, when he saw a book for sale –
'Enter Trubshaw'. Recognising 'Trubshaw' as Ian Fenwick's
favoured cartoon character, he bought the book for 5 rupees,
to discover ninety-six pages of his friend's drawings – including
the one of Will and Iris Edmundson, sketched during their
Devon holiday three years earlier.

'Trubshaw', in Ian Fenwick's Acknowledgement , was a
character -

   '...immortalised by David (Niven) in the film world and by me
in the cartoon world and by himself in his own world...'

In the Preface, written before he knew of Ian Fenwick's death, the film actor David Niven had written:

'At the age of nine I played in a children's tennis tournament and was beaten 6 − 0 and retired from tennis for ever. My conqueror was Ian Fenwick. Later we became great friends and many happy summer holidays were spent by the seaside taking the corks out of people's rowing boats and smoking blotting paper up trees...'

From an appended publisher's note, Stuart read:

'It is with the very greatest regret that we have to announce, since the sending to press of this book, the death in Action of Major Ian Fenwick'.

Michael Trubshaw, a real life character and one of David Niven's friends from pre-war army days, had something of a small-part film career himself. Together with David Niven, he was in 'The Guns of Navarone', 'The Best of Enemies', and 'The Pink Panther'. He also figured in many of Ian Fenwick's drawings.

Major Fenwick is buried in the cemetery at Chambon-la-Forêt, north-east of Orleans.

A number of Ian Fenwick's cartoons are reproduced in this book. Research, so frequently hampered by dead-end leads, benefited in this case from a series of unlikely coincidences. Stuart and Ian met through unplanned, adjacent postings with Auxunits, and spent a holiday together. After duty transfers which separated them by many thousands of miles, they were not to see one another again. But Ian Fenwick did arrange to publish the Trubshaw series of drawings before he went into action in France. The odds against a volume being on sale in New Delhi, and of Stuart Edmundson being there to buy it, are too great even to imagine.

The final piece in an improbable jigsaw was Stuart's post-war UK relocation from the west country to Suffolk, a pathway which led researchers to meet him. The Museum of the British Resistance Organisation wishes to record special gratitude to his sons, Will and Marcus, for loaning the original 'Enter Trubshaw', and their continued support for the Museum which Lt-Col. J W Stuart Edmundson, TD, opened in August 1997.

★   ★   ★

A famous photograph in David Lampe's 'The Last Ditch' − taken at Auxiliary Units' HQ at Coleshill under Colonel C R ('Bill') Major − shows the staff and his Intelligence Officers.

Standing alongside Ian Fenwick – looking equally youthful – was (then) Captain Charles Frederick Gordon ('Dick') Bond.

Dick Bond was born in 1912 and at the outset of WWII served in the Wiltshire Regiment, before joining Auxiliary Units as Intelligence Officer for the Sussex Area from October 1941 to July 1942. He was promoted Temporary Major, probably as an Auxiliary Units Special Duties Section Intelligence Officer, before commanding 'B' Squadron, 1 SAS, in 'Operation Howard', one of the final operations of the NW Europe campaign. In April 1944, his unit reconnoitred toward the German town of Oldenburg ahead of the Canadian 4th Armoured Division.

On 10th April, in the closing stages of the war – not expecting real opposition and failing to appreciate the extra danger of ambush once on German soil – the leading Jeeps came under heavy fire from nearby houses as they approached the small town of Burgerwald. Pinned down, the crews dismounted and took cover in a ditch. The remainder of the Squadron came to a halt and Major Bond and his driver moved forward to reconnoitre, using the ditch as cover. While crawling over a culvert, they were exposed to sniper fire.

Both were killed – probably the last SAS casualties before VE day.

Major 'Dick' Bond is buried in the large war cemetery at Sage, near Oldenburg, Germany.

★   ★   ★

'I certainly thank God I was one of the lucky ones to be spared against the terrible acts of War'.

(Company Sergeant Major Cyril Hall)

Burma – Jungle Town 1944, the Second 'Chindit' Long-Range Jungle Penetration.

Cyril Hall was brought up in Huntingdonshire. Conscripted into the Suffolk Regiment soon after the outbreak of WWII, his initial training was at Gibraltar Barracks, Bury St Edmunds. After promotion, he volunteered for GHQ Auxiliary Units, joining the Scout Section at the Mill Houe, Cransford, near Framlingham under Lieutenant 'Mac' McIntyre and time-serving Sergeant Jack Steward.

'Geoff Bowery was there too, and so were 'Slogger' Leach, Ralph Bailey, Oliver Bloomfield and Joe Middleditch. I well remember training specially selected local men, exempted from conscription – a fine group of crafty country lads prepared to put the nation before their own lives. I was proud to help train them for warfare behind enemy lines.'

In mid-1942, Cyril Hall was first re-drafted to West Africa. With his third stripe, he joined the 12th Battalion, 81st West African Division, 3rd West African Brigade, Nigerian Regiment. The next transfer was to India where, in 1944, the Nigerian Regiment prepared to enter the Japanese held Burmese jungle with the second long-range 'Chindit' penetration, commanded by Major General Orde Wingate and Brigadier Mike Calvert. His company was trained to handle mules – vital supply carriers but 'reluctant aviators'.

'In the cool of the evening of April 4th, I gathered my group of eight Africans and four mules waiting for the Dakota pilot. Half and hour later he walked over and said – "Who's ready? Where's it to be boys – White City via Aberdeen?"'

These code names were airstrips more than 150 miles inside Burma, cut from the jungle by the first invasion armada, volunteers from a dozen regiments and US Gliderborne Engineers. Cyril Hall – taking troops, mules and equipment in support – was in the second wave:

'The pilot gave his instructions – "Get those mules in first and make 'em happy. The rest of you get behind their crates, equal numbers each side to balance the ship".
None of the Africans had been inside a plane before. Neither had the mules. Nor had Cyril Hall!
'Two hours later, with No.1 Air Commando, USAAF, we were over 'Aberdeen'. Small lights were shining below like Piccadilly Circus. We bumped down on the rough strip, disembarked in one piece, and soon disappeared into the night to bivouac. The Japs were around somewhere. The next morning a reconnaissance patrol returned with orders to move to the 'White City' – which should have been called 'Red City' from the amount of blood that flowed there. It was a fortified road-block straddling the Japs main line of communication.
'To get there we had to cross a mile of open paddy covered by Jap machine guns. As we approached we heard the drone of approaching aircraft. It was our fighting boys of the RAF, six heavy bombers and nine fighters. They came in low on smoke markers laid by our mortars. The fighters let go 50-pound eggs and the bombers dropped parachute-retarded Bunker-Busters. It was a gift from heaven and kept Johnny Jap's head down as our column arrived.
'This campaign was nothing less than terrible. We were fighting

two enemies, the Japanese and the natural elements of the jungle, especially the dreadful monsoon rain.'

Fighting was continuous, violent and bloody. In the first Chindit raid, morale had suffered as British wounded were shot rather than remain abandoned to a cruel enemy. Now they could sometimes be evacuated by air – also their only means of re-supply. Early in May they received the long awaited order to abandon 'White City' and on the 10th, forty Dakotas flew in to land within a mile of Japanese positions and start the evacuation. The Japanese threw everything at them:

'The other enemy had fallen on us as well – driving Monsoon rains that turned tracks into leach-laden streams. After very heavy going, attacking and killing Jap patrols on the way, we arrived at a pre-arranged RV. Here we were ambushed by the enemy but drove them out...'

'When the ambush took place we were moving along a track through treacherous monsoon jungle. Several shots were fired and we halted and moved off the track and into the jungle. Sharpened bamboo panji sticks had been concealed at the side. One ripped a jagged hole in my thigh.

'After several days, the area of the wound was inflamed and sore. I had difficulty walking but had to push forward: it was a case of *survival.*'

Cyril Hall eventually arrived at a jungle airstrip which looked no more than 200 yards long. An American L5 pilot 'just dropped in' and picked him up. At a larger strip he was transferred to a Dakota and then to a base hospital back in India.

'At this time everyone was suffering from some sort of fever or illness because of the terrible monsoon conditions. I not only had my leg wound, which now looked like a piece of raw, stinking meat, but was full of fever, had sores on my feet, and a very painful right ear, where several abscesses had formed.'

He has nothing but praise for the RAF and US aircrew who supported the ground units, and particularly the US Air Commandos who flew out the wounded, as they claimed – 'Any time, any place'. He remembers the Nigerian soldiers too – 'valiant fighters and real comrades-in-arms'.

A post war medical board back in England, judged that Cyril had made a full recovery. That was not strictly true and his war wound still proves troublesome. Finally awarded a 40% disability pension after protracted claims in later life, this was reduced to 30% when he was eighty, in inverse ratio to his mobility and increasing need.

Not a man easily dispirited, however, he is in no doubt that his service and training with Auxiliary Units made a major contribution to his survival in combat.

> 'Although beating both the Japanese and the jungle, we felt forgotten at times – natural enough, I suppose, when we were unceremoniously dumped in a jungle clearing miles from base.'

Just like 'Highworth Fertilisers', he 'did his stuff unseen'.

'Lest we Ever Forget' by Cyril Hall

Why do you march old man, with medals on your chest?

Why do you grieve, old man, for the Friends
you laid to rest?

Why do your eyes still gleam, old man, when you
hear the bugles blow?

Tell me, 'Why do you cry, old man, for those
days so long ago?'

I'll tell you why I march with medals on my chest,

I'll tell you why I grieve, young man, for those
I laid to rest,

Through Burmese jungles of thickened growth
come visions of distant times,

When the boys of tender age moved forth to
distant places,

We buried them in shallow graves clothed in their
lightweight blanket,

Their young flesh shattered and blackened,

A communal grave with no record made,

Gouged in blood-stained jungle growth.

And you ask me why I march, young man,
I march to remind you all –

That but for those apple-blossomed youths,
You'd never have known freedom at all.

Don't ever forget, they did it for you!

CHAPTER THIRTEEN

Auxiliary Units, Special Duties Section

TOP SECRET & PERSONAL

The SPECIAL DUTIES Branch of AUXILIARY UNITS is organised to provide information for military formations in the event of enemy invasion or raids in GREAT BRITAIN, from areas temporarily or permanently in enemy control.

'All this information would be collected as a result of direct observation by specially recruited and trained civilians, who would remain in an enemy occupied area.'

C/o GPO Highworth
R M A Jones, Major
28 June 1944
Commander Aux.Units Sigs

★   ★   ★

David Lampe claimed in 'The Last Ditch' that Colonel 'Bill' Major, during his fifteen months as Commanding Officer, Auxiliary Units, created a second organisation with 'an entirely different purpose and entirely unknown to the Patrols'.

This was again only partly true. Unlike the operational Patrols, with a stage by stage evolutionary development from an MI(R) blueprint, the Special Duties Branch (more properly known as the Special duties Section) arrived within Auxiliary Units as a package, complete and ready to go, several months before Colonel Major took over. The best secret services plan well ahead and one authoritative spokesperson insists that 'sleepers' – that is enrolled agents waiting to be called – were in place before the war. However, it was certainly true that,

below the level of Group Commander and Key Man
respectively, operational patrols and SDS 'coast watchers' acted
independently and were unknown to one another.

The men and women of the SDS operated as civilian spies,
'observers', 'coast watchers' or agents, and not (after a false
start) as armed guerrillas. Although created as a saboteur force
to a format not dissimilar from the operational patrols, it was
not in the event how they would go to their secret war, which
was to collect and communicate intelligence about the
occupying enemy.

A different origin from the patrols is clearly indicated. The
SDS was very specially Top Secret and, as far as can be
discovered, the classification, although outdated, has never
been downgraded. Even less detail has been released from
official records – and that apparently in error – than for the
operational patrols, and information about them is still
unnaturally restricted. 'The Last Ditch' does have a partial,
and therefore defective, SDS summary, but includes no
acknowledgement, for instance, of Major Maurice Petherick,
who according to Brigadier Geoffrey Beyts was the 'genius
behind Special Duties'.

Researchers are confronted with little in print, the restricted
release of official archives, and a provocative lack of frankness
from Government departments – still sheltering behind an
imbroglio of secrecy. The Ministry of Defence still insists that:

> '...the high level of secrecy surrounding these (Auxiliary) units
> militated against the survival of official policy papers...'

Although this is taken as indicating that no further disclosures
can be anticipated, the wording avoids an all-important issue –
whether all Auxunit records have or have not been officially
destroyed. This evasive tactic certainly keeps interested
researchers in investigative mode.

Only a few SDS agents survive to provide eyewitness
evidence. Having been recruited mainly from the already
middle-aged, they were, man for man, older than the Patrols.
Most have now passed over to the Great Secret Intelligence
Service-in-the-Sky. Is it realistic to suggest that – when Cabinet
Office agreed in 1992 there should be 'no residual (National
Security) sensitivity' in respect of the British Resistance
Organisation – some smart Whitehall archivist thought they
were all dead? If so, even with access to the nominal roll – and
as the SDS all received a formal letter of stand-down in 1944 a
full SDS list of names must once have existed – he was wrong.

Some of the fortunate few, today's survivors, consider themselves free to tell discreetly 'self-edited' memories; others honour a commitment to six decades of secrecy, and still decline to come forward. Museum policy is to respect both points of view. One Norfolk lady telephoned to support applications by Auxiliers for the WWII Defence Medal. Tempted though she must have been to emerge into the open, perhaps even join former colleagues at reunions, she resolutely insisted on anonymity – identifying herself only as 'BOWLING FOUR'. It is no secret that the SDS radio network in Norfolk used the 'BOWLING' call sign.

The SDS was already an up-and-running cadre as war broke out in September 1939. It was not a product of Colonel Holland's think-tank although – according to SOE records – MI(R) already had authority to organise the 'collection of information by special means outside the province of other sections of the Military Intelligence Directorate'. These terms of reference would soon accommodate an essential change in the management and structure of the SDS as originally assembled.

With a common 'stay-behind' purpose, more than a thousand hurriedly recruited and partly trained agents were handed over during the summer of 1940 and absorbed into Auxiliary Units under the Commanding Officer at Coleshill for administration, co-ordination and future expansion. Major Nigel Oxenden, in 'History and Achievement', writes about weekly meetings of operational Patrols' Intelligence Officers at Whitehall Place in a paragraph headed 'Formation':

> 'On one occasion in July (1940) they found themselves with an equal number of strangers, officers and civilians, and even a woman. "You may as well get to know each other, gentlemen; you are all in the same game." This was the first contact between Ops and Special Duties, and was the last they were to see of one another for some time.'

Analysis would be pointless without considering the SDS genesis, but no sign is evident that any person at the baptismal ceremony wants to stand up and talk about the great day. 'Bill' Major was apparently willing to do so to David Lampe, although he was not actually there. This smacks less of those units working under the Director of Military Intelligence – such as MI(R) and the associated propaganda and deception agencies later amalgamated to become SOE – and more of long-term, professional secret services.

The finger of suspicion points firmly at MI6, normally

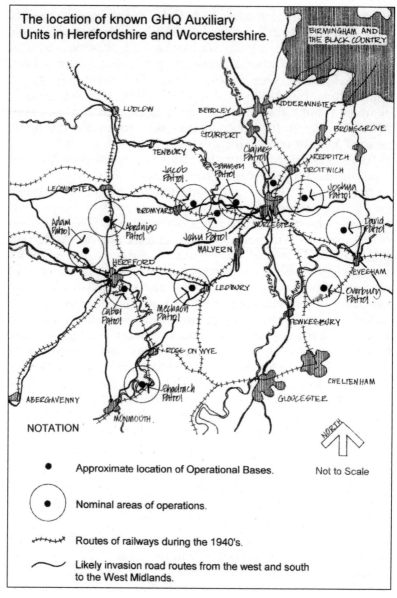

The location of known GHQ Auxiliary Units in Herefordshire and Worcestershire.

BIRMINGHAM AND THE BLACK COUNTRY

NOTATION

● Approximate location of Operational Bases.

Not to Scale

◉ Nominal areas of operations.

⌁⌁⌁ Routes of railways during the 1940's.

〜 Likely invasion road routes from the west and south to the West Midlands.

responsible for secret Intelligence operations overseas. Coming broadly under Foreign Office for finance and strategy, it was decided that occupied Great Britain should be regarded as overseas.

With new units appearing daily during the Dunkirk evacuation, all with urgent priorities in a national crisis for survival, some overlap, some changes to hitherto forbidden terms of reference, were reluctantly accepted by established departments as new operational guidelines proliferated. In a quiet reorganisational reshuffle, the Special Duties Section had to be orchestrated within emergency defence plans – and Colin Gubbins's Auxiliary Units, with existing access to GHQ, were ready-made as a front. Their subsequent significance to GHQ can often be detected and, even as breathing space was created when Hitler postponed Operation 'Sealion', the SDS continued to expand.

Some clues are discernible on the origin and pre-packaged status of the SDS, from a civilian network known as the 'Home Defence Organisation' – created by 'D' Section of the Secret Intelligence Service (first known as Section IX) under (then) Major Lawrence Grand, RE, after his secondment in 1938 to Admiral Sir Hugh Sinclair, KCB, then Chief of MI6, and originally housed in his HQ at 54, Broadway, London, SW1 before expansion and transfer to Caxton House, SW1 in April 1939. Enduring secrecy is a certain SIS trademark. For example, when SOE disbanded soon after 'VJ' (Victory over Japan) Day, their records were promptly absorbed by MI6 and a number of secrets gradually drip-fed to the public through selected authors and institutions. But not when they were of significance to the Secret Intelligence Service itself, who work to the watchword that:

'...to be effective a secret service must remain secret...'

– a bloodstained rule that is never negotiable. And 'never' means 'never ever'. Little doubt remains that the records of Auxiliary Units' Special Duties Section received the same treatment.

Another clue to the origin of Auxunits SDS comes with its radio communications – highly sophisticated for the agents and completely absent for operational Patrols. (Although rumours hint that some Patrols' OBs were linked to a radio network, not a single eyewitness has positive corroboration.) A complex and efficient communications system was soon on tap for the SDS from a technical specification drawn up early in the 1930s. The work of 'D' Section of MI6, according to SOE records, included:

'...Research...into other paths, such as the use of free balloons and the development of secure R/T, which had no future in SOE.'

Not only had an innovative transceiver blueprint been developed for Section 'D', it had the unique advantage of voice transmission (Radio/Telephony) and not slow-witted,

conventional Morse Code (Wireless/Telegraphy) used world
wide by the SIS itself. Following a systems 'break-though', a
technique known as the 'quench' principle ensured high-level
security. This dispensed with laborious and time-consuming
cryptography but, to make doubly sure, 'Bill' Major described
to David Lampe how his 'friend' developed an everyday code
for SDS use as well.

At the end of the war, with recognisably MI6 fingerprints, all
the sets were put beyond further use, and knowledge evaded,
avoided or denied by likely agencies. It would greatly stretch
the imagination to suggest that the secure R/T used by the
Special Duties Section under the (later) identifying acronym
'TRD', did not originate from that developed by Section 'D'.
While any old 'buff' will tell you all about it and make
confident promises to produce a set to display in the Museum,
once they have actually gone away to look for it they are never
heard from again.

At the end of the war they were all put beyond further use.
Not a single 'TRD' has been found.

★   ★   ★

Thanks to recent research in Public Record Office, many of the
mysteries surrounding the origin of Auxiliary Units' Special
Duties Section are less unclear now than ever before.

'D' (standing for 'Destruction') Section of MI6 had a
number of world wide responsibilities. As far as civilian 'stay-
behinds' in Great Britain were concerned, their project known
as 'D' Home Defence Organisation, was coded 'D/Y' and, after
a pilot scheme, went fully into action at the beginning of June
1940 under Winston Churchill's premiership and directly after
the Dunkirk evacuation.

Because of the difficulties experienced in setting up similar
organisations in territory already occupied by the enemy, it
was considered essential to prepare well in advance of
invasion. The D/Y organisation was based on the concept that
in homeland areas where British forces had been 'fought out',
a civilian leader would be waiting to co-ordinate underground
civilian resistance. This organisation, energetically created in
about seven weeks, depended upon comparatively tranquil
conditions behind the front lines and the cessation of fighting
resistance in the prepared areas.

The civilians were selected by 'Regional Officers' of Section
'D', attached to Regional Commissioners, through whom
introductions were arranged with chief constables,

universities, landowners, aristocrats, and the Church, in a fashion not dissimilar to that employed more or less simultaneously by MI(R) and the operational Auxiliary Units. Men and women were sought who would have very good reason, as civilians, to 'stay put' and attempt to carry out their normal life so far as their everyday work permitted, either in the country or in towns. Here was a significant initial difference with the Auxiliary Units patrols, which were overwhelmingly rural in concept.

'D/Y' envisaged comparatively tranquil conditions in enemy occupied territory, with their operations organised on a one off basis by selected 'Key-men':–

> '...who, by virtue of their local standing, could instil confidence and courage into that part of the civilian population which may still be alive after the battle has swept beyond them.'

Key-men knew the country well and were usually too prominent to be expected to take part in operations themselves, but assisted the enlistment of men and women who would. They knew the 'whole story' and helped Regional Officers to train and educate their agents and runners.

Regional Officers left London – well ahead of the Auxiliary Units – on 7th June 1940. By 16th June every region except London had been covered and introductions arranged to choose civilians and teach them means of 'Obstruction', the euphemism employed for sabotage activity – mainly by the use of incendiaries rather than explosives. By the 22nd July 1940, nearly 200 Key-men had been appointed and 1,000 dumps of material placed, including 1,000 bottles of sulphuric acid and enough petrol and paraffin to build 45,000 petrol bombs. The secret location of these 'dumps' was known only to the Regional Officer, his Key-man, and the dump owner himself. Those who were intended to carry out the 'Obstruction' were chosen from quarrymen and colliers with previous explosives experience, rather than personnel who needed to be trained.

Section 'D' operations were regarded as 'unavowable' and they looked upon the development of the 'Home Guard' patrols as comparatively overt. They certainly differed in concept. As the two units were to work in identical areas, Auxunits programme of continuous harassment was seen by Section 'D' as likely both to provoke reprisals against the local population and be counterproductive to the 'tranquil' conditions within which they intended to mount their own 'obstructions'. Moreover, Section 'D' was directly coordinated with military requirements, whereas Auxiliary Units' patrols – apart from some intermittemt contact through their Intelligence Officer – would be acting entirely as mavericks against targets of their own choice.

This operational overlap was immediately taken on board by Colonel Holland's newly formed Inter-Services Projects Board and on 14th July 1940 the stay-behind organisation imaginatively created by Section 'D' was withdrawn (effectively from 19th July) as a combatant force of guerrillas, their 'dumps' collected, forgotten about, or more usually assimilated with those of the ascendant Auxiliary Units' operational patrols, and the Key-men and their agents left temporarily in limbo until a new role was developed for them within the existing Auxunits' administration.   Unfortunately, the new head of the Secret Intelligence Service was not to hear about this for three weeks. He was not pleased. On 21st July 1940 – probably because he was a recipient of the transcripts of German messages coded on 'Enigma' machines' – he was, however, reassured that the military situation had so far improved that invasion was now unlikely.   Section 'D' themselves seem to have taken it all well – probably realising that their new role, largely within the burgeoning new Special Operations Executive, was likely to have a greater part to play in the war than the patrols of Auxiliary Units. They did decide, however, that:

> 'While obstructive activities of the 'D' Organisation are being gradually transferred to GHQ Auxiliary Units, it is considered necessary and desirable by GHQ and CSS (Chief of the Secret Service) *that the Intelligence side of the activities should be maintained and developed* (Editor's italics).

This role had already been outlined by Colonel Gubbins as 'the other side'. The Section 'D' network – formally transferred on 16th August 1940 – was reconstituted as an Intelligence gathering and communications network and, as such, the 'D/Y' civilian men and women recruits were retrained as spies, supplied with radio communications, given a protective security cover of cellular secrecy, and co-opted as non-combatants into a new Section of the Auxiliary Units. As the Special Duties Section this was to expand and achieve the highest standard of excellence in areas where invasion was a potential – and to do so entirely separately from their operational comrades and unknown to the men in the patrols.

No evidence has been found to explain how the transition of the powers-that-be took place from Section 'D' Regional

Officers to Auxunits' SDS Intelligence Officers. It is unlikely that survivors are still there to help out but, having been seconded from the army to MI6, it is unlikely that the Regional Officers would have jumped at the chance to transfer to Auxiliary Units (and the Directorate of Military Intelligence) who were seen – even if not exactly inferior, certainly as essentially part of a different military strategy. Although some may have done so, it is clear that within eighteen months Auxunits was appointing its own SDS IOs drawn either from HQ or the operational areas – men such as 'Bill' Harston, Stuart Edmundson, Anthony Quayle and 'Dick' Bond.

The Special Duties Section, as they were now known, would have men and women observers trained to spy on the enemy and, even as early as the 4th June 1940 and before their formal demise as saboteurs, a system of runners was organised to pass on Intelligence information. Early 1941 saw the production and issue of a communications transceiver much ahead of its time – and the enemy; with technical backup from soldiers of the Auxiliary Units (Signals) – most of whom were pre-war radio 'HAMS' – all integrated within the established administration of the GHQ Auxiliary Units.

David Lampe described developments accurately:

> 'The organisation of cloak-and-dagger ancestry was now going more intensively into the cloak-and-dagger business.'

Any questions, so far?

★   ★   ★

The status of the Special Duties Section – sometimes (even officially), confusingly called the SD. 'Branch' – was spelt out by Commanding Officer, Auxiliary Units, in a paper drawn up before 'D' Day, when SHAEF trawled for underemployed active servicemen to retrain and dispatch to the Normandy beaches. Eyes fell on Coleshill where, having identified a few spare soldiers, a comprehensive available manpower report was called for. It included this summary:

Special Duties Branch.
There are 10 Areas covering the coastal belt from the North of Scotland down to, but excluding, Devon and Cornwall and including parts of South Wales. Each area is under an IO.
(a) In each area an organisation has been built up of civilians able to transmit accurate information about the enemy in event of raids or invasion.

(b) There are well above 200 R.T. stations situated throughout the coastal areas – mostly concealed underground in dugouts capable of holding three men. These stations are known as OUT Stations and are manned entirely by civilians.

(c) These OUT Stations – which are 'fed' by Sub-OUT Stations in many cases – communicate with IN Stations which are manned by Royal Signals personnel and ATS officers.

(d) IN Stations are sited in depth with an inner system established at Headquarters of Commands.

(e) There are over 3250 civilians in this organisation...

Papers concerning SDS were highly classified (usually 'MOST SECRET'). Surprisingly, the Home War Establishment at Coleshill, effective on 25th November 1943, was downgraded to a lowly 'Confidential'. It contained useful details of 'Special Duties Branch' personnel then serving at HQ:

General Staff officers, 2nd grade	4
General Staff officers, 3rd grade	1
Intelligence officers (captains)	
(maybe Intelligence Corps)	9
Clerks ATS	
(may be civilian female shorthand typists)	2
Drivers, 1st Class, RASC	14
Cook, ACC	1
Batman	1

A total of 32 staff therefore managed the affairs of the SDS. The nine 'Intelligence Officers' were the SDS IOs (later ten, then eleven) in charge of areas. Under 'NOTES' on Page 3 of the same duty-state, the Signals contingent is aggregated:

'The following additional personnel will be allowed for the special duties branch *to be filled as and when required* (Ed's italics):

(i) Personnel	
Major)	1
Captain) (R Signals)	1
Subalterns)	5
Company quarter-master-serjeant	1
Serjeants	7
Corporals	20
Signalmen	41

The Officers retained Royal Signals designation but the other ranks, most of whom were to go to 'stay-behind' stations in the event of invasion were, according to their Pay Books, attached to GHQ Auxiliary Units (Signals).

Sixty ATS personnel included the officer-in-charge, one 'Senior Commander' and fifty-six 'IN Station' subalterns and second subalterns. Finally, four Royal Engineer subalterns were 'attached' – specialists designing the ingenious radio-station OBs built by sappers.

Total personnel (under 'NOTES') were one hundred and fifty-two.

HQ for the SDS until 1942 was at Hannington Hall, a few miles from Coleshill. In command was Major Maurice Petherick (the 'genius' referred to by 'Bill' Beyts earlier), responsible to the Commander, Auxiliary Units but operating independently. He and his senior Staff Officer, Charles Randell, at first Messed with the owners of Hannington Hall, the Fry's chocolate family. Another officer there was Subaltern Barbara Culleton:

> 'When I arrived at Hannington Hall, it was as a "billetee". We shared the Fry's accommodation and food. They still had fourteen servants! Luggage was soon unpacked and our beds turned down.
>
> 'Ma and Pa Fry sat at opposite ends of the enormously long refectory table. They always dressed for dinner – so we felt we should make an effort. But a change of shirt and/or tie had to suffice.
>
> 'Normally the four of us, including Maurice Petherick, were spread out down each side of the dining table but once army rations appeared we were bunched together in the centre.
>
> 'Then came the crunch – official requisition of one wing by the Area Quartering Commandant. Out goes all the comfortable house furniture – in come iron WD bedsteads with "biscuits" (Army issue mattresses), and a fold-flat wooden chair each. With no other furniture in the bedroom where could we hang our clothes? Maurice suggested coat hangers suspended from the picture rail! My room looked like a street market at times.'

Born in October 1894, Maurice Petherick had private addresses in London and Porthpean House, St Austell, Cornwall. Educated at Marlborough and Trinity College, Cambridge, his Clubs were the United University and 'Bucks'. A National Conservative, he was Member of Parliament for Penryn and Falmouth Division, serving from October 1931 until defeated in the immediate post-war Labour landslide of 1945. He was then Financial Secretary at the War Office and High Sheriff of Cornwall. Later he was a Director of the Prudential Assurance Co. Ltd until 1971.

Maurice Petherick served in the First Royal Devon Yeomanry

in WWI but, in 1916/7 'was in the Foreign Office'. In 1939 he was re-commissioned on the General List with the rank of Major. It does not require a genius to interpret this translucent biography. His WWI service in the Foreign Office suggests that he had long standing links with our friends in MI6.

He appears on Auxunits' HQ Duty state directly after his Commander, one from the top of the pecking order:

General staff officer, 1st grade   1

The officer who briefly led the SDS into Auxunits has not been identified. Maurice Petherick was probably the second to take Command – his successor being his GSO(i), Major Charles Randell. The final SDS CO was Major Peter Forbes, promoted and brought down to Coleshill (SDS HQ having relocated from Hannington Hall in 1942) in July 1943 from operational Patrol duties in Scotland, by the Commander Auxiliary Units, then Lieutenant-Colonel Frank Douglas.

Recent correspondence with the Ministry of Defence has produced unusually well-rehearsed evasions about documentation still held in official records. It is very fortunate, therefore, that a few clues are discernible from one of the papers that did escape the shredder. Dated 1st October 1943, and headlined – 'Part II Orders (Officers) No 39, HQ, GHQ Auxiliary Units Home Forces', it provides a list of officers' names who, from 1st October 1943 to 31st March 1944, were eligible to receive HRRA – Higher Rate Ration Allowance, probably awarded because their circumstances or duties required them to eat away from the Officers' Mess. (The obvious suspicion is that thirty-eight other Part II Orders may be lurking somewhere.)

The identities of SD Intelligence Officers can be isolated with help from a couple of clues. The first is their Regiment – the six in the Intelligence Corps must be certainties and, secondly their rank – with Majors otherwise favoured over Captains and Lieutenants. This leads to a selection from:

T/Capt. F B Childe	Int.Corps
T/Capt. E R Fingland	Int. Corps
T/Major R Fraser	Int. Corps
T/Capt. J Halley	Int. Corps
T/Major K W Johnson	Int. Corps
T/Capt. G Woodward	Int. Corps
T/Major G C L Atkinson, MC.	Royal Fusiliers
T/Major C F G Bond	Wilts.

Some of the 'Bulbasket' team under Captain John Tonkin *(seated, smoking his pipe)* in the Forest of Verrieres before the SS attack. John Fielding, former Norwich Auxilier, is standing, top right. *(Paul McCue/John Fielding)*

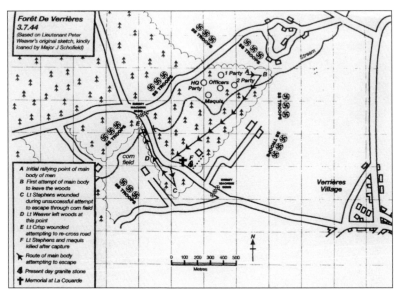

The dispositions of the SS attack on the morning of 3rd July 1944. Diagram prepared by Peter Weaver. *(Major Joe Schofield/Paul McCue)*

(top left) Trooper George Biffin, 'A' Troop, 'B' Squadron, 1 SAS. *(Credit: George Biffin)*

(top right) George Biffin in 1998 *(Mark Biffin)*

(lower left) Captain L Roy Bradford was Scout Section officer for the Devon Auxiliary Units before becoming Intelligence Officer for Sussex. Having dropped with SAS Operation 'Houndsworth' in the Morvan wilderness, Roy and REME Craftsman Devine, his rear gunner, were killed on 20th July 1944 while attacking a convoy of German soldiers. *(Geoffrey Bradford)*

In a remarkable display of airmanship by Flight Lieutenant A H C Boxer (later Air Vice-Marshal Sir Alan), fourteen *Bulbasket* survivors were evacuated from a short airstrip France on the night of 6/7th August 1944.

Soldiers from the East Dorset Auxunits' Scout Section were also volunteers for the SAS, operating with significant success behind the lines in France for 30 days in August and September 1944 in Operation *'Haggard'*. C ('Dusty') Beckford *(back row ,second from right)*, Leonard ('Blackie') Blackwell *(back row, fourth from left)*, Jack Blandford *(front row, third from left)*, Bob Burgin *(third row, third from left)*, Ron Handford *(front row, last on right)*, and Lionel Stonham *(back row, fifth from left)*, were joined by Monmouth Auxilier Fred Rowe *(third row, second from left)*. Major Joe Schofield *(front row, second from left)* now organises 'Bulbasket' reunions at Verrieres for the SAS Regimental Association.   *(Jack Blandford)*

(top left) Major Ian Fenwick, Auxunits' Intelligence Officer for Somerset, friend of David Niven and Stuart Edmundson. *(Will & Marcus Edmundson)*

(top right) Ian Fenwick at the wheel of a heavily armed SAS Jeep. *(Donald Brown collection)*

(lower left) Corporal Cyril Hall served with the Auxunits' Scout Section, Cransford, Suffolk. Promoted to Sergeant, Hall transferred to the Nigerian Rgt and fought in the 2nd Long Range Burmese jungle penetration with Brigadier Orde Wingate's 'Chindits'. Ambushed and badly wounded, he was flown to safety by the US Air Commandos. *(Cyril Hall)*

(top left) Auxunits, Special Duties Section, Jill Holman (now Jill Monk) was enlisted in 1941 as a 'runner' and travelled cross-country by night on her horse, 'Merry Monarch', to collect Intelligence messages from secret 'Dead Letter Drops' *(Jill Monk)*

(top right) Sixty years on, Jill Monk still breeds horses but now declines all invitations for adventurous night cross-country gallops. *(Ann Warwicker)*

(lower left) Dr Alec Holman, Jill's father, was 'Key Man' for the Intelligence gathering network in the Aylsham area of Norfolk, organised by John Collings. Dr Holman is seen here with his wife, the 'cypher queen'. *(Jill Monk)*

Mark, John Collings' 'War Dog Hero', is pictured here training with British soldiers at Inverailort. *(Captain Ken Ward)*

John and Ann Fielding at their Norwich home in 2001 *(Ann Warwicker)*

Bachelor's Hall at Hundon, Suffolk, where the first Auxunits (Signals) radio workshop was established early in 1941 – in spite of the absence of electricity.
(East Anglian Daily Times)

Captain Ken Ward *(top left)*, a Member of the Institute of Electrical Engineers, who served as a radio communications specialist with the Royal Signals and Auxiliary Units. He and his wife Thea *(top right)*, an operator in the pilot scheme, were involved with the development of secret radio transmissions even before the unit was absorbed into the Special Duties Section. *(Ken Ward)*

The Army No. 17 voice transceiver, was installed in up to 200 OUT-Stations in 1943/4. Not a single TRD, the Special Duties Section workhorse, has survived. *(BRO Museum collection)*

T/Major R F H Darwall-Smith	R. Sussex
T/Major W W Harston	Dorset
T/Major R M A Jones	R. Sigs.
T/Major N V Oxenden, MC	N'land Fus.
T/Major J W Edmundson	RE

Major R M A ('Spud') Jones, with a specialist role in Royal Signals, and Major Oxenden – posted directly to Coleshill after creating Auxunits Patrols in Norfolk and living with his family nearby – can be discounted. That leaves eleven probables. As stand down approached, there were eleven Command areas:

North Highland; Scottish; Northumbrian; North Riding; East Riding and Lincolnshire; Norfolk and Cambridge; Essex and Suffolk; South Eastern; Hants and Dorset; Southern and South Western; and South Wales.

The case of the late Major Edmundson is particularly intriguing. He was Patron of the Museum of the British Resistance Organisation – generously giving resources, exhibits and advice - and producing persuasive evidence that he left Auxunits Patrols (in Devon) in 1941 or 1942. He claimed that he then transferred directly to SOE. When evidence came to light that he was still on Auxunit records in 1943/4, and that his rank indicated a move to SDS first, he was positive enough:

'I know nothing of the Special Duties Section. It is strange, but a complete year of my life seems to have gone missing!'

Whoever inducted Stuart Edmundson into the arcane commitments of enduring secrets in the early 1940s would have been proud that he was prepared to take them to his grave sixty years later.

The Senior Commander listed under 'ATS' was Beatrice Temple, alias 'Belinda Blue-eyes', niece of the incumbent William Temple, Archbishop of Canterbury. She worked closely with Maurice Petherick from Hannington Hall, and was apparently accepted as a full member of the 'need-to-know' club. The ATS subalterns included Barbara Culleton, who appears (just) in the famous picture of Staff and IOs taken on the steps of Coleshill House and reprinted in 'The Last Ditch' and elsewhere. Although she and Beatrice Temple sat opposite one another across a desk, security was such that Barbara was never to know the precise terms of reference to which her Senior Commander worked.

Auxunits' Signals NCOs and other ranks were deployed from a workshop, first at Bachelors Hall, Hundon in Suffolk and, from 1942 at Coleshill, building, redesigning and servicing radios for OUT Stations and Control Stations manned either by ATS subalterns or other Signals personnel.

★   ★   ★

Men and women were originally recruited to the SDS to observe (or spy on) the invader. Their role would later be extended.

Those in–the-field were selected from an index of names, carefully drawn up and vetted, some before the outbreak of hostilities, drawing upon the personal recommendation of an Establishment inner circle connected by birth, or tradition, through Universities or the Armed Forces, Whitehall or prestigious London Clubs.   Others came more locally from Regional Commissioner-to-Section 'D' recommendation. This unglamorous, Registry 'trawl', is the essential workhorse of any efficient Intelligence organisation. The British, with world wide business contacts and agencies throughout the Commonwealth, have always shown commendable proficiency in this groundwork. They were the envy of competitors – such as pre-war Germany, where Nazi Party servitude was frequently mistaken for secret service competence.

As spies, SDS personnel were sworn to everlasting secrecy. Everlasting meant 'for ever' and not for as long as might be convenient. It was a binding commitment, not subject to later attenuation or compromise. In the finest British tradition, this dangerous, perhaps suicidal, work was unpaid, and undertaken on patriotic grounds alone. There is something about voluntary undercover work which should fascinate psychiatrists. It is dangerous, lonely, arduous, and demands continuous mental alertness and a capacity for duplicity. Is the imperative for spies some special, 'peeping-Tom' quality of a double life, with secrets unknown to friends and family – as well as the 'target'? Add a patriotic ingredient and you have the makings of a hero; without it you are looking, perhaps, at a confidence trickster. The hard-nosed motivation of professional agents who do it for the money is sometimes easier to understand than that of their amateur colleagues.

In the old days when spying was still a sort of scouting pastime, Lord Robert William Baden-Powell, with a personal record of secret service for MI6, wrote:

> '...for anyone who is tired of life, the thrilling life of a spy should be the very finest recuperator. When one recognises also that it may have valuable results for one's country in time of war,

one feels that even though it is a time spent largely in enjoyment, it is not by any means time thrown idly away; and though the 'agent', if caught, may 'go under', unhonoured and unsung, he knows in his heart of hearts, that he has done his 'bit' for his country as fully as his comrade who falls in battle.'

Fortunately for him, 'BP' was never to suffer interrogation by the Gestapo. Had he done so, the words '....time spent largely in enjoyment' would have been seriously avoided.

The SDS civilians did their work solely for King and Country. No visible recognition or reward was ever a consideration or inducement.

Inevitably, secrecy and security were on rare occasions less than 100% watertight. Nevertheless, the rules were sound enough. No agent was to know any other. None was to know the identity of his 'runner' or radio operator. None knew of the operational Patrols, or the Patrols of the SDS. No contact was permitted between the two organisations below the level of 'Key Man' – who, in addition to recruiting and training commitments, was probably responsible for coding and decoding OUT Station messages – and Group Commander. No manoeuvres took place jointly – their tasks remained entirely separate. SDS 'coast watchers' concentrated on early warning of invasion or enemy raids, and then the collection of Intelligence.

SDS personnel received limited training with small arms and a few were issued with handguns for final self-defence or self-destruction. They wore civilian clothes and once within the Auxiliary Units were never considered a combat unit. Operational IOs and SDSIOs in the same area were aware of one another but usually acted separately. Typically, when visiting agents or runners, they might distribute a small favour – such as a few, invaluable petrol coupons.

It was not 'cricket' to recruit women into operational Patrols – their saintly virtue might have been endangered by men in the close confines of underground OBs – but they were acceptable in the SDS where sex was not an issue, although torture by the enemy might well have been. Qualifications were, after all, different from the Patrols. It was not essential to be hardy and able to live off the land, or fire weapons or explosives, or be adept with the garrotte. Exemption from military service was necessary and this favoured middle aged recruitment. Elderly people were not adequately durable and, as a general rule, the young too unaware. Mobility within a useful radius of home or work was invaluable. Doctors, clergymen, policemen, tradesmen, agricultural suppliers, milkmen and management grades were ideal, especially if they were likely to be able to continue normal civilian activities, as cover, after enemy occupation. 'Runners' certainly required to circulate as freely as the occupying power was likely to allow, and they were the one SDS group to profit from conventional training – movement on foot by night, the use of cover, and the advantages of silence and stealth. In this respect they had to acquire some skills comparable with Ops.

So intensely secret was the SDS, that a case is recorded of one man being enrolled in a Patrol as well. The Home Guard was his front for the Patrol and the Patrol for the SDS.

Training was under overall supervision from the SDSIO and delegated at a personal level to his 'Key Men', These were the equivalent of Group Commanders in Ops and, similarly, unpaid. David Ingrams' father, Douglas, was a 'Key Man', and operated a radio Sub-OUT Station from Bewley Down in Devon. It was the furthest point for SDS operations in the south-west, and right on the Axminster-Bridgewater defence line – all Cornwall and Devon to the west, being scheduled, in early days, for abandonment to the enemy and from 1941/2 too far from the fountainhead of Wehrmacht invasion planning (much of which was being read through the Ultra programme) to be of Intelligence significance.

Douglas Ingrams maintained a folio of useful information, supplied and updated through his SDSIO. It contained silhouettes of enemy aircraft, tanks, and lorry transport. It had detailed drawings of German regimental insignia, and indications of rank. Shapes and sizes of enemy fuel containers, their bombs, grenades and mortars, rifles and machine guns, were all displayed together with essential operational data. This was the basis of his teaching to agents in the field, the spies, other radio operators – one at a time to maintain their anonymity – and occasional ladies from the Women's Auxiliary Territorial Service (ATS), subalterns manning IN Stations learning something of the practical aspects of 'OUT Station' work.

He may have operated from a modest, although secret radio Sub-OUT Station, but Douglas Ingrams' standing in Auxiliary Units' Special Duties Section was high. He was subsequently enrolled directly into the regular army, although this may have been a cover, and served as SDSIO in Norfolk, with the rank of major. (Admittedly, he is not on the 'HRRA' list.)

He was a specialist in 'Dead Letter Drops' (as they were then known) and had a demonstration kit of his favoured hiding places. Included was a disused five-bar gatepost hinge, extracted, bored out and fitted with a metal sleeve to hold a small piece of rolled notepaper; and a horseshoe doorknocker. The metal 'knocking' stud, when lifted from its fitting, had also been bored and sleeved to take secret messages.

Although official secrecy is still absolute, there have been many leaks at a personal level, the most recent – focusing on SDS activities in South Wales – through the medium of the Press. The attraction there was the extrovert first SDS Intelligence Officer in charge, Captain John Todd, alias 'Tommy Atkins' – and a unit led by pillars of the Church.

'Tommy Atkins', always in 'mufti', is believed to have been the only SDS and operational Auxunits IO simultaneously. He usually wore a hat with colourful fly-fishing hooks stuck in the crown. Todd was missing from the list of IOs in receipt of Higher Rate Ration Allowance in 1943/4 because he was by then detached to work for SOE in Madagascar. He swore-in his agents and runners – doctors, bus drivers, milkmen and midwives - on the spot with a pocket bible. Unusually, they were permitted to know one another and had a rifle 'to shoot collaborators'. The dead letter drops in Todd's area were in the bowl of a yew tree, in the hollow branch of an oak, in a culvert, under a removable stone in a churchyard wall, and inside a wooden plank on the door of a garage. For final delivery, messages were squeezed through a cut and into the interior of a tennis ball.

Three local vicars featured prominently in this imaginative set up and the altar of the church at Llantilio Croesenny, Monmouthshire, was the hiding place for their clandestine radio, the aerial being concealed behind the lightning conductor climbing the tower.

Instruction on SDS Intelligence gathering in general, and resistance to interrogation and torture, was supplemented by manoeuvres and field exercises. These were unremitting and became even more arduous as 'D' Day approached, and the agents' role was extended. SDS operations became highly organised and efficient along lines described by Douglas Ingrams' son, David:

'The spies, in position in their homes or at work, were hopefully beyond suspicion. They were specifically trained to identify information likely to be of value for Intelligence assessment at GHQ in the disposition of defence forces.

'Their findings were committed to slips of paper and discreetly

– preferably clandestinely at night or during busy daytime periods
if safe to do so – 'posted' in their specific 'Drop'. A runner would
later collect and re-post them secretly for the radio operator, who
would encode and transmit the information at a pre-arranged time.

'Some were deliberately trained and placed as provocateurs.
Agents were asked 'to keep an eye' on the movements, morale, and
actions of Allied soldiers. They tried to get them to talk about
things they should have kept to themselves and then report back
through the letterbox system. SDSIOs might produce photographs
of security suspects for agents to identify, sometimes when they
attended dances or social evenings.   Such tasks were usually
delegated to women of attractive appearance, responsible directly
to their SD(S)IO.

'This particular aspect of SDS work was ordered by the 'War
Office' as 'D' Day approached.'

Major Peter Forbes was the third GSO(2) at Coleshill under
Colonel Frank Douglas:

'Frank Douglas was of course responsible (for the SDS) but he
delegated and it had always been the tradition from the beginning
that the G2 mainly ran SD. I arrived in July 1943...and left for the
Staff College in March '44.   In this comparatively short time I
visited every SD(S) IO throughout the UK having written exercises
appropriate to their area.   The out-station civilians made up
messages based on the narrative and sent them through to the
'main station' (Control or IN Stations) where I sat with the IO and
(usually very attractive) ATS subalterns.

'...at the end of '43 the out-stations were given an important
new role; that of reporting rumours circulating from East Anglia
and all along the South Coast.. The War Office wanted to know
what was being picked up about concentrations for the invasion.

'These reports came to me for consolidation and were passed to
Douglas for onward transmission. In the end this was probably the
most important SD work.

'It was a pity, I think, that the patrol side and the SD were kept
entirely separate and secret from each other. When I later visited
the SD IO in my old Border area, I was amazed to find some of his
out-station OBs were very close to my patrol OBs. They could
have been a useful means of communication with Scottish
Command. There was a main station in Hume Castle where in
ignorance I had considered putting a patrol.'

It is now known that construction work on the Hume Castle
SDS radio station was the subject of complaints in the local

Press, where objections were raised to the deployment of troops on 'repair' work at the castle. Royal Engineers were in fact 'burying' a radio aerial in the ramparts for Auxunits (Signals). The official explanation offered was that engineers had to be trained in many skills and where better to practise for the benefit of the local community than on an important historical feature such as Hume Castle?

Generally, arrangements were highly secure. Both runners and spies were taught the skills of discreet operation and how to identify danger signals. In most cases, cellular secrecy and security cut outs were intended to prevent the disclosure of other agents if one was caught and interrogated under duress. Key Men, however, with their greater knowledge of other associates, may have represented a weak link. Radio transmissions were on a frequency unlikely to be monitored by listening enemy signals' intercepts and, in any case, were in (apparently) plain language, demanding only brief transmission time.

Coded messages were relayed to a Control Station, manned by Auxunits' Signals other ranks or ATS subalterns, and retransmitted to Coleshill or local Army Divisional HQ by radio or secure telephone line.

For its day, this was a highly efficient network.

★   ★   ★

The late David Ingrams made a special study of his father's service. With family connections in the SIS, he was well equipped for such analysis, drawing at times on his own boyhood memories. During one wartime summer holiday, he remembered seeing a squad of Royal Engineers digging a large hole in his garden. It was to become an underground radio station. His young curiosity was aroused and his father found it safer to include him in a few, low-grade confidences, under a personal oath of secrecy, than concoct implausible explanations. In post-war years more details of the SDS came his way and, eventually, he inherited his father's instructional memorabilia. His view is to be respected. He wrote:

> 'There is one more element that has never escaped from secrecy. Among the runners were a few especially courageous men and women known only as "the other side". They are those who had agreed to collaborate with the Germans knowing full well they could be shot by either side, prepared, in Mr. Churchill's words – "to perish in the common ruin rather than fail or falter in their duty".'

David insisted it was 'inconceivable that any organisation with such a firm secret service base as the SDS, would not have included trained collaborators among their number'. (It is not easy to understand why he identified them – generically perhaps – as 'runners' – who had a specifically different, if still covert task.) With a major imperative to collect every available scrap of intelligence about the enemy, 'above-ground' stay-behinds such as SDS agents, should certainly have included a nucleus of trained collaborators, probably German speaking, who might display apparently extreme right-wing sympathies on demand, although British and patriotic at root. This double-agent technique was adopted by SOE with such success that fifty years later controversy still raged in France, for example, over who was a hero and who a traitor.

The point is well made that they 'could be shot by either side'. As British spies, unless the enemy could have persuaded them to join a double cross, that would have been their certain fate once in Gestapo or SS hands. More profoundly, it has to be remembered that many Auxunit Patrols regarded themselves as Judge, Jury and Executioner when collaborators were identified and, having no knowledge at all of 'the other side', would have resisted any temptation to listen to voices of reason or pleas for mercy. The bottom line is that comrades would, unknowingly, have been executing comrades.

The distinguished WWII historian, Norman Longmate, was also informed of 'the other side' when he wrote in 1972 (for the BBC in '*If Britain Had Fallen*') about agents trained to collaborate with the enemy in 1940, although it was not apparently then known that Section 'D' of the Secret Intelligence Service, soon to become the Special Duties Section of the Auxiliary Units, was the name of the organisation he was describing.

Military analysis had concluded, presumably during defence reassessment by General Ironside immediately following the Dunkirk evacuation, that the Isle of Sheppey was of particular strategic importance to the enemy who, by its occupation, could threaten the Nore, the sea approaches to London, destroyer bases sheltered in the River Swale between the mainland and the island, and the vitally important Chatham naval dockyard itself.

Instant bunkers and pillboxes, not to mention trained soldiers, were not in position to prevent an early air or seaborne assault on the island. Instead and in complete secrecy - even to operational Auxunits patrols sited to 'stay behind' –

an intelligence gathering cadre was established remain and monitor the enemy at close hand even, it was suggested, by deliberate infiltration and collaboration.   In the absence of a secret radio network, the problem of communicating the intelligence from the island to British units on the mainland was solved in an unusually ingenious and innovative way.

In Elizabethan days, it is recorded, Catholic clergy were warned to take refuge from approaching inquisitors by hiding away in 'priest holes', that warning being given by sympathisers using pre-arranged signals displayed on washing lines set up specifically as beacons to give the red light.   Perhaps drawing upon this precedent, washing lines as communications links were hurriedly established across the Isle of Sheppey, with small items such as handkerchiefs representing dots in the Morse Code, and large ones – tablecloths or sheets – representing dashes.   From the north Kent coastline, the signal on the south bank of Sheppey could be seen through a telescope on a good day, and a pre-arranged single letter code – not unlike that then in regular use for signalling at sea – easily read and promptly retransmitted to army Intelligence officers.

Ironically, the Special Duties Section continued to expand and improve their techniques even as the threat of invasion, or enemy commando or parachutist raids, receded.   Complex exercises were developed to upgrade efficiency and maintain morale.   Results – called 'batting averages' – were competitive. This was at times counter-productive, with some units blaming poor performance on uneven playing fields if, for example, they had a large area to cover, or one less suitable for efficient radio-communication. This was pointed out in 'Secret' Monthly Notes to IOs No. 5, dated July 1943, when they were called upon to see that good public relations were re-established between the less successful batsmen and bowlers. Counselling was yet another of an Intelligence Officer's accomplishments, it seems.

Army No. 17 transceivers were issued as communications replacements when skills in modern, mechanised warfare increased and 'the runner-and-Dead-Letter-Drop' system became too ponderous. This radio set was never suitable for clandestine use, having been designed as short-range R/T communication between Anti-Aircraft gunners and neighbouring barrage balloon crew – or forward Artillery observers to their gunners.   Lacking built-in security, they would   nevertheless   have   afforded   SDS   agents   rapid communication with more secure, TRD-equipped onward-relay stations.

Standard Army No. 17 Sets were likely to be identified by the enemy and this was deliberately useful in the final SDS role as part of the grand, and eminently successful, deception campaign masterminded by MI6, to convince the German High Command of the presence in East Anglia of an entirely fictional American Army. Apart from dummy guns, tanks and lorries, and other decoys, carefully orchestrated radio traffic was activated to simulate the presence of a non-existent army, and SDS radio stations played a small part in this war game. As 'D' Day approached, some agents were encouraged to mix with Allied troops and British civilians and report through their established network on loyalty and morale, together with details of apparent dissidents or Nazi sympathisers. They 'listened to conversations in public houses and noted opinions about the forthcoming invasion of France, the location and movement of Allied troops, and where it was thought they were scheduled to land'. Information likely to be of Intelligence value was 'passed to the War Office'.

Although this may have been something of a game, it kept all units on the alert and at a high state of efficiency at a critical time. The coast watch role also allowed GHQ to release useful numbers of soldiers for the fight itself instead of guard routines.

After a long build up, the end was sudden:

> GSO(2) to CSO, dated 13th July 1944 – Special Duties Branch of Auxiliary Units is to be closed down forthwith.

Only five weeks after 'D' Day, the closure of SDS also freed a hundred or so Signals and support personnel for active service. As specialists with no experience in the field, the ATS subalterns were soon demobilised.

Amazingly, in April 1945, a copy of a message of thanks to the SDS from their Commander, appeared in 'The Times' newspaper. Ironically, it became public knowledge that:

> '...their work would allow of no public recognition...'

The public, however, preoccupied with Victory, hardly noticed and the powers-that-be were able to box it all away in a 'Most Secret' file. Just as the British public had been warned in a wartime poster campaign, so the SDS were persuaded:

'BE LIKE DAD – KEEP MUM!'

And, of course, as a general rule, they did.

CHAPTER FOURTEEN

Major John Collings &
his 'Special Duties' Team

'Life in those days was a serious business. People who can't remember it can't know. A dull slog most of the time. Dreary diet, cold houses, shortages. It all seems like another life.'

(Jill Monk on civilian life during WWII.)

★   ★   ★

Major John Collings, of the elite 5th Royal Inniskilling Dragoon Guards, was Auxunits' Special Duties Section Intelligence Officer for Norfolk. At Aylsham in 1942, he created an SDS unit and radio OUT Station staffed by a General Practitioner, his daughter, and a black sixteen-hand gelding called 'Merry Monarch'. Backup was provided by Auxunits' (Signals), Royal Engineers, the doctor's gardener and a 'TRD' Radio/Telephony transceiver.   Physical security was, ex-officio, delegated to 'Mark', a 'positively vetted' German Shepherd dog – a devoted Allied supporter in spite of his dubious national origin.

Half-a-century later, the late Arthur Gabbitas – a WWII non-commissioned officer in Auxiliary Units (Signals) – reassembled pieces of the secret puzzle, with help from Jill Monk, the GPs daughter, and Captain Ken Ward, a WWII Signals veteran. 'Mark' and 'Merry Monarch' (by 'King Arthur' out of 'Naughty Nun') had, by then, taken their secrets to the grave.

John Collings, a professional soldier, was also a skilled equestrian, horse trainer, and breeder. Born in Paris, he was bilingual, probably trilingual, having fluency in both French and German.   He was in a pre-war army polo team - ostensibly a collection of mad Englishmen who often competed in energetic chukkas abroad. Germany was his favoured battleground. Having a dual role, he was also reporting back to GHQ with Intelligence of Nazi preparation for war. As cover, it was typically British.

Following the outbreak of WWII, John Collings was in France, on active service with a 'reconnaissance' unit, operating ahead of the Allied front line in secret. During a few days' rest and recuperation, he was once an official observer with a French army unit specialising in dog-training. His eye fell on 'Mark', a German Shepherd type, and he approached the French Sergeant-Major with an offer to 'acquire' Mark for a thousand French Francs (then about £5) on an unspoken understanding that in wartime even the best dogs could sometimes go 'missing while on active service'. A few days later the demobilised dog was delivered to the hotel where John Collings was billeted. Within a few more, his new master had won Mark's confidence and retrained him as a fiercely implacable enemy of the Nazis.

Mark learned to keep 'doggo' at the sound of rifle and mortar fire. He became something of a hero when, scouting bullet-swept no-man's land for British soldiers missing in action, he led a stretcher party to six wounded men. In May 1940, as the German army advanced through the Low Countries, Mark was sometimes left on guard when soldiers of the reconnaissance unit were too exhausted to keep a proper watch themselves. Trained never to bark – just to growl at anything suspicious – he discriminated almost faultlessly between friend and foe. However, one night while on watch alone, and acting on his own initiative, he took the seat from the unit commanding officer's trousers as he crept up quietly to check their state of alertness. Both trousers and buttocks required extensive stitching from army specialists. The CO was not best pleased but it cured him of unscheduled visits.

Mark carried ammunition in specially-made pouches. In 1940, he was injured by German rifle fire – swimming with reserve supplies for a British unit isolated on a mid-river island. John was shot in the leg as he abandoned cover and went to the rescue. Later, medics escorted them both to Ostend, where they were placed with other wounded soldiers on board a crowded trawler heading for England – surviving a mid-Channel attack by German 'E-Boats'. At Dover, after a tranquillising morphine injection, Mark was smuggled ashore through armed guards, past Customs and Military Police, hidden under a groundsheet and borne on a man-size stretcher by reconnaissance unit survivors solemnly pretending to be bringing home a dead comrade.

On John's insistence, medical staff at Milbank Military Hospital, London, operated on both man and his best friend, obtaining an emergency blood transfusion for Mark from Battersea Dogs' Home.

They both recovered and served together during Major John Collings months as Auxiliary Units SDS Intelligence Officer for Norfolk.

It is believed that he recruited Dr Alec Holman, a veteran of the WWI Battle of Jutland and GP for Aylsham, through a local network of landowners and men of influence. A well-known public figure, Dr Holman was custom-built for secret work and, in 1942, his sixteen-year-old daughter Jill, on holiday from boarding school in Cheltenham, was also brought in as a runner for the Auxunits' SDS unit in which he had been enlisted as an observer and radio operator. Jill collected messages from secret dead letter drops for transmission through the SDS network. She recalled how it happened:

'I can remember now the awful cold feeling at the pit of my stomach when war broke out – what was it going to mean? We had seen newspaper photographs of bombing on the Continent – it was absolutely terrifying. Anyway, we settled down to rationing and all sort of shortages.

'John Collings used to come over and ride every spare moment he could – he rather liked my horse. He thought it might be a good idea for 'mounted messengers' and so I was enrolled. I was breaking-in local ponies and it was good cover for me to be out and about.'

Jill developed a personal admiration for the distinguished John Collings – and it firmed up her commitment to the risky work for which she was a volunteer.

Jill thinks her father was ideal for secret work:

'He was too old for the Naval Reserve but was ostensibly Battalion Medical Officer for the Home Guard and involved himself in all sorts of local affairs – such as the Red Cross and St John Ambulance. Doctors lived in the community in those days and were on call all the time. To get about, he ran a 1939 model Rover car.

'Colonel Purdy, another WWI veteran, lived locally and started the LDV and Home Guard. He and Dad were great friends and I suppose that is how he became involved. He had a uniform and a nominal Commission. He was used to dealing with casualties, of course, ever since WWI. Indeed, that is how he first met my mother – when she was badly injured driving an ambulance in the blackout during a Zeppelin raid on Great Yarmouth.

'The first approach to my father to work for Auxiliary Units is still shrouded in mystery. I have a suspicion that one of the local landowners put John Collings and my father in touch sometime in 1942. They definitely did not know one another beforehand. Dad *kept his HG uniform because it was a good cover.*

'I feel sure the Reverend Humphrey Berkeley, vicar of Southripps, near Cromer, was part of the network too. I believe he had a radio in the church belfry.'

At Axminster in Devon, Douglas Ingrams – acknowledging the

impossibility of keeping everything secret from David, his bright twelve-year-old son – had accepted that it was safer to involve him to a limited extent, at least.

In the same way, with the natural curiosity of the Doctor's family, friends, and staff, John Collings and Alec Holman could not expect to keep their clandestine activities exclusive. The problem became critical when Royal Engineers arrived in the front garden of 'The Beeches' in Pound Road (later renamed Holman Road in appreciation of their doctor's service to the community) to dig up the floor of the family's Anderson air raid shelter. With a detached house out of view from immediate neighbours and working discreetly, they might have been just another part of the extensive public works demanded for the war effort.

The public may not have noticed but the doctor's wife and children, and their gardener, could not be excluded. When the Auxunits' (Signals) arrived to install a radio transceiver under the shelter duckboards, the gardener – seeing what was happening, had promptly to be sworn-in under the Official Secrets Act. During the winter of 1942/3, Jill became involved too.

This was less than ideal security. Realistically, however, there was little likelihood of German invasion by that time although the possibility remained of diversionary raids by German commandos or parachutists. The SDS role in mid-war years was partly experimental – and there was much to learn. With limited active service commitments, they kept in training as coast watchers, in radio deception, and observation of potential traitors and defectors. Any risk to the Holmans was therefore acceptable. At the same time, they were making a useful contribution to the war effort.

It was still important to improve the security of the radio Station, however, and new plans were made between Major Collings and Dr Holman, and the Royal Engineers and Signals. The results were ingenious. Jill Monk continues:

> 'The radio transceiver was replaced in the cellar under the house. This was approached by lifting floorboards in the ground-floor billiard room. You pulled a ring in the floor and the thing folded upward. You went down the cellar steps and let the floor down behind you so – once the rug was replaced – it was not obvious you were there. It had originally been a coal cellar so they filled in the chute outside with concrete and cobbles – matching that already in the yard, and you couldn't tell where the old joined the new.
>
> 'Then at the bottom where the coal used to fall, they put the radio transmitter and receiver on a shelf. In front of it they fitted an electric stove which was on an asbestos board and you had to

know just where to put a very thin knife into the side to undo a catch and lift out the stove to get to the radio. The aerial was fitted to the chimney-stack, which was very high, and disguised as a lightning conductor.

'The rest of the cellar was fitted out to look like an air-raid shelter so that any German invaders would think that it was where the poor Brits were hiding from German bombers.'

Had the Germans arrived, they might well have permitted Dr Holman, as a GP, to continue his practice within a working radius of home. With transport to visit his patients, he would have the opportunity to go out and about to see what the Germans were up to at the same time. The results were to be radioed back through the well-rehearsed network. Jill Monk:

'We never knew where our radio messages went to. We never knew anybody else who was definitely in the same job. John Collings said if you don't know anyone else who is in it, in the event of invasion you can't give anyone away. Dad never showed us any papers except the Code we used to send messages through. I can't remember how often code-sheets were changed – either weekly or fortnightly. You placed a sort of plastic thing and picked out the words that made up the code. All our messages were in spoken language - we didn't use Morse. The code, as I remember it, did not alter one letter for another but one word for another. Occasionally I used to send messages for my father – they might have sounded sense to a foreigner but after being encoded they were a bit like gibberish to me. I think the substitute words we used were something to do with a patient or a sick-call my father was pretending to make.'

Dr Holman's radio station was probably part of the 'BOWLING' call-sign network reporting to Army Divisional HQ near Norwich. The unit was regularly visited by Signals personnel, who checked the set and charged the batteries at least every fortnight; probably more frequently. They brought replacement code-sheets with them. Jill Monk continues:

'They generally used to turn up around lunchtime, knowing they would get a decent meal. They came in uniform but this was not necessarily a breach of security. Our house was not overlooked in those days and, anyway, men in uniform were around everywhere. We got to know them quite well. I have no experience how the code-sheets were disposed of – and I was not aware that we were supplied with morphine tablets to self-destruct if caught. As my father was a GP that was probably a matter for him.'

Subaltern Barbara Culleton, responsible to Hannington Hall

for testing and tuning TRD radio sets as they were installed in Control Stations, clearly remembers the code sheets. She was once even instructed to eat one to convince herself it could be done. Printed on rice paper, it had an 'Ugghhh....' taste. She also remembers that operators could be issued with cyanide tablets wrapped in packets, with instructions how to use them if caught by the enemy.

Jill Monk – on the SDS work entailed:

'If I was riding, or out working, I would note troops on the move, or camped in woods, or anything of that sort. Immediately I went home we coded up a message to say who and where they were, because I would see their shoulder-flashes, and approximate numbers and what sort of armament and vehicles they had; were there tanks or bren-gun carriers; and did they have guns with them? The information was all coded up and sent through as an exercise to keep us in practice for the real thing.

'We were also involved in regular planned exercises. We had to listen to our radio at certain times in case there were incoming messages. They were usually just to warn us that there might be an army exercise going on and we would re-double our efforts to describe them. I don't know whether we had firearms but I was taught to use a revolver and rifle. We fired them locally in a weapons pit and rifle range on Marsham Heath. It is still in use.

'On one occasion, assuming our radio station had in some way been knocked out, I had to take a message over to a 'drop' in woods at Hempstead, near Holt. I went across county at night with my nice black horse – 'Merry Monarch' – which wouldn't show up in the dark. It was about two in the morning when I arrived and tied the horse up well away from the drop. I got over the gate into the wood and was grovelling about under a rhododendron bush looking for the drop when I heard a stick crack. I lay absolutely still as a man came walking up the main path. He leaned against a tree and lit his pipe. I was lying there hoping not to wheeze or sneeze and getting cramp in every limb. Eventually he went away. I never did know who he was but he was probably primed to keep a lookout for messengers such as me. I was so scared of being caught I just belted out of the wood and got on my horse and made for home. It was only an exercise, I know, but realistic, and John Collings had warned that if the Germans came and we were caught we would be treated as spies and the interrogation wouldn't be very pleasant.

'By the time the war was over, I had joined the WAAF. My older sister arrived back home to help my father. Army lads came along and took away our radio. My sister was there when John Collings was replaced as IO by Douglas Ingrams, who had moved up from Axminster. She was delighted recently to see a copy of the Western Morning News which showed the Axminster OB and Douglas Ingrams' son, David, nearby. She said she found it exciting that David was instantly recognisable as the exact spitting image of Douglas, even though it was more than fifty years since she had seen him.'

Captain Ken Ward, Royal Signals and Commander of the Auxiliary Units radio workshop at Hundon in Suffolk in 1941, remembered John Collings and his dog well; it was through Ken that Mark first came into the research scene. He was even able to find photographs of the dog in training at the Special Training Centre for commandos (and, later, SOE personnel) at Inverailort in Scotland, where he starred in a number of experiments.

For example a target, with a bunch of keys attached, was rattled along the length of a wire in a dark room. When a Bren gun was aimed in parallel with the dog's head, the target was invariably hit because dogs look *directly at the source of sound.*

Tests were made to put him off the scent. Literally. A demonstrator's boots were dipped in ammonia, or petrol or chemicals, and washed in soap and water moments before he walked off. Not a single ruse was discovered to distract Mark from his target scent. Disturbing lessons were also learned about his ability to hunt down underground OBs.

Jill also remembered him well:

'I had John's dog when he was ostensibly away on a training course. But I discovered in after years he had actually been dropped to some mission with the Maquis in France. I originally looked after Mark for a fortnight and it finished up for several months. One day, John was supposed to come and pick him up but he never arrived. Eventually his batman turned up and said: "He's got lumbago and couldn't come and it didn't half put him in a bad temper."

'What had actually happened, I found out years later, was that he had fallen foul of German patrols on his way out of France, had been injured during the air uplift, came home very much the worse for wear – and was still convalescing.

'My last sight of Mark was sitting on the back seat of the army car, gazing sorrowfully out of the back as it went out of the gate. I think he had enjoyed civilian life and all the riding out, and he hid behind me and refused to get into the car until I ordered him to. The batman was offended because Mark used to obey him before!'

John Collings is thought to have been in occupied France with a 'Sussex team'. Their bi-lingual agents were given short-term tasks on the ground to obtain operational and tactical information for British Intelligence.

Real war started again for Mark and John Collings on the evening of 'D' Day, when they landed together in Normandy in the British 50th Division sector. Mark – a pace ahead – detecting an anti-personnel mine laid by the enemy just below the surface – suddenly froze, with ears up and body 'on point'. But for his alertness, John Collings would probably have been killed.

Three weeks later, however, Mark's luck ran out when he was blown up by a landmine. He lost a leg and was blinded in one eye, but recovered enough sufficiently to accompany John Collings to post-war Germany with the Control Commission. Compromising with former enemies, Mark endeared himself to them too, and when he died in Westphalia in 1952, local Germans engraved his tombstone:

'MARK – EIN TREUER FREUND'

John Collings retired from the army as a Colonel and settled first in Holt in Dorset. Later he emigrated to Canada to breed, train and judge horses. He died in the Veteran's hospital in Toronto at the end of the 1970s, aged seventy-seven, and received a handsome Obituary in the 'Horse and Hound' magazine. He and Jill Monk were in touch for many years but he never told her that Mark had been so severely injured:

> 'Perhaps he didn't like to tell me, knowing how I had loved Mark. He used to take part in a play, rescuing a little girl from an enemy soldier. He would then go round collecting money in his ammunition pouches to buy comforts for half-starved children, old folk, or BAOR charities.'

She went on to talk of her wartime Auxunit service:

> 'Did our family ever get paid? Good God no! Certainly not. It was a voluntary thing. We were told we would have been considered as spies by the Germans and we knew what we were in for if caught.
>
> 'Would we do it again? Certainly! We just did whatever came to hand to get rid of Hitler and the war. Nothing high flown or romantic but just determination, like so many others, to avenge all the deaths - including my own brother.
>
> 'Life in those days was a serious business...'

In 1999, Jill Monk applied to Army Medals Office (and posthumously for her father) for the award of WWII Defence Medals to acknowledge their war Service for Britain.

She was redirected to Home Office. The application there was curtly refused.

CHAPTER FIFTEEN

Auxiliary Units - Signals

AUXILIARY UNITS SIGNALS are responsible for providing the communications to enable the civilian observers to pass their information to a military HQ.

28ᵗʰ June 1944   c/o GPO HIGHWORTH
                                         RMA Jones R Sigs
                                         Commander Aux.Units Sigs

★   ★   ★

If the Intelligence collected by Special Duties Section civilian observers (or 'coast watchers' or 'agents') was to have operational value after invasion, it had to be delivered to the officers who would analyse it without delay. Their 'product' needed prompt amalgamation with other data, to enable Commanders to arrive at informed decisions and issue the best orders.

The original SDS scheme required observers to write their discoveries on slips of paper and 'post' them, still un-coded, in a designated Dead Letter Drop (DLD). After collection by a runner they were redirected through a secret 'letter-box' to the OUT Station radio-operator, still in enemy held territory, of course. Often a 'Key Man', he converted the message into simple, plain language code for transmission to his Control – or 'IN Station' at a pre-arranged time, leapfrogging the front line. Keeping a twenty-four hour listening watch as the scheme expanded, IN Station ATS officers or Signals' ORs at Base wrote down coded messages and took them by hand to the duty Intelligence officer (probably a GSO2 or GSO3(i)) at nearby Static Divisional HQ, for decoding and assessment. A bicycle was the usual transport for 'URGENT' messages, if the distance between radio-station and HQ was too far to walk in a hurry. Selected communications were channelled directly to Coleshill for onward transmission, some by dedicated landline.

IN Stations, operated by ATS subalterns, were out of bounds to 'other ranks', except Signals' maintenance teams. However, passing officers sometimes justified 'operational' or 'supervisory' visits – the ATS subalterns were not known as

'Secret Sweeties' without good reason. Suspicion about their work was tempered by the pretext that they were using their 'Met' huts to collect meteorological data; at times they supplemented their cover with technical talk about weather prospects and a display of barometric charts.

To pass messages through the front line, radio communication was critical. With no time to train OUT Station operators in Morse – not all of whom were experienced radio 'HAMs' from the Radio Society of Great Britain (RSGB) – speech in plain language (Radio/Telephony) was a necessary prerequisite. It had serious shortcomings. Although in 1940 RT was not unknown, it was still an innovation. Range was limited by the available electrical power and – unlike transmissions in Morse Code by Wireless Telegraphy ('WT') – depended upon line-of-sight. While power was available in battery-banks carried easily enough in armoured vehicles or tanks, and line-of-sight was no problem to the RAF, neither advantage was available to ground units dependant upon lightweight sets and 'portable' power. Satellite communication and today's miniaturised 'walkie-talkies' were unknown, and the most frequently used electrical supply was the bulky accumulator – remembered by civilians as hook-up power for domestic wireless sets.

Security was a special problem. It was counter-productive to transmit vital information if the enemy intercepted the message and instantly became aware just how much (or little) was known. Here was a certain recipe for deception and ambush. The Royal Navy – plentifully supplied with electricity but, because of the Admiralty's own skills, more aware than most of the danger of signals' interception – preferred electronically impenetrable techniques as laborious as Semaphore, or Morse transmissions by Aldis lamp for close quarters' communication. The army, well aware since WWI of the fallibility of field telephones under shellfire, and runners in bullet swept terrain, had developed portable transmitter/receiver sets – such as the 'Stratton' (with power developed from a generator fitted to a modified bicycle) – with limited range and no built in security from a listening enemy.

Above all, the source of intercepted signals could be determined by direction finding, and stations and their operators soon identified and eliminated. During the late 1930s, according to SOE records, the Secret Intelligence Service through Section 'D' had been involved in the development of a lightweight, secure R/T transceiver. When the pre-packaged SDS became part of Auxunits in mid-1940, it was realised that a specially secure radio network would be required but was not in production.   Discussions between Colonel Gubbins and Major Peter Wilkinson for Auxunits, and Captain John Hills, Royal Signals, resulted in a suitable set being designed and built in a few weeks.   Enough were produced to set up an experimental network in Kent.

Small in size, the first sets had a range of 20/30 miles and transmitted speech clearly and with unprecedented security. Operating on a waveband unlikely to be intercepted by the enemy, transmissions could not be received on conventional equipment.   For further security, messages were sent in an effective – if rough and ready – code.

Whether or not the SIS development – through a Section 'D' input - was used to advantage in the design of Auxunits' sets is conjectural.   However, if not, the respective systems certainly progressed on remarkably coincidental and parallel courses.

★   ★   ★

Between 1933 and 1936, Ken Ward, reading Mechanical Sciences at Cambridge University, was recruited to an eight-man project under W B Lewis, later Head of the Technical Research Establishment at Malvern, to develop a speech, two-way radio '....for the War Office'.   The specification included signalling between artillery observation posts and gun batteries. Other services showed interest:

'The technique used was to have a set which couldn't easily be intercepted. It was for short-range communication, dry battery powered, and 'Quench' operated. It meant that the carrier was 'mushy' – you couldn't hear anything until you rectified that carrier a second time to hear the speech. So unless you had the second frequency built in to your receiver, you couldn't intercept it. It worked on line-of-sight on about 4-metres wavelength. We took it on army manoeuvres in 1935 and improved it with modifications.

'We used a microphone and headphones – the most successful was a Post Office headset – with a microphone in front of your mouth. The set was accepted and given to Signals Research Development Establishment at Christchurch to toughen it up for work in the field. After they rebuilt it – it didn't work. So further development continued after I left Cambridge. This was written up in "The Wireless Engineer".'

'Later, I was commissioned in the Royal Signals, and spent some time on the Reserve as a graduate apprentice with English Electric to get my Membership of the Institute of Electrical Engineers. I was then with 4th Division Signals in Canterbury (later retitled 2nd Army Signals) in charge of Operator Training – Wireless-and-Line. After the outbreak of war, we received 3,000 civilians – including most of Aberdeen Football team, a complete dance band, and a classical Octet. Operators were trained to the high standards needed by 'Y' Service Signals.'

'Y' is the phonetic abbreviation for 'WI' – or Wireless Interception.

In the mid-1990s, Sir Peter Wilkinson, originally second-in-command Auxiliary Units to Colin Gubbins, told researcher, Stephen Sutton:

'This (radio-communications) had only reached the planning stage by the time that Gubbins and I left Auxiliary Units in mid-November 1940. But he got hold a Captain Hill (*sic*) with the help of a friend in Signals Intelligence business, and I remember having long discussions with Hill in September and October 1940 about the nature of the network that we required – a 'short-wave' voice transmitter network, operating for the most part in visual range. Such equipment, in those days, was unknown in the Regular Army...Major (?) Hill was a young boffin who was able to take charge of everything, including the location and design of the sets, which were constructed under his supervision. The radio network did not come into operation until after I'd left Auxiliary Units.'

The 'friend in Signals' Intelligence, was Colonel F W ('Nick') Nichols (later Brigadier), then head of 'Y' Service. 'Major Hill' was definitely (then) Captain John Hills, Technical Maintenance Officer of the main Signals' Intercept Station at Harpenden, where he and Ken Ward first met.

If it was Gubbins's intention to provide radio communications for Auxunit *Operational Patrols* as well, it never came to fruition. Although there was some early inclination to do so, it is likely that Peter Wilkinson was discussing specifications for *SDS* communications and – on what he considered to be justifiable grounds of security – still dissembling with part-truths fifty years later.

While attached to XII Corps with 110 'B' Type Intercept Section, Ken Ward reported the Signals' product each week to the Divisional Commander, first General 'Bulgy' Thorne and, later, Bernard Montgomery. In December 1940 John Hills visited the Section. He was 'starting a new outfit' and invited Ken Ward to join him as Staff Captain – after 'giving a vague idea of what he was going to do'. Needing female operators, Thea Ward, Ken's wife was also co-opted.

On January 1st or 2nd 1941, Ken Ward got a Movement Order to report to Auxiliary Units (Signals) at The Bull Hotel, Long Melford, Suffolk, where John Hills was living with his family. Captain Freddie Childe (SDSIO – Suffolk and Essex), was there as well. Ken Ward:

'I was taken upstairs to a room converted to an office and

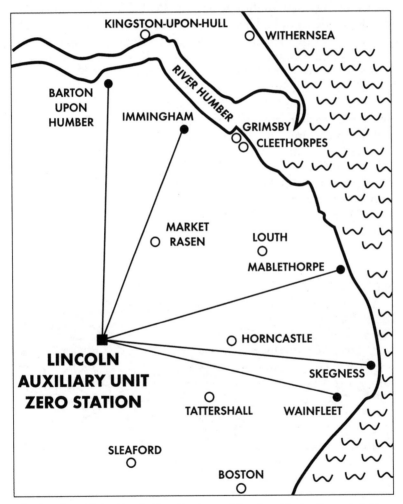

The Auxiliary Units Signals Zero Station at Lincoln with the five out-stations each operated by a civilian. A series of these network ranging from Scotland to Wales and all were capable of operating underground behind enemy occupation.

Freddie Childe read the Riot Act and made me swear to the Official Secrets Act. My billet was with the local baker.

'The unit comprised John Hills and, Lieutenant Tom Shanks in Kent, RASC corporals Chalk and Crawley, both forestry men, who had been installing the aerial/antennae in Kent for the pilot scheme – where there were also five ATS operators at a base (Call-sign 'MAIDSTONE'), and five or six outstations. The ATS were selected by the Queen 'AT' in South East Command, Lady ('Biddy') Carlisle and transferred to Auxunits (Signals).'

The station was at Tonbridge and the 'MAIDSTONE' call-sign a deliberate deception. This type of cover was adopted nationally as the network expanded. The pilot scheme, complete with radio communication, was operating in Kent before the end of 1940, even as Peter Wilkinson was disingenuously discussing project requirements with 'Major Hill'.

John Hills and Ken Ward had discussed the 'Quench' principle earlier (when intercepting German 'E-boat' R/T communications in the English Channel, using 8-metre receivers designed and made by John Hills at Harpenden). Perhaps referring to the published 'Wireless Engineer' article as background, John Hills designed a transceiver for Auxunits, and a contract for production was placed with Brian Savage and Parsons Ltd of Kingsbury. Forty or fifty were made by them. For security, they 'spoke' only to each other and,

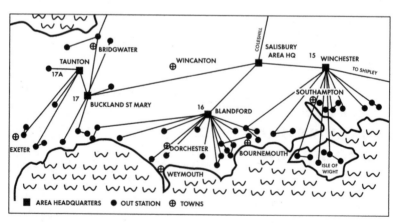

With Areas 1-11 entending from Scotland to Sussex, this map shows the extension westward to Area 15 (Omagh), 16 (Osterley), 17 (Chirnside), manned by Royal Signals, and Area 17a (Golding) and Area HQ, by subalterns of the ATS. Outstations were manned by civilians, who had a system of runners supplying intelligence information.

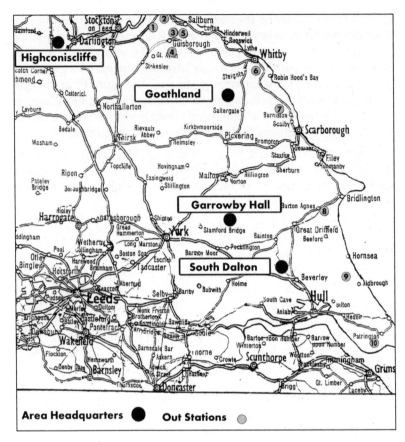

Highconiscliffe: 1 - *Flatis Lane*, 2 - *Coast Road*, 3 - *Errington Wood*,
4 - *Guisborough*, 5 - *Skelton*
Goathland: 6 - *Whitby*, 7 - *Cloughton*
Garrowby Hall: 8 - *Rudstone*
South Dalton: 9 - *Sigglesthorne*, 10 - *Sunk Island*

operating over a small frequency band, could be tuned free
from interference with other sets in the network. 'George'
came up at one spot on the dial – 'William' at another – it was
all very crude. Certain technical problems were inevitable and
– according to papers in Public Record Office - as late as 20th
September 1943, new frequencies (48,52,60 and 65
megacycles) were allocated for Auxiliary Units following a
report by Ack-Ack Brigades' from Southampton of 'dislocation
to radar equipment'.

During early test transmissions in Scotland, Les Parnell
recalled:

'Three of us sat on the highest point of the golf course using the 'call' Station A, whilst our Signal officer travelled round finding suitable sites. After two hours or so we found ourselves arrested by an armed patrol from the nearby AA battery. Every time we spoke on the air we apparently 'jammed' the entire Firth of Forth defence network operating on 56-mhz! We called in our officer as we had a 'problem' and he came along with the result that our frequency in Scotland was moved to 52-mhz forthwith.'

'Savage' sets had a hard life, working on SDS communications for up to twenty-four hours a day. Captain Ken Ward was tasked to set up a Signals workshop and organise their maintenance:

'We decided we wanted somewhere in East Anglia as Signals' HQ and workshop. For (SDS) coast-watchers that was the next area to be dealt with (January 1941), although our brief eventually was to establish similar networks along the coast from Berwick-on-Tweed to the Devon border. We discovered Bachelor's Hall at Hundon in Suffolk, already requistioned and then evacuated by the Manchester Regiment. It was isolated, had some grounds and barns suitable as workshops, and a hot and cold water system. The main disadvantage was lack of electricity. So lighting was by pressure lanterns. In the workshops, soldering irons were heated with blow-lamps.

'Before Colin Gubbins left for SOE in November 1940, he wanted this sort of communication network and caused the Kentish set-up (the 'pilot' scheme). However, when we applied for some Royal Signals' personnel to expand, we got a very firm 'No', and John Hills had a brilliant idea. Through John Clarricoats, secretary of the RSGB, we obtained details of radio 'HAM's already serving in infantry and non-technical units. By applying through the 'Battle Box' (the War Office) to transfer them individually, we were lucky enough to get 20 – 30 keen radio amateurs, as well as some RASC drivers and support personnel. They were transferred into Auxunits (Signals).

'Major T H ('Hugh') Winterborn took over from John Hills in the autumn of 1941.

'We did have a request later, probably mid-1941, to design a set for Auxunits' Patrols. There were various specifications we didn't like. It had to be on Long Wave and have a removable aerial. John Hills designed a set, which we tested, and it worked. The aerial was like the metal parts of an ordinary umbrella. The radio was never put into production as, on Long Wave, it could easily be intercepted. The IOs on the Ops side at Coleshill said they didn't want radio communications. They were very categoric.'

Personnel were not selected at random. When Auxunits' (Signals) expanded to include Berwick-on-Tweed to the north, and Somerset and South Wales to the south and west, 'MOST SECRET' Part II Order of 4thApril 1942 required:

'3. Furthermore, in view of the highly specialised nature of the wireless set and the most secret nature of their task, it is strongly recommended that personnel be carefully selected with an officer of the Signals branch, Auxiliary Units, taking part at the interview.

'Only men of responsible character and discretion should be entertained. Their medical category however need not be high except that their speech and hearing must be of a standard suited for R/T transmissions.'

This endorsed, and made official, HQ procedure which had been operative since January 1941.

The late Arthur Gabbitas, an NCO, was among those soldiers transferred to Auxiliary Units (Signals). In the 1990s he listed those he remembered with 'HAM' call signs –

G2AW Major John Hills	G2QV Captain Shanks
G8CK W E ('Bill') Bartholomew	GM8MQ Jack Millie
G8PP Les Parnell	GM2COI Jimmy McNab
G2KI George Spencer	G2FWX Bill Ayre
G2RD Ron Dabbs	G8JI Tom Higgins

This was not an entirely unsatisfactory posting; certainly an improvement on slogging about with the infantry. Bill Bartholomew still remembers:

'...the hot afternoons in Suffolk when we used to put our benches out in the orchard at Bachelors Hall. We had to go to Stradishall US aerodrome for our baths and some good American cheer – very different to our Spam and potatoes (HI). An American bomber came down one day just missing the house and G8JI fell downstairs head-over-heels as he thought the bomber was going to hit us – but it crashed in a field just past. The tail came off and the tail gunner scrambled out and ran pell-mell round the field screaming and waving his arms.'

The Savage sets, brilliant enough in concept, had minor intrinsic faults, creating a heavy workload of servicing and repairs at Hundon even after Ron Dabbs and Bill Bartholomew had removed some of the problems. Ken Ward remembers:

'We were responsible for everything right down to the Coast

Stations. We installed the sets and aerials. We taught operators how to use them, and the necessary procedures; and then serviced the sets and delivered charged batteries. Transport for the job was old Norton motorbikes with open sidecars.

'One of the upstairs rooms at Bachelor's Hall, equipped as a Base Station, worked to 'BUTTERCUP', Army Divisional HQ at Halstead, Essex, manned by my wife and Mickey Browne. Mickey was one of the first five in Kent (the pilot scheme). When we started at Hundon, John Hills brought her up because she had secretarial experience, and soon she took over the trainee operators. All new and repaired sets were tested on the 'BUTTERCUP' link, which was also used to voice-test potential ATS recruits. We requisitioned two cottages with smallholdings in Great Yeldham, built pre-war for unemployed miners. Mickey had one for the accommodation and training of new ATS intake. Freddie Childe lived in the other.

'We were all getting fed up with these Savage sets and one morning Sergeant Ron Dabbs and Corporal Bill Bartholomew were discussing the problems with me and then asked – "May we design a new set?". I said "OK" and they got on with it and, in about three weeks flat, submitted four prototype sets for test. We gave them a thorough trial. They worked well and the operators liked them.

'So the "TRD" (Transmitter/Receiver Dabbs) was approved for production, with an initial batch of 25 all made at Hundon.'

Bill Bartholomew, one of the self-styled 'Bachelor's 'All Gang', explained in arcane detail:

'...the TRD transmitters featured an RK34 twin Triode with top Anodes as a self-excited Oscillator for the transmitter, and an EF50, then an EF39 and a 6V6, in the receiver. The EF50 was to block the Super Regenerative squiggles from getting out and giving the game away.'

(Requests for more detailed explanation should be directed to the Royal Signals Museum at Blandford, please. HI! 'HI', it seems, is 'HAM-speak' for laughter. There is plenty in Bill Bartholomew's letters.)

His wife may not have been flattered to know that he referred to her as 'the XYL' – presumably an esoteric term for 'partner'. He also recalls:

'The equipments were given type numbers which included the designer's initials, such as 'TRWEB' or 'TRRD' – standing for 'Transmit/Receive/Ron Dabbs.'

However, official papers all refer just to TRDs or, after later modification, TRFs or TRMs.

Dipole aerials were 'T' piece in shape, three feet, ten inches each side, made from a flat, black twin lead – split down the middle and pulled to the required length. Bill Bartholomew described the installation:

> 'The feed for the horizontal dipoles was hidden under the bark of the trees in which they were mounted. It was Belling and Lee BL7 twin feeder, 80 ohm, black and thin. I use it to this day as feeders for my transmitting aerials. I bought a reel from the factory. (HI)'

Arthur Gabbitas merged research and memories of the TRD set:

> '...Bill Bartholomew designed the overall set; Tom Higgins and Ron Dabbs, the receiver; Bill and Jack Millie the transmitter; Les Parnell and Jimmy McNab the power unit; and John Mackie the metalwork. George Spencer and Bill Ayre completed the team.

> 'The resultant set was housed in a single metal case about 15" long, 9" deep and 9.25" high (whereas the Savage had a separate case for the power unit), powered by a large conventional 6 volt, 85 AH accumulator, the voltage being converted to 240 volts Alternating Current by a Mallory vibrator and transformer in the power pack, and with an output of approximately 1.5 watts. The frequency range was 48-65 m/cs, then rare but used by BBC1 television after the war.

> 'After extensive tests, an initial sum of £2,500 was allocated for the purchase of parts which generally were obtained from commercial companies or direct from the makers.'

Assembly of the TRD, concentrated initially at Hundon, was transferred to the Inter-Services Research Bureau as Auxunits' (Signals) workshops and laboratories moved to Coleshill early in 1942. It was there, in Nissen huts under the trees near the Great House, that TRF and TRM versions of the TRD were developed. The sets had the advantage of secrecy – admittedly not total but amazingly effective nevertheless. With an ordinary receiver, the carrier wave might be heard - but nothing else. Using the TRD, a rushing noise ceased automatically with voice transmission. Another development created a duplex set (avoiding the need to switch from 'transmit' to 'receive') – a necessity for unmanned repeater stations.

Repeater (or relay) stations, were required where the distance between the Met Hut and the Coast Station was too great for the sets' range, or where high ground intervened. The sets were modified TRDs, made so that they were normally on 'Stand-by', and tuned to receive from either direction. Once a voice was received from one direction, it energised the Transmitter to send the signal to the other station.

Usually sited in high trees to give maximum range, they were visited weekly by the maintenance teams for battery change and checking. This was particularly necessary in areas such as Yorkshire, for example, where signals could be blanked out by distances from coast to Divisional HQ, or intervening high moorland.

Modifications to the Savage blueprint were drawn and initialled RD/WEB, Sergeant Ron Dabbs and Corporal (and 'only war substantive at that', he writes) Bill Bartholomew. The modification and redesign of the TRDs was brilliant – and it is interesting to speculate why these other ranks received no official reward, recognition or appreciation?   Instead, they were later returned to Catterick for retraining, dispersal to units, and eventual anonymous demobilisation. There were no Reunions until Arthur Gabbitas went to work in 1990.

Thanks to him, much of the Auxunits (Signals) history may seem straightforward enough now.   But for researchers the radio network was even more than usually convoluted. At an early stage, something of its existence was disclosed by Suffolk operational Auxilier, Herman Kindred, who inadvertently headed the hunt away from the quarry when it was ingenuously assumed he was describing radio communication for his own Patrol network. Some considerable time later, it was realised that the unit he referred to had been that of his cousin, Charles Kindred, *separately enrolled locally as an SDS coast watcher/radio operator.* Although Herman knew something of this, and where the radio station had been secretly located, he had not clarified such vital detail to us.

Moreover, in spite of ever increasing evidence of R/T communication between *certain* Auxunits – and before the separate identity of Patrols and SDS was fully understood – technical experts all derided any possibility of portable, secure voice transceivers so early in WWII. Not one 'normal' channel of enquiry produced positive results and others, approached personally, either thought there was no 'need to know' – or more frequently, had genuinely never heard of the TRD.

Major R M A Jones's report of 28th June 1944 – when coast-watchers were about to be disbanded – shows that 250 TRD sets were manufactured, together with 28 modified TRMs and 36 TRFs.

None of these have ever been discovered (in spite of elaborate promises) and conflicting memories are evident about size and appearance. The approximate exterior measurement 9" x 9" x 15" is undoubted but opinions differ whether the metal case was 15" long or 15" deep. Bill Bartholomew, for example, is sure the *depth* was 15" to accept the MasterRadio Vibrator pack of that shape and size, with the few dials, knobs and switches set vertically in an almost square 9" face. Other witnesses remember the front as 15" *long*, with the dials sited horizontally. The power units – known as 'DAGS' (short for 'Dagenham') – with wooden carry handles, stood separately and were connected to the rear of the TRD.

In addition to a time lapse of sixty years, there are other explanations for differing descriptions. Like so many other aspects of Auxunits' history, the sets were different things to different people in different places. Several versions, including the 'Savage', developed after the 'pilot' sets in 1940. Further modifications appeared after the mainstream TRD and others were custom built for specific locations. Moreover, IN-Stations required a station dial – to transceive with a number of OUT-Stations – whereas the latter, communicating with just one IN-Station, did not.

Bill Bartholomew was firm about some aspects of the TRD exterior, which had previously defied investigation by buffs and researchers alike. The front edges, for example, were rounded while the back were left square. Sometimes the set was painted in a 'ripple black' but was more usually cadmium plated and 'passivated' to reduce the onset of mildew in damp locations. The resultant colour was 'goldish'. He is in little doubt that where Control (or IN-) Station operators recall 'searching the dials for radio transmissions by enemy agents, this was on an additional and more suitable set, the expensive American RCA Type AR 88.

200 No. 17 Army sets were also in SDS use in 1944. They had originally been requested by Geoffrey Beyts as he transferred out of Auxunits in July 1942 – but were never issued to the Patrols. (Just like Stuart Edmundson, he 'knew nothing about the Special Duties Section'!) They were eventually to have a dual role. Originally intended to replace the runner/DLD channel and speed up the communication of essential tactical intelligence, even at the expense of security –

the No. 17 had none of the built-in security inherent in the TRD. As 'D' Day approached, and MI6 co-ordinated and orchestrated numerous associated deceptions through the London Controlling Section, a new role was discovered for Auxunits SDS. Their increasingly frequent exercises using the No. 17 Sets, especially in East Anglia and Kent, represented a deliberate increase in the volume of phoney, *interceptable* radio traffic, intended to help bluff the Germans about the true location and focal points of the '*Overlord*' invasion.

At stand-down, the SDS radio network had expanded to:

'IN Stations' (also known as Control, Base or Zero)	30
'OUT Stations'	125
'SUB-OUT Stations	78

Only a few SDS radio operators survive and no single witness remembers the No. 17 Set in SDS use. It was confirmed that they were, however, in the July 1943 'Secret' issue of Monthly Notes for SDSIOs. Under 'Operations', it was noted:

> 1. No. 17 Sets.
> A further 100 of the above sets have been applied for and it is expected that they will arrive after the present allotment to areas have been absorbed and are working.
> No action for the siting of these further sets need be taken by IO's yet.

The August 1943 Notes reported:

> A further 100 17 sets have now been delivered to this HQ and will be installed in accordance with recommendations already made by IO's.
> Fresh sites will NOT be submitted until after the completion of the present programme, which calls for the establishment of some 170 of these sets.
> IO's will be asked for recommendations for further sites at a later date, and consideration will then be given to their installation in areas which at present are without them.

Some speculation about their importance to SDS is necessary. It is clear that they were suitable, if not ideal, for immediate IN Station communication over the short distance from 'Met-hut' to Divisional (or Corps) HQ – a mission previously undertaken on foot or by bicycle. Again, time was saved at the expense of secrecy. This might account for 30 of the 200 sets under issue, one at each IN Station – HQs having their own issue.

As the reasonably secure 'runner' to OUT Stations system in-the-field was too slow, and replaced by short-range radio communication, it could account for 156 No. 17 Sets – as 78 SUB-OUT Stations transmitted to 78 OUT Stations. With a further 12 in the reserve store, or under repair, some sense can be made of the 200 issued. The associated loss of security is circumstantial confirmation that pre-'D'-Day transmissions were deliberately phoney. Certainly, immediately the Normandy invasion beaches were consolidated, Auxunits' Special Duties Section was condemned to immediate death.

This is an admittedly mathematical hypothesis. Had it not been for conclusive evidence from the SDSIOs notes, deployment of No. 17 sets – as isolated breaches within SDS where nearly all else was secure and watertight – might have been dismissed.

It has to be seen in the context of an expansion of SDS personnel, from 1942, in inverse ratio to the likelihood of an enemy assault on our beaches. As a direct agency of GHQ, this could not have been policy decided upon lightly. As vigilant 'coast watchers', an SDS presence may sometimes have released useful numbers of trained soldiers from lookout duty, to be relocated and prepared for the Normandy invasion. The increasing activity of the SDS, their additional participation in exercises, and the extension of IN Station watch-keeping to twenty-four hours, was a strategic bonus for GHQ as well as a part of the grand deception to mislead German Intelligence.

The No. 17 Set was an ideal tool. Wehrmacht Signals no doubt found the traffic easy intercept and locate and, in doing so, were persuaded to confirm Hitler's dogged belief that the 'D'-Day assault would be across the Straits of Dover and into the Pas de Calais, rather than onto the Normandy beaches. This Allied stratagem helped delay the transfer of vital German armoured units to the invasion epicentre and allowed the Allies to establish real footholds in the Atlantic Wall. Credit for this went to the very (very!) secret London Controlling Section headed by the late Sir Stewart Menzies, chief of MI6.

Ron Dabbs, trained by Phillips Radio, had joined the TA pre-war. After Auxiliary Units, John Hills went to the far east war theatre with 'Y' Signals. He was succeeded at Coleshill by Major Hugh Winterborn, Major R M A ('Spud') Jones and, finally, Major Green. In 1944 there were seven officers and 69 other ranks on maintenance and watch-keeping duties with Auxiliary Units (Signals), and a further 57 ATS officers and three other ranks.

In December 1941, the Radio Communication Division of the Inter-Services Research Bureau agreed to take over the manufacture of TRDs needed for replacement or network extension and a Contract was later arranged by them with Peto Scott Ltd. In June 1940, the ISRB had been created, at War Cabinet level, as cover for research, development and manufacture of equipment for Special Operations Executive.

However, in spite of such an array of thoroughbred credentials, nothing could save the TRD when the Special Duties Section was stood-down in July 1944. Their hideaways and Control Stations were sealed up or destroyed and the sets collected into Ordnance, and then Ministry of Supply, stores.

Captain Ken Ward, himself recently released from secret work for SOE, was detailed to 'remove them from any possible future use', together with other specialist wireless equipment. Apart from a few radio units once seen, post war, by Bill Bartholomew in a West End ex-WD surplus store, they disappeared for ever.

Rather like the Colossus at Bletchley Park, they were too successful to survive. (HI!)

CHAPTER SIXTEEN

Auxiliary Units Signals - in the field

'King George for England – 'Kings Cross for Scotland'
(Auxunits (Signals) Radio Safety Check-Call)

It was not their fault, but the inclusion of men with radio communications' experience added further to already over-complicated Auxunits' terms of reference. With *their* own arcane jargon superimposed on official army phrasing, an almost impenetrable terminology developed. As could be expected, it increased the problems for 21st Century researchers.

Colin Gubbins and John Holland had initiated a strategic break-through which encouraged regular army commanders – reluctantly in many cases – to understand the potential value of irregular warfare. For the moment, paperwork would take second place to expediency. But in an organisation as hidebound and cost-conscious as the War Office, it could not go on indefinitely. For Auxunits, the first sign of reversion to formal administration came with the arrival of Colonel 'Bill' Major, replacing Gubbins as CO at Coleshill on 18th November 1940. This is how Sir Peter Wilkinson explained it to researcher Stephen Sutton:

> '...Bill Major...had an altogether less speculative mind. In my opinion, the great weakness of Auxiliary Units after we left, was that Major tried to organise it along military lines which, in my experience, is almost invariably fatal for a clandestine organisation for reasons of security.'

'On military lines' or not, continuity was never a feature of Auxunits' vocabulary – as official papers from Public Record Office demonstrate. Operational Patrols (or guerrillas or saboteurs or 'stay-behinds' or 'our Home Guards'), trained by regular army Scout Sections (or Scout Patrols, or even 'Home Guard Scout Patrols'), functioned from Operational Bases (or 'funk-holes' or shelters or hideouts). Special Duties Section agents (or 'civvies' or spies, or Intelligence gatherers or observers or 'coast watchers') reported through SUB-OUT-

Stations (or shore stations or coast stations or radio 'holes' or hideaways) to OUT-Stations and on to 'IN-Stations (Zero Stations, Control – or Base-Stations. Or Met-Huts).

If such everyday definitions were not standardised at HQ, the arrival of Radio HAMs and Signals' personnel – with relays, vibrators, boosters and oscillators – did nothing to help. Another restriction was the 'need-to-know' barrier, always in evidence with Signals' Intelligence.

On balance, Signals' other ranks (ORs) In-the-field, tended to describe their set-up as 'civvies' (or 'coast-watchers') working through SUB-OUT-Stations and OUT-Stations to IN-Stations.

But sorting it out was not easy.

   ★   ★   ★

When Ken Ward joined Auxunits (Signals) in January 1941, the SDS – according to Nigel Oxenden – had already been running for at least six months. Without radio communication the Intelligence collected was worthless and, after a successful pilot scheme in Kent, a Contract for the construction of Savage sets – based on Major John Hills' designs – was under way. These were installed from the new Signals' HQ and workshops at Hundon.

Stan Judson was sent to Hundon after initial training:

> 'I was called up in October 1940, joined the Royal Signals, and qualified as an electrician/Signals at Catterick. Four of us were posted to Auxiliary Units, but when we arrived at Sudbury in Suffolk nobody in the town had heard of them. After an overnight kip in an empty shop we managed, with the help of an officer, to telephone Bachelors Hall and a big staff-car took us to Hundon.

By early summer 1941, coast-watchers in East Anglia were already equipped with radios and the scheme was extending northwards along the East Coast, and in Hampshire and Dorset. Security was tight and twenty-six Signals' instrument mechanics and electricians – happy in their work at Hundon – were not intended to know much about their comrades out in-the-field, the ones installing radio sets and aerials, or servicing those already in position. As soldiers, they were bound, of course, to hear rumours and get to know something of the networks and site installation requirements.

The field units, working seven days a week, enjoyed specialist status and remained happily apart from restrictive army routines. They had transport, and private billets where civvy 'Mums' provided bed-and-breakfast and evening meals at War Office expense. Having to find their own lunch – they conspired to arrive at promising destinations around midday mealtime, if they were likely to be invited to the family table. If not, they headed for the robust alternative – a local 'British Restaurant', respected during food rationing for the size of affordable portions – although making no claim to *'haute cuisine'*.

Coast-watchers were identified and selected by Special Duties Section Intelligence Officers, using a network of contacts from the MI(R) card index, leading through Regional Commissioners to police chiefs, aristocrats, landowners, squires and the clergy. Candidates were approached discreetly and vetted – according to one report – by Special Branch units with access to Security Service records through their Chief Constables. Patriotism was an essential prerequisite, together with personal integrity, local knowledge, a sharp intelligence, and practical reasons to be near areas of potential enemy invasion or raids. The probability of remaining at work after enemy occupation was another asset.

No financial inducements were on offer – they were days when invitations to participate in risky operations for King and Country were more likely to be accepted than refused. Captain Freddie Childe, of the Intelligence Corps, and Captain John Collings, 5th Royal Inniskilling Dragoons, usually dressed discreetly in mufti, were archetypes of early SDS 'powers-that–be' responsible for recruitment and training in Essex and Suffolk, and Norfolk respectively.

At this stage Auxunits (Signals) entered the scene. The 'civvies' selected to man radio stations were given voice tests and, if successful, taught to use the sets. Corporal (later Sergeant) G2KI George Spencer – working through and sometimes alongside G8CK Captain Tom Shanks from Hundon – would visit a new coast-watcher's area with the SDSIO. To maintain anonymity he was probably the only OR to meet him. Secrecy was of prime importance and George Spencer never divulged his WWII work for Auxunits even to his immediate family. A survey of the selected coast-watcher's operational area followed, usually with G2KI deciding where the radio station would be best placed, taking into account accessibility; the nature of the landscape between it and the base station; and the likelihood of discovery by other civilians, or regular army or Home Guards on manoeuvres or, most importantly, the invading enemy.

Finally, height above sea level was needed to maximise transmission range, with dipole aerials then being secured high

in trees or chimneys or, in a few cases, church steeples or
factory buildings.

Signals' ORs tried to visit one or two OUT-Stations each day
with newly charged batteries. Three men went to some 'IN-
Stations' – all of which were equipped with a recharging
generator – one remaining on radio watch as two visited an
OUT-Station. After invasion, IN-Stations and the few suitable
OUT-Stations equipped with a mains battery charger, would be
self-sufficient but for the majority there would be no further
chance for battery replacement or recharge. Obviously, the
better the supply, the longer the potential life of the OUT-
Station after the balloon went up.

Arthur Gabbitas:

> 'The stations were usually hidden in woods but we had to be
> careful where we left the scout car so that it didn't attract
> attention. Having heavy batteries to carry, we sometimes
> compromised with security and had a problem if we saw anyone in
> the vicinity. Some stations were in private houses, in an attic or
> hidden in the toilet perhaps. We always kept a lookout for
> neighbours.'

In buildings, down-leads from aerials were hidden in chimneys
or disguised as lightning conductors. In trees, they were
concealed by removing a strip of bark and carving a runnel to
take the wires. The bark was tacked back with panel pins or
adhesive. Inadvertent discovery was unusual and the cables
often remain invisible to this day.

As Arthur Gabbitas remembered, tree climbing became an
essential skill if aerials were to remain in effective service.
When displaced from a narrow directional band, reception was
adversely affected, interception more likely, and security
compromised:

> 'One soldier in Suffolk was killed. He fell when his climbing
> rope parted. We found later it had been weakened by battery acid
> leaking into the back of the car.
>
> 'The tree used at Lincoln, an elm with no low branches, was the
> worst. One day the officer insisted on an aerial check and you needed
> a double length extension ladder to get within 15' of the nearest
> branch. You then threw a weighted light line up and over, and
> watched for the hammer or whatever when it swung back. Next, you
> hauled yourself up the main rope to the first branch – and then
> started the climb! I was up there seven hours, fixing the aerial, rather
> than come down for a rest and have to climb up all over again.'

It was not always straightforward at ground level either, as Stan Judson discovered:

'The operator at Woodhall Spa, Lincolnshire, was the local doctor and we put the set under the floor of his dog's kennel with the dog's bed resting on top of the trapdoor. We couldn't get in without his Red Setter escaping and rampaging round the garden, alerting the gardener and everyone while we were trying to remain unobtrusive.

'The aerial was in a tree behind the garage but the army put an ack-ack unit nearby and their cook used our tree to chop his firewood and severed our wire. We chose another tree but there was an armed guard marching up and down and we had to try and re-install the whole thing every time he moved out of sight. It was like escaping from a PoW camp. Then the guttering broke over our station and when it rained the set got wet. We decided to relocate the station inside the house.

'It worked fine there until Jerry came over and bombed it flat. That one gave us more trouble than all the rest.'

Teams of two or three soldiers on maintenance worked under an NCO. As the radio network expanded during 1941, it became impracticable to travel from Hundon and men were billeted with civilians in their work area. Transport was usually either a Norton motor-cycle and sidecar, or army truck. Corporal Stan Judson, 6'2" with matching legs, was one of the lucky ones:

'After a while I was posted to Lincolnshire and billeted with the Vicar of Wispington, near Horncastle. I was a corporal and our unit had two lance/corporals and a driver, working under Captain Shanks – usually called 'Tom' away from HQ. He was the contact with the SDSIO. We tested locations and installed the sets. Originally, there was little digging. The sets were contained in boxes like small coffins, metal lined inside with a lid and they were sunk in the ground, usually well hidden. The operator lifted the lid and worked on the surface.

'The station at Donnington-on-Bain was in woods. There were two operators – one the manager of a knackery and the other the village coal merchant by the name of Grey. One evening, an RAF officer and a WAAF were doing a bit of courting in the wood when they heard this phonetic transmission – "Able, Baker" and this sort of thing. One of them crept down and alerted the local army unit who surrounded the wood. The operators concealed the set but got arrested at gunpoint. Tension was high and some of the army blokes were all for shooting them out of hand because they thought they were fifth columnists. They were released the next morning after a call to the Chief Constable.

'After that the set could no longer be operated and it was decided they would need purpose-built Operational Bases. An Auxunits' Sapper Section, stationed near Coleshill, usually came to do the digging and construction if they were underground.

'For transport, we used little two-seater Austin open cars. The only snag with them was they used more oil than petrol and you had to put a new engine in every 12,000 miles.'

With War Office administrators soon firmly in command, authority for this was noted in 'Most Secret' War Establishment review, dated 4th April 1942:

> II. In order to conserve manpower and to safeguard security, Royal Corps of Signals personnel will be employed in the driving and maintenance of the Cars 2 seater, 4 wheeled, utility, other than those allotted to the RE officers, and motor cycles.'

The joint SDS/Signals network continued to expand from 1942. As the likelihood of enemy invasion decreased, GHQ worked it out that the probability of raids would increase proportionally and, instead of posting armed soldiers to guard the length and breadth of the country, decided that much vulnerable coastline should be kept under adequate and cost effective surveillance by unpaid civilians.

With Control (or 'IN') Stations – manned either by ATS subalterns or Signals' other ranks, but never both at once - the scheme extended from Berwick-upon-Tweed clockwise to Winchester; and from 30th March 1942, Montrose to Somerset. The final expansion was from Elgin in Scotland to Devon in England and, by late 1943, along the South Wales coast to Carmarthen.

Cornwall was excluded, perhaps because it was too remote from the focus of events leading to 'D' Day, or because the original 'stop-line' from Axminster to Bridgwater was still intact and regarded as 'impregnable'.

It is known that Major Geoffrey Beyts flew more than once to Scotland to liaise with SOE on sabotage training, and the Northern Isles to meet Captain A G Fiddes-Watt, Intelligence Officer for operational patrols in the Outer Hebrides. Indeed, during one he made a night assault by revolver on the crew in the conning tower of a German U-boat, calmly recharging batteries in a sheltered bay. Records confirm, however, that

SDS radio-stations were confined to the mainland. Twenty networks were about the maximum, with a Control Station at Army HQ, Taunton, the furthest west in England. From August 1943, in areas identified as vulnerable to enemy raids, IN-Stations were manned 24 hours a day, sometimes with ATS subalterns watch-keeping by day and Signals ORs by night.

Later, each area had an administrative number – Taunton, for example, was 17A – and the associated radio network identified with a call sign. Control Stations were usually equipped with an emergency, fallback base underground, called a 'Zero Station', serviceable, with rations for 28 days and regularly checked, situated near the main centre of daily activity – the Met Hut. In the event of enemy assault, the Met Hut was to be abandoned, the door left swinging and radio sets destroyed – all hopefully leaving the impression that the station had been abandoned in a panic. The operators would, however, have moved only a few yards to the hidden, *underground* Zero Station to continue the collection and dissemination of Intelligence for as long as they could survive without discovery. The entrances were – to usual RE/Auxunits standards – ingeniously constructed and camouflaged and Bill Bartholomew remembers one Zero Station shaft that was hidden under the outdoor toilet, and entered by activating a hidden lever which rotated and lifted the whole seat assembly to reveal the hatchway descending.

The call sign for the Control Station at Cheddon Fitzpaine, Somerset, was 'GOLDING'. At Parham Museum, it was hoped imaginatively that 'GOLDING ONE' would turn out to be the Met Hut and 'GOLDING ZERO' an indication that the operators had gone-to-ground. Alas this was not so – both were 'GOLDING ONE'. This network stretched to an attic in the Hare and Hounds public house at Ottery St Mary in Devon ('GOLDING ONE-ABLE'). The Buckland-St-Mary network ('CHIRNSIDE') included the ingenious SUB-OUT-Station at Bewley Down, operated by the late Douglas Ingrams. He was subsequently commissioned into the army, promoted Major and posted as SDSIO for Norfolk, where the Norwich call sign was 'BOWLING'. As a deliberate deception, call signs were usually selected from genuine locations elsewhere in Great Britain, whereas the originals had used flowers – 'BUTTERCUP', for example.

Others networks identified by Arthur Gabbitas included:

OTLEY' – at Alnwick; 'BARNACK' – at Edinburgh; 'GOREY' at

Ousden, Suffolk; 'HARSTON' – at Shipley; 'OMAGH' - at
Winchester; 'OSTERLEY' – at Blandford; 'HARCOURT' - at
Abergavenny'; and 'BRAMLEY' – at Crwbyn, Carmarthen.
'ORMSKIRK' and 'STEYNING' were also allocated but their
location not identified.

Stan Judson sorted out another grey area - the cipher used for
everyday message transmission.   Surviving ATS subalterns
could never remember much about it. Jill Monk and her sister,
operating with their father from the OUT-Station at Aylsham in
Norfolk, remembered a regular delivery of new code-sheets –
weekly or fortnightly – by the Signals team detailed to service
their radio set.

Colonel Major was reported (in *The Last Ditch*') to have
prepared a list of five hundred military phrases most likely to
be used by his 'observers' in Britain, while his 'friend' produced
a list of five hundred words to match the phrases. This was the
basis of a crude cipher, not intended to fool the enemy for
long. Jill Monk remembers that her father's code involved the
use of medical jargon and, elsewhere in East Anglia, farming
and agricultural terms were favoured. No doubt both were
modifications to meet local circumstances.

Stan Judson explained:

> 'The code-sheet had the alphabet down the side – and along the
> top too. It was all divided into squares or oblongs and in each were
> descriptions – tanks, trucks, aircraft, etc. The operator would say
> 'Able Baker' and the person receiving would look on the code and
> it would say '50 tanks', or something. All sorts of things were in
> the squares so you just related the top and the side letters and that
> gave the clue. I suppose you could pass a map reference too. It
> never changed as far as I remember.
>
> 'It was something like playing battleships and cruisers.'

If the main sheet never changed, the regular delivery by Signals
personnel must have involved alterations to the marginal
references. In general, it all seems to fit the phonetic
transmission overheard by the RAF courting couple. The use of
this simple code was never intended as a long-term barrier for
enemy code-busters, if they were listening – 'Quench' security
was adequate enough. This is fully confirmed in the SDSIOs
'Secret' Notes for July 1943:

> 'The second thing to remember is that our cipher is of the
> lowest grade (for the sake of simplicity), and that it provides

security for a limited time only. Tactically, therefore, it is secure because by the time it will have been broken the info. will be out of date or action will have been taken by the appropriate military command.

'A very different picture would be given to the enemy if, during present training, a daily interception of our practice traffic were taking place.

'The code we use can be broken quite easily by experts, so even in code messages great care should be observed and reference to the functions of this organisation should never be made, even if they are enciphered.

'Despite the above, one IO has recently (presumably to save time and trouble) transmitted from the IN-Station to 11 OUT-Stations in his area, the provisions of the new 'captured' drill and how it works! Any further comment is unnecessary except to express the strongest disapproval of such stupidity.'

Will the Intelligence Officer with the red face please stand in the corner?

'Captured' drill was a secret indication from one operator to another that he had been taken prisoner and was transmitting under duress. Auxunits (Signals) had their own 'captured' drill. Entirely as a personal initiative, opening calls from a Signals-manned 'IN-Station' were:

'King George for England!'

The response expected from the OUT-Station was:

'and Kings Cross for Scotland!'

– unless, of course, the operator had been captured and had the barrel of a Nazi revolver pressed to the back of his neck! (HI)

Although code was regularly used to pass operational messages, test transmissions, which comprised the bulk of Control Station radio traffic, were usually 'In Clear' – and often selected poems or readings from books. Thea Ward's favourite was 'You are old, Father William, the young man said...'

from 'Alice in Wonderland'.

If this descriptive sequence is as nearly true as we shall get, it also explains why ATS subalterns never *quite* manage to recall the code-system. The deduction may be that they received 'jargon' messages in coded plain language, and promptly took them to the duty Intelligence Officer at nearby army Divisional HQ. And so *he* usually did the decoding.

Captain Ken Ward says that the Germans may have heard the general radio traffic (and in 1944 were *intended* to do so) but there was no evidence that transmissions were otherwise intercepted or radio stations located.

For the seven officers and sixty-nine ORs employed in 1944 on maintenance, watch-keeping and training 'civilian personnel', this special way-of-life came to an abrupt climax soon after 13th July when General Staff (Operations), GHQ Home Forces, informed General Staff (Special Duties) of the 'closedown of SDS and associated Signals forthwith'.

And asked for their men back.

CHAPTER SEVENTEEN

Auxiliary Units Signals
& SDS Operational Bases

'...the Signals organisation in the country is divided into areas
which closely correspond to existing Command areas...In the area
there are varying numbers of maintenance parties (3 men each);
...These maintenance parties are responsible for manning an IN
Station, and for maintaining all OUT and SUB-OUT Stations in
their own areas...

R M A Jones, Major, R Sigs
Commander, Aux.Units Sigs

Burying Auxunits' Special Duties Section radios in boxes with
lids was seriously insecure and no way to fool an intelligent
enemy. As soon as this was understood, permanent new
arrangements were worked out. Each of the 125 OUT-Stations
and 78 SUB-OUT-Stations, had to be properly hidden, as well
as the thirty Control Stations. Some of the OUT-Stations
could safely go in sheds, or attics or barns or other cleverly
thought-out hides; and Control Stations were disguised as
'Met' Huts anyway. But the majority had to be replaced into
underground Operational Bases.

These were ingeniously designed by Royal Engineers,
carefully sited by Royal Signals, and strenuously hammered,
dug and cement-mixed by Sappers and Pioneers. In spite of
admittedly inadequate corroboration, the odds are 'evens' of
another clever ingredient, although it is unclear whether it was
an idea germinated at Cabinet level, or from the War Office, or
even the Deputy Director of Military Intelligence himself.
Perhaps it was simply developed by SDS Intelligence Officers
over pre-prandial pink gins in the Officers' Mess – and later
disseminated through Secret Monthly Notes?

In any case, someone with clout seems to have decided that
chickens were a sure way to forestall German Army Signals'
intercepts.

The 'cackle-factor' occurs in significant disproportion to the total number of OBs, and too frequently to be mere coincidence. It is often possible within military or quasi-military administration, for some aspirant to achieve promotion with a bright idea – in this case by dedicated study of the genus – Rhode Island Red.

For example, in one published account summarising OB locations, SDS radio stations were discovered on top of the mausoleum folly in Brocklesby Park in Lincolnshire and in a summerhouse on the roof of a mansion in Ottery St Mary, Devon. Another, at Axminster, Devon, was run by – '*a chicken farmer who entered his bunker by..........*' Further indicators were evident in Suffolk where, the radio OUT-Station at Great Glemham was situated behind a false partition in *a mobile chicken shed* – one of those heavy duty affairs on sturdy iron wheels, frequently seen fifty years ago being pulled around the field by a horse in harness. The operator crouched his way into the chicken shed door, poked his finger through a knothole in what looked like the end wall, pressed a hidden catch to release access to the false partition and crawled into a tiny radio room. The aerial of his set, typically, was ducted into the bark of an adjacent Spanish oak – and is still there. The 'post-box' was under a rusty old ploughshare which the operator, Charles Kindred, reached by lifting out a floorboard without leaving the chicken-house.

Another chicken shed hid the TRD radio used by Bert Daniels at nearby Swefling. Bert Daniels and Charles Kindred – patriotic, resourceful, and interested in pre-war amateur radio work – were typical of the calibre of civilian recruited and, as farmers, exempt from military service. Who can doubt they were good with chickens too?

Major David Wemyss, with Auxunits for nine months, was apparently SDSIO at Carmarthen. He wrote to Arthur Gabbitas:

> 'Sergeant Jack Millie was my right-hand man. I remember little about the outstations......I only remember constructing two. One was in a golf club locker at (I think) Newport golf club, where the back of the locker consisted of a second (secret) door - with the batteries under the wooden floorboards in front of the locker. The other was at Bridgend, which was made from an old red GPO van situated in the middle of a large wire-netting cage which housed masses of chickens. The radio was in the back of the van under the floor - which had neither engine nor axles. I seem to remember that the old scrap van was uplifted during the night from a dump!'

Here was an example of British innovation and opportunism, with the 'cackle' factor in tandem. It didn't stop south of the Border, as Stan Judson told us:

'In John O'Groats in a crofter's cottage, we had a bit of trouble with his set and Lieutenant Bradley and myself were sitting in this chicken house, operating the set, with a row of chickens perched above us. They were not house trained either.'

Radio network locations centred on the Winchester Control Station ('OMAGH') were abbreviated, in recovered records, to 'D/O' – for dugouts – at Shorwell, and Wickham. In the Buckland St Mary net ('CHIRNSIDE'), they were in 'hut/boxes' at Puriton and Puckington and elsewhere in farmhouses or attics. Please step forward with best guesses for Setley and Denmead, both listed as 'Ch/ho'. (HI!)

And if the case is still 'Not Proven' turn to page 125 of 'The Last Ditch' and read about;

'One clandestine radio operator, Adrian Monck-Mason, a chicken farmer who lived on a hilltop outside Charing, Kent, was once going to his radio hideout, under his chicken houses, when he saw...'

Can there still be doubt about it?

★   ★   ★

The late Douglas Ingrams was recorded as a 'chicken farmer near Axminster'. The words were inadequate to describe him – or his family or their splendid property at Bewley Down, backed with Scots Pines towering high above picturesque valleys. In addition to breeding chickens, Douglas, an inter-war Territorial Army Gunnery Officer and Special Constable, ran fifty acres of mixed farmland. With these credentials, and a thorough knowledge of the locality, he was easily identifiable as a prime Key-man and radio station candidate by Captain Cecil Coxwell-Rogers, MC, the first Special Duties IO in the area.

Coxwell-Rogers, owner of Rossley Manor Country Club near Cheltenham and said to have pre-war Security Services' connections, had his HQ at 17, Mount Street, Taunton. Taken ill in 1942, Douglas Ingrams was his replacement IO – for a time combining these duties with travel and training, as well as farming. In 1943 he attended a full-time advanced training course 'somewhere near Ipswich', and then took over the Norfolk SDS network from John Collings. He was eventually posted to secret work in the Canal Zone of Egypt and is known to have made a 'political foray' into Palestine before returning with Major's rank in 1947.

Before his own death in 2000, his son David described what happened in 1941 when he came home from prep-school for Easter:

> 'To my astonishment at the bottom of the garden, beside the old original privy, an enormous hole was being dug by seven or eight soldiers. They were keen to barter a can of Spam for a steaming pot of tea. They came and went each day in a closed furniture van with just a couple of little air vents in the top – they hadn't a clue where they were. I was sworn to secrecy by my father and when I returned in the summer the garden was in its original state and looked as though nothing had ever been disturbed.
>
> 'For a while in 1943, we had two ATS subalterns billeted with us, Mary Alexander and Priscilla Badgerow (now Aston). Aged twelve, I fell madly in love with them both.'

'Billeted' was one way of putting it. These ladies were Control Station personnel from the Met Hut at Divisional HQ, Taunton, learning something of everyday life in the Auxiliary Units' SDS radio OUT-Station which the soldiers had been building. Priscilla Aston recalls that they also 'did-their-bit' for the wartime 'Dig-for-Victory' campaign, helping gather in the Ingrams' harvest in their spare time.

For reasons of essential secrecy, David would never know 'the civilians, the clergyman, the postman, the vet., the doctor, milkman and perhaps a lorry driver or two', the men and women recruited locally and trained to collect Intelligence and send messages to the radio station through Dead Letter Drops. Neither could he identify the runner who brought those messages. But he did discover how the unit worked and that his father's favoured DLD was:

> '...a spike driven into a telegraph pole and drilled hollow. All telegraph poles have a metal disc or plate with a number on them. If the runner saw the plate upside down, a message had been left in it by an agent. Taking care he was not seen, the runner would cautiously pull out the plate, lift the message from the hollow tube and replace the plate with the number the right way up. The agent would realise the message had been collected and the DLD was ready for reuse. Of course, this was only ever done as practice. The Germans never came, but the system was proved and perfected and ready to go into action if they did.

'Other DLDs in my father's area were in hollowed tethering rings for horses, house knockers, and five-bar gate hinges.'

It was now the runner's duty to get the message to the radio OB but, although obviously close by, he never knew the precise location. Trained to move stealthily at night, he walked from the local hamlet in the valley, using hedgerows for cover and avoiding skylines. A final climb took him to the outer market garden of the Ingrams' property and past a refuse dump where, deliberately placed among discarded children's toys and other household remnants, he would find an old tennis ball with a cut in it. When squeezed open, the message, still in plain language, was inserted. With pressure released, the ball reverted to normal shape. Moving through a garden gate and up a few steps to a laurel hedge – the runner arrived at a well-disguised letterbox:

'In the laurel hedge there was a tree stump. It was about nine inches across and three feet high and had been cleverly adapted by Royal Engineers. When grasped and twisted, the top six inches swivelled to reveal a hole just big enough for the tennis ball. He would drop it in, close the tree trunk 'lid', make sure nothing was out of place, and go back home.

'The ball fell down the hollowed tree trunk and rolled along a system of glazed, earthenware, four-inch water pipes, buried underground.

'The next leg of the Intelligence conduit was to code-up the message and transmit.'

Although the tree stump has rotted away, the pipe installation is still in full working order.

The OB was located under the 'thunder-box' of the outdoor privy. With its whereabouts cunningly disguised, a right to enter was reserved for the Ingrams' family, Captain Coxwell-Rogers, and Auxunits' Signals service and supervisory personnel – including Arthur Gabbitas, working for a time from the IN Station at Buckland St Mary. Also on the approved list were a local man and woman – never unidentified by David Ingrams – who helped to man the radio room when listening time increased to 24 hours a day in 1943. Usually, there was just one person at a time below ground, and they monitored a sophisticated alert system to identify anyone trying to gain entry.

Those few with a need-to-know operated an actuator - David Ingrams remembered an air pump like a blood-pressure bulb, hidden at ground level by the foot of a nearby rose arbour – lighting an overhead bulb in the OB, probably linked to the accumulator system.   Each pressure produced a flash.   A simple Morse Code group was changed each day. If the correct group flashed, the duty operator would prepare to receive 'friends'.   If incorrect, or someone tried to obtain admittance without actuating the signal at all, the operator 'was ready to meet the enemy with his hand-gun'.

The inside of the privy, entered through a low door, was entirely normal in its day – a bucket-and-chuck-it, two-seater, wooden thunder-box. Inside to the left, were three cup-hooks used as coat hangers. One was false and could be pulled and turned – if you knew about it – to operate a Bowden cable buried in the flint and concrete wall, releasing a catch.   A system of levers and lead counter balances then came into play allowing the whole toilet assembly, and suitably watertight contents, to be eased up about four feet, revealing a block and concrete down-shaft with built-in wooden ladder.

The down-shaft ended in a confined, horizontal tunnel. A few crouching paces brought the visitor into standing headroom, with corrugated elephant-iron roof bolted to a block plinth, and a small table, stool and sleeping bench. This was the map-room, with wall-mounted Ordnance Survey.

Also the code and decode area, and with Intelligence data in dossiers, the map room contained a food and water supply for two weeks or so – likely to be the maximum that Douglas could expect to hold out before invaders zeroed in. As the operator sat at the table, his right shoulder was close to vertical railway sleepers apparently forming the end of the OB.

However, a small lever was hidden underneath the table. When pulled, it released the catch securing a secret access cover, allowing a second system of weights and counter-balances to activate.   These lifted a disguised hatch, and permitted access to a smaller, one-person radio room *behind* the sleepers.

On the floor was a saucer shaped metal fixture where the tennis ball rested.

Essential air circulation was ducted through pipes in the roof to hidden ventilators outside. Light was by Tilley lamp – with warm air rising to assist air circulation. Heat came from a paraffin stove but, with an ever-present danger of asphyxiation, this was used only when absolutely necessary. David Ingrams considered that the hidden radio room gave the operator a few invaluable extra moments' transmission time if finally tracked down. Aerials for the TRD were buried in the bark of the Scots Pines close by. Their height, and that of the site above sea level, gave useful line-of-sight transmission range. Unusually for an OUT-(or SUB-OUT) Station, and perhaps indicating the significance of the operator, there were three separate hidden aerials, each specifically targeted.

Bewley Down SDS OB was of above average importance. The map of the final network drawn up by Major R M A Jones in June 1944, when the scheme had achieved its greatest scope, gives an indication of only one radio communications link but evidence of three is indisputable – so there may have been a relay station function as well. The aerial down-leads are still in position and, where the three trees have grown faster and further than the wires could expand, have snapped and popped out at right angles to the trunks.

Probably the best-known survivor, the Bewley Down OB is well-preserved and now protected by an English Heritage order.

Pretty well the most westerly in England, this Devon OB was not dissimilar in design to an OUT Station at Normanby in Yorkshire, surveyed and drawn for this book by Dennis Walker of Redcar. Some continuity of design was obviously shared among Royal Engineers in different parts of the country, but enquiries to uncover their records have been ignored.

Other imaginative OB examples are on record. Stan Judson, for example, described one which his team serviced in Lincolnshire:

> 'The entrance consisted of a flat platform supported on two metal tubes with pulleys and counterweights, so that the platform was raised vertically by the release of a concealed catch, thus retaining its horizontal position, together with the undergrowth which concealed it. The interior of the bunker consisted of a small room lined with storage racks from floor to ceiling, which were stacked with items to give the impression that it was an underground storage depot for the Home Guard. Actually one set of racks was a blind as, on the release of a concealed lever, it could be swung open to reveal the entrance door to the transmitting room.'

In a Scottish Estate Office, Stan found the radio set hidden in a big roll-top desk. It looked normal but the back was false and when a hidden spring was released the set 'just slid out'. In another dugout, a wooden panel was nailed into position. When a particular nail was pressed – 'it went in, released a catch and the door came open.' One east-coast radio station had the TRD hidden in a safe behind the manager's desk in a gasworks. The whole safe slid out when a catch was released, to reveal the radio – with the aerial hidden up the chimney.

Wilhelmina Morrison-Low transmitted on the 'BARNACK' network, near Perth. She wrote to Arthur Gabbitas from Fife in 1996:

> '...was a secret wireless transmitting centre for use in case of invasion, manned by Major R W Purvis of Gilmerton (died 1956) and Miss H W M Purvis (Dowager Lady Morrison-Low). The centre was in a wood on Kinaldy. It was underground, about 8ft deep, entered by a trapdoor. This was covered by leaves etc and released by an underground wire, the end of which was about ten yards from the trap-door and had to be pulled to release the catch which held the trap-door closed.

> '...we went about once a week to send messages – imaginary, as if here had been an invasion. These I dictated using the alphabet – "Able, Baker" etc. Occasionally, there were night exercises when messages were sent by other centres to headquarters. I suppose this was run by the Signals. A captain certainly called occasionally to see us. ...I have no idea where the other centres were or how many...'

Survival time for operators after invasion can only be a guess. Control Stations had:

> '...concealed dugouts in which station crew can, if necessary, live without coming above ground at all for three weeks at a time. This includes provision for battery charging, feeding, etc.'

Roy Russell was an officer with Auxunits (Signals) in the south east of England. He describes the entrance to a Zero Station, probably at Harrietsham, one of two for which he had responsibility:

> 'The trapdoor was a circular metal tray, with a sod of earth cut to fit and slightly overlap. When opened there was a wooden ladder down to the Station, which had cover as an ammunition dump. When a hidden wire was pulled, shelving opened to reveal a secret interior entrance.

> 'A long screw or worm activated the trapdoor lid. From the exterior it was necessary to find a flat stone, lift it, and a four-sided fixture for the crank was revealed. This swung the trapdoor upward and to one side.

'It was so well hidden on an airfield that a Mosquito once parked on top and we couldn't get access. I had to confide in the RAF Station CO to get his aircraft moved.

'Ventilation was through a channel, with air extracted by a petrol driven pump activated by a pull on a hidden wire, so that it could be switched on and off from inside as required – and when it was safe to do so.'

Three or four weeks was therefore the optimum lifespan. But with more than 200 OUT- and SUB-OUT Stations, tracking them *all* would have presented the enemy with a hugely complex and time-consuming use of resources. Moreover, torture of captives could not have produced betrayal – the agents were not known to one another.

And some of the vital Intelligence that Auxunits SDS was trained to collect, would still have been speeding to the men at HQ who really needed it.

★   ★   ★

Control Stations, the hub of the communication network, were often manned by ATS subalterns using 'Met' Hut cover, and usually situated in a quiet spot in the grounds of Army Divisonal HQ. Underground, fallback, last-ditch Zero Stations waited nearby and the ATS received elementary firearms training to defend themselves. Subaltern Marina Bloxham at the Ousden, Suffolk Control Station, had a revolver and was told it was to shoot herself with to avoid capture - but she had moral objections against taking her own life, even under such a threat.

The theory was that these ladies would 'stay behind' but, in the event, they were unlikely to be abandoned to the searching enemy. Stan Judson certainly assumed that male other rank Auxunits' Signalmen were considered more expendable'.

'Met' Huts were cover for HQ transceiving stations. Sometimes they were purpose built War Office wooden huts and sometimes Nissen Huts. Initially intended for one or two operators, they needed space for three at any one time as the system expanded and watch hours increased from 1941. The War Establishment was for three operators with two radio sets, and five when there were three. None of the huts survived the 1944 War Office stand-down order for destruction.

Zero-Stations were permanent structures, built of concrete by Royal Engineers. Usually with three chambers – the first a small entrance and store; then the radio installation and quarters for two or three soldiers or ATS; and finally a room for a petrol driven generator, and an escape route along a tunnel constructed of heavy duty concrete culvert pipes about 30" in diameter. After early trials, and the usual hiatus with exhaust fumes and asphyxiation, the end chamber was redesigned and effectively sealed off with asbestos cladding. Pumps were installed to duct exhaust gases through the tunnel, or along purpose built systems, with ventilators concealed outside.

Each with up to a dozen OUT-Stations, Zero Stations were equipped with sleeping, cooking and toilet facilities. The Winchester OB doubled as a Relay Station to Divisional HQ near Salisbury and was Arthur Gabbitas's first field posting. One of the team of three kept a listening watch for OUT-Stations scheduled – except in an emergency – to make short transmissions at fixed routines, while the other two travelled out with recharged batteries. Lightly armed, they expected the order to stay behind after invasion:

> 'We didn't use these Zero Station OBs regularly but had frequent exercises in them. I don't ever remember receiving instructions what to do in the event of possible capture. I take it they believed we should have been capable of using our own ideas whether to join up with local forces or try to get back to our own lines. The escape tunnel at the Winchester OB came out under a large tree twenty or so yards away and was well hidden.
>
> 'On one occasion two officers came to supervise the exercises and I was sent off to get some gear. When I got back, my friend Alf Ellis had collapsed due to carbon-monoxide from the generator. We had the devil of a job to get him out of the main entrance. It was a straight up ladder to the hatch, which was hidden under the cold frame of the market garden. To get in you had to slip the frame to one side and lift out a tray of pot plants. I tried to drag Alf up while the officers pushed from the bottom. I went to get their Staff-car and of course the driver was not there. Alf finally came round and we took him to the military hospital, but there were no staff on duty. So we finished up at the civilian hospital. Alf and I were kept in for observation.
>
> 'Annoyingly, the officers spent most of the night at the other end of the Ward chatting up the attractive red-headed night nurse.
>
> 'Back at the OB, we decided the dry weather had shrunk the earth round the outside and allowed fumes to leak in.'

His next posting was to Buckland-St-Mary where the OB was

at the end of the Blackdown Hills, on an old Roman site. The dugout was let into the rim of a natural hollow and this gave some protection from discovery. Another Control Station was at Hume Castle, near Edinburgh. According to Stan Judson:

> 'Close to the 'M' Station (or 'Met' Hut), was a little back-of-the-garden lavatory.
>
> 'By lifting the lavatory you had access to the underground station through a tunnel made of great large circular drainpipes. They had an escape that went under the wall of the castle and the door was made of imitation rock – the same as the castle – so it couldn't be seen from outside.'

Most of the Control Stations – or IN-Stations, Base or Zero Stations – and all the Met Huts, were demolished at stand-down in 1944. Fortunately, a few OUT-Station OBs were missed in part, and at least one Control Station is intact.

It is again important to emphasise the danger of standardising available knowledge to fit predetermined hypotheses. Frequently, OB construction depended upon available materials, Engineers' skills, and IOs' initiative. To establish the point, detailed drawings of Signals' OBs in Yorkshire, formally confirmed as radio OUT-Stations, have been provided by researcher, Dennis Walker. The OUT-Station establishment would usually presuppose one or two civilian operators for each but – in respect of size, construction, layout, ventilation and, in one case the position and size of the escape tunnel – they appear substantially the same as the Control Station OB at Winchester, manned by three or four soldiers.

They have little resemblance to the OUT-Station at Bewley Down in Devon, and were constructed with know-how collected from earlier trial- and-error in the south and east of the country. The most probable assumption is that – overlooking coastline vulnerable to raids or counter-invasion – the Yorkshire sites had a disproportionately important role as manpower-saving guard-and-observation posts and personnel adequate to man them.

★　　★　　★

The 'cackle-factor' was never, of course, a serious reality. But the whole OB network, the 'genius' of Maurice Petherick and his Special Duties Section, the innovations of Royal Engineers, and the steadfast patriotism of the men of Auxiliary Units (Signals) and the ATS women, were above all a thoroughly British product.

Do we really have to find our backs to the wall before developing such special talents? And why were so many men and women anxious volunteers to talk about it over half a century later?

Could it be that they were peeved because nobody got any credit for it?

CHAPTER EIGHTEEN
Auxillary Units ATS
'The Secret Sweeties'

'Nor run with raving Cries to fill the City,
But rather whilst your Brothers, Fathers, Friends,
Pour Storms of Fury on our fierce Invaders,
Do you implore kind Heav'n to shield your country,
With silent Earnestness and calm Devotion.'
('*Old England to her Daughters*' –
a Broadsheet Address to the Females of Great Britain.)

★   ★   ★

Another unorthodox introduction into this Special Duties' Section Intelligence gathering army - of which the pilot scheme before the end of 1940 formed an important part – was officially called GHQ Auxiliary Units (ATS). Once again, operational 'Top' secrecy was absolute and lasted even after they were officially laid to rest a year before the end of WWII. And – apart from David Lampe's flirtation with a chapter on the 'Secret Sweeties' in '*The Last Ditch*' in 1968 – that was where they were intended to remain.

Fortunately, however, documentary evidence emerging from Public Record Office confirms the existence – although not much about their role – of a number of women who wore ATS Officers' uniform, even though only a few were, for the duration of their Auxunit service, lady soldiers as conventionally remembered. Lacking eye witnesses or research in PRO, David Lampe – knowing only what he was told – bundled them together with Auxunit Special Duties Section and Signals. In fact, although an integral part of the SDS network, they worked in almost complete isolation from both.

The recollections of survivors, supplemented by serious analysis based on recently rediscovered papers in PRO, is assembled here for the first time.

In the absence of certain critical detail – such as a full nominal roll – it would still be unwise to attempt too many definitive conclusions. Two things are absolutely certain, however. Firstly, Auxunit Operational Patrols and the ATS were not in any way connected. The women had an SDS communications' role, communications being conspicuously absent for the saboteurs/guerrillas hidden in underground OBs. Secondly, although many of the ATS wore Royal Signals' insignia on their uniform and were commanded by Major John Hills – from the Corps himself – they were on a GHQ Home War Establishment and never Signallers in a formal sense. Neither were they trained as such. Indeed, 'Royal Signals' was one of several fronts used to disguise their true role and identity, and it was Auxiliary Units HQ which smoothed an irregular pathway to promotion and ensured officer status for them outside normal administrative channels.

One of the few ATS ladies who for a time did come near to conventional service was Sergeant E M ('Willie') Wilmott. She was not either first in or last out of Auxunits; nor did she serve with them in-the-field. Although an 'other rank', as personal secretary to the Commanding Officer, Colonel Bill Major in 1941 and 1942, she was at the Coleshill fountainhead:

> 'I joined the TA soon after Mr Chamberlain announced in September 1938 that a Women's Army was being formed, and was called up to Southern Command HQ at Salisbury on 27th August 1939. I served as secretary to the Major General (Administration) and was drafted to France with six other ATS to join the British Expeditionary Force. However, on arrival at the ship at Southampton, an indignant Sergeant Major screamed – "We don't want women, we want tanks!" Dunkirk was just beginning so we all had to go back to our Units with tails between our legs and much mickey-taking...
>
> 'I arrived at Coleshill after Colonel Gubbins had moved to Baker Street (with SOE) and taken his secretary, Margaret Jackson, with him. Colonel Major took over with me as his secretary. There were only four ATS there at the time. We lived in the house – so did the officers – and other ranks were in the stables. Maurice Petherick and his secretary came over every morning, though I had no idea where they came from (They were five miles away at Hannington Hall. Mary Burton was probably his ATS secretary – shared with Captain Charles Randell: Editor). Although I worked in the Coleshill library with Colonel Major every day, I had to leave when Major Petherick arrived.
>
> 'One day, John Todd, the IO for Cardiff came to say goodbye and I wrote to him later saying I had no idea where he was going but was there any possibility he wanted a secretary? The sparks flew. I was called in by Colonel Major – whom I had come to

loathe – on a Charge. "Don't you know it's against King's Regulations for Other Ranks to communicate with an Officer?" I did not, and went through Hell for a few weeks while John Todd and Colonel Major argued the toss. I overheard John Todd say – "...after all, she's singularly unattractive." Colonel Major replied "...Oh, I don't know, John, I've seen worse!"

'Anyway, I got my transfer but had to resign from the ATS first. I served with Special Operations Executive in South Africa – organising the Vichy French surrender of Madagascar – then Cairo, Baghdad, Colombo and Kuala Lumpur, before being discharged in 1946 in India.'

John Todd (alias 'Tommy Atkins'), the Intelligence Officer for South Wales, and possibly Hereford and Worcester as well, was the only Auxunit IO responsible for both Operational and Special Duties networks at the same time. (Anthony Quayle, Stuart Edmundson and Peter Forbes, among others no doubt, worked both with Operational Patrols and SDS – but not simultaneously.) Under Todd's command, the remarkable 'Vicars' SDS network was formed near Abergavenny (see Chapter XIII). Maurice Petherick was, of course, the head of the Special Duties Section, operating from Hannington Hall together with ATS 'Queen Bee' – Senior Commander Beatrice Temple, often known affectionately as 'Belinda Blue Eyes', and Subaltern Barbara Culleton.

After the war, 'Willie' Wilmott was a founder member of the Special Forces Club in London, and she and Barbara Culleton are enthusiastic and generous supporters of the Museum of the British Resistance Organisation at Parham.

★   ★   ★

A 'pilot' Special Duties Section radio network, operating in Kent at the end of 1940, has already been identified. Two of the five or six ATS other ranks (soon to be second-subalterns) operating with a 'MAIDSTONE' call-sign, were Mickey Browne and Thea Ward. Yolande Alston (nee Bromley) – with Kitty Hills and probably Margaret Whiting – was another of 'the six', being co-opted early in 1941, well before the majority of the other 'Secret Sweeties'. She served later at Thornham Magna, Suffolk, the home of the Henniker-Major family, and it was through Lord Henniker (who himself had distinguished WWII service with SOE) that the Museum was fortunate enough to be put in touch with Yolande at her home near Stowmarket:

'Having completed my education and a secretarial course, I

joined the ATS in York in January 1940. I applied for service overseas. After horrible injections and being issued with tropical kit, I was told 'Monty' refused to have women in the Middle East.

'I was drafted to XII Corps and, after reporting to Major John Hills at Tunbridge Wells, was billeted in an 'ATTERY'. He told us only what we needed-to-know, but checked that we were numerate and tested our voices for clarity. I was joined by Kitty Hills, the OCs wife. Our job was to become radio operators and pass on Intelligence reports, as well as learning some of the arts of spying. At times the training was intensive, including self-defence and survival practice; at others a bit boring. I don't know whether XII Corps was even there! I never saw a soldier.

'The network was already in existence round the bit of coast then most likely to be invaded; we could therefore contact other stations. A need for secrecy was instilled. It was understood that we were expected to stay-behind to work our radio stations after invasion, even if the army had to retire. We were clear about "do-or-die" expectations. I was persuaded against telling even my family about the work.

'I never did know how I was selected, although they had a CV and I may have come to notice by applying for service overseas. The six of us were sent to OCTU in Edinburgh, two at a time, for two weeks – we couldn't be spared for the usual six.

'To get us, our OC had quite a fight with the ATS Commandant – who had no idea what work we were doing. In order to move about the country without restriction, we needed to be officers.'

Phasing women into a man's world, before the nation was socially and culturally prepared, presented numerous problems. Today, unisex operations are normal enough but in 1940, even as the nation prepared for total war, Victorian embargoes preserved women from enforced proximity to men, especially those of a certain class. Women, for example, were never considered for service underground with Auxunit Operational Patrols.

Stan Judson, with Auxiliary Units (Signals), understood that:

'...the idea of staying behind in an OB with women was not entertained...it would have created insoluble toilet problems.'

Working from the back of an army truck during one lengthy exercise, Auxunits ATS officers protested when a cylindrical object was delivered with the rations. Explaining that they proposed to cope without an Elsan chemical toilet, they were abruptly told:

'You are officers. You've got to have one!'

ATS Director, Dame Helen Gwynne-Vaughan, laid down firm disciplinary guidelines. 'A bit of a fuddy-duddy who had been a big white chief in WWI', she decreed that ATS other ranks should – for self protection – never be posted in contingents of less than ten where men were in the same establishment. The British Empire would protect its women, and was not diverted by powerful imperatives to win the war. This admirable aspiration was underwritten by direct Instructions from the War Office. In consequence, as individuals, or groups of only three or four at the most, Auxunit ATS ladies working in-the-field had to be officers. Civilian ladies became ATS other ranks, then Auxunits Second-Subalterns. Later they got a second 'pip'.

The rules were 'adjusted' for the 'Coleshill Four' – ATS other ranks who slipped through the net. They were not, however, out 'in-the-field' but living safely in the Big House with male officers. Although these included specialists in thuggery, assassination, stabbing, booby traps and dirty tricks generally, fortunately for the War Office not one was a serial rapist. Even though there was a war on, the culprit would still surely have been in breach of 'Good Order and Military Discipline?' At least.

Still at Tunbridge Wells on 10th May 1941, Yolande Bromley was busily training and listening out:

'At night I picked up this freak signal on the 'CAULIFLOWER' network all the way from Scotland – a range unheard of in those days. I wrote it down in plain language for the OC. It was a report that Rudolf Hess (Deputy to Adolph Hitler) had landed by parachute in Scotland.

'We never used Morse Code – there would not have been time - and we spoke as if we were talking on the telephone. We didn't say "over and out" in the usual official way – for the Germans to recognise. There was a sort of code, rotated or 'adjusted' daily – I don't remember deliveries of new code sheets or books. You called tanks something like "bulls" or "cows" and if our calls were intercepted they were intended to sound like country women chatting.'

After OCTU at Edinburgh and a short posting to Eastern Command HQ at Hatfield Peverel in Essex, Yolande went in June 1941 to Thornham Magna, Suffolk, then HQ of 15th (Scottish) Division, working alongside Margaret Whiting. Kitty Hills made up the complement of three. Major Hills told her she was no longer an 'AT' and instructed her to wear Royal Corps of Signals badges as cover. Operating from a hut with a dark green radio set, she 'searched the dials' for suspect stations, as well as making and receiving routine calls through her own network. The Suffolk dialect was sometimes a problem but - having only four panel controls – using the TRD was simple enough:

On/Off switch
Send/Receive switch
Receiver Tuning
Volume.

One of the OUT Station operators was a District Nurse, but she never met any of them directly. All messages were taken to the GSO(2), the Staff Officer responsible for Intelligence, and handed over personally. With a 'rolling' code moving along each day, she was responsible for coding and decoding messages. In this respect, Thornham Magna differed from other stations, where code work was left to the Intelligence Staff.

Three operators were not enough to listen out full time. One evening, on a quiet 24-hour solo stand-by, she chanced a bath. Unexpectedly, she was called to report to her station in a hurry:

'I shot out and got on my bike. At night the camp was closed and I had to go the long way round. As that would take too long, I picked up my bike and went through the wire in a rush and tore my stockings and things. I got on duty and took some calls. The next day the OC asked me if I knew what it had all been about?

King George VI was listening at the other end – and it was a demonstration for him!

'We had to carry gas masks everywhere and I kept my lipstick and powder in the case. One colleague used to keep her knitting inside as well. Beatrice Temple was known as the "Queen Bee". I was at work before she was posted to Auxunits. For example, I applied directly to John Hills for leave – and I don't ever remember meeting her. Captain Freddie Childe was our local officer.'

In 1942, Yolande received a telegram from John Hills inviting her to volunteer for India, where he was setting up a new radio network. Keen to travel but still undecided, she confided in local landowner, Donald Alston, when he took her to dinner:

'I told him I was off! He said – "I was going to ask you to marry me". It was an awful decision and, thinking I might be able to do both, I asked him if he would wait? But he replied – "No".

Yolande and Donald were married on 7th July 1942. After a month's leave, she opened a new Control Station at Bury St Edmunds, with both a 'Met' Hut and under-ground Zero Station. She was demobilised in April 1943. Donald died on

26th June 2001.

(Yolande, in all good faith, cannot recall ever meeting Senior Commander Temple – whereas the Beatrice Temple diaries indicate more than one direct contact. In itself, this is not of significance but it is another typical example of recall differences after a sixty-year interval.)

⋆   ⋆   ⋆

Someone in ATS headquarters in the War Office once asked Miss Temple, 'What exactly do your officers do? We hear that they sit in caves all day and knit.'

Miss Temple smiled. 'That's what they do.'

⋆   ⋆   ⋆

During 1941, Special Duties systems improved, and continued to expand for another two years. Coast watchers' recruitment extended from the south-east, to East Anglia; then north through Lincolnshire and north-east England, into the east coast of Scotland; and simultaneously westward as far as Devon. The final addition was along the south Wales coastline, with a Control Station at Abergavenny.

TRD radio transceivers were rolling from the assembly line at Hundon, and Auxunits' Signals teams installing and servicing them in-the-field. In the early days, formal ATS administration was set aside because of the sheer urgency of getting an SDS network rolling before the Germans arrived. This may well have been encouraged by the Secret Services – more interested in retaining an innovative, hybrid task within their control than handing it over to bureaucratic, routine War Office financing and regulation.

The senior officer chosen in November 1941, as the arbiter to re-establish formally structured supervision and administration, was Beatrice Temple, the niece of the Archbishop of Canterbury. She is on record as 'pretty' – an undoubted asset in an unsmiling military hierarchy - and carried the title of Senior Commander. With official accommodation at Hannington Hall, she had easy access to Auxiliary Units HQ at Coleshill. Miss Temple's responsibilities included frequent visits to subalterns in-the-field, to assure herself of their welfare, adequacy of accommodation – some being in official quarters and others in approved lodgings - and the arrival of pay in good time.

Known as 'the Battling Bantam', her Assistant (or Adjutant) was Subaltern (later Captain) Barbara Culleton, TD, – whose official Service Record gives encouragement to anyone petitioning the Ministry of Defence and rating his or her recall more accurate than theirs. With incomprehensible inaccuracies, the record states that on 27th June 1941, she was posted to 'Auxiliary Platoon, Edinburgh', then to OCTU and on 7th September 1941 to HQ – Auxiliary Units, Edinburgh. The existence of an Auxunits Platoon or HQ at Edinburgh is certainly news to everyone outside the MoD. On 18th September 1941, she was attached to HQ 1st Division, Hundon. While the MoD will never admit to inaccurate records, hers are at times entertainingly unclear. Especially to Captain Culleton herself.

Lack of inches rarely held her back but she was later disqualified from SOE service. They found her too short to leap quickly into and out of aircraft hatches.

During early autumn 1941, having mastered the uncomplicated operation of a TRD radio at Hundon in Suffolk, she was rocketed by staff car (either a Humber or Armstrong-Siddeley, affectionately known as an 'Um-Tum-Tiddley') – or army truck if the country going was rough – to unidentifiably remote locations, setting up and testing radio communication in new Control Stations. This required contact with linked-up OUT-Stations, and systems' adjustment until perfect voice communication was achieved. She was then whisked off to the next station ready for action – 'Somewhere-in-England'.

Life was not all grimly desk-bound. One evening the two Commanders unwisely accepted an invitation by 'Jack-the-Lad' Captains Charles Randell and A R C Anderson for a trip to London Town. Unexpectedly, they found themselves in a Soho night-club famed for saucy showgirls and often frowned upon by the local authorities, who were still merciless in clamping down on anything hinting of 'good times'. As a rumour spread that the police vice-squad was preparing to raid the premises, the two women displayed properly expected initiative by disappearing through a small window in the Ladies' room and exiting smartly into the blackout – thus avoiding scandal on their own account and, vicariously, the Archbishop of Canterbury. They may also have wrong-footed the eternal watchdog of propriety, the News of the World – even in those intoxicating days vigilantly searching for 'all human life'.

Also at the end of 1941, GHQ decided to operate some Control Stations with women officers. As they were not immediately available from the ATS, it was Beatrice Temple's job to recruit them; she took advantage of several channels to find young women, mainly civilians, able to conduct themselves

Four of the Auxiliary Units' (Signals) NCOs. G2RD Ron Dabbs *(top right)* and G8CK Bill Bartholomew *(bottom right)*, specially selected for Auxunits as pre-war radio 'HAMS', were instrumental in a brilliant redesign of the SDS secret voice transceiver, eventually recognised as 'TRD'. Stan Judson *(bottom left)* and Arthur Gabbitas *(top left)* were in-the-field and it was Arthur whose research first penetrated the post-war iron curtain of absolute cellular secrecy which led to a number of reunions. *(Stan Judson)*

(top left) Captain Barbara
Culleton, ATS (Auxiliary Units).
(Barbara Culleton)

(top right) Specially recruited
lady Control Station radio
operators received subaltern's
rank in ATS (Auxiliary Units).
Yolande Bromley (now Yolande
Alston) participated in the pilot
scheme. (Yolande Alston)

(lower left) A rare photograph
of Colonel Frank Douglas,
Commander of Auxiliary Units
from 1943 until close-down in
January 1945.
(Mick Wilks collection)

(top) 'Secret Sweeties'. Unpopular though this sobriquet may have been, it is hardly a mystery how it was coined! Here are Dorothy Monck-Mason, now Dorothy Rainey, and (possibly) Ann Ellis-Hughes, taking a mealbreak from their Blandford, Dorset, Control Station.
(Dorothy Rainey)

Geoff Bowery stops mercifully short of assassinating a once-only volunteer (the Editor), in a CQC demonstration to a TV crew.
(Lion Television).

Disbandment started in 1944 and 'Stand-down' group photographs suddenly proliferated. Not surprisingly, however, no photographic record has been discovered of the Special Duties Section. Among this November 1944, formal stand-down group of AU (Signals), readers will identify many names familiar from the narrative – Mackie, Gabbitas, Bartholomew, Judson, Ellis, Spencer, Shanks, Thimont, Dabbs, Millie and Parnell, for example.

(Stan Judson/BRO Museum collection)

Suffolk Auxunits' veterans Reginald ('Rex') Chaston *(left)*, of the Carlton Patrol, and Geoff Bowery, Cransford Scout Section, describe the use of some of their WWII guerrilla paraphernalia to a TV crew.

(BRO Museum collection)

Fifty-five years later, Herman Kindred views the main OB chamber of elephant iron still, incredibly, intact. *(Ann Warwicker)*

Many tons of earth, mostly heavy Suffolk clay, were removed with bucket-and-chuck-it techniques before this exit was clear.

The underground tunnel of a classic OB at Sibton was revealed, and a rebuild organised. *(Ann Warwicker/BRO Museum collection)*

Appropriately, Lord Ironside – pictured here with Lady Ironside and Museum Director, Andrew Taylor - is Patron of the Museum. *(C Jack Grice)*

Herman Kindred is seen advising Colin Durrant (Chairman) and Andrew Taylor (Museum Director) during an initial survey of the collapsed underground tunnel to his WWII Operational Base near Parham.

(Paul Mothersole/Museum collection)

Some of the veterans present at Parham for that reunion. (Credit: Paul Mothersole/BRO Museum collection)

in selected company, with intelligence, good clear voices, an understanding of the essence of secrecy, and personally resourceful. These were still the days when it was accepted that people from aristocratic, public school, middle or upper class backgrounds, were free from any inclination to treachery. In the case of Auxunits ATS, the assumption was fully justified.

The names of some suitable recruits may have surfaced from Secret Service lists of trusted contacts. Sources such as the better girls' schools, families of serving officers, and influential landowners and aristocrats, would selectively have been a focus to recommend names on a confidential basis. A trawl was also made within the ATS under the authority of Chief Commandant, The Countess of Carlisle, sometimes known as 'Biddy', then Assistant Director ATS, South-Eastern Command, and specifically the ATS Signals School opened in June 1941. Serving FANYs (the First Aid Nursing Yeomanry – not only a useful service involving the right young women in the war effort but also a long-standing recruiting ground for the secret services), such as Marina Bloxham, were also short-listed. The total considered was variously reported to number from ninety to one-hundred and thirty.

After security 'vetting', Beatrice Temple made the final choice – regularly conducting interviews in the challenging ambience of the tea-lounge at Harrods-of-Knightsbridge. Dorothy Rainey believes her name was put forward by her (then) husband, Adrian Monck-Mason, a coast watcher with a radio OUT Station outside Charing in Kent:

> 'Toward the end of 1941, my WVS canteen work in the London blitz was coming to an end and I was invited to go and meet Beatrice Temple in Harrods. There she was in the Rest Room in mufti, with a red rose in her buttonhole as arranged, and we had a somewhat devious and conspiratorial conversation amidst ladies taking tea. Nothing specific was discussed but she asked if I would be interested in something which was sort of secret. After a short tea party I said "Yes" and was told I would have to sign secrecy papers.'

Women already serving were also encouraged to recommend suitable friends.

Priscilla Badgerow lived in Earls Court when war broke out and – probably during the winter of 1941/1942 - was still a civilian when she recognised Mary Alexander in the street one day. They had been at school together:

> 'She told me a little of her work, without mentioning Auxiliary

Units or anything specific. She asked me what I was doing – as 'they' still required more people. I went home and waited for somebody to write to me, as Mary said would happen.

'When the letter came it invited me to report to a Miss Temple at an address in Hyde Park Corner – in the process of being turned into an ATS Club. I can remember thinking they won't want me because I have got the most awful chilblains, and when the Porter pointed out Miss Temple I thought – "that's done it" as I hobbled across. Anyway she could not have cared less about the chilblains!

'The next thing I had was a Travel Warrant with a letter telling me to report to a place called Hundon. When I got off the train from Liverpool Street, I was met and taken to the Rose and Crown for lunch. Later the same day I went to Bachelor's Hall, before going home to wait for another letter. I joined the ATS as a private. I remember a ghastly uniform. It didn't fit anywhere!'

Miss Temple was not directly responsible for training – this was organised through Auxunits (Signals) HQ at Hundon – but she did assist in the organisation of courses when they were transferred to Coleshill from March 1942.

At Bachelor's Hall, Hundon, the first priority was a voice test by radio through the 'BUTTERCUP' network. With secrecy uppermost, and a total prohibition against talking about their work, if challenged the ATS had a War Office telephone number to hand over as a last resort. Even this did not always work effectively. Barbara Culleton was once detained by 'Redcaps' – the Royal Miliary Police – at Kings Cross Station for more than an hour when they wouldn't accept it.

The next step in the call to the colours was usually a shortened course for Officer training (OCTU) at Craigmillar, a castle in Edinburgh. Technically, at first, still a civilian in this short-circuited process, Dorothy Rainey was there:

'We went in mufti, three or four of us. It was a huge place with about 2,000 ATS, mostly sprucely turned out NCOs who were being promoted and 'au fait' with everything. As 'direct entries' we were a motley little bunch in our slightly shabby civvies, who hadn't the slightest idea about drill, or Part I Orders or anything. It was some time before we were kitted out.

'Even in the bitter mid-winter, there was absolutely no heating whatsoever – the windows didn't fit, there were stone corridors and we were sleeping on iron beds. When we were tacked onto the end and taken out on our first parade through Princes Street, the four of us in civilian clothes hadn't the least idea what was happening. The rest were marching along smartly when three senior officers came out of Crawford's Restaurant and we, at the back, didn't 'eyes right'. It was all a bit ridiculous.

'Shortly after we had been given our uniform, we had to lie down in the snow in our khaki knickers and shirt and do exercises.'

After OCTU, Priscilla Badgerow went home to wait for her first posting – which turned out to be an old people's home at Broadwater Down in Tunbridge Wells, Kent where, unlike many other billets, 'they were delighted to have us'. This was followed by a transfer to the Control Station, with Met Hut and OB/Zero Station, at Cheddon Fitzpaine outside Taunton, Somerset, equipped with another Auxunits'(Signals) technical modification developed to ease the strain of long hours on radio watch. Although GPO headphones were worn in the ordinary way, the No.13 microphone was held at a comfortable level on a round wooden base with central vertical tube and four anti-vibration springs.

A 'chums' arrangement was encouraged and Priscilla and Mary Alexander always worked together. Although of the same rank, Mary was senior in length of service. Billeted in a farmhouse with 'a very hostile family', they had a five-minute walk to work. It was understood they would 'stay-behind' at their station after invasion. The Intelligence Officer was Captain Coxwell-Rogers:

'He was never in uniform. He used to arrive when we had exercises which sometimes went on all night. He would sit behind us listening to whatever we were broadcasting which was, I think, always in code. We wore uniform and sometimes worked from our dugout. One operation lasted a week. We never came up from underground at all. We were training the chaps in the outstations to use the code. We had to keep up a continuous flow so that they could recognise our voices.

'I can't remember Douglas Ingrams, although I met his family at Bewley Down. We never went to his radio station but I do remember baling his hay! Mary and I may have stayed overnight but, as I recall it, we usually returned each time by train to Taunton, and cycled back to our billet. My next post was back at Edinburgh, working from a Met Hut on a golf course, and then down to Dynes Hall, Halstead, with both a hut and a bunker.'

That was where Priscilla met John Aston, whom she later married. He was there with the 51st Highland Division, preparing for the Normandy campaign. After the SDS stand down in 1944, she reverted to normal ATS duty and was demobilised from St John's Wood barracks in north London:

> 'There was no 'demob' suit of clothes for women. I met another
> officer who wanted to go to Harrods. We shared a taxi. I went
> home to Earls Court and that was that!'

Dorothy Rainey's first posting, in 1941, was to Doxford Hall,
Alnwick in Northumberland, the home of Lord Runciman,
who lived at his other home on the Isle of Eigg. The ATS trio
was billeted in the servants' hall and had a batwoman. The
Intelligence Officer was Captain Victor Goss. He later found
special favour with Barbara Culleton during one bitterly cold
night exercise at Coleshill, where she and Beatrice Temple were
involved as 'umpires'. Returning to a cold and unheated room
in the early hours, Captain Goss's arm appeared discreetly
round the door offering a blessedly warm pair of knitted socks.
(Tragically, he was later killed in action in North Africa.)

The ATS subalterns lived in some style on bounty from Lord
Runciman's market garden, and from his gamekeeper, and
butler. Other delicacies sometimes appeared unexpectedly:

> 'We wrote up practice messages and coded them for the
> outstations to work out and they did the same. I talked to one jolly
> chap and he sent a message through – "did I like salmon?" I
> replied – "Of course" and he told me in code that he would put
> one on the train from Berwick and I could pick it up at Alnwick.
> Which I did – and we had a wonderful feast at Doxford Hall.
> Some time later in a Berwick haberdasher's, an upstanding chap
> came to serve me. I recognised his voice and later found he had
> caught the salmon himself on the River Tweed.
>
> 'I next went whizzing down to Blandford, where I stayed in a
> lovely country house belonging to Colonel and Mrs Percy Brown.
> We carried out the same sort of exercises from the Control Station
> in nearby woods. We covered the Dorset and Hampshire area to
> the coast, with Captain Owen Hall-Hall the IO, working from
> Tarrant Hinton. We wore one or two pips but I don't remember
> any insignia at all. Our pay went directly to our bank account.
>
> 'After this came Wilton Castle in Southern Command, with
> Anthony Quayle (the actor, later Sir Anthony) as IO. He was a
> gorgeous man and we all fell in love with him – but he was very
> happily married!'

Barbara Culleton points out that, after Beatrice Temple's
arrival as CO, it was less likely that the ATS would have worn
the cap and lapel badges of the Royal Signals as cover, but
might have had the flash of their attached HQ on their sleeve.

Dorothy's final posting was to Halstead in Essex:

'I went there in a hurry for a major exercise. I was supposed to be going to Scotland for a wonderful New Year's Eve Hogmanay party. In fact I was whisked off to Halstead and, on the way, stopped off at the Berkeley Hotel in London, with all my luggage, including a trunk and bedroll on top of a taxi, to see if any friends going to Scotland were there – to tell them I wasn't going to make it. When I came out the taxi had driven off with all my luggage. I was in full Dress uniform and had lost everything else!

'When I got to Halstead, every hotel was full for the New Year and I was dropped in a requisitioned house – unfurnished and unheated. I fell asleep on a pile of newspapers. At midnight the telephone rang. My mates in Scotland managed to find me to wish me a Happy New Year. I could hear the Haggis being piped in. Can you imagine anything more bitter?'

Although always a minority commitment, increasing emphasis was placed on searching the wavebands for possible transmissions by enemy agents, unlikely though it was, and the whole scheme generally continued to expand. On 25th November 1943, 56 subalterns were recorded on Auxiliary Units Home War Establishment.

Whether or not Divisional HQ would ever have given the 'stay-behind' order to ATS Subalterns is a matter for conjecture; in the final analysis the Commanding Officer of the moment was responsible. But the 'Secret Sweeties' certainly believed they would be left and none was in doubt of her vulnerability or that a personal last-ditch decision to carry on operating might be called for when the enemy surrounded the trapdoor of their Zero Station. Should they then crawl hopefully through the escape tunnel, or give themselves up – with the certainty of interrogation and the probability of torture and execution? A cyanide tablet in a sealed packet was available to lone operators in isolated locations, as a final contingency to self-destruct when no alternative remained.

Not all the thirty Control Stations were manned by ATS subalterns. Some had Auxunits (Signals) NCOs. Mid-war moves to replace all the subalterns with either soldiers or ATS other ranks were robustly resisted from Coleshill. Some of the evidence is still in a 'grey' area and it would be unwise to attempt definitive conclusions but Arthur Gabbitas, from a privileged point of view, found on the balance of probabilities that, after invasion, the whole network would have been immediately handed over for direct operation by Army GHQ, including dedicated telephone lines hooked up in advance, running from selected Control Stations to Hannington Hall and designed then to be automatically switched over to GHQ.

He also distinguished between Control Stations, manned by Auxunits (Signals) NCOs, and HQ Control and Zero Stations, with ATS subalterns. In the face of conflicting evidence, precise responsibilities and lines of distinction are not clear cut, especially as some personnel interchange took place between ATS and Signals' NCOs. Procedures also changed sometimes after local trial and error experimentation.

It is certain, however, that proposals to introduce ATS other ranks as radio operators were firmly vetoed.

In 1943, Dorothy Rainey transferred to different secret work. On 'D' Day in 1944, she was working in the Operations Room of Southern Command and, typically, had no further contact – 'absolutely nothing' – with Auxiliary Units.

In June 1944 there were still fifty-five ATS subalterns on Auxiliary Units Establishment but stand-down was imminent. Part II Orders (Officers ATS), Serial No. 42, 'POSTINGS OUT – STRENGTH DECREASE', gave a list of the final twenty subalterns 'Posted from Auxiliary Units to No.1. War Office Holding Unit' with effect from 25th July 1944 and 'Struck off the strength of Auxiliary Units'. They included Mary Alexander and Kitty Hills, the wife of the founder of it all – John Hills. If Personal Numbers are any indication, 196514 Subaltern M L Barden was the longest serving and 301325 Marina Bloxham the shortest.

The unit had been organised in secret cells and – knowing the identity of only a few colleagues – the ATS were effectively prevented from post-demobilisation contact. One of the very few to know every 'Secret Sweetie' – for a time at least – was Beatrice Temple and the fact that she never organised any sort of reunion must have been calculated policy rather than personal choice. The men of Auxiliary Units (Signals) gathered at Coleshill for a stand-down group photograph, and were then similarly dispersed. It effectively created a security vacuum round their WWII service.

In *The Last Ditch*, David Lampe attributes the origin of the title 'Secret Sweeties' to the male officers in the divisional HQ mess at Doncaster, where the women from one of the Yorkshire stations lived.

One other fact is absolutely copper-bottomed.

It was a nickname all the ladies hated!

CHAPTER NINETEEN

Stand Down

By 1942 there seemed to be no really compelling reason for keeping a Resistance organisation at the ready in Britain, and yet a stand down of the Auxiliary Unit patrols or of the espionage network at that time, would have been, at the very least, incautious.

('*The Last Ditch*', page 136)

★   ★   ★

High level fear of 'incaution' – in the form of enemy invasion or raiding parties – helped Auxiliary Units Ops Patrols to remain more-or-less intact until official stand-down in November 1944.

But in April 1943, when withdrawal of regular Scout Section soldiers was announced, Sergeant Bill Webber, leader of the Firle, Sussex, operational Patrol, thought – 'it was the beginning of the end for us too'. With hindsight, September 7th 1940 (when the 'Cromwell' Stand-to was sounded throughout Britain), was perhaps an even more appropriate date - although only a very few knew it at the time.

Towards the end of summer 1940, RAF aerial reconnaissance over Continental North Sea and Channel ports disclosed the collection and conversion of canal craft suitable for invasion, and the preparation of extensive minefields to protect them from the Royal Navy. There was admittedly no specific Intelligence of the date and time of attack. Indeed, the 'Cromwell' stand-to – based on favourable tide and weather predictions – was more the product of a threat assessment. As we now know the Germans did not take that opportunity and, miscalculating again, left it to *Feldmarschall* Göring's Luftwaffe to force Britain into the Conference room.

Perhaps just the very few top people, those with access to increasingly bulky transcripts of Hitler's secret radio communications, could distinguish between the pretence of an imminent attack on Britain, and his real determination to head east to Russia at the first opportunity. It was Hitler's hope to force Britain to negotiate as the loser – after defeat in France – and then bargain for British neutrality, while he prepared to attack the Soviet Union. In the event, his failure to subdue Britain in 1940, left him fighting on several fronts and, after the entry of the United States in December 1941 and Churchill's persuasive arguments that Germany should be dealt with before Japan, Hitler had effectively lost the war. However, that would take four more years and many millions of lives.

This may now seem obvious, but it was unknown at the time to the British people – who remained in fear of invasion or seaborne raiders or parachute attack until Second Front success in Normandy was clear to see.

Nigel Oxenden noted:

CRISIS IN SEPTEMBER (1940). When Hitler's invasion barges were driven into port by gales in September, and there bombed by the RAF, it was believed by some that all immediate danger was over, and the continuance of Auxiliary Units was in the balance. Rumour had it that its abandonment was avoided by a timely dinner at the Cavalry Club. In any case, the Commander (still Colin Gubbins) set about strengthening its position, as well as its striking power, by the permanent attachment of regular personnel.

Typically, Gubbins preferred attack as the best method of defence. A flurry of secret correspondence, signed C McVean Gubbins (before he adopted the better known 'Colin Gubbins'), resulted in the creation of Auxunits Scout Sections. Oxenden describes the thinking:

'By Christmas 1940, Colonel Gubbins considered that most of the danger of invasion had blown over and left the unit, selecting as his successor Lt-Col. C R Major, then GSO (1), Eastern Command.'

Auxiliary Units were still vulnerable, however:

EXPANSION. When Hitler attacked Russia (22nd June 1941) and the chances of invasion in the west receded still further, it was clear that the unit must either go on or go under. This second crisis was successfully overcome and the War Office agreed to expansion to the tune of about a hundred patrols, to include the hitherto untouched areas of the Border, Northumberland, and Durham.

With the expansion, Areas were increased from 14 to 22, later settling at 20, and Auxunits operational role was revised. Principally still 'stay-behinds', Auxiliers' experiments with new skills - living underground and off the land, their increasing aptitude with explosives, time pencil fuses, and the development of ingenious booby traps and mines of their own - were valuable experimentation for the Special Forces proliferating before 'D' Day. Moreover, Patrols were part of the coast-watch scheme. Although this was principally the remit of the Special Duties Section, the presence of independent, well armed Patrols was another factor as the General Staff planned the release regular troops for active service.

Above all, perhaps, Gubbins recognised that they cost the country virtually nothing.

Changes were introduced in step with expansion. Patrols now trained as groups and, from 1941, Group Commanders (and Assistants) were Commissioned within the Home Guard, sent to Coleshill on special courses, and took over some training and increasing amounts of administration. This relieved Intelligence Officers of a burden. The Patrols, originally 'recorded on the back of an envelope', were now coming under the full bureaucratic scrutiny of an unhappy War Office, not yet accustomed to private armies. A proposal to share OBs with the SDS was abandoned. Gelignite replaced the prized plastic explosive. Morale raising competitions were organised locally, as well as nationally through HQ.

Norman Field, IO for Kent in 1940 and 1941, assumed that his clerk had a nominal roll, but could not remember seeing it himself. The first *national* nominal roll was compiled in 1942 (and released to Public Record Office in 1998) – as Colonel Major was handing over command to Colonel The Lord Glanusk. The names of some Auxiliers already enrolled in the Home Guard were removed from their rolls and personal records destroyed to guarantee 'stay-behind' secrecy. A few Intelligence Officers moved on to active service, being replaced, sometimes successfully with former Scout Section subalterns and, at others less so, with older men.

The crisis of survival was still far from finished, however, even though a further weapon was added to Auxunits' armoury – as 'Oxo' recalls:

THE RAID ROLE. In the early summer of 1942 the Home Guard was warned that local raids might be expected upon our priority coasts, and all units worked out their raid roles.

'This warning was a gift to IOs for although no universally applicable directive could be ussued from HQ, they were able to formulate their own (directives) in conjunction with their local military commander, and the rumour of a renewed threat to our shores was a wonderful tonic for fading enthusiasm in the ranks. Sceptics wondered whether it was ever intended as anything more. The effects, with careful nursing, lasted for the next two years...

Lord Glanusk was still in command – comfortably removed from the real war and enjoying his wine cellar and stimulating hunting, shooting and fishing conversation in the Coleshill Officers' Mess. His Adjutant cantered (on horseback) at speed round the grounds. Some Guards officers bet heavily on 'the Gee-gees', sometimes placing 'three figures' over the HQ telephone network. The news, intercepted at the exchange, spread rapidly through the other ranks, some of whom – seizing the opportunity of freebee insider information – placed a 'few-shilling' bets with their own bookies.

The next attack was mounted in a 'MOST SECRET' report to 'CGS' (Chief of General Services), signed by E C Beard on 6th January 1943 (reference – HF/72/52/1/G (SD). The terse wording clearly indicates an attempt to penetrate and undermine Auxunits HQ complacency and return *all* serving officers and men to General Duties:

1. I do not think the proposals made by Commander, Auxiliary Units, are at all satisfactory...
2. It is no argument to say that some of the personnel are low category and that they are therefore no use to the rest of the Army...
3. As I see it, the degree to which we are justified in retaining the Auxiliary Unit organisation, must be measured by:-
The likelihood of invasion.
The 'vital area' if invasion came.
As regards (a) we are working on the assumption that invasion is not possible in 1943. It is highly unlikely at any future date.
As regards (b), Home Forces recent appreciation showed that nothing serious could be attempted (by the Germans) outside the area, roughly Norfolk – Hampshire.
4. The deductions from these two facts are that –
Auxiliary Units are unlikely ever to be required; and
If they were required, they would only be necessary in, and possibly slightly overlapping, the flanks of, the 'vital area'.

Within two months, Lord Glanusk was taken seriously ill (and replaced by his GSO (1), Colonel F W R Douglas, Royal Artillery), but his response to this direct attack on his personal fiefdom must by then have been successfully repulsed, probably with heavy casualties. Unfortunately, we do not have *all* the papers, but some concessions to compromise and modification were obviously agreed. The number of Auxiliers dropped. Nearly 200 courses had been held at Coleshill – including 100 for Auxiliers, 25 for Patrol Leaders, and 15 for Scout Sections – but they were eventually abandoned and replaced in Areas by a training 'circus' of the few remaining regular soldiers. Attempts to introduce arms drill proved universally unpopular. The patrols' existence was no longer a close secret and Auxiliers appeared in uniform at Church Parades and on exercises jointly with the army and Home Guard. OB disciplines slackened noticeably too. Administration became centred on Territorial Army Association HQs at Inverness, York and Reading, as three Reserve Battalions were organised – 201 included Scotland and Northumberland; 202, southward to a line from the Wash to the Severn; and 203 south of that.

On 7th November 1943, GHQ Home forces sent a 'MOST SECRET' instruction to all UK Commands, standardising the previously hit-and-miss security classifications allocated for Auxunits:

> 1. Knowledge of the existence of Auxiliary Units should be confined to persons who need it in the course of duty. As however a considerable amount of correspondence of a purely administrative and non-committal nature refers to these Units, it is not necessary for documents containing a bare reference to them to be marked SECRET.
> 2. The functions of Auxiliary Units are MOST SECRET and any documents which refer to, or in any way, suggest their function, or give any indication of their strength, will be graded MOST SECRET. Correspondence referring to their functions will be addressed personally to one of the officers specifically...

This can only be seen as a move to downgrade the *existence* of Auxiliary Units, while keeping the *functions* at 'MOST SECRET' level. Previous correspondence had been classified randomly and without formal guidelines, usually at the highest grade.

From 1942, GHQ thinking was centred upon the invasion of Europe. IOs now dealt directly with the TAA and the name Auxiliary Units never again appeared in Part III Orders. Auxiliers simply belonged to 'this or that' GHQ Reserve Battalion.

But, even with many of their best men in demand for active service, Auxiliary Units were not yet entirely consigned to the military waste-bin.

In a TOP SECRET 'Note' by the Commander, GHQ Auxiliary Units, dealing with 'ECONOMY IN MANPOWER', probably dated early in 1944, Colonel Douglas first summarised the position of the Operational Branch. With 20 Areas extending from Thurso to South Wales, there were 'rather more' than 640 patrols with some in the Hebrides and Shetlands – comprising 4,200 'Home Guards' spread over

44,000 square miles, and one IO for each Area, with six or seven administration and training staff. In addition, the War Establishment allowed for 10 officers and 139 ORs at HQ. To help with active service requirements, Colonel Douglas proposed swingeing cuts in Officers, other ranks, and ATS subalterns, but when it came to Auxiliers, he defended robustly:

> '...I wish to state emphatically that there is no possibility of running the Operations Branch entirely under Home Guard auspices.
>
> 'For nearly four years Auxiliers, who were hand-picked men, have had rubbed into them that they were a part of the regular Army and GHQ Troops and as such were expected to give at least two or three times the amount of time to training that the HG did.
>
> 'This they have willingly and selflessly done and achieved an esprit-de-corps second to none. They regard themselves, quite properly, as a corps d'elite and something superior to any Home Guard. They have had repeated assurances that they would never be asked to revert to Home Guard.
>
> 'You might just as well expect a Guards regiment to amalgamate with the Salvation Army. It isn't on!...'

With this resounding claim, Colonel Douglas secured another temporary lifeline for the patrols although, on 12th July 1944, the War Office insisted on the return of most of the regular personnel. Just a few were left at HQ to allow the unit to retain its identity to the end. In a 'SECRET' letter to the Under Secretary of State at the War Office, dated 11th November 1944, the C-in-C, Home Forces explained that, as the OC Auxiliary Units was 'personally responsible for the supervision of the withdrawal of all stores and equipment', it was necessary for him to retain the rank of Temporary Colonel. With this went a Special Allowance of 3/- (15p) a day.

Under 'varying arrangements', stores – mainly meaning weapons and explosives – were being returned either to Ordnance or TAAHQs.

Four administrative Groups with appropriate staff had been created and the C-in-C explained to the civil servant in charge of the purse strings:

> 6. It is considered that this apparent misappropriation of personnel is necessary to prevent very large losses of equipment and weapons.

Auxiliers admit that life was never the same again. Some from Hampshire, others from Northumberland, joined Isle of Wight patrols – who according to Jim Caws, had been ordered to stand-by in their OBs to counter a threat perceived at GHQ from German troops garrisoned on Jersey – to protect Pipeline – Under-the-Sea ('PLUTO') installations. They entertained themselves, firing their Tommy Guns at oil drums bobbing around in the sea.

Others on the lookout for raiders, patrolled their own patch of coastline. Usually, they just drifted along, winding down. Manoeuvres were created to sustain their interest and, as 'perks', Colin Cooke led three or four of his patrol to Huntly in Scotland, officially for night exercises, with a flight in an RAF Wellington aircraft as a bonus. Returning by train, they saw 'Gone with the Wind' in a 'London flea-pit'. Considering themselves inadequately trained and without the language, like others they rejected a half-hearted idea to be parachuted into France and fight behind the lines.

Weapons and explosives were finally collected. Some Auxiliers still displayed initiatives expected of specially selected men, this time with a hypodermic syringe. Even without formal permission, many managed to sample the contents of their sealed gallon jars of rum – one for each OB. With deftness and dexterity, some patrols extracted the contents without removing the cork. Cold tea was the ideal replacement. Stand-down parties were consequently often enjoyed with robust gusto. While the OC Auxiliary Units was, of course, personally responsible for losses, it was TAA Quartermasters throughout the country who tried to balance books showing a shortage of rum against a bewildering surplus of cold tea.

An enormous crater, now water filled, can still be seen near an OB at Sibton in Suffolk. It is at the precise map reference given in writing by Lieutenant Denny, the local Group Commander, for his Patrols' final operational rendezvous. It was also the location of a one-man Observation Post which – ideal for the final fling – was filled with 'surplus' gelignite and gun cotton and anything else that would make a great bang, and then expertly exploded. After it all went up and came safely down, a dozen very happy men retired to a cosy hostelry to celebrate stand-down, throwing away empty hypodermics as they went.

In June 1944, seventeen-year-old engineering student, Geoff Bradford – one of the last recruits into the Devon 203 Reserve Battalion (and probably one of the last in the land) – dramatised a Home Guard battle course with 'special effects' activated by pull-switches to the right and left of the advancing platoon. With a skilfully timed charge for a finale – he drenched them all with the murky contents of the pond round which they had unwisely paused to recover their breath.

As Allied armies broke from the Normandy bridgehead, Herman Kindred blew up old tree stumps on his farm in East Anglia; but still had some 'specials' when the USAAF left the nearby aerodrome:

> 'I climbed the water tower with five firepots, time-fused to go off together. While the airmen were shooting off all their spare ammunition and having a great party, the firepots suddenly exploded high above them.
>
> 'How those old Yanks did cheer!'

★   ★   ★

Formal Stand-down was dated 30th November 1944 and, according to the Adjutant General's Directorate of the Ministry of Defence, disbandment was on 15th January 1945. Most Auxiliers received a Reserve Battalion lapel badge and a copy of a letter to Colonel Douglas, dated 18th November 1944, from the C-in-C Home Forces, Sir Harold Franklyn. In a personal letter, Colonel Douglas concluded:

> 'In view of the fact that your lives depended upon secrecy, no public recognition will be possible. But those in the most responsible positions at General Headquarters, Home Forces, know what was done, and what would have been done if you had been called upon. They know it well. It will not be forgotten.'

These were fine words. However, in the summer of 1945, daily papers published fanciful 'Betty the Barmaid' stories of the British 'Maquis' and 'The Times' ran Editorial comment about Auxiliary Units which, overwhelmed by the volume of end-of-war events, went largely unnoticed by their readers. Some officers were recognised with Honours, including Brigadier Geoffrey Beyts and several Group Commanders with MBEs; and a few Patrol Leaders were awarded the BEM.

The rest, honouring personal commitments to silence, were soon conveniently forgotten. Apart from some grudging expenses, they had never been paid a penny.

★   ★   ★

The civilian men and women of Auxiliary Units, Special Duties Section, were also unpaid. Activated early in the war, their numbers and role expanded right up to 'D' Day. It was all very specially 'MOST SECRET' and the statement in SOE records that Auxunits were one of Britain's nine Secret Services (rather than one of the many hundreds of services that were secret), applies principally to the SDS.

The nominal roll has not yet appeared and is unlikely to do so now. But the record shows that 3,250 agents, runners, and radio operators were finally co-ordinated into a massively efficient Intelligence network, operating from homes and offices, hideaways and radio OBs, trained to feed vital data rapidly to GHQ Home Command.

Surprisingly, in view of the secrecy, the SDS *was* briefly described in the 'Secret Sweeties' Chapter of '*The Last Ditch*', and documentary evidence of its existence is now in Public records. Until recently, this lacked serious content and, without doubt, the SDS has long-term security cover. The general public was never intended to be in the picture and it is surprising that information has leaked at all.

That post-war '*Times*' leading article, and the confidences imparted to David Lampe by the highest Auxunits ranks, including Colin Gubbins and 'Bill' Major ('...my most important single source of information...'), were extraordinary lapses – if that was what they really were? The first PRO papers were mainly reports summarising SDS manpower, with only occasional hints of their *function*. Even in the latest tranche – which does expand upon their selection and training and how the branch was funded, together with an explanation of the SDS role – there are still no agents' names. Speculation is consequently inevitable. It is unlikely, however, that an official spokesman will appear from behind the camouflage to set the record straight. Or *straighter,* shall we say?

The latest evidence supports the statement in SOE records that the SDS was a Secret Service in its own right – so it was not initially funded by the War Office. It was handed over from the control of Section 'D' of the Secret Intelligence Service to the Director of Military Intelligence as an embryonic, going concern after Dunkirk, and operations, retraining and administration delegated to HQ Auxiliary Units. If the SDS was then controlled by Maurice Petherick as both a Secret Service *and* for the War Office, it would not be a surprise. The network of communications – running from 'vital' areas of the coastline, through OUT-Stations to IN-Stations with the unique TRD transceiver, and then either directly, or by means of a dedicated telephone system, to GHQ – was mainly the product of what Brigadier Beyts described in a uniquely unguarded moment as the 'genius of Maurice Petherick'. His secret credentials have already been described.

In any event, the SD Section, after working at frenzied speed in preparation for 'D' Day, was then instantly brought to a standstill. At the beginning of 1944 there were 10 Areas, each under an Intelligence Officer. More than 200 OUT-Stations fed IN-Stations manned by Auxiliary Units (Signals) other ranks and ATS officers – the whole administered by 14 officers and 16 ORs. When considering economy of manpower and the possibility of closing down the organisation, the OC Auxiliary Units suggested that the branch could be dealt with differently (from the Ops side):

> '...being composed entirely of civilians, there are no SD civilians outside the organisation to be considered.
>
> 'If considered desirable it would be possible to close down all except the Wash to Dorset and the North of Scotland, thereby effecting a considerable saving.'

Interpretation of these coded paragraphs is again speculative but probably not all that far from the mark. 'Scotland' and 'The Wash to Dorset' were presumably vital areas of enemy counter-raid potential and therefore of interest to GHQ. The remaining Areas were not (it can be assumed), and as the 'civilians' were never part of the 'War Establishment', they could be closed down with no administrative hassle because – although having potentially benefited from the Intelligence they provided – there was no War Office financial or administrative responsibility for SDS demobilisation.

Perhaps they still 'belonged' to the Secret Intelligence Service? The civilians of the SDS certainly fitted the pattern approved by Colin Gubbins – they cost the country nothing. The evidence here *is* clear enough. They were recruited and trained, and stood prepared to put their lives at risk – and the only motive was patriotism.

The success of the Normandy invasion proved to be the end for the SDS, and it was closed down four months before the Operational branch. Just one month after 'D' Day, General Franklyn wrote to Colonel Douglas:

GHQ Home Forces
4th July 1944

> It has been decided by the War Office that in view of the shortage of manpower and the fact that the danger of invasion had receded, it is no longer possible to retain (Editor's italics) the 'Special Duties' organisation.
>
> I realise that each member of the organisation from the first 'invasion days' beginning in 1940 voluntarily undertook a hazardous

role which required both skill and courage, well knowing that the very nature of their work would allow of no public recognition.

This organisation...has been in a position...to furnish accurate information of raids or invasion instantly...

In recent days, while our own invasion forces were concentrating, an additional heavy burden was placed on those of you responsible for the maintenance of good security, to ensure that the enemy was denied foreknowledge of our plans and preparations. The security reports regularly provided by Special Duties have proved of invaluable assistance to our security staffs.

As no public recognition can be given for this job, it is my wish that a copy of this letter be sent to all members of the Special Duties organisation as my own acknowledgement of the value and efficiency of their work.

(signed) H E Franklyn
General, C-in-C

Colonel Douglas did as he was asked and sent copies to all those on his nominal roll – and added:

'...I must tell you how much we have admired your disinterested loyalty which has made constant demands on your time, energy and initiative, all of which you have so generously and selflessly given.'

Colonel Douglas's letter tells us little, but General Franklyn's, once de-coded, gives a number of strong hints.

The War Office had decided that SDS numbers, albeit unpaid, were disproportionate to the risk of enemy raids, and even the few regular soldiers involved could be more productively employed elsewhere. It can be read that 1940, the 'first invasion days', was also the SDS effective start-up date – the pilot radio scheme then operating in Kent is confirmation. Next comes a clear instruction (repeated later) – that no 'public recognition' would be possible and (although not specified), he undoubtedly meant 'for ever'! The penultimate paragraph obliquely acknowledges SDS participation by watching for lapses in pre-Second Front Allied morale and spying on potential dissidents, as well as their small part in the strategic deception game played to confuse the Wehrmacht about the true destination of the invasion armada.

From this moment, the SDS marched into apparent oblivion. The cellular structure ensured that no one knew either the identity or function of anyone else. Post war secrecy soon took over and was not easy to crack.

What explanation can there be for perhaps the most

significant phrase in General Franklyn's letter?

'...it is no longer possible to retain the Special Duties organisation...'

Could this indicate that it was not intended to *disband* the SDS, only to return them - again as a composite unit – to their roots in the Secret Intelligence Service? If so it may not be prudent to speculate what for or why? A post-war role could, however, account for the super-secrecy which has directly protected the SDS ever since and. obliquely perhaps, their operational colleagues at the same time.

★   ★   ★

The paid members of Auxiliary Units working with the Special Duties Section also went quietly. But a different stratagem was employed to ensure their everlasting silence. With them it was divide and rule.

Intelligence Officers returned to their units or other special duties; and the men of Auxunits (Signals) were posted separately to regimental duty or the Royal Signals depot at Catterick for retraining and re-posting. They never worked together again – limiting the chances of a Comrades' Association or reunion.

In the 1990s, Arthur Gabbitas set out to trace his colleagues. They were all dispersed in civvy street; by then many were dead but a few managed to get to his Signals' reunions. It is a tribute to the efficacy of cellular secrecy that, in 1994 when Geoff Bradford and Peter Wilcox organised an Auxunits reunion at Highworth, neither was aware even of the existence of Auxunits (Signals) – and Arthur had some difficulty in satisfying them of his credentials.

As intended, TRD secrets remained securely locked away.

The subalterns of Auxiliary Units (ATS) were temporarily absorbed into the mainstream ATS – of which they had absolutely no experience or knowledge. Neither did they know much of the Royal Signals, Morse Code, or Auxiliary Units Operations Patrols; or the SDS agents with whom they had spoken over the radio and from whom they had been successfully separated as a matter of security.

Then, the 'Secret Sweeties' too, were individually quietly demobilised.

Without their knowledge, however, they had been at the epicentre of a War Office battle of sex and class at the same time. Only fragments of the 'MOST SECRET' correspondence have been discovered in public records but they are illuminating enough. Here is a summary of the volatile

numbers of direct entry ATS officers on the radio network
Establishment, and some of the reasons:

1940		6	(in the pilot scheme)	
March	'42	135	(Part II Orders)	MOST SECRET
Feb.	'43	31	(Part II Orders)	MOST SECRET
Dec	'43	56	(War Establishment)	Confidential
July	'44	20	(at Stand-down)	Unclassified

These figures indicate a tug-of-war that went on between the
War Office and Coleshill; the main protagonists, the subalterns
of the ATS and other ranks of Auxunits (Signals) were entirely
unaware of the fight.

The women were, as a rule, stationed at static Divisional HQ
Control Stations, and the men at other Base Stations, as well as
being responsible for maintenance and battery charging. The
War Office wanted their men back and Lord Glanusk preferred
ATS subalterns. The War Office apparently proposed a
compromise, the withdrawal of both – and their replacement
by ATS 'other ranks'.

Lord Glanusk brought big guns into action with a 'MOST
SECRET' letter to GHQ, Home Forces, dated 1st February 1943,
proposing an 'increase in ATS Officers in the Signal Section':

2. The principal of Auxiliary Units employing ATS Officers as
opposed to R.Signals ORs has already been accepted...

Experience has proved that a mistake was made in reducing the
number of ATS Officers from 135 to 31 as R Signals (i.e., men
other ranks), while technically desirable, are not necessarily a
satisfactory substitute.

While not wanting to lose his ATS officers at all, if Glanusk had
to have other ranks he wanted men:

A (men). The men on these detachments always have a car, as
this is essential for their work. Billets therefore do not have
necessarily to be within walking or cycling distance. The men are
attached for pay, etc, to the nearest military unit, and can use the
car to attend pay parades.

B (ATS). ATS detachments are not provided with a car. Billets
must therefore be within walking or cycling distance, which very
greatly limits the choice of accommodation. The Officer of any
unit to which the Auxiliaries (other ranks) were attached for pay
would have to make a special journey to pay them.

He summarised the problems. Accommodation was extremely
difficult to find for officers and would probably be equally
difficult for other ranks. Theoretically, householders could be

compelled to billet ORs, with subsistence reimbursement, but in practice this often 'turns out to be literally a physical impossibility'. But in similar circumstances, 'arrangements are made for the ATS Officers to become members of the local male Officers' Mess, but it is obviously undesirable that 3 ATS ORs alone should be fed in a soldiers' dining room'. There was no chance of ORs eating with officers. On matters of Pay, Clothing, etc., ATS ORs would have to be attached to the nearest ATS Unit, but the question did not arise for officers. Discipline and supervision of ATS other ranks in isolated detachments could not be adequately carried out...except by the nearest ATS Officer who, 'for reasons of security would have no access to the place of duty'. The only way of overcoming these difficulties would be for:

(i) The War Office ruling of no (ATS OR) detachments under 10 to be waived.

(ii) the Auxiliaries (ATS ORs) to be allowed, if necessary, to feed in soldiers' dining rooms,

(iii) Pay, and all necessary supervision, to be made the responsibility of the local military unit.

Lord Glanusk pointed out that these three conditions were contrary to ATS Policy and proposed that:

'As Security is the over-ruling and vital factor, the employment of ATS Officers is therefore essential.'

Very soon afterwards Lord Glanusk suffered a heart attack, but he had won the battle. The establishment of Auxunits' Signals (men) other ranks was maintained, while that of ATS subalterns increased from 31 to 56. ATS other ranks were never employed in-the-field.

Some members of the military hierarchy must have completely forgotten there was still a war to be won!

The Museum of the British Resistance Organisation at Parham has been fortunate (thanks to researcher Tony Evans) in obtaining from Public Record Office, a copy of the full WAR DIARY of HQ Auxiliary Units.

Dated 15th January 1945 and classified 'SECRET', it consists of one entry – Highworth. Jan. 15 1800 hours. On instructions from GHQ Home Forces the Headquarters was finally closed down on disbandment of Auxiliary Units.

(signed) Frank W Douglas. Colonel.

It really was the end of the end!

CHAPTER TWENTY

Would it have worked?

'We were trained in all aspects of warfare. We were trained to kill with our hands in unarmed combat. We were trained in all weapons from machine guns down to pistols. We were given knives and taught to kill with them. We were taught to use all forms of explosives with different varieties of fuse. We were taught to set booby traps. We were taught what targets to look for, how to get ourselves away from the target area, and take care of ourselves for as long as possible. I think the powers-that-be rather thought that our life span might not be too long!

'...the point was – we were not going to let Germans run around our country.'

(Peter Boulden, a farmer of Aldington,
a WWII Kentish Auxilier and post war Mayor of Ashford)

★ ★ ★

Auxiliers' resolve has never been in doubt. Individually selected, they were a civilian *Corps d'elite*. Operational Patrols were thoroughly trained and equipped, well concealed in OBs and they and the other 'stay-behinds – the Scout Sections – were generally well led. Major R F Hall, MC, writes:

'Yes, it would have worked. It would have encouraged other resistance. The men I met had the Fairbairn/Sykes 'know-you-are-going-to-win' spirit...'

As they were never called into action as a unit, judgement has to be made from the accounts of survivors; the battle worthiness of OBs; and the opinions of authors – not only David Lampe, but the many others who have written summaries of their local research.

No evidence has been discovered that the Germans knew of Auxunits specifically — although they had draft plans to prohibit resistance, with the death penalty for offenders. Referring to armed insurgents, the draft order included:

'If the population initiates active operations after the completed conquest of a locality, or in places behind the fighting front, the inhabitants involved in the fighting will be regarded as armed insurgents. When taking hostages, those persons should if possible be selected in whom the active enemy elements have an interest.'

It is possible to lose some of the thrust in the translation. However, the oblique threat to Auxunits is clear enough. As operational patrols were selected only from local men, hostages taken as reprisal for their acts of mayhem were likely to include their own families and friends – although the relationship may not have been known to the enemy. If the men in the OBs became aware of their plight, it might well (and entirely reasonably) have undermined their enthusiasm to continue the fight. Moreover, although the patrols' cellular structure was reasonably watertight at first, serious security defects developed.

The weakness of the Group system has already been thoroughly examined by Andrew Taylor in Chapters III and IV; of some administrative value, it allowed overworked IOs to delegate routine paperwork to Group Commanders and patrols to participate in joint manoeuvres. The problem was that real core, cellular security, was discarded. The capture of one Auxilier by the enemy would inevitably – by means of interrogation, deception, or torture – have led to priceless information, not just about half-a-dozen immediate colleagues, but *all those in the Group* – perhaps thirty men or more. This is not to undervalue the fortitude of the men themselves but – although some prisoners can tolerate more pressure than others – nothing can guarantee a man's silence when subjected to extremes of physical or psychological violence.

Auxiliers were never to suffer the weakness of Continental counterparts such as the French Maquis, who often had to hold certain political or religious opinions and, conversely, to accept applicants of suitable 'correctness', irrespective of their aptitude as guerrillas.

But other potential weaknesses can be seen in Auxunits' patrols basic structure. If captured, for example, immediate leads would have been evident to their interrogators. Once identified, the attention of enemy investigators would have focused in the right area, and their homes and those of their relatives, searched as a matter of routine. Even more vulnerable, perhaps, were those 'pals' patrols assembled from men in the same factory or workplace Again, the capture of one would inevitably have pointed toward his colleagues – by work records and intelligent deduction alone.

Some Auxiliers accepted the possible imperative to kill their own family, *in extremis*, in order to save themselves, because they were taught, rightly enough, to understand their function as an integral part of a grand scheme of defence against an evil foe. In total war, such extreme acts can be essential. But, in the same way that WWI 'Pals' Battalions sometimes led to the annihilation of *all* the young men in a given locality, so the group of Auxunits hiding below ground were more vulnerable to collective detection than they ever imagined. Such a possibility was not in their minds – so completely did they trust the protection offered by their 'powers-that-be'.

Nigel Oxenden, in his 'History and Achievement', gave a number of significant recommendations for the future, based on four years' experience. He approved the careful siting of each Patrol in areas where they should prove useful – near to likely target areas, for example, rather than in some safe but remote – and therefore useless – location. He advocated the careful selection of Patrol leaders, and four to six trusted men. The role of the Group Commander was considered useful for morale and administration, but *'in action they should never take precedence over their Patrol Leaders'.* In other discussion of the role of Group Commanders, he concludes *'...in action they can have no definite role'.*

He was doubtful of the value of woodland as cover for OBs – on the logical assumption that it was the most likely location to be selected by the enemy to hide his own supplies and equipment. While approving the choice of a slope to assist drainage and ventilation, he preferred concrete construction, instead of iron, to reduce the chance of discovery by metal detector.

His impressive summary for survival was based on common sense and trial and error. Auxunits Patrols' chances of discovery may have been increased by using elephant iron for OB construction (in most cases), and detection by dogs was a problem never successfully mastered, although some patrols did store their own urine and experiment with its selective distribution near trapdoors as a diversion to canine trackers.

Major Oxenden's most positive guidelines for the future were about personal weapons and the use of explosives. His revolutionary conclusions about firearms were based on the opinion that night operations could be betrayed by the noise of just one shot. He made a strong argument against taking firearms at all.

This said farewell to the Tommy gun, the Sten, and the rifles:

'The only weapon that could be used without wrecking the chances of the attackers is one that is silent and fitted with luminous sights. Such a pistol has been produced under the name of 'Welrod.'

The Welrod was an invention from the SOE experimental station at Welwyn, Hertfordshire. (Others needing no further explanation include the 'Welsub' and the 'Welbike'.) Some were more successful than others – but the 'Welrod' – a close quarters and comparatively silent hand-gun, was to have a long Service life. The Mark I, 7.65mm was later modified to 9mm. An American derivation was called a 'sleeve gun'. A single shot handgun, with butt magazine, the muzzle velocity (1100-fps) was below the speed of sound, with consequent reduction in the noise of discharge. Each time the weapon was fired, it required re-cocking by rear movement of a knurled, rounded, cocking lever. Although bulky when assembled with its silencer, it could be taken apart and hidden under normal clothing. The Welrod – not entirely silent – was quietest from behind and at its best *when held against the target!* It was only of real use in eye-to-eye combat. It was not, of course, available until mid-war years.

Even more controversially, perhaps, Oxenden proposed the withdrawal of all custom built explosives and their replacement by a pre-prepared, standard, half-pound charge, with time pencil fuse delays of either about one and a quarter, or four hours.

For defence, he selected the grenade:

> 'The No. 77...would prove most useful on patrol. There is no indication of the point from which it is thrown, and there is no chance of taking cover from it. It would always baffle pursuit.
>
> 'In short no arms are needed but the Welrod for attack and the 77 for defence.'

Smoke Grenade No, 77 Mark I, a fearsome weapon ordered in tens of thousands for Auxunits, contained White Phosphorus in a green, lightweight metal housing. Like the Welrod, Oxenden favoured it for its silent operation, when compared with conventional high explosive grenades. The best were made, it is claimed, in Canada. The object was to incinerate a target rather than blast it.

These conclusions were revolutionary enough and disposed of much of Auxiliary Units' training and equipment in an instant. The Patrols had, of course, developed from scratch in 1940 and the reason for outlining his conclusions here is to highlight their vulnerability. Even given the men's resolve, their extensive local knowledge, and the remarkably unorthodox capabilities they developed in the employment of stealth under cover of darkness, the conclusion is irresistible that much of their training, weaponry, and explosives would have been seriously unsuitable. Indeed, if Oxenden is correct, much of it might have been positively counter productive to clandestine activities. Auxiliers were never intended to participate in open attacks or firefights – so why all the weaponry, he would argue? And the benefits of assembling their own explosive charges would have been considerably outweighed by the time needed to construct and place them. Prepared charges, although lacking one-off, custom built specification for each target, would have much enhanced the speed with which they could be laid – and chances of escape proportionately improved. Booby trap construction was therefore, he thought, unnecessary.

By the time he came to assemble his conclusions - in a few months before mid-January 1945 – Nigel Oxenden was the beneficiary not only of the results of Auxiliary Units' experiments but also the experience then available to an inner core – of which as Colin Gubbins cousin he was one, from four years' subversive activities by Special Operations Executive.

With numerous Patrols sited in potentially critical areas of invasion, some would have escaped detection even in the long term. The likelihood was probably in proportion to the number and frequency of their aggressive operations for, without transport or any fallback hideaway, there was nowhere to escape. The majority, however, would have been detected at an early stage – and indeed that is just how GHQ saw it. Auxunit Patrols were never intended as a long-term resistance organisation.

Their plight would have been compounded by lack of radio communication, information on the progress of the war, or even the whereabouts of the front line. An ardent enemy was unlikely to make it easy for them to take the day off and return home to listen to BBC news broadcasts on the 'Beetle' network – and then continue the campaign suitably informed and refreshed. Writing about his patrols on the Borders, Major Peter Forbes suggests:

> 'Again with hindsight, I feel my patrols would have been blind sitting in their OBs as to where targets were. They could not have reconnoitred by day. What was needed was an "outside man", unconnected with and not knowing the patrol, who could have observed and dropped information in a dead letter box.
>
> 'No one at Coleshill seems to have issued tactical advice on these lines.'

Worst of all, perhaps, was the absence of preparation for contact with Intelligence Officers – in whom they all placed such great faith. According to the considerable evidence available, their role after invasion was confused. Some IOs intended to revert to GHQ duty; others, under Corps Command, might have been dispatched through the front line with orders for their patrols. Geoffrey Beyts, aware of the hazards involved, proposed the issue of standard War Office No 17 Radio sets for such communication. This definitely did not take place. Other IOs intended to live with their men in the field, but their own staff were largely untrained – remember there were only four courses for them at Coleshill in four years – and OBs rarely prepared for them, although plans were outlined at one stage in 1942, and funds sought.

Peter Forbes, one of the IOs who planned to stay behind with his patrols, suggested:

> 'It was a pity, I think, that the patrol side and the SD were kept entirely separate and secret from each other...they (the Special Duties Section) could have been a very useful way for communicating with Scottish Command.'

All in all, it must be concluded that in the 'Blaze of Wild Priority' in 1940, the best possible efforts were made for Auxunits' Patrols, and they may with luck have had some limited effect in one or another of their roles. Even until 1942, Geoffrey Beyts was still endeavouring to formalise their fighting position in the grand strategy of defence. It never was clarified and it is reasonable to assume, never could. With the course and outcome of set-piece battles so impossible to predict, the possibility of doing so with guerrilla forces must be even more difficult. No doubt it will always be the same.

It is fair to bet that once the United States and Soviet Russia joined in the fight against the Axis, the development of the Patrols was of little more than academic interest to GHQ. Their usefulness from then was experimental but it is doubtful whether the secrecy which has enveloped them for more than half a century was justified by the results. Indeed, even at an elementary level, their findings were ignored by units such as the SAS – who should have had access to the wealth of practical know-how they had amassed. But when it came to organising small, underground, 'stay-behind' groups of troopers in Eastern Europe during the Cold War, the SAS fell into the trap not only of failing to ventilate their OBs, but constructing them of 'long, hooped sheets of corrugated metal for the roof'. Tut-tut!! Somewhere, there was Nigel Oxenden's brief and, if that was mislaid, a thousand or more Auxiliers still living and well qualified to put them right.

Colin Gubbins, discussing Auxunit operational patrols, told David Lampe:

> '...they would have justified their existence: to what degree would have been entirely dependent on the circumstances. But my

judgement is based heavily on the fact that they were costing the country nothing either in manpower or in weapons... These patrols in their left-behind missions, out of all contact, entirely on their own, with their caches of arms and stores would have given some account of themselves in the invasion areas but their usefulness would have been short-lived, at the longest until their stocks were exhausted, at the shortest when they were caught or wiped out. They were designed, trained and prepared for a particular and imminent crisis: that was their specialist role.'

The other 'inside' expert, Sir Peter Wilkinson also insisted that the patrols were never intended to exist long-term – so there can be little doubt about it. The 'warriors' were to select their own targets, make their own decisions, and perhaps even execute collaborators or their family or colleagues. Their longevity would have depended upon luck, the duration of their stores, and the vigour of their operations. Everything was left to the quality of the patrol leader – he was in charge, an amateur with professional responsibilities, and no one to refer to.

Most Auxiliers think they would have made a useful contribution to the defence of Britain. Many expected to die while doing so.

Can there now be any doubt about it?

★ ★ ★

Rules and roles for the Special Duties Section were different.

It is fair to summarise Auxiliary Units operational patrols as an idea from pre-WWII Military Intelligence (Research) – with initial backup from Section 'D' of the Secret Intelligence Service and General Andrew Thorne of XII Corps – and put into effect by the Director of Military Intelligence for Army GHQ.

But the description could never apply equally to the SDS, whose origins developed independently within the Secret Intelligence Service. They amalgamated with Auxiliary Units for administrative rather than operational convenience, retaining their own HQ, Intelligence Officers, ATS and Signals section, and selection and training processes but - other than a partly formal army structure, and an unpaid, stay-behind role for enrolled civilians in-the-field – little else in common with the patrols.

Although less is known about the SDS, enough has emerged to be sure of most of the picture. Civilian 'coast–watchers' – even though generally from an older age group than the patrols, had not all passed-on when public questions were raised in the 1990s. Post war secrecy was draconian in spite of a few Press leaks after 'VE' Day. Apparently, it was not a breach of the Official Secrets Act for a senior army officer (presumably) to brief the editor of the '*Times*' newspaper in 1945 whereas – with typical MoD double standards – it might well be for a coast watcher to mention his WWII service today over a pint in a pub.

Although patrols were sometimes able to organise quiet reunions, that was not within the gift of the SDS, for they were unknown to one another - and no nominal roll has ever been published. Intelligence Officers dispersed after the war, comforted by continuing access to an old-boy Intelligence network which, while supportive, eventually left them behind as new minds were called for in a new and, this time, Cold war.

The weak links (or strong, depending upon your point–of–view) in everlasting secrecy were a few independent minded other ranks of Auxunits (Signals). Remaining as serving soldiers until demobilisation, they were then distributed piecemeal into post-war austerity. Can there be any doubt that Whitehall 'thinkers' – trying hard to keep the lid on the SDS – concluded they would never surface again? They were wrong, and the secrecy dam started leaking in the early 1990s, just in time for Signals' survivors to get together for a few drinks and many a laugh (HI!).

Although none went into print in the market place, some of their memories and technical know-how did appear miraculously – it now seems – in respected, quasi-official publications on the fringes, for example of both Royal Signals and Bletchley Park. They drew ATS Auxunits from obscurity too. The fact is that, following a number of well publicised, post-war high-level and unprosecuted Official Secrets breaches, several soldiers and some ATS justifiably felt free, after fifty years, to look realistically at their role and ignore some of the secrecy to which *they* had originally been committed. They were undoubtedly right and well-intentioned, but disapproving officials discussing matters in secret Whitehall committees must have kicked themselves. However, almost all the men and women enrolled through the influence of secret services, such as SDS Intelligence Officers, still went to their graves insisting they knew 'nothing about the Special Duties Section'.

Thankfully, therefore, enough written evidence is now available through Public Record Office to confirm those eye witnesses who felt confident enough to speak out. It is not any longer necessary to make the guesses into which David Lampe was lured when he researched '*The Last Ditch*' in 1967 and 1968. It is not clear why he was told about the SDS at all and the strong clue from his source acknowledgements is that 'Bill' Major spilled some of the beans. Lampe, grateful no doubt for what he was given, was in no position to ask questions but the breach may not have pleased everyone. Indeed, it can perhaps be interpreted as a deliberate leak, part of the then ongoing unfriendliness which continued to plague relations within the secret services. Lampe also put the 'Secret Sweeties' on the map and others could quite rightly then ask – 'Why not me too?'

For better or worse, '*The Last Ditch*' – whether intentionally or not, was certainly the watershed. But important facts were kept from David Lampe and he was led to the conclusion that:

> 'The Special Duties Section of Auxiliary Units was beyond doubt the part of the organisation that would have collapsed most quickly after the Germans got a foothold in Britain, for underground broadcasting from fixed stations is untenable. The out-station operators would have been in great danger, but not in as great danger as the control station operators who had to remain on the air until their hideouts were penetrated. The secret sweeties accepted this fact'

No observer would doubt that ATS Auxiliary Units, ordered to 'stay-behind' in their Zero-Stations, would have been dangerously vulnerable. Although they always accepted the probability, it cannot be certain that the order would have been given at all. It is far more likely that, when the balloon went up, the other ranks (men) of Auxunits (Signals), would have been ordered to remain instead. They did have basic training – at least – as fighting soldiers. For final communications fallback - while no project diagram has been traced – dedicated telephone lines leading to GHQ through Hannington Hall, already existed; indeed some men of the Signals were involved in the installation.

Nevertheless, a potential breakdown in the transmission of Intelligence is obvious once Divisional HQs were obliged to retire and establish a new location. These could only have been planned if retreat was organised in advance, and the enemy would have had something to say about that. It seems likely that it was the responsibility of the SDSIO to keep the information flowing. Perhaps Auxunits (Signals) could promptly re-orientate the TRD aerials? Perhaps the men and women manning the Zero Stations would have been expected to set out on foot with a package of memorised information – but the problems of doing so in the front line area are too obvious to need recounting? In any case, Arthur Gabbitas, was certain he had never received specific instructions or training to do so. Perhaps some IOs intended to penetrate the front line to get the information personally? If so, the delay involved would have rendered it virtually useless for tactical decisions.

Coast watchers, as well as the staff of the Control Stations, had advantages obviously unknown to David Lampe. The system was so secure and cellular, that the capture of one could not have led to the detection of others. They were securely unknown to one another. Moreover, their radio communications operated on the 'Quench' principle. According to the best information, this certainly greatly reduced, and perhaps eliminated entirely, the danger of interception by the enemy. Wavelengths employed were unlikely to be targeted; OUT Station transmissions would have been rare – in many cases of short duration, and not necessarily at prearranged times; and the arc over which signals were sent was only a few degrees anyway. Hence the need for regularly fine tuning the dipole aerials.

It is true that the 200 No. 17 standard War Office sets distributed among the coast-watchers for 'SUB-OUT' to 'OUT-Station' communication were notoriously insecure and easy enough to intercept. But they were not issued until 1942 and 1943, well after all realistic danger of invasion had passed and it is highly probable that, as SDS radio traffic expanded in inverse proportion to that danger, this was deliberate.

A decision on the efficacy of the SDS is not as clear cut as David Lampe believed. There is a confusion of information. As with most war-oriented agencies, the SDS was imperfect in some respects and not, in the event, put to the test under active service conditions. The original role as coast watchers and collectors of intelligence may have failed but not by reason of easy enemy interception. As invasion became improbable, the revised role for SDS as *agents provocateurs* among the Allied armed forces and informants on public morale did undoubtedly work and may have been useful to strategists.

But if, as David Ingrams firmly believed there was a deliberate role for some specially trained agents on the SDS 'other side' to collaborate with the enemy, they were certainly in double jeopardy whether it worked or not. If their double-agent role was detected by the Gestapo, they were doomed. On the other hand, if they were suspected of disloyalty by the men of the Patrols, they were on a short list for execution by them!

Was it a surprise that it was to be kept 'Most Secret' for ever?

But not, of course, for the benefit of the men and women of the Auxiliary Units themselves!

CHAPTER TWENTY ONE

Werewolves, 'Gladios', & Auxunits

by Geoffrey Bradford.

'Only a people's war, blazing up all over the country, can rob the victor of the fruits of his victory.'

(General Ludendorff)

★　　★　　★

From the previous chapters, it will be seen that in May 1940 – showing unusual and remarkable foresight – the British High Command created the Auxiliary Units. This volunteer army came into being at a time when a successful German invasion was more than probable.

Much later in the war, the German High Command (OKW) was forced to consider the possibility of Allied Forces setting foot in the Fatherland. By the late Spring of 1944, leaders of the Nazi Party, with most to lose from an Allied success, finally realised that they could lose the war in spite of Hitler's continued declarations of victory. In desperation, they turned to the German people, wrongly believing they possessed the same degree of fanaticism and that, in a frenzy of patriotism, they would rise against the invader.

The *Herrenvolk* were, however, beginning to suffer the effects of war. Shortages of everyday essentials, heavy casualties on the Eastern front and devastating bombing of their cities, were all having an increasingly adverse affect on civilian morale. Despite this, German propaganda hoped to engender the same 'They can take it!' spirit shown by the British earlier in the war. Inspired by this hope, a Citizens Army was created – the Werewolves. Unlike its British counterpart, the very name was designed to produce an element of fear and superstition among Allied troops. How better to describe a normal civilian by day – but one transformed into a vicious killer by night?

The Allies became aware of the existence of this secret army when Goebbels announced details of Werewolf missions in a radio broadcast. It is unlikely that this was unintentional – he was too much of a professional propagandist. More probably he wished to create an impression of a large and well-organised army of guerrilla fighters, supported and assisted by a public loyal to the Nazi cause.

Although conceived by the Party, the Werewolves were operated by the OKW. As well as having the same functions of sabotage, guerrilla attacks and intelligence gathering as the Auxiliary Units, the Werewolves were given additional duties. They were to undertake local propaganda by distributing leaflets, painting slogans, and bill-posting in an endeavour to bolster the resistance of the German people, even in areas already occupied. The leaflets gave hints on how to commit sabotage, pointing out that such acts would require the enemy to deploy front-line troops to protect his supply lines. Using the same maxim as Lawrence of Arabia, they encouraged the destruction of enemy equipment, this being more difficult to replace than men.

A more sinister duty was the assassination of any German that accepted office under the Occupying Powers or assisted the Military Government. Although the Auxiliary Units were equipped with high-powered silenced rifles, these were mainly to deal with sentries and guard dogs – or to live off the land – rather than specifically for the execution of collaborators. There is no doubt that 'Quislings', as such traitors became known - would have existed in Britain as they did in all the conquered countries. Although many Auxunit patrols had a definite understanding of how they should be dealt with, no specific instructions were issued – as far as is known.

Very few records relating to the Werewolves exist – most were destroyed in the later stages of the war to protect their members - and for many years survivors displayed the same reticence as Auxiliers, probably due more to a fear of retribution than adherence to an oath of secrecy.

The Werewolves were formed in the Spring of 1944, and it is interesting to compare and contrast these units with their British counterparts. Like the Auxiliary Units they were all volunteers, initially recruited by personal invitation, forming a nucleus that increased as its existence became known to members of the Nazi Party and Hitler Youth. Sufficient volunteers came forward to avoid the need for conscription. They were trained by members of the SS Jagdverlande, experienced in anti-terrorist operations in Russia, Yugoslavia and France, and who could pass on partisan skills to the recruits.

By July 1944, five training centres had been established, the largest at Hulcenrath, an ancient Rhineland castle.

The first course lasted for up to five weeks and, as well as training in sabotage, recruits were familiarised with German and Russian weapons and taught survival skills and fieldcraft. Great emphasis was placed on physical endeavour and the ability to withstand pain and hardship, whilst political indoctrination ensured loyalty and blind obedience to the Third Reich.

Werewolves operated in small patrols of five to six men. Up to ten such groups could gather together for major operations, although these were rare. Underground depots were constructed, and maintained by the German equivalent of Auxunits' Scout Sections. Although they contained explosives, weapons food and clothing, no provision was made for living accommodation.

The volunteers were expected to prepare their own hides or foxholes, and a training manual entitled 'Werewolf – Hints for Hunting Units' – illustrates how this was to be done. It shows a volunteer, dressed in civilian clothes, sitting upright and clutching his rifle, in a cramped excavation accessed by a trapdoor. Recruits do not appear to have been uniformed or badged in any way and therefore, being denied protection under any Geneva Convention (for what it was worth!), could be treated as terrorists and summarily executed if captured.

In action, for obvious reasons, they were expected to sever all connection with their families and former lives, and were provided with false identities to avoid reprisals should they be caught. They were also taught secret recognition signals to enable them to identify fellow combatants. Werewolves provided their own signals section and were trained to operate radio equipment.

Since the first area of Greater Germany to be invaded was Austria, initial Werewolf activity was mainly directed against the Red Army as it crossed into Austria at the end of March 1945. Werewolf patrols, strengthened by Austrian volunteers from the Wehrmacht, were to report Russian troop movements to their Austrian HQ although, at this stage of the war, the information would have been of little value to the High Command. Other Werewolf groups were active on all sections of the Eastern Front, their successes against communications and transport causing the Russians to deploy considerable numbers of troops in anti-partisan operations.

On the Western Front, Werewolf attacks were directed more against American troops than the British. The reasons for this are unclear, but it is thought that the British were advancing through the North of Germany, where Protestant inhabitants had never supported the Nazi cause to the same extent as those in the Catholic South. However, one of Montgomery's Liaison Officers was killed in an ambush by a group of Hitler Youth Werewolves. Although wounded, he fought back with his revolver until overwhelmed. Other attacks against British armoured divisions were less successful when small arms and grenades were pitted against tanks.

The Americans met greater opposition from Werewolf groups and found it difficult to come to terms with the fact that their enemies were often little more than children. Having heard Goebbel's broadcast, the Americans were persuaded that a national uprising was imminent. When, in March 1945, the Lord Mayor of Aachen was assassinated, they concluded that Werewolves were well-organised and ruthless killers. German propaganda further strengthened this understanding - as did references to the Alpine Redoubt where, supplied by underground weapon factories, the German Army and it's Fuhrer intended to make a victorious last stand.

This immense bluff caused General Eisenhower, as Supreme Allied Commander, to drive his armies southwards towards the mountains, although Montgomery advised a push onwards to Berlin.

One particularly successful Werewolf tactic was to string wires across roads at head height to decapitate dispatch riders or the unprotected drivers of Jeeps (a tactic not unknown to the Auxiliary Units!). To defeat this, vertical lengths of angle–iron were welded to the front bumpers of Jeeps.

American attitudes to the Werewolves hardened further when the Commander of their 3rd. Armoured Division was assassinated at Paderborn. From then onwards, any attacks by civilians were treated as Werewolf actions and dealt with ferociously. Boys of 12-years-old were tried by Courts-Martial and sentenced to life imprisonment, whilst two teenaged members of the Hitler Youth - allegedly snipers in Aachen – were executed in June 1945.

Following the death of Hitler, Germany's new leaders sued for peace. Realising that continued partisan activity would result in delayed and more punitive peace terms, Keitel, as head of OKW ordered that all Werewolf actions should cease. After the

German surrender, the hunt for Werewolves continued – the British and French being particularly successful, while the Russians had never shown mercy anyway to anyone likely to endanger the lives of their troops.

It is certain that the very presence of a partisan army had some effect on the Allied conduct of the war as, no doubt, the Auxiliary Units would have had in similar circumstances. These two civilian armies had much in common but, since both lacked the essential requirements of long-term guerrilla warfare, namely a permanent supply base and a steady source of recruits, their effectiveness had a limited life span.

Werewolves were not the only imitators of the Auxiliary Units. During the Cold War period (1950 – 1990), Allied 'stay-behind' units – code-named 'Gladios' – were created to provide a guerrilla resistance organisation in the event of Soviet invasion, or communist take-over in any of the NATO countries. These 'irregulars' – conceived and largely funded by the CIA – had secret training camps and hidden packs of weapons and explosives, an example of which can be seen in the Imperial War Museum in London (Special Forces exhibit).

Activities were directed by a NATO Committee, amongst whose members was the late Sir Colin Gubbins, founder of fhe Auxiliary Units and commander of the wartime SOE. Gladios were particularly strong and active in Italy, where they were linked to political assassination and acts of terrorism. Their story is complex, detailed, and yet to be revealed in full.

In November 1990, a Resolution was passed by the European Parliament condemning the existence of this clandestine network, which operated completely outside the law, and may have interfered illegally with the internal affairs of Member States.

It should have led to the demise of the 'Gladios'.

Part I

Auxunit research was hampered from the outset by a minefield of confusion – some was calculated and deliberate.

Although it is no surprise that little was clear-cut in 1940, when the overwhelming imperative for the nation was naked survival, it seems strange still to be confronted with a security smokescreen fifty years later. The conclusion is obvious – this confused state of affairs is not discouraged by the commanding authorities, neither the Ministry of Defence nor the Secret Services. A smart philosophy such as this could well indicate something to hide, it might be concluded and so, counter-productively, researchers were inspired to keep digging even when rock bottom appeared to have been reached.

It was admittedly no help that the 1940 genesis for the Patrols was a three-strand effort, with General Andrew Thorn and the Kent Observation Units; Foreign Office Section 'D' and 007-type hidden arms and supply dumps; and John Holland and Colin Gubbins with their Auxiliers, all creating 'stay-behinds' during the same crisis with more or less skill, more or less authority, but with only Auxiliary Units at first coming immediately under GHQ control. It is not forgotten that C-in-C Home Forces was *aware* of the Kent Observation Units; they were however a localised expedient, the direct inspiration of General Thorne, Commander of XII Corps, and never established as an integrated part of Home Forces. As for Section 'D', the word 'maverick' remains appropriate.

Rarely before this has there been any detailed distinction between the Patrols, the Special Duties Section and Auxiliary Units (Signals). Where it existed at all, the restricted information available on each was allowed to overlap without clarification and – in *'The Last Ditch'* – deliberately encouraged to do so. As each unit worked in secure capsules unknown to one another in-the-field at least, the result was simply additional misunderstanding, *even* – perhaps *especially* – among surviving Auxiliers themselves.

Under the threat of imminent invasion – the focus of all military planning from June 1940 – other circumstances were conspiring to generate long-lasting confusion for 'stay-behind' research. Sheer urgency – a blaze of wild priorities – was in command. Soldiers of the BEF were on leave after Dunkirk – a desperate gamble by the War Office with enfeebled Home Forces, inadequately equipped and untested. With munitions' production lines still only in first gear, there literally was not a moment to lose in preparing Britain against invasion. Under such conditions, it could admittedly hardly be expected – fifty years on – to find every early-day move by the Auxiliary Units carefully documented and recounted by some impeccable war diarist.

To add to the problem, there was no *precedent* for the creation of stay-behind guerrillas by British High Command, either with 'regular' forces or civilians. The British had hitherto believed in 'clean' warfare, even after suffering numerous campaign setbacks from irregulars in various Indian campaigns, with the Boers and – more recently – the Irish Republican Army. It is interesting to speculate whether 'Jo' Holland's acknowledgement of the efficacy of Michael Collins's IRA 'Auxiliaries' in the 1920s, inspired the title for Gubbins's 'stay-behind' civilian 'Auxiliers'.

Between the wars, Holland and Colin Gubbins developed a new operational creed for British *irregular* forces based on those military setbacks. After enemy occupation of home territory, they argued, properly trained and controlled guerrillas could be deployed as significant irritants to the occupying enemy and to our advantage.

Of necessity, the implementation of their plans in 1940 was essentially experimental and not always committed to paper in formal War Office fashion. Consequently, it was just not there for easy reading in the last decade of the century while Auxiliary Units' veterans were literally dying off – as their families and friends started to show belated interest, as well as historians and researchers. However, enough official papers are now available in Public Record Office to show that as early as midsummer 1940, Gubbins was starting to generate formal correspondence – with for example those Commanding Officers who had helped him by providing manpower for his Scout Sections – and in doing so falling in line to some limited extent with the long standing administrative practices expected by the War Office.

It can now be argued that enough standard army administration and rank structure – undoubtedly an essential ingredient for systematic and, in other circumstances successful control of operations – *did* exist but that some could have been *operationally catastrophic* to men of the Auxiliary Unit Patrols after invasion. Much of Gubbins', Wilkinson's and Beyts' time, as well as that of their Intelligence Officers, was at first dedicated to getting things done quickly, by the avoidance of red tape. in a system until then unused to either speed or informality. With the main imperative clearly in focus, they were selecting and training their 'warriors' faster than they could be administered and – at the same time – with the obligatory secrecy essential for both operational and legal security.

In general, War Office systems were unsuited to the urgency with which Auxiliary Units' Patrols were created by Colin Gubbins and Peter Wilkinson. It may have seemed necessary to the War Office in Whitehall to have a Commanding Officer and HQ, Staff, Intelligence Officers, Patrol 'Sergeants' and Auxiliers (or 'other ranks') – that was how it had always been in the army and to some it was the only way to operate – whether it helped win the war or not. His personal authority is demonstrated by the frequency with which Gubbins – prompted by MI(R) and backed by GHQ – managed to 'buck' the system.

Operationally, however, much of the experiment was flawed, and would fail exclusively at the expense of Auxiliers left behind in their OBs. Perhaps this is why the authorities have been so evasive? Have they worked it out too, possibly as the result of later SOE experience, and decided it was in someone's best interests to let the bad news wither away, to avoid serious investigation, to refuse recognition and publicity for Auxiliers, or at least make it all extremely difficult, and to do so by hiding behind implied commitments under the Official Secrets' Act and a long-term, largely unnecessary veil of secrecy?

Whatever the thinking was, it is certain that those collectively in authority did not have the best interests of operational Auxiliers in mind for, when 'action stations' was called, the strategy would *not* have favoured their survival. They would instead have been left mortally exposed. With no communications or plan for relief or reinforcement, the Patrols would have been ruthlessly and knowingly abandoned and then, either killed in action or captured, interrogated, tortured and probably executed. Nothing less than a successful counter-attack by Home Forces could have saved them. While some did admittedly have limited briefing on the nature of their suicide mission, this could never be in the context of savage reprisals and hostage taking – the hallmark of the Nazis in occupied territories.

Let us examine the facts and the role of the powers-that-be.

Part II

The formal Auxunit operational set-up was based on conventional armed forces lines, officers and other ranks. 'Other ranks' – Auxiliers – were almost completely without experience of active service, particularly after a few WWI veterans had been weeded out in what may be termed the second phase; but they were universally trustful, often in awe, of the 'powers that be', as they warmly remember their regular officers.

It was was, however, debatable whether those officers would 'stay behind' with them when the balloon went up. Although there were no written orders, a few IOs were definitely under the impression that they were intended to remain with their patrols. One, Peter Forbes in the Borders, *assumed* he was expected to stay-behind and Norman Field in Kent, did have two OBs to retire to, together with his staff. But the overwhelming evidence supports Stuart Edmundson's conviction that:

> 'As soon as the enemy landed my job with Auxunits would have come to an end. I would have reverted to regimental status and withdrawn with Home Forces.'

This is amply supported by Major Geoffey Beyts' correspondence when he left Coleshill in 1942, which not only pre-supposed that most IOs would remain with Divisional or Corps HQ as the balloon went up – rather than in-the-field – but also sought funds for IOs OBs if they were ordered to remain *with their patrols*. On the other hand, Scout Section officers definitely were to stay and carry on the fight from one of two OBs, each created to house half a dozen soldiers.

In view of the fact that the fatal weakness for Auxunits Patrols - isolated with their Leader in individual OBs – rested in a complete inability to communicate with their IO, it is important to pursue this aspect of their function in more detail. Before – and after – the ill fated Group System, patrols were to go to ground as the enemy approached, allow him to pass overhead, and then emerge to observe targets and, finally, destroy them, returning to the safety of their OB before their explosive charges fired. All that was fine as long as the battle status remains unchanged.

But to make sensible plans and carry on the fight, they needed vital, tactical information each day. Where, for example, was the front line and were the British planning to counter-attack or retire to (say) Scotland? Without radio communications they were absolutely dependent for this information on contact with their IO – who should have been briefed from Divisional or Corps HQ. They had no way of getting to him and *he* could only pass on vital messages by crossing the front line. Major Beyts was in no doubt that, while the IO might have got away with it once or twice, there was no chance whatever of making it a regular feature of his day (or night). Even then, with cellular arrangements, he would have been forced to visit each of his patrols one by one – being the only operational officer who knew where they were.

It was clearly unworkable in anything but the very shortest term.

Overwhelming evidence exists that Auxiliary Unit patrols were not seen as long-term survivors. The gist of Sir Peter Wilkinson's message to the final Reunion at Parham in July 2000 was:

'They were never intended as a *permanent* resistance movement'.

This approach demonstrates nothing but short-term expectations for Patrols. Further survival limitations were evident. Auxiliers' supplies of food, weaponry and explosives were finite – limited by storage space and accessibility – and they were left with no means whatever of re-supply other than living off the land and stealing enemy munitions. When stocks were exhausted – with enemy aircraft nothing more than smoking ruins at the dispersal point, supply and petrol stores destroyed, and Tiger tanks immobilised – Auxiliers were supposed, it may be assumed, to declare their war over and return to home and workplace under the gaze of an understanding enemy?

The prospect is plainly ludicrous but no evidence has been discovered of any plan to bring them to safety. Effectively, they were expendable and abandoned. (Indeed one speculation, admittedly uncorroborated, is that their presence behind enemy lines, isolated underground, would have been a bargaining point used by Winston Churchill *in extremis* to try to persuade President Roosevelt and the United States to enter the war before Japan did the job for him. From experience, it would be unsafe to bet too heavily that Cabinet papers will not one day be released to sort it all out.)

What *is* absolutely definite, however, is that Auxunit Patrols had no *upward* communication – and it is here that the essence of the organisation would have been catastrophic. Under no other circumstances in those times can it be imagined that groups of recently trained soldiers, let alone civilians, would have been placed in such supremely dangerous circumstances without either an officer to refer to or means of getting signals through in pursuit of orders. Too much was expected of them and no backup provided. The nature of their special task, with emphasis on local knowledge and self-sufficiency, guaranteed that Auxiliers were often working men more used to taking orders than giving them. Now they were on their own with no one to tell them what to do and no means of knowing front line dispositions or even whether the fight was still on.

Auxiliers who realised their role was suicidal *at the time* never dramatise the fact today. It is obvious that success or failure would have been mainly in the hands of the Patrol leader. If he was good enough they might have had a brief chance. Where he was not they had no hope – and no officer to refer to. With no relief, re-supply, or reinforcement, they would have been effectively in isolation.

In war, Auxiliary Units were to be sacrificed as nothing more than a short-term provocation to the occupying power; and in peace as part of a long-term cover up.

This is far from all. Although most Auxiliers were never to realise the fragility of their legal standing under the Conventions of War, it seems very much as though there were others who did.

Part III

In warfare, Rule One is simple enough. If you win your leaders are heroes; if you lose – *war criminals*. After WWII, it was the Dock at Nuremberg that was full, not the Old Bailey although there must have been times when even Allied forces were provoked into acts of retaliation better forgotten?

War is a dirty business and, in spite of fine words, all that counts is winning. Great Britain, was a signatory to a 1930s Agreement – together with France, Germany, the United States and others – not to be the *first* to use poison gas in any future conflict. With the horror of a million dead men in WWI as the incentive, the theory was that if no one used gas *first*, such mass annihilation could never again happen. And yet, according to James Hayward in 'Shingle Street', an author who researched this subject in depth, confronted by Germans preparing to cross the 'big river' toward Kent in 1940, a military recommendation was put to the War Cabinet that, as soon as the enemy set foot ashore, they were to be counter attacked by that very same poison gas.

The rules of war take a positive point of view about belligerents in uniform and the vulnerability of who are not. In general, if a fighting man in uniform has identification tags and a Paybook, for example, and is part of an identifiable, disciplined unit, with rank structure and officers, he is entitled to Prisoner of War status if captured and certain associated rights and commitments.

A fighting man without these recognisable symbols can be treated as a 'franc tireur' – that is as a guerrilla or terrorist or sabotThe idea *was approved*, although the final decision to fire remained with the War Cabinet and therefore became political as well as military.

(There has been speculation about the siting of Auxiliary Units' OBs as a result. It is a fact that they were, in the main, not *on* the coast, as might sometimes have been expected, but usually inland; the proposed use of poison gas, known at GHQ, may have been confided to Intelligence Officers who therefore positioned OBs to avoid the danger of gassing their own men?)

In any case, not many Britains would disagree with such a 'last-ditch' plan, even in these days of political correctness. The point is that we were prepared to survive by throwing rules overboard and, in that respect, were not a lot better than many others. It did not stop there.eur with no rights at all but the prospect of being shot out-of-hand without trial. Indeed, from their early days, even British Commandos - regular troops in all respects but with irregular methods of fighting - were the subject of Hitler's specific Directive withdrawing their rights as combatants - and authorising their immediate execution (See Appendix THREE).

The Rules of War are often arcane, unclear, and subject to interpretation - usually by the victor. Those considered *after* WWII, appear to provide that irregulars, in order to enjoy recognition as legitimate, belligerent forces, shall:–

(a) have at their head a person responsible for his subordinates
(b) wear some fixed distinctive badge recognisable at a distance
(c) carry arms openly and
(d) conform in their operations to the laws and customs of war.

The rules, however, also provide that, in case of invasion, the inhabitants of a territory who on the approach of the invading enemy *spontaneously* take up arms to resist it, shall be regarded as belligerent troops if they carry arms openly and respect the laws and customs of war, although they may not

have had time to become organised in accordance with the
above provisions.

In respect of Auxiliary Units, this invites detailed legal
analysis and it is not within the scope of this book to follow
that path. However, it must be clear that they fail to qualify as
regular troops on any number of counts.

It is with this background that the position of the men of
Auxunits' Patrols has to be considered. They were the creation of
the British military authority – let us say the War Office. It is on
record that a memorandum dated 8th August 1940 was seen by
Prime Minister Winston Churchill, detailing progress with their
formation. So, very soon after Dunkirk, there is confirmation of
both political and military knowledge of the Patrols' existence.

And yet, they broke accepted conventions of War. Auxiliers had
none of the necessary identifying features of a conventional force
– no pay or Paybook, no identity tags – not even a name on a
nominal roll, no disciplined structure, no uniform in early days,
and above all, perhaps, no officers on-the-spot. Had Britain lost
the war, would their existence have been a war crime?

Auxiliers themselves were unaware, even disinterested in
such hypotheses; they were in the deep end and training for the
real thing. The men were, technically at least, volunteers for
high-risk operations, but rarely had a full understanding of just
what was meant by a 'suicide mission'. It was one thing to be
dropped by parachute to assist the Franch Maquis, properly
educated and well-read, after careful selection, a
comprehensive course of instruction and specific briefing on
the dangers; absolutely another to be a farm worker, bored
with life in the Home Guard and invited to participate in
something 'special' as a sort of prank. Auxiliers were never to
get a full description of their legal vulnerability from IOs or
Group Commanders – they didn't know much about it either.

But there is evidence to show that *someone* did. For example,
there was a race in 1942 to list Auxiliers on a national Nominal
Roll for the first time. Not only were they by then sometimes
in uniform, instead of the denims which had been their early
trademark, they also had identifying County tabs and rank
'stripes'. There was further identifying uniformity when 'front'
HG Battalions were created early in 1943. In this way they
were moved from the totally covert to the partially overt. Was
someone worrying about their very legality at last?

Significantly, research by Steven Sutton in his Dissertation
(copied to the Imperial War Museum) while reading for a BA
(Honours) Degree, suggested that General Alan Brooke,
successor to Field Marshal Lord Ironside as C-in-C Home

Forces, although fully and officially aware of the existence and role of Auxunits:

> '...did not want its existence recognised or acknowledged in an official policy document?...'

From the first, General Brooke was well enough aware, not only of the Auxunits irregular operational patrols, but also the embryonic Special Duties Section. His diaries show a visit of inspection to Kent and Sussex on 29th August 1940, a visit well remembered by the patrols' Intelligence Officer, Norman Field. To his very considerable surprise, General Brooke diverted from the planned schedule to visit a cottage, staffed by ATS subalterns – part no doubt of the SDS 'pilot scheme' – the existence of which had hitherto been entirely unknown to Captain Field, although very much within his sphere of responsibility.

Steven Sutton explains Brooke's resistance to Auxunits' 'acknowledgement' as 'subterfuge' in the good cause of operational secrecy. Another possibility is that the C-in-C, with more time than his predecessor to think about it, had decided he did not wish to contribute evidence against himself if the war went badly – and there was still a real possibility of that – and he was later hauled up as a war criminal. Together, undoubtedly, with other scallywags such as Winston Churchill and Colin Gubbins!

The evidence does not stop there. The Patrols' stand-down letter directed that, because of the necessarily secret nature of their work:

> '...no recognition would be possible'.

Auxiliers' reaction, as usual, was belief in the judgement of their officers and if they said 'don't talk about it', then they didn't. They all believed themselves committed by signatures on Official Secrets' Act forms – the existence of which the Ministry of Defence now denies; no formal Associations were created either and Auxiliers were never invited to national Armistice Day Parades. When recent arrangements to do so were concluded on their behalf with the Royal British Legion, it was not a surprise when survivors showed positive disinterest.

But in any event, the 'no recognition' order was enforced and their war service ignored by, for instance, deliberately keeping the nominal roll secretly within Army Medal Office at the Ministry of Defence for for *fifty years*.

Moreover, Auxiliers were not admitted to the Special Forces

Club in London, in spite of a recommendation from Colin Gubbins. (After a submission by Geoffrey Bradford, they *were* finally accepted in 2002.) Auxiliers in south Wales did hold regular reunions, entirely as a local initiative. Albert Cocks wrote a chapter in 'Churchill's Secret Army'. Books by local researchers rather than Auxiliers, proliferated as more became known.

At very best, however, the history of Auxiliary Units was drip-fed.

With no long-term resistance role the Patrols were nevertheless expected to create havoc behind the lines for a few weeks. Success would have been in proportion to the skill, luck and dedication of the Patrol Leader.

If there was a secondary role to provoke acts of retaliation by the Nazis, none of the Auxiliers interviewed was aware of it. However the possibility exists that their guerrilla activities could have led to cruel retaliation by the Germans and this might in turn have hardened civilian attitudes against the invader. Such a policy was successfully devised by Michael Collins, the Irish hero – or terrorist – in the 1920s, and known about by Holland and Gubbins. In support of Mike Calvert's theory, it may even have been one ingredient of Auxunits' HQ strategy, intended to provoke worldwide propaganda backlash and condemnation against the Germans.

As there was no invasion it was easier for the authorities to remind Auxiliers of their commitment to silence and then ignore their illegality, rather than face the issue. Consequently, Defence Medal-worthiness was too late for most of the men, half-hearted as it was and linked unswervingly to service in the HG – which had always been only a front.

The belated medals' offer – most men having by then died – shone some light upon the few survivors but further complicated their security status.

It is of interest to note, in spite of repeated 'offers of understanding' to Departments of the Ministry, that *not one* claimed that Auxiliary Units were kept secret long after the war *for operational reasons*. This is a further testament to deliberate, official Auxunits' marginalisation. Nobody wanted post-war responsibility, and the easy way out was to capitalise on the innate, patriotic trustfulness of the men, and allow time erode the problem.

Add the implied confidentiality of Official Secrecy – and Auxunits would just disappear.

And they very nearly did. At the expense of the 'Warriors'.

As usual.

Part IV

Scout Section regular soldiers and those of Auxiliary Units (Signals) had a 'stay-behind' role as well as the civilian patrols.

Signals, after withdrawal from various units – often resulting from pre-war registration as 'HAMS' with the Radio Society of Great Britain – and transfer to AUs, remained in uniform, with conventional ranks, and a Paybook stamped 'Auxiliary Units (Signals)'.

In spite of this, if the later treatment of troopers in the SAS is any guide, the invader would no doubt have identified both Signals and Scouts as irregulars or Special Forces behind his lines and treated them without mercy; they would have been lucky indeed to receive formal recognition and benefits from PoW status.

Signals' ingenious work in support of SDS has never before been adequately documented and, had it not been for the dedication of the late Arthur Gabbitas, the unit would have passed into oblivion at the end of the war, and disappeared with the Patrols. Both they and the Scout Sections, having worked in small groups, did not find it surprising to be dispersed and demobilised in a routine way.

It was not until Arthur set about reuniting his comrades annually, and writing some of their WWII history for specialist publications, that they came together and a broad picture emerged.

But the same was never to happen to the Scout Sections. Fortunately there are still survivors to tell their general story – and of the Dorset Sections' unique status with the Special Air Service Regiment. Without these leads, they would probably remain as unknown today as they did to David Lampe in 1968.

ATS Auxiliary Units

The carefully selected subalterns – the 'Secret Sweeties' – were specifically equipped to 'stay behind' after invasion and some had limited firearms' training. It was never intended they should fight to the death, however.

It will be recalled that they had a Control Station – a working 'Met' hut usually in the grounds of an Army Command HQ – and a fall-back 'Zero Station' underground and independently equipped for a lengthy stay. In the event of HQ evacuation, they would either have closed down their Control Stations, thus paralysing the SDS network, or continued working from Zero Stations, relaying incoming intelligence to the site of the new Army HQ until inevitable capture.

Here was a serious 'Catch 22' situation. They could either leave with the army and lose valuable contact with SDS, or remain at work until certain capture. Treatment as PoWs was not guaranteed and would very much have depended upon the invader. With the SS or Gestapo they were unlikely to survive, if precedents with women radio operators in SOE were followed, although they would have had the great advantage of uniform and insignia. Officers of the regular German Army might have been more understanding.

The decision to stay would have been with Army Command. The ATS (Auxiliary Units) *were* adequately briefed on 'stay-behind' risks but it remains questionable whether local commanders valued the quality of incoming Intelligence so highly they would have ordered them to do so.

Another option was possible. To leave the radio stations in the hand of the men, other ranks of Auxunits (Signals).

The Special Duties Section

David Lampe in '*The Last Ditch*', assured that the radio network would have been quickly penetrated by enemy direction finding units, considered the SDS to be of 'untenable' value.

He was fortunate to have been briefed, on the only post-war occasion we can trace, with certain information about the working of the Special Duties Section, but it is not clear from the Acknowledgements in his book precisely who provided him with this unique opportunity. However, with the SDS and (Signals), working separately but entirely in harmony with a master plan, it is difficult to conceive that his fear of communications' interception was not taken into account at an early planning stage by Auxunits' GSO(2), Major Maurice Petherick.

David Lampe believed what he was told but did not ensure corroboration through research. It is undeniable that he succinctly described Special Duties' activities; nearly every word is confirmed by our own crosschecks. However, he was apparently unaware of the very special nature of the radio communications network described earlier in this book. Either he was deliberately mislead or it was sheer guesswork for him to deny the potential of SDS reconnaissance and intelligence communication on the grounds of the enemy's skill in radio direction finding, and he has entirely overlooked the real breakdown point as we see it – namely at the IN-Station.

It was unfortunate that Lampe was unaware that this was, as far as we can tell, the only radio network operating with the 'quench' principle, using Radio Telephony on an improbable frequency. This is not to say it would not have been detected by the enemy in due course but it is a very reasonable proposition indeed that the SDS would have been in a position to continue spying and communicating with GHQ for a significant time, *providing the IN-Station link was maintained by the ATS.*

SDS agents, operating individually and under 'Most Secret' conditions were less likely to get caught than the men of the provocatively equipped fighting Patrols. Moreover, if one was detected, the domino effect was improbable for the simple reason that he or she knew no one else in their cell other, perhaps, than the Key Man and the Intelligence Officer. It is unlikely therefore that severe interrogation and even torture could have forced betrayal of the network.

Whereas rewards for the patrols were never in evidence, if precedents of other contract work for the secret services are anything to go by, a few men and women of the SDS could reasonably anticipate post-war recognition or benefits of a kind, either directly or indirectly. Coming, as they more frequently did, from the professional and educated classes they would have entered into a commitment with SDS only after a full explanation of the hazards and a commitment to the total and everlasting secrecy involved. In return there might be an indirect sprinkle of Honours in due course, probably in recognition of 'public service'; or further – and perhaps paid – employment for one of the secret services, even emoluments distributed as 'expenses'. As they were 'released' and not disbanded, some may have found help with future employment or family education.

They could reasonably expect to find, from time to time, that someone was watching over their good fortune. However, these men and women would from the outset never have expected *visible* recognition.

It may be assumed that Colin Gubbins was being deliberately disingenuous when he told David Lampe (p.149 – '*The Last Ditch*') that he was then 'so sure that some higher authority had decided that the full story of the Auxiliary Units Organisation must remain secret that he told no-one about his own connection with it until the first time he saw the organisation mentioned in print...'

Although the SDS probably arrived at Coleshill after he left, it is inconceivable that Colin Gubbins was not a significant part of that very 'higher authority'.

Part V

Conclusions

If Great Britain had lost the battle, Auxunits' Patrol and Scout Section personnel would have been eliminated on active service sooner or later. Group Commanders might have gone down fighting with them. As non belligerent units, it seems a fair bet that the Special Duties Section, Signals, and ATS subalterns might have got away more or less intact, for a time at least.

Intelligence Officers, together with Colin Gubbins and Peter Wilkinson and other senior officers, as creators of irregular units of civilians, would probably have been arraigned as war criminals with death sentences or long periods of imprisonment resulting.

Fortunately for us all, the British – having reluctantly entered into conflict anyway, were to show singular genius for winning! GHQ Auxiliary Units were a special part of that genius and the whole nation should still be breathing a sigh of relief on their behalf.

A final matter for discussion focuses on the continuing post WWII secrecy – perhaps *obfuscation* would be a better word? – imposed upon Auxiliary Units' history. After the end of the Cold War, Auxunits' papers started to appear in Public Record Office. If the official proposition is that this post WWII delay was because lessons learned in WWII were still of operational value in Cold War planning and training, it is not supported by the evidence.

There is not, for example, any indication that 'stay-behind' units such as the Special Air Service learned anything from Auxunits' experience, particularly in respect of their OBs. The 'Welrod' is still security classified but was not a weapon exclusive to the patrols – indeed it was never issued to them and obviously came directly to Nigel Oxenden's knowledge following its success with Special Operations Executive.

The development of the Special Duties Section, and the later disappearance of the TRD radio transceiver, have the fingerprints of the secret services rather than the War Office. As a matter of long-term policy, neither of our best-known services would have encouraged publicity. A few 'coast watchers' may have been called upon again, post-war, this time to work covertly at home as counter-subversives.

Auxunits Patrols, the SDS, ATS and Signals – each was intended to be kept under wraps and it would not require much imagination to suggest that the leaks to David Lampe in 1968, for 'The Last Ditch', did not receive the unanimous approval of either the Security Service (MI5), or the Secret Intelligence Service (MI6).

It all conspired, anyway, to ensure that Auxunits were to remain unrecognised for half a century and that, just as originally intended:

'They did their stuff unseen!'

Even today, things are still not all that much different. Auxiliers, knowingly or not, had to conform to Secret Service rules!

The Museum of the
British Resistance Organisation
Parham, Suffolk

This Museum, dedicated to the WWII GHQ AUXILIARY UNITS, is a part of the 390th Bomb Group Memorial Air Museum, and occupies the control tower on the former Framlingham Airfield, a base for USAAF B-17 Flying Fortresses. The two units operate with one Committee and are registered as a charity.

The MBRO was added to the 390th in August 1997 and opened by the Late Lieutenant-Colonel J W Stuart Edmundson, TD, one of the first Intelligence Officers to be called for briefing in Whitehall Place by Colin Gubbins and Peter Wilkinson in July 1940.

The long established 390th, owed its existence to the generosity of the landowners, Suffolk farmers, the Late Percy and Herman Kindred. When enquiries about the Auxiliary Units started locally in 1992, it was discovered that the Kindred brothers had been WWII members of the Stratford St Andrew Patrol.

As a gesture of thanks to the Kindred family, the Committee and Members of the 390th Bomb Group Memorial Air Museum unanimously agreed to create a new section dedicated to the Auxiliary Units. They also hosted the final national Auxunits Reunion on 2nd July 2000, thought to be the 60th Anniversary of the formation under Field Marshall Lord Edmund Ironside, GOC Home Forces.

His son, the present Lord Ironside, Patron of the Museum, was guest of Honour at the Reunion.

The President is Peter Kindred, Percy's son.

★　　★　　★

AUXUNIT NEWS – www.auxunit.org.uk – is a website dedicated to the Auxiliary Units. It was established in 1999 by David Waller, whose father Raymond served with the Brotton Patrol in North Yorkshire.

The Medals' Fiasco

In 1996, someone in Whitehall tried to direct kindly light upon the Auxiliary Units. If it was intended to benefit the men of the Patrols, it succeeded in a limited number of cases. Unfortunately, it was cruelly unkind to a minority.

As usual, it was the confused Auxunits background that highlighted the problem. It is surely now beyond dispute that there were half a dozen branches, all marshalled under one Auxunit HQ administration, with a coordinated objective – but different origins.

Although it is now on record that Auxiliary Units were one of Britain's nine WWII Secret Services, as opposed to merely being a service operating in secret, it was really those sections generated by Section 'D' of MI6 that gave rise to this high security classification and its attendant embargoes. This directly embraces Auxunits (Signals), the ATS Subalterns operating radios from IN-Stations, and the Special Duties Section.

Intelligence Officers, Scout Sections, Group Commanders and the Patrols, developed from a more orthodox background – the War Office in general and, in some cases, the Directorate of Military Intelligence in particular.

Bundled together, they formed the GHQ Auxiliary Units of WWII.

The ATS and the SDS were certainly fully aware that no overt recognition would ever be a possibility. IOs, as officers, would have had a clear understanding too. This was not necessarily so for the other ranks of the Scout Sections and Signals but – as we have seen – they were split up, and dispersed to demobilisation without a murmur.

As civilians, Auxiliary Units Patrols – a special case – were allowed to languish in more or less secrecy until the bright light shone in broadsheet newspapers in 1996. By that time the majority had died and the rest had come to accept that they would take the secrets of their WWII service to the grave.

The 'Times' presented an article by Michael Evans, Defence Correspondent, on 7th September 1996:

'Honour at last for elite force whose hour never came...

'...The Ministry of Defence confirmed yesterday that the Army Medals issuing Office at Droitwich, near Worcester, would award the former secret commandos (Auxunits, that is), provided they could prove they had completed three years' service...If they were with the Home Guard, they would get the Defence Medal.'

Even accepting that someone in the Establishment at last wished Auxiliers to have tangible recognition, this was a ham-fisted way of going about it. We can only guess how many were still alive, or how many read the *'Times'* (or *Daily Telegraph*). Moreover, it was a leak to the media rather than an official announcement and, as such, never appeared to have the encouragement or formal backing of the Ministry of Defence.

The Historical Branch of the MoD soon wrote, rather condescendingly – as though everyone must know – that as members of the Home Guard, Auxiliers had *always* been entitled to the Defence Medal. Although perhaps unaware of the inference, they were seen as naughty boys and it was clearly their own *fault for not bothering to apply.* It looked like a cop-out when Army Medals Office was later too overworked and short of time, to report the number of applications prior to 1996. The answer, of course, was Nil. Many Auxiliers never realised they had ever been in the Home Guard at all. There was also the significant fact that they all been warned never to expect recognition.

The next MoD shot in the foot was the claim that there was no nominal roll – although within two years, they lodged it in Public Record Office for all to read. Someone, it seemed, did not approve of Auxunits.

An undisclosed number of applicants were successful. The three-year-service rule within which Army Medals Office was obliged to operate, was rigorously applied to the disadvantage of some eligible applicants. It is farcical to pretend that Auxunits' administration was in any way coordinated in the early days of the war or could be depended upon now as absolute corroboration of Service – indeed, it was not until 1942 that the first national nominal roll was collated from previous local records, often cobbled together on the 'backs of envelopes'.

Moreover, it was compiled for a very different reason than the post war issue of medals.

On the basis of that very imperfect nominal roll, several applications were improperly refused – and no quarter was given by AMO in their decision making. They took it upon themselves to ignore any interpretation of the evidence other than their own and showed exceptional aptitude for economies of the truth. If it is desired to be fair to them, they were probably staffed at a level that did what it was told. They suffixed each refusal with the specious :–

'...although I know you will find this a disappointment...'

but their communications sometimes seemed to radiate bureaucratic satisfaction that there was nothing they could, or wished to do about it and that there was no other channel of appeal or accountability. They were the masters.

As far as accountability and appeals are concerned, they were absolutely right. In order to rectify unfair refusals in East Anglia alone – attempts to co-opt help from Downing Street and ten members of the Palace of Westminster, both Lords and Commoners, have come firmly against dead ends with – in some cases – strong hints to discontinue the application.

One refusal affected an Auxilier enlisted in 1940 – but whose enrolment form signature was not called for until 1942. Another, had his HG enrolment papers torn up by an officer, for secrecy, when he enlisted in Auxunits in 1941. A third was admittedly *two days short* of three years service after a wait of fifty years. While the Ministry is very sharp off the mark to claim that approval of these applications would merely devalue those already granted, they are impervious to the hurt and humiliation their generation brings upon unfairly deprived, elderly applicants who are not unaware that elsewhere the Defence Medal was issued to telegraph boys, clerks and canteen assistants. This will be a great discouragement when the next call for volunteers is sounded.

Would the man who shone the kindly light in 1996 kindly step forward and promptly set up a meeting with the Adjutant General's Branch – and all the other interested parties – to get proper recognition for the survivors and not take 'No' for an answer from the men or women that M R D Foot wrote about – those responsible for the:

'...bureaucratic inertia which thrives on Whitehall's cult of secrecy.'

Hitler's Commando directive
(*Kommandobefehl*)

1. For some time our enemies have been using, in their warfare, methods which are outside the International Geneva Conventions. Especially brutal and treacherous is the behaviour of the so-called Commandos, who, as is established, are partially recruited even from freed criminals in enemy countries. From captured orders it is divulged that they are directed not only to shackle prisoners, but also to kill defenceless prisoners on the spot at the moment in which they believe that the latter, as prisoners, represent a burden in the further pursuit of their purposes, or could otherwise be a hindrance. Finally, orders have been found in which the killing of prisoners has been demanded in principle.

2. For this reason it was already announced, in an addendum to the Armed Forces report of 7th October, 1942, that, in the future, Germany in the face of these sabotage troops of the British and their accomplices, will resort to the same procedure, that is, that they will be ruthlessly mowed down by the German troops in combat, wherever they may appear.

3. I therefore order:
   From now on, all enemies on so-called Commando missions in Europe or Africa, challenged by German troops, even if they are to all appearances soldiers in uniform or demolition troops, whether armed or unarmed, in battle or in flight, are to be slaughtered to the last man. It does not make any difference whether they are dropped by parachute. Even if these individuals, when found, should apparently be prepared to give themselves up, no pardon is to be granted them on principle. In each individual case, full information is to be sent to the OKW for publication in the Report of the Military Forces.

4. If individual members of such Commandos, such as agents, saboteurs, etc., fall into the hands of the military forces by some other means, through the police in occupied territories, for instance, they are to be handed over immediately to the SD. Any

imprisonment under military guard, in PoW stockades, for instance, etc., is strictly prohibited, even if this is only intended for a short time.

5. This order does not apply to the treatment of any soldiers who, in the course of normal hostilities, large-scale offensive actions, landing operations and airborne operations, are captured in open battle or give themselves up. Nor does this order apply to enemy soldiers falling into our hands after battles at sea, or to enemy soldiers trying to save their lives by parachute after air battles.

6. I will hold responsible, under Military Law, for failing to carry out this order, all commanders and officers who either have neglected their duty of instructing the troops about this order, or asked against this order when it was to be executed.

★　　　★　　　★

General Franz Halder's 'Most Secret' decree for the occupancy of England

Including:

Armed insurgents of either sex will be dealt with with the utmost severity. If the population initiates active operations *after* the completed conquest of a locality, or in places *behind* the fighting front, the inhabitants involved in the fighting will be regarded as armed insurgents. When taking hostages, those persons should if possible be selected in whom the *active* enemy elements have an interest.

I warn all civilians that if they undertake active operations against the German forces, they will be condemned to death inexorably.

Bibliography

Acton, Viv	*Operation Cornwall 1940-44*, Landfall Pubs., 1994
Andrew, Christopher	*Secret Service*, Heinemann, 1985
Angell, Stewart	*Secret Sussex Resistance*
Beatrice Temple	*Diaries* (Private collection)
Beyts, Brigadier Geoffrey	*The Kings' Salt*, Haslam Printers, 1983
Billiere, Sir Peter de la	*Looking for Trouble*, Harper Collins, 1995
Bright-Astley, Joan	*Gubbins and SOE*, Leo Cooper, 1997
Brown, Donald	*Somerset v Hitler*, Countryside Books, Newbury, 1999
Calvert, Michael	*Fighting Mad*, Airlife, 1996
Carpenter, Edward	*Romney Marsh at War*
Carter, Derek	*Operation Cornwall 1940-44*, Landfall Pubs, 1994
Cassidy, William	*The Art of Silent Killing*
Cave Brown, Anthony	*Bodyguard of Lie,* Robert Hale, 1991
Cave Brown, Anthony	*The Secret Servant*, Sphere, 1989
Chinnery,Philip D.	*March or Die*, Airlife, 2001
Chinnery,Philip D.	*Any time Any Place*, Airlife, 1994
Cocks, Albert	*Churchill's Secret Army*, Book Guild, 1992
Croft, Andrew	*A Talent for Adventure*, Spa, 1991
Dunning, James	*It Had to be Tough*, Pentland Press, 2000
Fenwick, Ian	*Enter Trubshaw*, Collins, 1945
Fleming, Peter	Invasion 1940, Pan Books, 1975
Foot, M.R.D	SOE, Mandarin, 1990
Foot, M.R.D	*Resistance*, Eyre Methuen, 1976
Hamilton-Hill, Donald	*SOE Assignment*, Kimber, 1973
Harrison, D.I.	*These Men are Dangerous*, Cassell, 1999
Hayward, James	*Shingle Street*, LTM Publications, 1994
Hayward, James	*The Bodies on the Beach*, CD41 Publishing, 2001
Hoare, Adrian	*Standing up to Hitler*, Geo.R. Reeve, 1997
Ironside, The Lord	*The Ironside Diaries*, Constable, 1962
Kemp, Anthony	*The SAS at War 1941–45*, Penguin, 1998
Lampe, David	*The Last Ditch*, Cassell, 1968
Lowry, Bernard	*The Mercian Maquis*, Logaston Press, 2002
Mackenzie, Prof. S.P.	*The Home Guard*, Oxford University Press, 1996
Mackenzie, William	*The Secret History of SOE*, St.Ermins Press, 2000
Macrae, Col. R. Stuart	*Winston Churchill's Toyshop*, Roundwood Press, 1971
McCue, Paul	*SAS Operation Bulbasket*, Leo Cooper, 1996
Melton, H. Keith	*The Ultimate Spy Book,* Dorling Kindersley, 1997
Niven, David	*The Moon's a Balloon*, Penguin, 1994

Royal Signals Magazine *The Wire*
Schellenberg, Walter *Invasion 1940*, Little Brown, 2000
Skillen, Hugh *Enigma Symposium 99*
Stafford, David *Camp X*, Viking Press, 1987
Stafford, David *Britain and European Resistance 40-45*, Macmillan, 1979
Stevenson, William *A Man Called Intrepid*, Macmillan, 1976
Taylor, Andrew *Auxiliary Units – History and Achievement*, BRO Museum, 1998
Verity, Hugh *We Landed by Moonlight*, Harrap, 1950
Ward, Arthur *Resisting the Nazi Invader*, Constable, 1978
Whittaker, Len *Some Talk of Private Armies*
Wilkinson, Sir Peter *Gubbins and SOE*, Leo Cooper, 1997
Wilks, Mick *The Mercian Maquis*, Logaston Press, 2002
Winterbotham, Fred. W. *The Ultra Secret*, Weidenfeld and Nicholson, 1974

Index

A

Alford, John; 4

Alanbrooke, Field Marshal Lord; see Brooke, General Alan

Alexander, Subaltern Mary; 208, 225, 227, 230

Alston, Donald; 222

Alston, SubalternYolande; 219, 221

Anderson, Captain A R C ('Andy'); 61, 174, 224

Andrew, Christopher; xxvi, 21

Asche; see Schmidt, Hans-Thilo

Ashby, Lieutenant William; 76

Ashley, Alan George; 130, 133

Ashley, Lord; 4

Aston, John; 227

Aston, Subaltern Priscilla; 208, 227

Atkinson, Major G C L; 160

Auchinlech, General Claude J E; 69

Ayre, Bill (G2FWX); 187, 189

B

Bachelor's Hall, Hundon, Suffolk; 57, 161, 186-8, 196, 226

Baden–Powell, Lord Robert William; 162-3

Badgerow, Priscilla; see Aston

Bailey, Eric; 16

Bailey, Ralph; 145

Barden, Subaltern M L; 230

Barffe, Alfie; 74

Bartholomew, William E B ('Bill') (G8CK); 187-90, 194, 201

Beaumont-Nesbitt, Major General Frederick J ('Paddy'); xxix

Beckford, C ('Dusty'); 139

Beddington-Behrens, Major Edward; 4, 98

Bell, Percy; 115

Berkeley, Reverend Humphrey; 173

Bertrand, Captain Gustave; 12

Beyts, Brigadier Geoffrey H R ('Billy'); 20, 38, 59-60, 62, 70, 77, 81, 83-4, 107-10, 119, 150, 159, 191, 200, 238-9, 250, 261, 263

Biffin, George; 4-5, 123, 127, 133, 136

Bird, Eric; 115

Blackwell, Leonard; 139

Blair, David; 63

Blandford, Jack; 139

Blaxall, Ernest; 90

Bloomfield, Oliver; 145

Bloxham, Subaltern Marina; 213, 225, 230

Bond, Major Charles F G ('Dick'); 145, 157, 160

Boulden, Peter; 245

Bowen, David; 90

Bowery, Geoffrey; 65, 73, 75, 145

Boxer, Air Vice-Marshal Sir Alan; 129

Bradford, Captain Roy; 140-1

Bradford, Geoffrey; 137, 237, 242, 255, 268

Brain, Captain Geoffrey; 139

Bridgeman, Major-General The Viscount; 70

Bromley, Yolande; see Alston

Brooke, General Alan; 69, 267

Browne, Subaltern Mickey; 188, 219

Bulbasket, SAS Operation; ix, 123-133, 136, 139, 143

Burgin, Bob; 139

Burnell, Kenneth E; 56

Burton, Mary; 218

C

Caddy, Jack; 90
Calendar 1937;29, 40, 47-8, 97
Calendar 1938; 40-1, 47-8
Calvert, Brigadier Michael ('Mad Mike'); xiii, 66, 69, 79, 102-6, 138, 146, 268
Camp 'X'; 83
Carlisle, Lady ('Biddy');184, 225
Cassidy, William; 78
Caws, James; 84, 97, 99, 236
Chalk, Corporal, RASC; 184
Chamberlain, Neville; xx, 2, 218
Chaston, Reginald F J ('Rex'); 85-6
Chevalier, Captain; 140
Childe, Captain Frederick B; 160, 183-4, 188, 197, 222
Churchill, The Rt Hon. Sir Winston; xxvi, xxix, xxx, 12, 23, 30, 69, 88, 98, 100, 264, 266, 268
Clarricoats, John; 186
Cogger, George; 130
Coleshill House, Wiltshire; xxxi, 12, 31, 53-64, 133, 138, 144, 151, 157-61, 116-7, 180, 187, 189, 193, 195, 200, 218, 221, 223, 226, 228-30, 233-4, 243, 249-50, 263, 272
Collings, Major John; 61, 171-8, 197, 207
Collins, Michael; 10, 268
Colquitt, Tom; 74-5
Cooke, Colin; 237
Countryman's Diary, The; 47-8
Coxwell-Rogers, Captain Cecil; 207, 227
Crawley, Corporal, RASC; 184
Croft, Colonel Andrew; 3, 26-7, 33, 121
Culleton, Captain Barbara; 159, 161, 176, 219, 224, 226, 228

D

Dabbs, Ron (G2RD); 187-90, 193
Dalton The Rt Hon. Hugh; xxx

Daniels, Bert; 206
Darwell-Smith, Major R F H; 161
Defence Medal, The WWII; Appendix TWO
Delamere, Lord 'Tom'; 54, 59, 61
Delaney, Private; 61
Denniston, Commander Alistair; 15
Denny, Lieutenant; 237
Devine, REME Craftsman W H ('Andy'); 140-1
Dingley, Captain John; 6
Douglas, Colonel Frank W R; 44-5, 50, 59-60, 63, 100, 122, 160, 166, 234-6, 238, 240-1, 244

E

Eden, The Rt Hon. Anthony; xxix
Edmundson, Lieutenant-Colonel Joshua W S ('Stuart'); xxxii, 1-10, 59, 91, 93, 107, 114, 137, 140, 142-4, 157, 161, 191, 219
Edwards, Len; 76, 124, 139
Eisenhower, General Dwight D; 258
Enigma; 11-13, 15-17, 22, 156

F

Fairbairn, Major William Ewart ('Dan'); 58, 77-84, 86, 88, 245
Fairbairn/Sykes fighting knife; 83, 99
FANYs; see First Aid Nursing Yeomanry
Fenwick, Major Ian; 58, 141-4
Fiddes-Watt, Captain A G; 200
Field, Lieutenant-Colonel Norman; 69, 72, 74, 81, 101, 104, 107-8, 111, 233, 263, 267
Fielding, John; 76, 123-5, 127-8, 130, 139
Fingland, Captain E R; 160
First Aid Nursing Yeomanry; 225
Fleming, Ian; 4
Fleming, Robin; 67, 104
Fleming, Major Peter; xxx, 1, 3-4, 66-7, 69, 74, 81, 101, 104
Foot, Prof. Michael R D; xxvi, 277

Forbes, Major Peter; 59, 71, 100, 107, 160, 166, 219, 249-50, 263

Ford, Roger; 138

Franklyn, General Harold E; 238, 240-1

Fraser, Major R; 160

G

Gabbitas, Arthur; 171, 187, 189-90, 198, 202, 206, 209, 212, 229, 242, 253. 269

Gain, SAS Operation; 142-3

Gallwey, Nigel Vernon; see Oxenden

Gammell, Major General J A H; 68-9, 72

Garth, The Bilting, Kent; 4, 66, 81

Gaulle, General Charles de; 18

GCCS; see *Government Code and Cipher School*

Gladios, The; 255, 258-9

Glanusk, Colonel The Lord; 39, 45, 54, 58-60, 109, 233-4, 243-4

Goss, Captain Victor; 228

Government Code and Cipher School; 12, 15

Grand, Major General Lawrence; xxvii, 9, 66, 111, 153

Gray, Eric; 55, 57, 88

Green, Major, RCS; 193

Gregson-Ellis, Maj. Gen. P G S; 108

Gubbins, Major General Sir Colin McVean; xiii, xxiii, xxiv, xxv, xxvi, xxix, xxx, xxxi, 1-4, 6, 9-24, 29-30, 32, 34-5, 47, 53-4, 60, 66-70, 72, 78, 83, 98, 100-1, 104, 108, 117, 119-20, 137, 142, 156, 181-2, 186, 195, 218, 232-3, 239-40, 249-50, 259-62, 268, 272

Guerrilla Warfare, The Art of; 10, 53

Gwynn, Captain John N W, MP; 4

Gwynne-Vaughan, Dame Helen;221

H

Haggard, SAS Operation; 139, 140

Hall, Cyril; 73, 137, 145-48

Hall, Major R F ('Henry'); 77-81, 83-4, 86, 103, 245

Hall-Hall, Captain Owen; 228

Halley, Captain J; 160

HAM Radio operators; 157, 180, 187-8, 196, 269

Hamilton-Hill, Maj. Donald; 3-4, 137-8

Handford, Roy; 139

Handscombe, Donald; 100

Hannington Hall, Wiltshire; 57-8, 120, 159-61, 176, 218-9, 223, 230, 253

Harston, Major W W ('Bill'); 157, 161, 202

Hayward, James; 87, 265

Henderson, Maj. The Hon. Michael T; 4, 54, 75

Henniker, Lord; 219

Higgins, Tom (G8JI); 187, 189

High Explosives, How to Use; 10

Hills, Subaltern Kitty; 219-21, 230

Hills, Major John; 181-4, 186-8, 193, 196, 218, 220, 222, 230

Hitler, Adolf; xviii, xix, xx, xxiii, xxv, 11, 88, 105, 118, 130-1, 141, 153, 178, 221, 232, 258, 283 *Commando Directive;* Appendix THREE

Hitler Youth; 256-8

Holberton, Captain J W; 74

Holland, Maj. Gen. John F C ('Jo'); xx, xxii, xxiii, xxiv, xxvii, xxix, xxxi, 9-10, 195, 260-1, 268

Holman, Dr Alec; 171, 174-5

Holman, Jill; see Monk

Home Defence Organisation; xxix, 153-4

Houndsworth, SAS Operation; 140

Hume Castle; 166-7, 215

I

Ingrams, David; 164, 167, 209-10, 254

Ingrams, Major Douglas; 165, 174, 177, 201, 207-9, 227

Inter-Services Projects Board; xxvii, xxx, 10, 156

Inverailort Special Training Centre, Scotland; 67, 78-80, 83-4, 103, 177

IRA; see *Irish Republican Army*

Irish Republican Army; 261

Ironside, Field Marshal Lord William Edmund; xiii, xiv, xxviii, xxix, xxxi, 9, 66, 69, 97, 105, 168, 267, Appendix ONE

Ironside, The Lord Edmund; xiii-xiv

ISPB; see *Inter Services Projects Board*

J

Jackson, Margaret; 218

Jedburgh team 'Hugh'; 131

Johnson, Major K W; 160

Jefferis, Major General Sir Millis; xxiv, 40

Jones, Major R M A ('Spud'); 161, 191, 211

Joyce, W A; 52

Judson, Stanley; 196, 199, 202, 207, 211, 213, 215, 220

K

Kidner, 'Tiny'; 138

Kindred, Charles; 206

Kindred, Herman; 25-7, 30, 33, 89, 93, 96, 99, 101, 190, 238, Appendix ONE

Kindred, Percy; Appendix ONE

Kindred, Peter; Appendix ONE

Kinnivane, John; 127, 132-3

L

Lawrence, T E; 256

Leach, 'Slogger'; 145

Lewinski, Richard; 13, 16

Lewis, W B; 181

Long, Leslie; 74, 127, 130

Longmate, Norman; 168

Lovat, Lord; 67, 104

Lovat Scouts, The; 104

M

Mabel Fable, The; 56, 87

MD1; (see *Winston Churchill's Toyshop*)

Mackenzie King, Canadian Prime Minister William L; 83

Major, Colonel C R ('Bill'); 32, 34, 39, 60, 81, 84, 119, 144, 149, 151, 154, 195, 202, 218-9, 232-3, 239, 253

Mark, The War Dog Hero; 171-8

Marks, Leo; 19

Mayne, Colonel 'Paddy'; 138

McGinn, Sergeant C ('Maggie'); 141

McIntyre, Lieutenant 'Mac'; 73, 75, 145

McNab, Jimmy (GM2COI); 187, 189

Melville House, Fife; 63

Menzies, Sir Stewart G; 12, 15, 20-1, 193

Merry Monarch; 171, 176

'Met' Huts; 180, 196, 205, 213, 215

MI5; see *Security Service, The*

MI6; see *Secret Intelligence Service,*

Middleditch, Joe; 145

Milice; 129, 132

Military Intelligence (Research); xxiii, xxiv, xxvii, xxix, xxx, 2, 10-11, 13, 24, 26, 32, 40, 53, 66, 83, 102, 111, 149, 151, 155, 197, 251, 262

Mill House, The, Cransford, Suffolk; 73-5

Millie, Jack (GM8MQ); 187, 189, 206

MI(R); see *Military Intelligence (Research)*

Monck-Mason, Adrian; 207, 225

Monck-Mason, Dorothy; see Rainey

Monk, Jill; 172, 174-6, 178, 202

Morrison-Low, Lady Wilhelmina; 212

Muggeridge, Malcolm; xxvi

Museum of the British Resistance Organisation; Appendix ONE

N

Nichols, Brigadier F W ('Nick'); 182

Niven, David; 80, 143-4

No. 17 Army radio transceivers; 109-10, 169-70, 191-93, 250, 254

No. 77 Smoke Grenade; 48, 248

Norrington, Colonel; 3
Norrington, Iris; 2

O

Observation Units, XII Corps; xxix, 70-1, 260
Ogg, Joseph; 124, 127, 129-30, 133
Oxenden, Joy; 61
Oxenden, Major Nigel V ('Oxo'); xxx, xxxi, 2, 5, 7, 24, 28, 30-2, 34-5, 39, 41, 44, 46-9, 55, 59, 61-3, 69, 72-5, 93, 97, 110, 113-23, 151, 161, 196, 232, 247-50, 273
Oxenden, Pat; 115

P

Parnell, Leslie (G8PP); 185, 187, 189
Partisan Leaders Handbook; 10
Pascoe, Henry James ('Sam'); 127, 129-30, 133
Petherick, Major Maurice; 58, 150, 159-61, 215, 218-9, 239, 271
Phantom; 130, 139
Pike, Lieutenant Percy; 75
Pleydell-Bouverie, Mary; 54
Pleydell-Bouverie, Katharine; 54
Pleydell-Bouverie, Lady Jane; 12
Purdey, Colonel; 173
Purvis, Major R W; 212

R

Radnor, The Earl of; 12, 54
RAF, 161 Special Duties Squadron; 130, 132
RAF, 2 Group, 140 Wing; 131-2
Radio Society of Great Britain, The; 180, 186, 269
Rainey, Subaltern Dorothy; 225-6, 228, 230
Randell, Captain Charles; 159-60, 218, 224
Rejewski, Marian; 12
Rideout, Jim; 129
Ritchie, Brigadier N M; 68-70
Robins, Peter; 77, 82, 84

Roosevelt, Franklin D, President of the US; 83, 264
Rowe, Fred;124, 139
Rozycki, Jerzy; 12
RSGB – see *Radio Society of Great Britain*
Russell, Lieutenant Roy; 212
Ryland, Sydney; 130

S

SAS; see *Special Air Service Regiment*
Sandwich; 15
Sandwith, Commander Humphrey; 15
Sandys, Captain Duncan; xxxi, 1, 98
Savage Sets; 186-8, 196
Savage and Parsons Ltd, Kingsbury; 184
Schmidt, Hans-Thilo; 12
Schofield, Major Joe; 127
Scott-Moncrieff, Captain G; 74
Scout Sections; 66-76; Suffolk; 36, 69-70, 73-5, 145; Devon; 6; Dorset; 126-7, 130, 138-9, 270
Seabrook, Keith; 99
Secret Hunters, The; 131
Secret Intelligence Service, The; xvii, xxvii, xxix, xxx, xxxi, 5, 12, 15, 18, 20, 66, 105, 111, 151, 153-4, 156-7, 160, 162, 167-8, 170, 180-1, 192-3, 239-40, 242, 251, 273
Secret Sweeties, The; 180, 217-230, 239, 242, 253, 270
Section 'D'; xxvii, xxix, 5, 13, 66-7, 105, 111, 153-6, 162, 168, 180-1, 239, 251, 260, 275
Security Service, The; xvii, 119, 197, 273
Shanks, Captain Tom (G2QV); 184, 187, 197, 199
Simpson, Fred; 24-5, 27, 29, 49, 51
SIS – see *Secret Intelligence Service*
Smith, Sam; 125-6, 128-9, 132
SOE - see *Special Operations Executive*
Special Air Service Regiment; 13, 63, 66-7, 74, 92, 104, 123-5, 127-33, 135-6, 138-42, 145, 250-1, 269-70, 273

Special Operations Executive; xvii, xviii, xxii, xxvii, xxix, xxx, xxxi, 3, 8-9, 11-13, 17-22, 47, 66, 78, 83, 98, 101, 111, 120, 137-9, 142, 151, 153, 156, 161, 165, 168, 177, 180, 186, 194, 200, 218-9, 224, 238-9, 248-9, 259, 262, 270, 273

Spencer, George (G2KI); 187, 189, 197

Spens, Professor Sir Will; 105

Stark, Charles; 139

Steed, Norman;89, 101

Stephens, Lieutenant Twm; 129, 132

Stephenson, Sir William;16

Steward, Doris; 73

Steward, John ('Jack'); 73, 145

Stoneham, Lionel; 139

Straker, Jack; 139

Stranks, Mabel; 56, 87

Sussex team; 177

Sutton, Stephen; 97, 104, 182, 195

Sykes, Major William ('Bill'); 79-80, 83, 86, 88, 99, 245

T

Taylor, Andrew; xxxi, 23, 43, 87, 113, 246

Telfer, Lieutenant-Colonel M; 92

Temple, Snr Commander Beatrice; 161, 219, 222-3, 225, 228, 230-58

Thorne, General Andrew ('Bulgy'); xxix, 1, 66-7, 182, 251, 260

Todd, Captain John; 165, 218-9

Tonkin, Captain John; 123, 125-6, 128-9

Torrance, Hamish; 4

TRD transceivers; 154, 169, 171, 176, 188-9, 191-2, 194, 206, 211-2, 222-4, 239, 242, 253, 273

Trubshaw, Michael; 143-4

Turing Machine, The; 11

Twelves, Sergeant Major; 61

U

Ultra; xvii, 12-15, 17-8, 21, 164

USAAF, No. 1 Air Commando; 146

W

Ward, Captain Ken; 171, 177, 181-4, 186-7, 194, 196, 204

Ward, Subaltern Thea; 183, 219

Weaver, Major Peter; 126-7, 129-30, 132-3

Webber, William; 76, 231

Welrod, The; 248, 273

Wemyss, Major David; 206

Werewolves; 255-8

White, Victor ('Chalky'); 74, 127, 130

White, Sgt, 'A' Squadron, 1 SAS; 141

Whiting, Subaltern Margaret; 219, 221

Wiart, VC, General Carton de; 11, 13, 15

Wickham-Boynton, Major Marcus; 59

Wilkinson, Lieutenant Colonel Sir Peter; xxiv, 1, 3-4, 13-4, 18, 20, 29, 35, 98, 105, 137, 181-2, 184, 195, 251, 262, 272

Wilcox, Peter; 242

Wilmott, Miss E M ('Willie'); 218-9

Wingate, General Orde; xiii, 146

Winston Churchill's Toyshop; xxiv

Winterborn, Major T H ('Hugh'); 186, 193

Woodward, Captain G; 74, 160

Worby, Sergeant 'Bottles'; 70

Z

Zero Stations; 65, 183, 196, 201, 212-5, 223, 227, 229-30, 253, 270

Zygalski, Henryk R; 12